GW00770997

Warp and Weft

Chinese Language and Culture

By

Keekok Lee

Eloquent Books
New York, New York

Eloquent Books
An imprint of AEG Publishing Group
845 Third Avenue, 6th Floor - 6016
New York, NY 10022
www.eloquentbooks.com

ISBN: 978-1-60693-247-6
SKU: 1-60693-247-0

Printed in the United States of America

Book Design: Roger Hayes

Dedicated

To all who may wish to understand an ancient culture and civilization which still live on and whose heirs today constitute a sixth of the world's population

Contents

Acknowledgements

I wish to thank several friends, in particular, Delia Davin, Bao Hu Lingtai, Hu Jingling, and Zhang Yu, who have so generously recommended as well as procured books and articles not readily available in the UK, and suggested relevant websites to help with the essential research of this work. To Zhang Yu and Fan Qing, I owe gratitude for having tracked down so thoroughly the various ancient Chinese fonts available on certain internet sites; and to Yang Fan for having so expertly downloaded them to my laptop as well as so patiently explained how to apply them. I must also express heartfelt thanks to numerous members of the University of Manchester IT staff, in particular, to Sarah Tischler, to whom I constantly appealed to get me out of technical “dark holes.” I am also grateful to Daniel Oi and Zhang Yu for helping me to track down a certain astronomical matter. However, to Hu Jingling, I owe a very special debt for her noble offer to read through the entire text, painstakingly pointing out errors, both great and small, suggesting clarifications and improvements as well as co-operating so generously in solving several thorny theoretical questions arising from the deconstruction of certain characters/words. I also benefited from Chen Guang’s comments and suggestions to improve Part I, for which many thanks. Last but not least, I must thank *Xiaolaowai* who made me promise that I would use plain English – I did my very best not to deviate from this “riot act” she read me. Without their respective contributions, this book either could not have been written at all or even if written, would have been a far inferior work.

The author wishes to acknowledge, with heartfelt thanks, permission to use the following two images: on the front cover, reproduced by courtesy of the University Librarian and Director, The John Rylands University Library, The University of Manchester; the Shang ceremonial axe on page 287, reproduced by courtesy of the Asian Art Museum, East Asian Art Collection, National Museums in Berlin. Permission is also acknowledged for use of the Gem Heap Sutra image on page 204 by the British Library.

Manchester
Summer 2008

Playing Chinese Charades

Linguistic excavation

Have you ever wondered why we buy beef, but not cow-meat, from the butchers? In English, we call the animal which gives us beef, "cow."Traditionally, the person, who looked after cows, was called "cowherd." To understand this distinction between the cow and its meat, we have to dig a little into English as well as French history. We have all heard about the Battle of 1066, the Battle of Hastings, in which King Harold of England was killed by a very "wicked" French arrow, which pierced his eye. Thus began the reign of William the Conqueror (the Duke of Normandy) on English soil, bringing momentous changes in its wake. Here, we are only concerned with the linguistic legacy of the Norman Conquest. French became the court and official language of England. The aristocracy, old and new, all spoke French in their daily lives, unlike the ordinary people who continued to speak English. The lowly jobs continued, naturally, to be done by the common folks, the natives, so to speak. Hence, the cowherd remained "cowherd," and the animal he looked after continued to be called "cow." People like him could not afford to buy and eat the meat of the animal, as this was very expensive and destined for the table of the elite who all spoke French. In French, as we know, the word for cow-meat is *boeuf*. The cowherd and the kitchen maid could not quite manage that sound and so turned it into something like "beef." This bit of "linguistic excavation" accounts for the fact that a cow is called "cow" (and not *vache*, the French word for "cow") and beef is "beef." The next time you go to the butchers, or more likely, the supermarket to buy a piece of beef steak, you would recall (if you do not know it already) that the word "beef" carries a slice of English and French history with it.

Here is another instance of "linguistic digging." Every one knows that the term "hocus-pocus" means "nonsense, something unintelligible," although, perhaps, not every one may know its origin. To understand that colorful expression in full, we need to go back to history, to Henry VIII and "his merry wives." The pope of the day did not exactly oblige Henry in helping him to sort out his complicated marital affairs. As a result, the English king defied Rome, and declared himself Defender of the Faith in England. By doing so, he set in motion what today is called the English Reformation, when the Church of England became the established church. Of course, that was not the main or only reason for the rise of Protestantism in England, but it did play a role. Amongst other grievances against Roman Catholicism, one commonly cited was that the church services were held in Latin, a dead language which only the priests and a tiny minority of educated people could understand. The common people wanted to communicate with their God in their own language, English. The main service in the Roman Catholic Church was the mass. A crucial part of the mass was the consecration, when the priest (literally according to the teachings of the Church) turned the bread and wine into the body and blood of Christ by uttering certain words over them. The words are: "this is my body, this is my blood." In Latin, "this is my body" comes out as: *hoc est corpus meum.* Imagine the following scene at mass in a cathedral in those days. The congregation stood in the main body of the cathedral. The people were separated from the priests at the altar, who were carrying out the service, first by a screen, which blocked a considerable part of the view, then the choir stalls (where the choir sang). The altar was far away beyond the screen and the choir stalls, in a part of the cathedral which only the clergy could go. The service was conducted in a language the people could not understand. All they could hear was some mumbling from the altar as the priest, bent over the unleavened bread and the wine, uttered softly over them the words, which turned them into the body and blood of Christ. To the new Protestant spirit, all this was, indeed, unintelligible superstitious mumbling, which it nicknamed "hocus-pocus." The Protestants made it into an effective political/ideological slogan for ridiculing and challenging the authority of the pope in Rome. At least, this is an account often recounted of the origin of "hocus-pocus."

We invite you to join us on a similar journey of "linguistic excavation" of the Chinese language, to make it yield equally interesting information about ancient or traditional Chinese culture and history in which the language is embedded. The notion of linguistic excavation is analogous to an archaeological dig. Archaeologists excavate a site not simply to uncover buried artifacts but also to get as much detailed understanding as possible about them and of the context in which the objects were made, and then later came to be buried. What were the objects used for? Were they merely things with a practical function? Might they not be ordinary wine vessels but wine vessels to make sacrifices to the gods? Were the objects buried for a special purpose, such as to serve the needs of the dead in the next world? Or could they simply be part of an ancient landfill or rubbish dump? Or did an earthquake, a volcanic eruption stop existence in its track? These and similar questions are what we hope archaeology would be able to answer, at least ideally, when the evidence unearthed is sufficiently full and intact. Circumstances may not always be ideal and no one convincing conclusion may emerge, although more than one plausible hypothesis or interpretation may.

Instead of digging in the ground, we shall be deconstructing Chinese characters (Chinese being written in what are commonly known as "characters" but, as we shall see in Part II, that a Chinese word often consists of more than one character), in their various historical forms, taking them apart to reveal the different components out of which they could be constructed. One of these components could tell us how the character (roughly) sounds, others what they could mean, which might even be able to throw light on the context in which the character/word was embedded. Yet others might tell us what the objects they refer to actually looked like in ancient times. Often, too, as in archaeology, the evidence might not lead to only one indisputable interpretation, but to competing plausible interpretations given by different scholars. Occasionally, we even have our own hypotheses to offer. When we do so, we would hang a "health warning" label on them so that you would know that they would not have any authoritative status, but are mere speculations on our part.

Some scholars, especially in the West, have dismissed such an activity as "folk etymology" (etymology is the study of the origins of words). Playing folk etymology is considered trivial, leading nowhere. While one should be on one's guard against wasting time in this fashion, there is no need, however, to embrace the extreme of condemning all speculation. That attitude would be carrying the avoidance of folk etymology to absurd lengths so as to become a vice. We like to play detectives. Hypothesis-making is, after all, the most characteristic of human traits. There is no need to stifle our creativity and our imagination in fashioning hypotheses including linguistic etymological ones, provided we do not foolishly believe that all hypotheses are equally convincing, or equally well-grounded. They are capable of being tested against evidence. Some evidence may not be forthcoming straightaway; provided the stab at explanation is plausible, one should bear it in mind until future evidence might settle, on the whole, for it or against it. It is in this spirit that the Chinese have long played this "game" regarding their language. Sometimes, one might have to wait a fairly long time before any evidence becomes available. For instance, when the ancient Shang script (of the Shang Dynasty, ca. 16th – 11th century BCE) was finally discovered right at the cusp of the twentieth century (as we shall see in Part II), Chinese scholars speculated that as it was such a mature system of writing, it could not have emerged ready made during the late Shang period, but that it must have an earlier history. This seems to be a very plausible hypothesis to make, but some skeptics were tempted to dismiss it as no more than a piece of Chinese chauvinism which need not be taken seriously. Yet, after a century of further discoveries and investigation, Chinese scholars have produced evidence to back up this claim.

Aims and intended readers

We have entitled the book: ***Warp and Weft: Chinese Language and Culture***, in order to demonstrate the interwoven fabric of writing, on the one hand, and history and culture, on the other. The warp is the metaphor for the former and the weft for the latter. Later in Part III of the book (***Precious as the warp***), we shall show in some detail why this metaphor is apt in characterising the relationship involved. The cultivation of silk worms and the manufacture of silk and silk products almost define what constitutes Chinese civilization itself, at least, in the eyes of non-Chinese, through the ages. Silk is woven; all weaving on a loom requires two sets of thread, one called the warp and the other the weft. The overland Silk Route carried the precious silk and other luxury goods from China to Europe through Central Asia and what we call the Middle East today, while one branch of the maritime Silk Route carried similar goods to South East Asia, India, and beyond, and the other to Korea and Japan. Furthermore, as we shall show in the book, the very character for "warp" in Chinese itself, which is 经/經 *jīng,* stands also for the character "classics," or "scripture." Silk for centuries in Chinese civilization and culture had enjoyed a special status; so too, have certain classical texts, great works of philosophy such as those of Confucianism, Daoism as well as Buddhism. Is it not curious that the Chinese should have used the character for "warp" to stand for them? Our book will unravel this puzzle.

In the process of deconstructing some key characters and concepts, conceived thematically, such as those of war and peace, rites and rituals, kith and kin, leisure and pleasure, and so on, we hope to reveal, amongst other things, certain aspects of:

- ancient Chinese religion, cosmology, philosophy, political theory, law, medicine, astronomy, physics, geography;
- their grasp, on the part of the ancient Chinese people, of human reproduction, biology and physiology, psychology, biochemistry, even neurology of the brain;
- what constitutes Chinese identity, the core values of Chinese culture, the essential glue holding their society together;
- their daily existence, such as their food and drink, the houses they lived in, the furniture they used, their chief modes of transportation, etc.

The Chinese language is unique as a living language, especially in its written form, as it is non-alphabetic. This attempt, to unravel the interweaving between the written Chinese language, on the one hand, and the history and culture in which it is embedded, on the other, will also reveal other specific ways in which it can claim to be unique.

Clearly, it is not meant to be a textbook or a specialist book on the nature of Chinese writing. It is simply a general account written primarily with three kinds of readers in mind. Those, whose work, whether in business, journalism, diplomacy, politics, government, and non-governmental organizations, involves liaising with their Chinese counterparts, might benefit from this attempt to help them better understand Chinese culture of which the language is such an important part. Members of the global English-reading public, who find Chinese fascinating because it is so different from other languages, too, might welcome this kind of approach. Students, who are already learning Chinese, might like to know something more about its history and background to enrich their understanding of a language which they are in the process of mastering. We also would like to interest those who may be thinking of starting to learn another foreign language, one which is less familiar, more "exotic" perhaps and in that sense more challenging.

Chinese Charades?

Charades are not something which people, who do not know the Chinese language, would immediately associate with it. All the same, let us introduce you to Chinese in the most playful way we can think of. We invite you to look at charades and riddles which the Chinese have always loved to play. Their tradition of charades and riddles is a very long one indeed. However, before doing so, we must say something about charades in some European languages, so that you would be able eventually to compare the game as played in an alphabetic language with that in a non-alphabetic one, and to see where the similarities and differences lie.

There are charades and charades. Charade is understood today in English to be a kind of pantomime, acting out each word of the phrase or the whole phrase which is supposed to be behind the action, and getting your audience to guess what the phrase is. The better an actor you are, the easier it is for others to guess it. A charade is not necessarily played like this historically, in its original form. In Europe, the French have been credited for introducing it in the eighteenth century. Victor Hugo (1802-1885) – novelist, poet, playwright – considered the most important of the French Romantic writers, adored charades. Here is one of his easy ones.

> *Mon premier est un métal précieux*
> My first is a metal precious
> *Mon denier se trouve dans les cieux*
> My second is found in the heavens
> *Mon entier est un fruit délicieux*
> My whole is a fruit delicious.

The answer is *orange*. As the clues are lost in the translation, a small explanation may be called for in case your memory (those who learned French at school some time ago) may require some jolting. The precious metal is gold, *or*, in French. What is found in the heavens above is (an) angel or *ange*. The last clue is that the object referred to is a fruit. The three clues taken together lead you inevitably to conclude that the word must be *orange*, which is the same in French and English, as we all know.

The English took to charades in a big way when this game came across the Channel from France. For instance, Jane Austen made great use of it in her novel, *Emma*. A very-well known charade in the story runs as follows:

> My first doth affliction denote
> Which my second is destined to feel.

And my whole is the best antidote
That affliction to soften and heal.

The solution: "my first" is "**woe**"; "my second" is "**man**"; "my whole" is "**woe-man**," hence "**woman**." We leave you, readers, to decide how good you think this famous charade really is!

For those who are not familiar with this historical form of the charade, the format involves giving a clue in each line of the verse, yielding in each case a letter of the alphabet or part of the word which, put together, make the whole word. The final line makes it obvious what the word is. There is also an attempt to make the endings of the lines rhyme.

In other words, a charade is really like a riddle, but played according to specific rules. Furthermore, the word "charade" is French and so sounded "posher," more refined to that stratum of polite English society in the eighteenth century in which "the drawing room" increasingly played an important part in its social life. Playing charades in the drawing room became a standard pastime. Although a riddle gives clues, it is not cast in the form just described. Here is an example. The answer is "bookworm," in the literal, rather than the metaphorical sense.

A moth ate words.
I thought it was quite curious, that a mere worm, a thief in the dark, ate what a man wrote, his brilliant language and its strong foundation.
The thief got no use for all that he fattened himself on words.

This is an Old English riddle. Its spirit, though not its form, is that of a charade. That is why it may not be altogether correct to say that the notion of the charade was absent in England until it arrived from France in the eighteenth century. A charade is just a more stylised kind of riddle, a word-game all the same. Charades, played as mime, by English-speaking peoples today, are derived from the original version as riddle. By emphasising pantomime, the English appear to have turned charades into mere entertainment, whereas the French have continued to focus more on their original verbal character, using them as an entertaining, but nevertheless, serious educational tool to help students in schools get a better grasp of French spelling, vocabulary and grammar.

Of course, French and English are alphabetic languages. Their charades and riddles necessarily involve letters of the (Latin) alphabet. Chinese is not alphabetic which renders it unique today. This uniqueness appears to have given rise to a lot of problems to Western European peoples and scholars in trying to understand it, ever since they came into systematic contact with China and its language in relatively modern times, from the late sixteenth century onwards, as we shall see in Part II. We shall also see that it caused a lot of heartache and agonising on the part of Chinese intellectuals in the first half of the twentieth century when they diagnosed their country's ills as caused, in the main, by the non-alphabetic character of their writing. For China to shake free of its weaknesses and the humiliation it suffered at the hands of Westerners and others, to become strong again, they thought that the country must first liberate itself from its "archaic" idiosyncratic form of writing to embrace something "more modern," "more Western," the Latin alphabet. We shall also see in Part II that this, in the end, is not to be the fate of Chinese writing; some other is in store for it. If the Latin alphabet had been adopted in the People's Republic of China after 1949, then, this book, which you are reading, would, at best, only have curiosity value, as the characters we shall be examining and deconstructing would belong to the past, they would be part of a dead language. But they are living characters with a very long ancestry, having descended from more archaic forms of writing.

You must be wondering how one can play charades at all in a non-alphabetic language. In order to remove your puzzlement and to understand their game, we must first say something very quickly about the way in which a Chinese character is constructed. Unless we understand how it is constructed, we cannot begin to deconstruct it to solve any riddle or charade.

Every character is constructed through strokes, the simplest has only one stroke, such as the character for "one" which is written 一, pronounced *yī*. At the other extreme, there is a character with 72 strokes, now hardly used except as an example of a curiosity. Reducing the number of strokes is the aim of a project initiated after 1949. Take just one example here as illustration of the reform which will be discussed in detail in Part II – the strokes for the character for "body" have been reduced from 22 to 7, from 體 to 体 *tǐ*.

A stroke is what one makes with a brush or pen in one continuous motion. Very broadly speaking, strokes can be constructed out of three basic elements: **dots**, **lines** and **hooks**. Below is a chart showing how they occur in the construction of a character. The character chosen is pronounced *yǒng*, meaning "forever," "always" and is a favorite used in teaching brush calligraphy.

An example of **dots** is 1 in the diagram below and an example of **hooks** is 4. **Lines** are more complicated and may be spelled out as follows:

- ★ they may be horizontal, always written from left to right, such as 2 or 5;
- ★ they may be vertical, always written from top to bottom, such as 3;
- ★ they may slant downwards left such as 6 and 7 or they may slant downwards right such as 8.

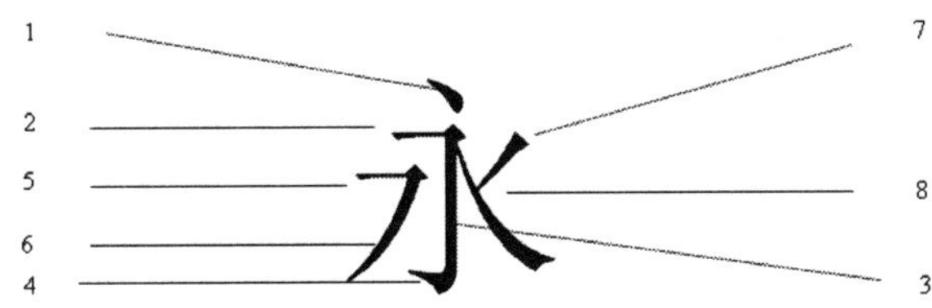

A second thing to grasp is that a Chinese character, in general, save the simplest with one stroke, is made up of different components. Here is an example of how you may build up a character, first from one element, then another character by adding an extra element to it, then yet another new character, by adding further elements to the second character, and so on:

- ★ write on the page the horizontal line 一, from left to right (like 2 in the diagram above). As it stands, it is a character which means "one," and is pronounced *yī*, as already mentioned above;
- ★ add a vertical line (from top to bottom, like 3 in the diagram) bisecting the horizontal line to create another character, looking like this: 十 *shí* meaning "ten";
- ★ add, on the left, a slanting line downwards (like 6 or 7 in the diagram) and, on the right, a slanting line downwards (like 8 in the diagram). You have created a

new character looking like this 木 *mù* which basically means "tree," but is often used in its derivative meaning as "wood" or "wooden";

★ put two of these 木 *mù* or trees together, and you create yet another character, looking like this: 林 *lín*, meaning "grove" or "wood" as in 树/樹林 *shùlín*. The logic behind this kind of construction is that two trees huddling close together represent many trees grown together, though not densely so, which amounts to a grove or wood.

★ Add another of these 木 *mù* to 林 *lín*, and you create another character, looking like this 森 *sēn*, meaning "full of trees," and hence "forest" as in 森林 *sēnlín*. It also means "dark and gloomy." If you have ever walked in a forest; especially a pine forest, you would know how dark and gloomy a forest is. The leaves at the top of the tall trees shut out the sunlight. That is why the *Grimm's Fairy Tales* tell us how frightening forests can be, especially when such forests have wolves and other fearsome beings in them.

You may also think of Chinese characters as bits and pieces of a lego set. If you want to build a lego tower, you first find a piece to act as a suitable base, then you add further similar pieces, stacking them up. When you have built such a tower with several such pieces, you may get bored, and you may fancy adding a different piece from the set, looking like the blades of a windmill and stick it on the stack, turning the tower into a windmill. By merely adding a different piece to the stack, you have changed the construction from a mere tower to a windmill. If you use a piece looking like a cross instead of the blades, you would have altered the tower to a church tower. Should you use a lantern as your topmost piece, you would have created a lighthouse instead of a mere tower, a windmill, or a church tower. Chinese characters are just like lego constructions, except that lego pieces are primarily squares or rectangles. The Chinese writing tool kit, instead, contains horizontal pieces, vertical pieces, slanting-downwards-left pieces, slanting-downwards-right pieces, dots and hooks. Ultimately, even that notorious character with 72 strokes mentioned earlier can be built systematically from these basic pieces in the writing tool kit. Looked at in this way, no one need feel intimidated by Chinese characters, no matter how complicated they may look at first sight, as the logic behind their construction is clear and simple.

The third thing to bear in mind is this: Chinese scholars have called a certain part of a complicated character, usually the component on the left hand side 部首 *bùshǒu*; in English, it is called "radical." In an early dictionary of nearly two thousand years ago, 540 radicals were listed but by the early eighteenth century, this excessive number has been trimmed down to 214. This is the figure often cited and used today after it was incorporated in another very important dictionary issued in 1717, called the *Kangxi Dictionary* (康熙字典). A radical is a component which enters into the composition of a good many characters. For instance, the radical for "metal" is 钅/金 *jīn* and it occurs in over a hundred characters, such as 钟/鐘 *zhōng* ("clock"), 铭/銘 *míng* ("inscription"), 铁/鉄 *tiě* ("iron"). The same holds true for the silk radical 纟/糸, which enters into the composition of between roughly 150 and over 300 characters (depending on how large the dictionary you may be consulting) such as 细/細 *xì* ("fine"), 线/綫 *xiàn* ("thread"). 木 *mù* ("tree" or "wood") can act as a radical, and is a very common one, as it enters into the composition of even more characters than in the case of the other two radicals already mentioned. So many things, after all, are made of wood or related to trees – for a start, nearly all the fruit trees sport that radical. Chairs in the past were made of wood, hence the character for "chair" would have the "wood" radical (on the right) and is written as: 椅 *yǐ*.

A radical may sound strange at first sight, but actually an analog of the radical can be found in many European languages, such as English, which borrows heavily from Latin and, to lesser extent, Greek to enrich its vocabulary. Take the words "photograph," "photogenic," "photocopy." They appear each to be made up of two elements and could be written as "photo-graph," "photo-genic," "photo-copy." You can see straightaway that the element common to all three words is "photo." Should people so wish, there is no reason why they should not borrow the term "radical" or *bushou* to talk about this common element. In Greek "photo" means "light" and other European languages have borrowed the Greek word as an element in making up new words in their own vocabulary. The word "copy" has existed in the English language for a long time. To copy something in the past meant that we either wrote out exactly on another sheet of paper the words we saw in the original document, or we painted on another canvass exactly what we saw in the original painting. But our technology today enables us to use a photocopier to reproduce the original. The electronic machine copies but not in the same way that a human being using pen or brush copies. It copies with the help of light particles or photons. Conveniently in Greek, the word for light is "photo." By putting "photo" in front of "copy," a new word has been created. Any word with "photo" as an element in its composition has something to do with light. In this way, Chinese is no different than English and some other European languages. (We do apologise that our examples come, in the main, from European languages for the simple reason that our knowledge of other non-European languages is even more limited.)

Bearing these few rules in mind, we can now return to the game of Chinese riddles or charades and see how it is played. Listen to the following charming story. This concerns supposedly a very talented family in the Song Dynasty (960 CE – 1279 CE). The oldest was Su Shi (苏轼/蘇軾), commonly known as Su Dongpo, 苏东/蘇東坡, one of China's greatest poets and wits, although as an official, his career did not go smoothly as he often displeased the emperor. He had a similarly very gifted younger sister, but as she was a woman, she had, of course, no career to pursue except to get married. (In reality, the historical Su Shi did not have a sister, only a very talented brother who alone, apart from himself, survived infancy, amongst all the children born to his parents. However, the legend that he had such a sister had taken firm root in people's imagination for many centuries.) One day she said to her husband (also a scholar-official like her brother) that she had made up a charade to test him. If he could not unravel the riddle, the penalty would be a repeat of what happened on their wedding night – he would have to stand the whole night outside the *boudoir*! Her charade runs as follows:

两日齐相投 /兩日齊相投
四山环一周 /四山 環 一周
两王住一国 /兩王住一國
一口吞四口 /一口吞四口

We are not translating it just yet, as it would make little sense to do so right here. As the story proceeds, its meaning would soon become clear. Her husband studied it but could make no sense of it. After a while, he had the bright idea of running to his brother-in-law who, he was sure, would solve it in a flash. He sneaked out of the house to make sure his wife would not know that he would be cheating. He arrived at Su Dongpo's house, just before meal time, explained his mission and showed his brother-in-law his wife's charade. Su Dongpo glanced at it quickly, smiled but said nothing. Instead, he invited the visitor to join him for the meal, and ordered an extra dish from the kitchen, a whole steamed fish, freshly caught from the lake. When the two men sat down at table, Su Dongpo lifted his chopsticks, and with them he removed the head and the tail of the fish. It was precisely at this point that it dawned on his guest what his wife's charade really was all about. He left the table straightaway, thanked his clever relative profusely, and rushed back home to tell his wife that he had solved it. Thus, he was spared the pain and the embarrassment of having to spend the night outside the bedroom door.

Now what exactly was revealed when Su Dongpo removed the head and tail with his chopsticks, leaving only the body of the fish on the plate? The answer is the character 田. Instead of explaining to his brother-in-law the clues in the charade his sister had dreamed up, Su Dongpo thought it simpler to mime the charade for his benefit. Hence he got his cook to serve up the steamed fish, as the character for "fish" is written 鱼/魚 *yú*. Study carefully in particular the version on the right of the slash (as that was the version which the historical players were "playing with"), and you would see that it has three major components: top, middle and bottom. When he detached the head of the fish with his chopsticks, this is equivalent to removing the top component of the character 魚, namely, ⺈; when he removed the tail, this is equivalent to removing the bottom component of the character, namely, 灬 . The middle or body of the fish left on the plate after the topping and the tailing is equivalent to the middle component of the character, namely, something looking like this 田. This turns out to be the character for "cultivated field," pronounced *tián*. The clues in the charade about the character 田 *tián* had obviously passed over the head of Su Dongpo's in-law, and Su Dongpo, obviously, could not be bothered to explain them patiently. Instead he thought of the brilliant device of topping and tailing a fish at table to tell his relative what the key character in the charade was. This story, you can see, is a perfect illustration of the combined talents of the Su family at work – the (legendary) sister dreaming up a tease for the (legendary) husband, and the brother using an effective alternative to enlighten her not so quick-off-the-mark but tormented husband as to what the charade was really all about. In other words, this charming tale contains two charades, not one – the first provided by sister is entirely verbal or written, and the second by brother amounts to miming the character. Just as in European charades, the mimed charade in Chinese is a derivative of the verbal game.

Now what exactly are the clues contained in his sister's charade which enabled Su Dongpo in a thrice to work out what character sister had in mind? For ease of explanation, we reverse their order. Like Su Dongpo's brother-in-law, we would also cheat a little, and propose to do a bit of "reverse engineering." With the help of the distinguished poet and wit, we, like his relative, know that the character is 田. You will notice first that it is made up of 4 small squares. However, if you were asked how many squares there are in the character before you, the smart answer would be 5, not 4, as you must count not only the 4 small ones but also the big square within which the 4 have been incorporated. A square in Chinese is the character for "mouth" 口 *kǒu*; hence the last line of the charade – 一口吞四口 *yì kǒu tūn sì kǒu* – may be translated as: one big mouth swallowing four smaller mouths. We can guarantee you that as a result of having decoded this line of the charade, you would never forget how the character 田 is written.

However, imagine for a moment that we did not have the benefit of Su Dongpo's miming of the charade. Could we do better than his brother-in-law and tumble to the character 田 ourselves, relying only on the verbal clues of the charade? We can, provided we work on them. Begin with the character for "mouth." If we do not already know what it is in Chinese, we must first look it up in an English/Chinese dictionary. We find that it is pronounced *kǒu* and looks like a square. It is actually built out of four lines, two vertical (1, 3) and two horizontal (1, 4), as shown below:

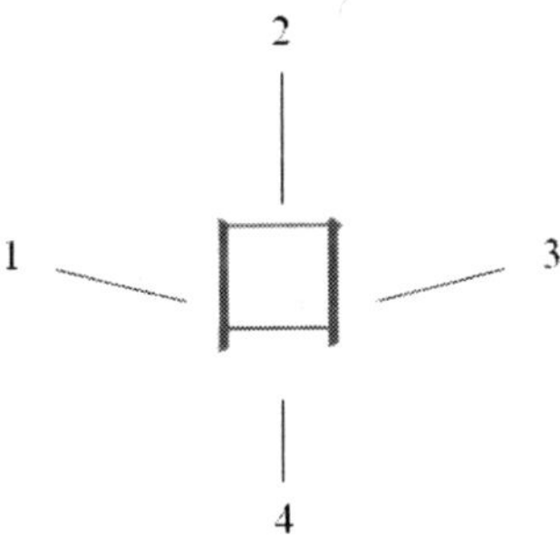

Next imagine yourself creating the character using lego pieces: choose one vertical (1), then add a horizontal (2) to the vertical, next add the second vertical (3) to the other end of the horizontal, and finally, add the second horizontal (4) to close the gap. You have now constructed one character for "mouth." Make three more. Put all the four characters for "mouth" together, not by stacking them one on top of the other, but by making sure that they are pushed together on a flat surface to form a big square. Thus assembled, they will look like the character for "cultivated field," *tian*. You can see then at a glance that besides the four little characters for "mouth" you have deliberately constructed, you would also, by assembling your lego pieces in this way, have unwittingly constructed one more character for "mouth," a great big one, looking as if it has swallowed the four little ones, just as the clue says. The character, constructed out of imaginary lego pieces, consists of three vertical lines (1, 3, 5) and three horizontal ones (2, 4, 6):

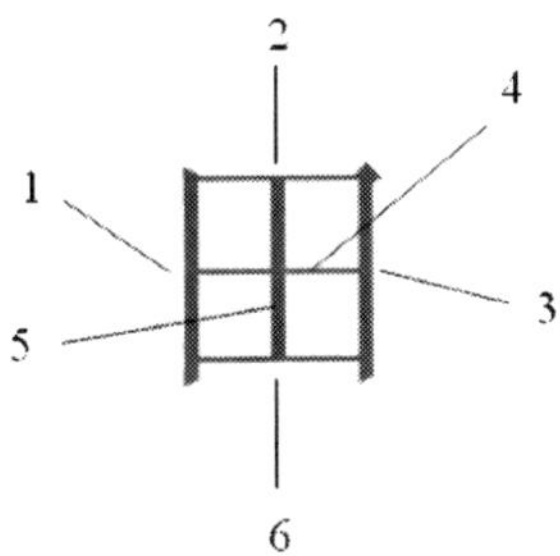

Take another clue, the one found in the penultimate line of the charade, 两王住一國 *liǎng wáng zhù yī guó* which may be translated as: two kings residing in one country. Imagine again that we do not have the benefit of Su Dongpo's solution and we are starting afresh. First, we look up "king" in our English/Chinese dictionary and we find that the character is pronounced *wáng*, looking like this: 王. It consists of one vertical line (3) and three horizontal ones (1, 2, 4) as follows:

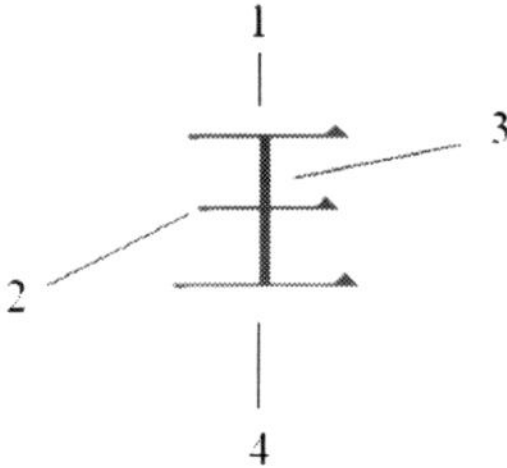

Make two of these. According to the clue, we must find a way of making them both fit together to form one territory or country. By playing around with them a bit, it would soon be obvious that the first should stand upright while the second lie on its side as if someone has knocked it over, looking like this: . The character 田 would appear. In other words, we have constructed 田 out of two characters for "king." To check, highlight the upright one in yellow and the lying sideways one in red. We have, so to speak, found two kings residing in one country, just as the clue says. This statement may not be politically or constitutionally correct but is, certainly, linguistically accurate.

The third clue says: 四山環一周 *sì shān huán yī zhōu*, which may be translated as: four interlocking mountains within a range. We go through more or less the same moves as we have done before. We, first, find out from the dictionary that the character for "mountain" or "hill" (pronounced *shān*) consists of three vertical lines (1, 3, 4) and one horizontal one (2):

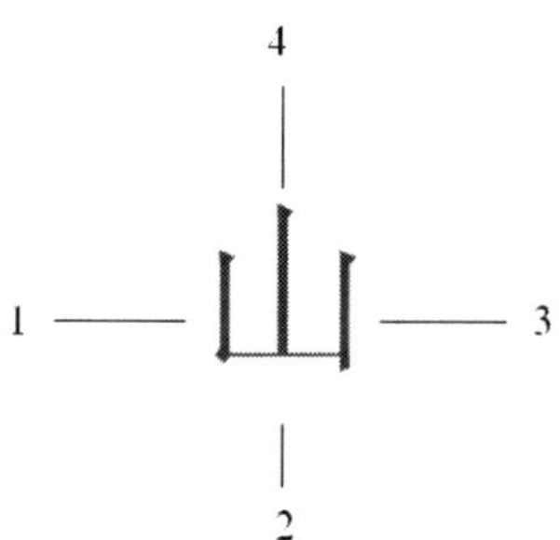

Next imagine playing with pieces from your imaginary Chinese lego writing tool kit. Also imagine the pieces not to be made of thick plastic as real lego pieces are but of thin cardboard. First build your first character for "mountain" in the way indicated above, then build three more, so that you have four altogether, as the clue mentions that number. Next you assemble them in such a way that they interlock with one another. By trial and error, you should eventually get to 田, bearing in mind the key word "interlocking"; in other words, the four constructions for *shan* partly overlap. To see that the character 田 does, indeed, contain four interlocking mountains, let us do a check: we suggest that you use four different color highlighters. The most obvious one to spot is the one upright, on top, staring you in the face 山 : color this one yellow. The next one you can readily locate is the upside down one, sharing the base with the first: color this red. You have now located two. Where could the other two characters for "mountains" be? It would then occur to you, that these are lying side by side, one on your left (color this blue) and the other on your right (color this green), again sharing the base with its neighbor. You can try even yet another way of checking by locating the four mountains as follows: with a piece of paper, cover up first the bottom half of 田 to get your first "mountain," then the top half to get your second, the right half to get your third and the left half to get your fourth. All these methods together should convince you beyond reasonable doubt that the four characters for "mountain," indeed, do interlock with one another to form a range within the character 田, exactly as the clue says.

We now get to the original first clue of the charade which says: 两日齊相投 *liǎng rì qí xiāng tóu* which may be translated as: two suns amiably sharing the same sky. Our dictionary tells us that the character for "sun" is pronounced *rì* and looks like this: 日. We construct it from our imaginary Chinese lego writing tool kit as follows with two vertical lines (1, 3) and three horizontal ones (2, 4, 5):

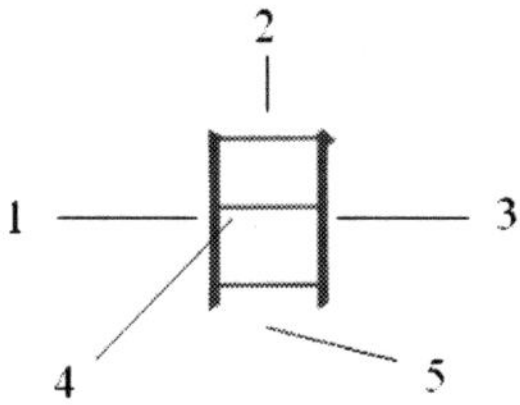

Make two of them, as the clue tells us two are involved. Suppose we put these two constructed "suns" side by side, then we push them together as close as possible. Well, by so doing, the character 田 appears again before our very eyes. The clue is trying to tell us that two instances of the character for "sun," 日 *rì*, lying side by side, make up a new character, and that new character is 田 *tian*.

Now you know how Chinese charades are played. They are the same in spirit as European charades except for the fact that as the language is non-alphabetic, the game correspondingly is structured differently. One can take a character apart in terms of other characters; by the same token, one can also construct a character out of existing characters. In other words, decomposing and synthesising are two sides of the same coin. These techniques, too, are employed in the construction of charades in European languages such as French and English. To be more precise, we can spell out the differences and similarities between the two specific examples of charades without, however, pretending that one can make vast general claims based on their particularities. Take Hugo's example of *orange*. The first thing we observe is that Hugo decomposes the word into two separate words, *or* and *ange*. His clues are constructed according to what these mean as well as what they refer to. The player by synthesising them get to the targeted word which the last clue then confirms, as *orange* in certain contexts means and refers to the fruit by that name. The second is that the charade does not work when translated directly into another language, such as English, which also uses the Latin alphabet. Translating and then following Hugo's clues would end up with "goldangel," not a recognisable word in English, and whatever it might refer to, it would not refer to what the English word "orange" refers to. To make the clues work, one would have to embellish the translation by saying something to the following effect: My first is a precious metal in French. This presupposes that the player knows French. In other words, it remains a French charade essentially. What works in French does not work in English, in spite of the fact that the word "orange" is spelled in an identical manner and refers to exactly the same thing in both languages. The English charade author might think of building clues by splitting the word into "o" and "range," but not "or" and "ange" for the simple reason that although "or" is undoubtedly a word in English, "ange" is not.

The author of the simple Chinese charade examined, also using the techniques of decomposing and synthesising, plays upon the fact that 田 can be decomposed in terms of 日、山、王、口. S/he then focuses on each respectively in the four clues, instructing the player to synthesis or put together either two or four instances of the specified decomposed character in order to get to the targeted character/word 田. It is unlike the *orange* charade where each of the two major clues gives a portion of the targeted word only.

This particular Chinese example shows that one may be able to translate the clues directly into another language which uses the same script as Chinese, such as *kanji* in Japanese. A Japanese reader reading the clues in Japanese would successfully be able to work out that the targeted character is 田, irrespective of whether 田 means "cultivated field" in Japanese (although as a matter of fact, it does mean that, too, as in 水田, meaning "rice paddy"). The difference between the Hugo and the Su Dongpo charades amounts to this. In the former, although both *orange* (in French) and "orange" (in English) refer to one and the same thing, the fruit in question, it remains true that one cannot translate the clues directly from one language into the other. In the latter, the four decomposed characters 日、山、王、口 as well as the targeted character 田 all happen to stand for the same things in both Chinese and Japanese. One must, however, not generalise from these two relatively simple examples of a European and a Chinese charade to make vast claims about their respective natures. Furthermore, Chinese charades and riddles use techniques other than those of straightforward decomposing and synthesising in the way indicated – there are more subtle versions involved. These all raise large issues beyond our remit.

The French and the Chinese have this in common: they both use their respective kind of deconstruction as well as construction not merely for entertainment, but also as educational tool. Should you, in future, ever find it difficult to remember how a particular character is written, see if the Chinese technique of constructing clues in their charades would help, and if it does, make up a line (like the line in the charade) as an *aide-mémoire*. Or just for fun, for those who are already learning the language, choose a character which catches your fancy and see if you can make out in the character, how many other characters it may contain. Try this example to see how you get on: 梨 *lí* (pear). See also if you can pick out which bit of the character functions as the radical. You should be able to find, at least, one character, which is also the radical, as this has already been mentioned in the discussion so far.

We have up to now focussed on the role played by the three basic elements of dots, lines and hooks which enter into the construction of Chinese characters. We have in passing also drawn attention to how a stroke is understood, that it is written in one continuous motion of the brush or pen. We now need to say a bit more about what a stroke consists of. At its simplest, a stroke may, indeed, be a free-standing dot, a horizontal line, a vertical line, a slanting-left-downward line or a slanting-right-downward line. However, it may also be a combination of two or three of these simple basic elements. An example of the former occurs in the character 田 which when written with a brush or pen is written with five strokes, in the following order: [1], [2, 3], [4], [5], [6]. In other words, horizontal line 2 and vertical line 3 are always written in a single continuous motion of the brush or pen, counting as one stroke, according to the rules of writing characters as taught in schools or to beginners. An example of the latter may be found in the character 永 which when written with a brush or pen is written with only five strokes in the following order: [1], [2, 3, 4], [5, 6], [7], [8]. In other words, the second stroke of this character embraces a horizontal line (2), a vertical line (3), and a hook (4). The order of the strokes in writing this character also shows how a horizontal line (5) and a slanting-left-downward line (6) constitute a single stroke. (Chinese brush calligraphy as an art form, however, has its own conventions which may not necessarily accord with any of the normal rules briefly discussed here.)

The exercise of deconstructing the charade is meant to help you understand the logic according to which a Chinese character may be constructed, stroke by stroke; how another character may be created by adding more strokes to it; and even how by putting two or more characters together, one could form a whole new character, with a totally new meaning. In similar spirit, given any character, one can take it apart, or decompose it into its component characters or parts, which we did, when going through the clues of the charade. We shall be doing a lot of that in Part III, when we look at specific clusters of characters which deal with particular themes.

We hope you have found Chinese charades and this activity of composing or decomposing characters fascinating and would happily stay with us during the rest of our exploration of other Chinese characters to get them to tell us other equally fascinating tales about the long history and culture in which they are embedded. You will see how some characters which are still used today are able to tell us about the nature of archaic Chinese society, which was very different from the feudalism of traditional ancient China which succeeded it, not to mention life in contemporary China. Like a very long bolt of silk, Chinese writing on the one hand, and Chinese history and culture, on the other, are inextricably interwoven.

Conclusion

Before we end this Part, we must draw your attention to some boring editorial conventions we have adopted. You may already have noticed that we represent Standard writing in two forms which we separate using a forward slash, such as 国/國, 鱼/魚. The first in each of these two pairs is in the Simplified script (called *jianti*), used in the continental part of the People's Republic of China (1949 –) and other countries such as Singapore. The second character after the slash is in the Traditional script (called *fanti*), used primarily in Taiwan, but increasingly less so in Hong Kong and Macau. If you see a character in one form only, this would mean that it has not been simplified and that the same form holds in books and newspapers today whether published in Beijing or Taipei. Where the context demands, we provide the pronunciation of a character in romanised form (called 拼音 *pīnyīn*), but using the italics font, thus: 鱼/魚 *yú*. As the pronunciation is the same whether in Beijing or Taipei, one set of sounds suffices.

As we constantly have to refer to key periods and dates in Chinese history, we have included a general chart, but we shall also as a rule put the dates in brackets when a dynasty, an important event or personage is mentioned. You will find that we have adopted the convention of BCE, "Before (the) Common Era" and CE, "(the) Common Era," instead of the more usual BC and AD after dates. Chinese history is a long affair. In a non-specialist book of the kind we are trying to write, it would be extremely tedious to distinguish between the various important periods in which the history is normally divided. We simply confine ourselves to three main divisions: Neolithic (New Stone Age, ca. 8000 – 2000 BCE), archaic/ancient (Xia Dynasty, ca. 21st – 16th century BCE, right to the end of the Shang Dynasty), traditional/ancient (Zhou Dynasty, ca. 11th century – 221 BCE, unified China since the Qin Dynasty, 221 – 207 BCE, to the end of the Manchu Dynasty, 1644 – 1911 CE, when the political/social order was feudalistic). When the term "ancient" or "archaic" is used, the context usually makes it clear which of these two huge periods which we have chosen to divide Chinese history. It bears repeating that this is not the normal way in which the subject is categorised and treated. We have simply used either the word "archaic," "ancient" or "traditional" depending on the context but making it clear which period of general history the context is situated.

We have also included three maps of China – one linguistic, two archaeological – showing some of the more important areas mentioned in the book.

We hope such boring but necessary editorial details would not stand in the way of your enjoyment of our telling the tales of Chinese characters or writing.

We wish to remind our readers yet again that this is not a textbook in the normal sense nor is it intended as one. It is a supplementary read which we hope you would find interesting. That is why we have not provided references in the usual manner, or attributed specific views to specific authors that a specialist scholarly book is expected to provide. To do so would alter the character of the book. We have included a very small bibliography in English for those who may wish to pursue the matter in a more academic way with regard to some aspects of Chinese writing talked about in this book.

We would also like to make it absolutely clear that there is nothing original in this book in terms of primary research. It relies entirely on secondary sources, on the contributions of scholars, experts in the various relevant fields of knowledge, such as linguistics, palaeography (the study of archaic writing), archaeology, art history, not, only, today, but through the ages, particularly in the case of Chinese scholarship itself. To all of them, past and present, we wish to say a big thank you. And for good measure, we would wish to take responsibility, in the normal way, for any errors and defects which might arise in the way we have handled the material, should we have misunderstood them and, unwittingly, have misrepresented the views of the original scholars. In this presentation in English, addressed primarily to readers who either do not speak or read Chinese, our claim to originality lies in the way we have structured our chosen themes to illustrate the intimate intertwining of the script on the one hand and history and culture on the other.

Part II – ***Chinese Language: Linguistically and Historically*** – is a short history of the nature of Chinese writing recounting: the date(s) of its origin, the various different kinds of scripts invented through the millennia showing the evolution of the character from archaic forms to the present as well as the various language reforms both past and recent. In this part, too, we endeavor to make good our claim stated at the outset that Chinese writing is unique in several ways: it is the oldest living language today; it is probably the oldest language in the history of human writing that we know of so far; it is the major, if not the only, non-alphabetic language in current use.

Part III, which follows, entitled ***Exploring Themes: Words Tell Fascinating Tales***, requires no special comments as it just deals with the chosen themes and clusters of concepts to explore the relation between the "Warp" and the "Weft."

Do not feel obliged to sit down and read the whole book at one go. It would probably be better to dip into it whenever time permits and mood dictates. Although the book is structured in such a way as to enable certain ideas to unfold step by step, nevertheless, that structure should not dictate that you read it from cover to cover. As far as the themes in Part III are concerned, it would not hurt if you were to choose to read first those which interest you more.

To those readers who are not actually learning Chinese, but would just like to know something about the language as well as the history and culture in which it is embedded, we offer an apology for cluttering up the text with Chinese characters, apart from the translation. You may find some of the Chinese text distracting, but may we suggest that you simply skip those bits which get in your way so that they will not disrupt the flow of your own reading. Unfortunately, there are some bits which you may have to pay some attention to in order to get the hang of the story. However, do use your own judgment as to how much detailed attention you wish to pay to them. On the whole, the story line is clear even if you were to give the Chinese characters a miss. The Chinese text is, in the main, only relevant for those who are studying the language actively.

Chinese Language: Linguistically and Historically

Aspects of language

Imagine you have a friend whose mother tongue is French. She had been brought up in north India and had Hindi-speaking playmates, as a child. Your friend understands Hindi and speaks it fluently, but she cannot read and write the language. Imagine another friend, who simply bought himself a Teach-Yourself Hindi book, and mastered the reading and writing of it, but has no clue as to how to speak it, nor is he able to understand anything when he hears it spoken. Imagine yet another friend whose mother tongue is Hindi and is educated in Hindi. These three friends all know Hindi, but they know it to varying degrees. People who can neither read nor write in the language may, strictly speaking, be said to be illiterate in the language. Certainly people who have not mastered reading and writing their own mother language are regarded as illiterates. But what about someone who can only read but not write their own native language? Such cases today are probably very rare, but in the past, at least with regard to Chinese, it might not have been so unusual. We used to know someone who fell into this more unusual category. She was born in China before the fall of the Qing Dynasty in 1911. Her family was enlightened with regard to the education of its daughters but, unfortunately, a fortune teller had predicted that grave misfortune would befall the family should the daughters be taught to read and write. As a result of this dire warning, the family compromised and instructed the tutors to teach them only to read but not to write. They were highly literate in one sense, as they could read and understand all the classics, use literary expressions and idioms, but alas, they could not write as they had never been taught to wield the brush.

All human beings (with very few exceptions) can speak their mother tongue, as all natural languages are spoken. Not all natural languages have evolved ways of writing. Experts disagree amongst themselves as to what counts as a language. If speech is universal, then surely, a language which is spoken but is not written should be language just as one which has devised a script. Yet other people take the more restrictive view that for a language to count as "proper" or mature, it must have a script, even if the script might not be an original creation but a borrowed one. The Chinese language would qualify under this strict requirement as it does have a script, indeed, an original non-derivative script.

This book is merely an attempt to explore certain characters/words in Chinese in order to show the inter-weaving between the language and the culture through the ages. It is a very limited exercise, and necessarily cannot begin to do justice to the very many complex problems which arise in the study of the Chinese language. However, this book will have to touch briefly on the relationship between sound, meaning, and writing in general, in order to illustrate the intimate link between them and the cultural features embedded in them.

Before going any further in this direction, we must briefly turn to another pretty complex matter regarding what we mean when we talk about "the Chinese language."

China and its linguistic diversities

China presently contains more than a billion and a third people, and constitutes roughly a sixth of the world's population. The number of people in the world who speaks some form of Chinese would be greater than this figure, as one would have to include, on the one hand, the population in Hong Kong and Macau, and on the other, the Chinese of Taiwan as well as people of Chinese descent in various other countries around the globe.

We naturally associate the Chinese language with people who live in China. In one important sense, we would be right to do so, although this assumption is an over simplification, a partial truth, for a number of reasons. We need to bear in mind that China has many different ethnic groups, of which numerically, the largest is often called the "Han people." The demographic details of China's population is briefly summed in the release of the most recent census figures in March 2006 by China's National Bureau of Statistics: there were 1,306, 280, 000 people on 1 November 2005; that by the end of 2005, the figure would have risen to 1,307, 560,000 people. (The figure excludes Hong Kong, Macau and Taiwan). The Han people constitute 90.6% of the total, registering a 2% increase; while 55 ethnic minority groups constitute 9.4%, registering a 15.9% increase, since the census of 2000. The language of the Han group is what we commonly call "the Chinese language" (中文 *Zhōngwén*). People in China also call this language the "Han language" (汉语/漢語 *Hànyǔ*). The mother tongue of each of the minority ethnic groups is not Han; some groups use scripts for their respective languages which are different from the

Han script. The Uygur in Xinjiang at the western end of China speak Uygur, a Turkic language, and today use a modified form of the Arabic script, while the Tibetans, whose language belongs to a branch of the Sino-Tibetan family of languages, write in an alphabetic script which is derived from the ancient Brahmi script, and so bears similarities to some Indian alphabets. Some very small groups, such as the Li (黎) in Hainan, had no script at all historically although one based on the new romanised script (*pinyin*) has been created in 1957 with the help of the government. (Paradoxically, certain countries in the Far East, such as Japan and Korea which had never been part of China in the political sense, nevertheless, came profoundly under Chinese cultural influence, and as a result, historically, adopted the Han script for writing in part, at least, their own languages – one of Japan's scripts is called *kanji* which is Japanese for *hanzi*, meaning "Han words," while the Koreans only devised their own script, Hangul, in the mid fifteenth century under their exceptionally able ruler, King Sejon.)

Even amongst the Han, the linguistic situation is not simple. In the past, the official Chinese language ("official" in the sense of being spoken by high-ranking officials in the Chinese bureaucracy) was called Mandarin in the West; it is today called 普通话/話 *pŭtōnghuà* ("common speech") in the PRC but 国语/國語 *guóyŭ* ("national language") in Taiwan. *Putonghua* (including rough variations of it) is spoken by two thirds to three quarters of the Han population while the remaining quarter to a third speak seven different "dialects" but which, according to some scholars, are not dialects but even different languages, comparable to the Romance group of languages in Europe (French, Italian, Spanish and Portuguese). In China these are called 方言 *fāngyán* ("regional speeches"). They include Shanghainese (吴语/吳語 *wúyŭ*, spoken in Jiangsu and Zhejiang provinces and Shanghai), Cantonese (粤语/語 *yuèyŭ*, spoken primarily in Guangdong, parts of Guangxi, Hong Kong and Macau), and Fujianese or Hokkien (闽/閩语/語 *mĭnyŭ*, spoken in Fujian, Hainan, and Taiwan). *Putonghua* is based, in the main, on the *fangyan* of Northern China and uses Beijing pronunciations as its standard, although it does not adopt all the peculiarities of Beijing speech. The native speakers of *putonghua* in its various forms (there are seven dialects and forty two sub-dialects) cover a large geographical area, stretching in a great arc from North East China through north and central China to the south western provinces of Sichuan and Yunnan and the north western provinces of Gansu and Ningxia. (See Map 1.)

Let us take a quick look at some of the major differences in terms of sound, vocabulary and sentence structure between *putonghua* on the one hand and, say, Cantonese on the other. “Quick” or “fast” is written as 快; in *putonghua* the character is pronounced as *kuài* but *fai* in Cantonese. We next compare a sentence in English with its translation in Standard Chinese as well as in Cantonese.

I	give	him	some money	
我 *wo*	给 *gei*	他 *ta*	钱 *qian*	
我 *ngo*	俾 *bei*		钱 *cin*	佢 *keoi* (to him)

You can see straightaway that the word order in the first two sentences is identical, and that this differs from that in Cantonese. It may surprise you to find that in this aspect, Standard Chinese sees eye to eye with a foreign language, such as English, but not with one of China’s own regional speeches. For this reason scholars hold that the way Cantonese differs from Standard Chinese is analogous to the way that English, for instance, differs from French. So let us compare the English sentence with its translation in French:

I	give	him		some money
Je		*lui*	*donne* (give)	*de l’argent*

Another significant difference between the two kinds of Chinese is the vocabulary – in the sentences above, you can see the verb “give” as well as the pronouns “he” and “him” are not only pronounced differently but are also different characters altogether.

The difficulties of communication in China are obvious should speakers use only their own regional speeches which can often be mutually unintelligible. Since the establishment of the People’s Republic of China in 1949, *putonghua* – as well as the Standard written Chinese associated with it – has been assiduously promoted as the language which all Chinese should learn and use in communicating with one another.

How old is Chinese writing? What sort of writing is Chinese writing?

Any thing one may say on these two subjects could be controversial. One claim which is uncontroversial is that the Chinese script has the longest history of continuous use in world civilizations. Should one argue that Chinese is the oldest script in the world, this would be regarded as deeply problematic, if not outright false by certain scholars. It was commonly held, until very recently, that Sumerian cuneiform writing in Southern Mesopotamia had that honor, dating from over 5000 years ago (roughly 3300 BCE) just ahead of the Ancient Egyptian hieroglyphs. However, the latest find of clay labels in 1998 put the date of the latter's origin to roughly 3400 BCE. Authoritative books (in English) published twenty years ago and even today would claim that the earliest ancient Chinese writing dates from about 1200 BCE in the late Shang Dynasty (ca. 16th – 11th century BCE). At the same time such accounts might also indicate that there is a claim dating its origin to a much earlier period in China's pre-history, based on certain inscriptions on Neolithic painted pots found at Banpo (半坡), near today's Xi'an (西安) in Henan (河南) Province, belonging to the Yangshao Culture (仰韶, ca. 5000 – 3000 BCE). These pots have been carbon-dated to 4800 – 4200 BCE. Such evidence would be considered to be at best provocatively interesting but would be dismissed as flimsy, as the marks are not writing but might simply be squiggles made by the potter in order to identify ownership of the artifact.

Scholarship in China based on archaeological finds has made great strides in the last two decades, constantly adding new knowledge with which some publications, especially in Western languages such as English, have not yet caught up. Let us look at a few instances. In the early 1960s, in Shandong Province (山东/東莒县/縣) in north China, some Neolithic pottery wine vessels were uncovered. At that time, there was speculation that the drawings on them were early forms of writing, but that remained mere speculation until some twenty years later, in the 1980s, when thirty tombs belonging to the late period of a Neolithic culture, called the Dawenkou Culture (大汶口文化, 4500 – 2500 BCE) were excavated in the same area. In these tombs, pottery wine vessels were found with more than twenty stylised pictures of physical objects drawn on them. They depicted sacrificial rites of the people living at that time who seemed to worship the god of wine and the god of the land. In 2000, after nearly two decades of study, archaeologists and palaeographers (those who study archaic scripts) announced that they could recognize fourteen of them as characters. They have succeeded in deciphering seven including 凡 *fán* (ordinary),

南 *nán* (south), 享 *xiăng* (enjoy). The experts are able to do this because these symbols are similar to an archaic type of Chinese writing in the late Shang Dynasty both in form and meaning. If so, then they could be a precursor of Shang writing. This would push back the history of Chinese writing by some two thousand years.

In March 2003, an expert on painted Neolithic pottery at the Gansu Research Institute came across a pot with seven marks on it. These, too, are identical to those found in Shang writing. Upon closer study, they turn out to be seven different ways of writing the same character. This is yet another piece of evidence to convince Chinese scholars that the Shang script indeed had an earlier history.

Even more recently, in May 2007, Chinese scholars have made public their results of another set of studies. This involved the rock carvings at Damaidi 大麦/麥地, in North-west China's Ningxia (宁夏) Hui Autonomous Region. The site covers an area of fifteen kms, with a core area of six square kms, within which one thousand and eighty nine carvings can be found, featuring over four thousand individual figures. The earliest of all the carvings on the entire site were ten thousand to eighteen thousand years old, depicting not only heavenly bodies such as sun, moon and stars as well as hunting or herding scenes, animals which include sheep, dog, deer, and tigers, but also human figures, dancing and performing sacrificial rituals. A geologist happened to stumble on them in 1988. What is of more astonishing interest from the point of view of Chinese writing is that after nearly twenty years of study, scholars have now concluded that some two thousand drawings or marks are characters, dating to between seven and eight thousand years ago. What has impressed them is the fact that these are not isolated but systematic symbols.

If these claims turn out to be truly correct (and not mere pieces of "chauvinistic scholarship"), then this would, indeed, put back the origin of Chinese writing to an even earlier period of time, at least three thousand years earlier than the dates of other texts and inscriptions. It would also mean that Chinese writing would not only be the oldest in continuous use but also the oldest in the history of civilizations, roughly eight thousand years old.

What sort of writing is Chinese writing? We all know what it is not – it is not based on an alphabet such as the Latin, the Cyrillic, or the Arabic alphabet. This much is uncontroversial.

A related set of general claims has recently emerged which appear to throw some light on its nature. First of all, these claims are not themselves linguistic but biological. They have been endorsed by scientists and linguisticians studying the activities occurring in the brain when an individual is engaged in reading. MRI (magnetic resonance imaging) scans throw up images of certain portions of the brain used when a person first learns to recognize written signs, then to associate sounds with them. Such research also shows that languages with different types of scripts appear to create their own distinctive networks in the brain. Learning to read Chinese, a non-alphabetic script, involves the laying down of a set of neuronal connections somewhat different from those in reading an alphabetic script such as English. This is revealed through the study of fluent bilingual readers – after a stroke, such a person would no longer read Chinese but would continue to be able to read English. It appears that while the neuronal connections which decipher Chinese are destroyed, those responsible for decoding English would remain intact. It also appears that people brought up reading Chinese would continue to use the "Chinese" neuronal networks when they first attempt to read English.

We next need to look at Chinese from the linguistic standpoint rather than that of evolutionary biology. Linguisticians classify languages into family groups. For instance, there is a vast group called the Indo-European group. Some modern scholars maintain that Chinese belongs to a group of three of which two are now dead languages. These are Sumerian and Mayan (the script of the latter, according to the latest research published in 2006, is said to date from around 400 BCE, and was the most sophisticated system of writing in Mesoamerica). What unique feature has this particular small group of languages, which despite their obvious differences, would justify putting them into one category? Given the gap in space and time, it is very likely that each of them stumbled upon a similar technique of coping with a key problem of transforming spoken words to become written words independently of one another. They have invented a particular kind of writing which has been called by various names such as "word-syllabic," "morpho-syllabic," or a "meaning-plus-sound" system. What this exactly means in the Chinese context will be made clear as soon as we have cleared away some thick undergrowth, and demolish a few myths along the way about what Chinese writing is still commonly, but mistakenly, perceived to be.

One persistent myth is that it consists of pictograms or pictographs, or that it is essentially ideographic in character. In other words, it is made up simply of different pictures, each trying in some way to capture the reality out there, whether it is a tree, a bird, the sun or the moon. Over the millennia such pictures have evolved to become more stylised, ending up with today's symbols, which seem to bear little or no resemblance to the original pictures. We shall see later that this claim as it stands is just simply false since, at best, only a very small portion of Chinese characters are pictographic in origin. One leading Western scholar of the Chinese language talks about "The Ideographic Myth." This myth can be traced to European Catholic missionaries (especially French and Italian ones), who went to China from the sixteenth to the eighteenth centuries and foisted their own mistaken interpretation on what they saw there. They thought they had found an exotic system of writing totally different from those they were familiar with, which was devoid of phonetics or sounds (unlike their own languages), but still capable of conveying ideas directly to the mind. The myth is harmful for the simple reason that no true writing could make do with only pictographs without proceeding to a way of incorporating sound with meaning – a language with only pictographs would lead to a dead end. Chinese writing is no dead end.

The Ideographic Myth, however, is a powerful one which seems not to go away. Standing behind it and sustaining it could be the observation that the script appears meaningful to any literate Chinese no matter what regional speech (*fangyan*) he speaks. A Shanghainese speaking Shanghainese and a Cantonese speaking Cantonese might find each other's speech unintelligible, but surely all would become clear once they write what they are saying on a piece of paper. While speech divides, script unites. This is only true up to a point. As we have seen, should a Cantonese choose to write in Cantonese and not Standard Chinese, it is not so obvious that everything would be crystal clear to a non-Cantonese. Standard written Chinese is based on *putonghua* (Mandarin), and the Cantonese people have to learn it with greater effort than northerners whose mother tongue is a dialect of *putonghua*. In colonial Hong Kong, some children were educated exclusively in Cantonese. They were taught to read and write in Cantonese only. As a result, they would have difficulty in reading and writing Standard Chinese; *vice versa*, those educated in Standard Chinese would not find written Cantonese readily intelligible. The first Qin emperor, who unified China militarily and politically in 221 BCE, also standardised the writing, but the standardisation was in terms of the Chinese of the Central Plains (中原 *Zhōngyuán*). The term *Zhongyuan* refers to the middle and lower reaches of the Yellow River

(黄河), an area traditionally considered to be the cradle of Han culture and civilization. In today's terminology, this Chinese language would really then be the *fangyan* of Northern China.

Another source sustaining the Ideological Myth is that some general writers in the West find that pictographs serve marvellously to grab the attention of their readers and audiences, as these look so obviously different from their own alphabetic scripts. They themselves may mistakenly conclude from the existence of such pictographs that the entire language consists of nothing but these. Their misleading presentation may implant and reinforce the myth in the minds of their readers and hearers. As a result of these factors, the myth becomes endlessly perpetuated and propagated.

We now introduce you to a very important scholar, Xu Shen (许慎/ 許慎) who lived roughly 58 – 147 CE during the Eastern Han Dynasty (25 – 220 CE). He was the first in Chinese history to compile a systematic dictionary called *Shuo Wen Jie Zi* (说/說文解字). There were other dictionaries before his but they were not quite so systematically organized. His dictionary is probably also the world's first known major systematic dictionary. He had completed it in 100 CE, although for political reasons it was only presented to the Han court by his son in 121 CE. His dictionary was primarily based on a particular style of writing called *xiaozhuan* (小篆) which was being promoted as the official script by the government of the day and about which more would be said later. For our immediate purpose, the important thing to note is that Xu Shen was the first to apply systematically six principles of formation and use (六书/書 *liùshū*, which literally means "the six writings") in analyzing the characters in his dictionary. Although it is true that he was not the first to identify and articulate them (these were already in current use by the Warring States Period, 475 – 221 BCE), his systematic use of such a classification has profoundly influenced later Chinese scholars for nearly two thousand years.

Sinologists (non-Chinese authorities of the Chinese language) appear on the whole not to be too impressed by "the six writings." Their complaint amounts to this: the principles, if at all helpful, must be understood as an exhaustive classification which assigns each and every character to one of the categories. Unfortunately, as a character sometimes falls into more than one category, these critics say that they are not all that useful. To us, the criticism seems needlessly strict, demanding that the classificatory principles themselves be dismissed altogether as worthless. One could distinguish a more defensible claim. There is no contradiction between saying that Xu Shen and earlier scholars had correctly identified six major relevant principles in terms of which one may classify Chinese characters and admitting that some possess characteristics which show that they fall into more than one of the categories. Whatever the perceived flaws and limitations, it remains true that if people knew about these six principles, they might not have been so easily led into propagating or accepting the Ideological Myth.

The six principles yielding six categories are:

1. Indicator (指事 *zhǐshì*)
2. Pictograph (象形 *xiàngxíng*)
3. Semantic-phonetic compound (形声/聲 *xíngshēng*)
4. Meaning compound (会/會意 *huìyì*)
5. Mutually interpretive (转/轉注 *zhuǎnzhù*)
6. Phonetic loan (假借 *jiǎjiè*)

We shall say something about each in the following order: 1, 5, 6, 2, 4, and 3.

The **indicator**, *zhishi* category has very few members which include the numerals such as "one," "two," "three" (一, 二, 三 *yī, èr, sān*), and prepositions such as "above," "below" (上,下 *shàng, xià*) .

The **mutually interpretative**, *zhuanzhu* category also has few applications. Some (Western) scholars often omit it from Xu Shen's list of principles on the grounds that it is somewhat obscure. We shall be looking at one such interesting example in Part III (***Happiness is piggy-shaped***).

The **phonetic loan**, *jiajie* category is a technique which involves a character being transferred to another unrelated in meaning but which in ancient Chinese sounded alike or nearly alike. The character for "foot" is used to write "suffice." Both then would be written as 足 *zú*; but the meaning of 足 zú when it refers to feet is totally different in meaning from 足 zú when it means "enough" or "ample." One can talk of 秀丽/麗的足 *xiùlì de zú* "dainty feet," and one can say 足吃足喝 *zú chī zú hē* "plenty to eat and to drink, a bountiful life."

The **pictograph**, *xiangxing* category, as one can see at a glance, is only one of six categories. This alone should have alerted people to the fact that Chinese writing could not possibly consist of nothing but pictographs. Some oft cited examples of pictographs are the signs for "sun" or "moon." Xu Shen relied primarily on a script in which the two characters look like this: , . Today, nearly two thousand years later, they look like this: 日, 月. In two scripts said to be older than the one Xu Shen used, they look respectively like this: , (Shang script) and this: , (Bronze script). It is obvious that these two more archaic scripts as well as Xu Shen's *xiaozhuan* (Lesser Seal script) render the characters more pictographic than the modern version. But the most pictographic of the four versions is the one, which makes the sun round and the moon crescent. This is the Shang script in which certain objects in ordinary life during Shang times are commonly represented as pictographs, and it is often said that the clearest pictographs are their earliest expressions in Shang writing. Here is an example of the character for "horse" 马/ 馬 in the Shang script to demonstrate the point:

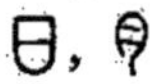

You have to move the page anti-clockwise, away from yourself, until the character is no longer vertical but horizontal to see what it really looks like. You can, then, see clearly the horse's head on the left, the body in the middle with legs attached, a mane on the spine, and a long swishing tail on the right.

The **meaning compound**, *huiyi* category is formed from existing characters. A standard illustration is the character for "bright" which is 明 *míng*. Two characters are combined to form a new character with a new meaning: 日 *rì* ("sun") and 月 *yuè* ("moon") are put together thus to form 明. The component characters may be pictographs, (*xiangxing*). However, the general principle behind this technique for creating a new character is probably not unique to Chinese as it is found in other languages. For instance, in Old English and Old Norse (the language in which the Icelandic Sagas are written), it is called "kenning."

Unlike in Chinese, these languages used it to create a striking new word entirely for poetic effect. For example, in Old English, the sea is called "sail-road," and also "whale-road" (in the epic *Beowulf*, the word is '*hronrãde*'); a sword is "battlefriend," and the body "bonehouse." By using such invented words instead of their everyday equivalents, the poet presented a new vision or idea of the objects talked about. Imagine a poet describing the aftermath of a battle, where bodies were strewn all over the place; the word "bonehouse" would drive home most effectively the idea that flesh decayed and ultimately the corpse would simply be a skeleton. The word "kenning" comes from an Old Norse phrase which means "to express a thing in terms of another." It seems plausible then to claim that the technique of creating meaning compounds (*huiyi*), in Chinese is analogous to that of kenning. In the Chinese context, it is not meant to create phrases with a magical ring to them, whereas in the Old Norse or Old English context it was used precisely to enhance the magical poetic effects of certain phrases. In this respect, Chinese may be more like Arabic – for instance, the word for body in Arabic translates literally as "bonehouse," or even like modern English. In Part I, we have given the examples of "photo-copy," "photo-genic," and "photo-graph" to discuss another point, but we can use them again here to illustrate the general principle behind the technique of creating meaning compounds. "Photo" means "light," while "copy," "genic," and "graph" each have their own respective meanings. By combining "photo" with each of them, English has created three new words with meanings different from those of their respective components.

The **semantic-phonetic compound,** *xingsheng* category is, in the opinion of modern linguistics, what renders Chinese undeniably a true system of writing, and is definitive evidence that it is a gross mistake to subscribe to the Ideological Myth. In this category, the character has two components: the one on the left hand side usually gives the meaning while the one on the right gives the sound. Take the following example, the character for "sweet," written like this 糖, *táng*. The left element is something we have come across already in Part I. It is the radical (部首, *bùshǒu*) and in this case, it is the character for "cereal foods," 米, *mǐ*. The right element is also a character in its own right, 唐, *táng* whose sole function, however, in this context, is to lend its sound to the new character 糖 ("sweet").

The sound of Chinese characters in *putonghua* comes in four main tones. The four are marked in *pinyin* as shown in the following examples:

1st	妈 *mā*	(mother)
2nd	麻 *má*	(hemp)
3rd	马 *mǎ*	(horse)
4th	骂 *mà*	(scold, swear or curse)

Sometimes the sound component donates to the character not only the sound but also the tone to go with it; in the case here of *táng*, it is the second tone. At other times, the sound component only donates the sound, but, not also, the exact tone.

The technique of combining sound and meaning enables new characters to be created almost indefinitely. Some Western scholars maintain that of the two components, the more important is the sound rather than the meaning component. This is because a native hearer could identify what is meant more readily *via* the sound element. They also argue that while the meaning element is not without significance, it does not, all the same, have that much significance, as the radicals contain minimal information, at best indicating very roughly what kind of object is involved, whether it is animal, vegetable, or mineral. If the radical is 木 *mù*, you would know that the object has something to do with trees or is made of wood. If the radical is 艹 *cǎo*, you would know that the object is about grass or shrubs. If the radical is 钅/金 *jīn*, you would know that the object involves metal. If the radical is 石 *shí*, you would know that the object belongs to the family of rocks. These scholars claim that while this kind of information is well suited to the game of "Twenty Questions" on radio or television shows, it is of no real earth-shaking value to the understanding of Chinese characters.

Is this correct? It appears not. Imagine you overhear someone on a bus saying: *ta chu zia le*. This sentence in *pinyin* is deeply ambiguous and can mean a number of things. Suppose that the lady on the bus is talking to her friend about her daughter. What you have overheard can then mean one of two things. The first is:

she　has got married
tā　*chū jià le*

You will notice that *jià* is in the fourth tone.

But suppose you think you hear her use the first, not the fourth tone in *jiā*, then you will be correct in thinking that the good lady is telling her friend not that her daughter has got married but she has just become a nun!

she has joined the convent
tā chū jiā le

The mere difference of the tone alters entirely the meaning of the character. As a matter of fact, it may not be so easy to distinguish between the first and fourth tones in *putonghua* when the speaker utters them indistinctly or quickly. After all, not every one speaks clearly and most people talk rapidly. One must also bear in mind that even *putonghua*-mother-tongue speakers could be speaking *putonghua* in several versions of *putonghua*, not all necessarily with the clarity of the "received pronunciation" of program presenters on central Chinese radio and television transmissions. If one were guided by sound alone, it may not always be clear.

The ambiguity would be dispelled on seeing the two sentences in their written forms:

she has got married
tā chū jià le
她 出 嫁 了

This *jià* in the fourth tone has the radical for "woman," 女 *nǚ* , added to 家 (meaning "home") to indicate a female leaving home to get married, rather than leaving home to become a nun, which is in the deeper sense of leaving family behind, as joining the religious life means abandoning home and family for good. A woman leaving her parental home upon marriage is not turning her back on ordinary life, but simply for another home and another family, her husband's.

She has joined the convent
tā chū jiā le
她 出 家 了

This *jiā* is in the first tone and the character is written without the radical for "woman." If the two meanings were to be represented by exactly the same expression, namely, 出家, the reader could be left wondering whether the woman in question had just got married (出嫁) or had become a nun (出家). It was to avoid such an ambiguity that the written difference in the two contexts had evolved.

Today even with near universal education in *putonghua* in China, Chinese television still flashes up the text as it is being spoken. Surely it is to ensure that ambiguities do not arise through misunderstanding the sounds. On the point as to which is more important, sound or meaning, it would be fair to conclude that both are equally important. After all, the unique feature of the category of semantic-phonetic compound (*xingsheng*) lies precisely in its ingenious technique of combining meaning and sound in the single character. That is why Chinese is said by modern linguistics to be morpho-syllabic, a meaning-plus-sound language.

There are additional complications to the example we have examined and to which it may be worth drawing your attention. When you hear someone say *ta chu zia le*, you cannot be sure if *ta* refers to a woman or a man. The lady on the bus could be talking about her daughter or her son. *Tā* has the same sound as well as the same tone, the first, and is gender-neutral. When written, modern Chinese distinguishes between the genders in this way: she is 她 and he is 他.

Imagine that you are pretty sure that the lady is talking about an offspring having left home to join the religious life, yet you cannot be sure whether she is talking about a son having become a monk or a daughter having become a nun. When you see the two possibilities written out, there would be no room for misunderstanding.

she has become a nun
她 出家了
he has become a monk
他 出家了

In other words, the two utterances *tā chū jiā le* and *tā chū jià le*, heard indistinctly and out of context, can give rise to misunderstanding in numerous ways. You can hear it as:

a woman having married
a woman having entered a convent
a man having joined a monastery

Now, you may think that we have left out a fourth possibility, hearing it as:

a man having married

This possibility does not exist in the Chinese language. The native hearer would not commit the mistake of thinking that someone's son has just married! The character 嫁 carries a very specific meaning within the Chinese cultural context in which it is embedded. The word "marry" in English, "marier" in French, or "hieraten" in German is gender-neutral. In Chinese, this is not so. 嫁 *jià* is used only in the case of females; in the case of males, the character is 娶 *qǔ* , meaning "to get a wife." (In Part III, ***In the twilight snatch the bride***, we shall be telling you precisely how, historically, the male got a wife.) Imagine a non-Chinese person who has just learned via *pinyin* that *jià* means "marry," but has not been told specifically that it is only used in the marriage of a woman. She might then cause initial puzzlement and then amusement when she announces that she, too, has a child who has recently "*chū jià le*," showing her new-found Chinese friends, photos of her son's wedding!

The discussion above reinforces the point that it is a mistake to assume that the sound component stands simply for the sound but with no meaning to contribute to the overall meaning content of the character. The meaning comes not only from the radical, 女 *nǚ* in the case of 嫁 *jià*. The meaning of the entire character comes from both its two components. The right hand component, 家 *jiā*, is there not only to give the sound but also to contribute meaning. It is to say that the woman in marrying leaves her parental home for that of her new husband. It is to say that this character 嫁 *jià* is only used to talk about a woman, but never a man, getting married.

We should resist asking the question: which is more important, the meaning or the sound component? Meaning and sound are intimately bound up in all the relevant aspects, that both components are equally important in the deconstruction and understanding of semantic-phonetic compounds (*xingsheng*). In cases where a component of a character donates both sound and meaning, the entire character itself is no longer simply a semantic-phonetic compound (*xingsheng*), but also a meaning compound (*huiyi*). This in turn shows that it would not be wise to dismiss flippantly Xu Shen's six principles, as a good number of characters, such as 嫁 *jià*, belong to both the *xingsheng* as well as *huiyi* categories. It would be wrong to assume that the radical exhausts the entire cultural baggage of a character; the cultural baggage is carried by the entire character including its sound component which may also carry meaning.

Regarding Xu Shen's six principles, except for the semantic-phonetic compounds, (*xingsheng*), the other five categories had, overall in the course of several millennia, made no outstanding contribution to the Chinese vocabulary in terms of volume. From Xu Shen's dictionary in the late Han Dynasty to the *Kangxi Dictionary* of 1716 in the Qing Dynasty (with 47,035 entries), the characters in numbers which could be classified under them remained more or less unchanged. The indicator, the phonetic loan, and the mutually interpretive between them account for the least. The really fruitful technique is hence the fifth, the semantic-phonetic compound (*xingsheng*). Even during the Shang Dynasty which well preceded Xu Shen's time by more than a thousand years, this principle already accounted for 34% of Shang characters. Since then, it had become predominant in yielding new vocabulary. One scholar in 1923 said that 90% of Chinese characters belonged to this category. Today, it is said to account for at least 97% of the Chinese vocabulary. In contrast, in Xu Shen's dictionary, which contained 9,353 characters, only 364 or about 4% were pictographs (*xiangxing*). Not all scholars give precisely the same breakdown in numbers for the categories for key compilations over the millennia. Although the figures do vary, they all bear out the tendency that while the percentages for the other categories decline as the vocabulary grows in volume, the percentage for the category of semantic-phonetic compound (*xingsheng*) steadily and even dramatically increases.

However, another conclusion should also be emphasized: even in Shang times, Chinese writing had never been predominantly pictographic (standing at only about 23%), and that the writing over the millennia progressively used less and less pictographs, relying more and more on a technique which combines sound with meaning to generate new characters. However, do remember that in many cases the sound component also carries meaning; this means that the category of meaning compounds (*huiyi*) is also a not insignificant technique in Chinese character creation.

Below is a chart which summaries Xu Shen's six categories, showing how the characters would look like in *xiaozhuan* (Lesser Seal), the script relied on primarily by Xu Shen himself as well as in Standard script used today.

Category	*Xiaozhuan*	Standard	Meaning	Sound
Pictograph	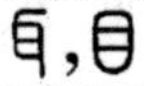 耳, 目	耳, 目	Ear, eye	*ěr, mù*
Indicator	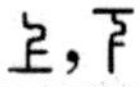 上, 下	上, 下	above, below	*shàng, xià*
Meaning compound	 日 + 月 → 明	日 + 月 → 明	Sun + moon → bright	*rì + yuè → míng*
Phonetic loan	足	足	Foot → sufficient	*zú*
Semantic-phonetic compound	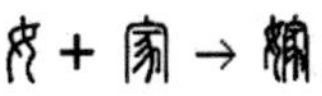 女 + 家 → 嫁	女+ 家 → 嫁	woman + house → marry	*nǚ + jiā → jià*
Mutually interpretive	 樂	乐/樂	music → pleasure	*yuè → lè*

Characters, words and syllables

So far we have talked about the written Chinese language, mainly, in terms of characters. The term "character" may not be the best term to use, but for want of a better, we have stuck to it, in spite of certain drawbacks to its use. A distinct drawback is that it appears to be intimately bound up with the Ideographic Myth. When the first Western European missionaries and scholars came into contact with the Chinese language, we have seen that they were so struck by the difference in appearance between their own (Latin) alphabetic writing and Chinese writing that they thought it fitting to call what they saw written on a page "characters," rather than "words," to mark their peculiarities. Part of their peculiarities lies in the fact that what the visitors saw was in a particular style of writing (楷书/書 *kǎishū*), introduced towards the end of the Han Dynasty (206 BCE – 220 CE) in which each stroke of the character is clear and separate, and each character also stands alone occupying the same area of space within a kind of imagined square box. A character of one stroke as in 一 *yī*, or two strokes as in 人 *rén*, is written in the same (imagined) size box as one with numerous strokes such as 娶 *qǔ*. The clarity of *kaishu* probably made it the preferred style for official documents especially with the invention of first block printing between the fourth and seventh centuries CE during the Tang Dynasty (618 – 907 CE), and later of movable type printing in the eleventh century during the Song

Dynasty (960 – 1279 CE). *Kaishu* has been in continuous use for about two thousand years.

Furthermore, these early missionaries and scholars noticed that each character has a sound attached to it. Of course, the sound is also uttered in a certain tone, one of four in *putonghua*. From these correct observations, it appeared that they inferred that Chinese as a language is essentially mono-syllabic, with one syllable to each character. Their propagation of this inference constitutes another myth.

To undo this myth, first, we need to sort out a terminological matter. For our purpose, we shall simply state how we use the terms "character" and "word." Let us agree that the term "character" simply refers to any free-standing item one sees when one opens a Chinese book. Let us imagine that we spot 中 in the middle of a certain page – it is a character.

It turns out quite unusually that the sound of this particular character is capable of having two different tones – the first is *zhōng* and the fourth is *zhòng*. The first tone *zhōng* means "middle," "center"; the fourth tone *zhòng* means "to hit," "to fit exactly." When a character has a sound with more than two tones, this really amounts to saying that the character stands for two different words with two different meanings. This makes it analogous to the English word spelled "bow" with two different ways of pronouncing it as well as possessing more than two different meanings. It can be pronounced as in "bow" of a ship as well as in a musician taking a "bow" at the end of a recital, or it can be pronounced as in a "bow " referring to something made out of a length of ribbon, as in the musician's bow, which is tied round his neck. The two different sets of pronunciation lead, however, to four different meanings – the ship's bow is very different from a stage bow, which is very different from a bow on a fair damsel's head, which in turn is very different from the bow with which one plays the cello. And who says that Chinese is a difficult language to learn and to master!

Let us say that the sound uttered in a particular tone associated with a character is a syllable, and that a character with a meaning, with a syllable with a particular tone attached to it, is a word. This then is to say that *zhōng* with the first tone is a word ("central", "middle"), so is *zhòng* with the fourth tone a word, but a different word ("hit" or "fit exactly"). They are two different mono-syllabic words, in other words.

Although all Chinese characters are mono-syllabic, not all Chinese words are so; to say that they are is to propagate, as we have seen, a myth. How, then, does the language create, say two-syllable words, of which it has an abundance? The most obvious method is simply to put two mono-syllabic words together to form a new two-syllable word, with a meaning different from the respective meanings of their components. Take the word 中国/國. How is it put together? Put 中 (1st tone) together with 国/國, and you create a new two-syllable word, namely, 中国/國 *Zhōngguó* "China," which refers to that country with a sixth of the world's population. We already know that 中 (1st tone) means "middle"; 国/國 *guó* means "country," "state," or "nation." That is why the literal meaning of the name 中国/國 is "Central Country." Suppose you put 中 (with the fourth tone) together with another word such as 暑 *shǔ* ("great summer heat"), you would have created another two-syllable word 中暑 *zhòngshǔ* ("to suffer from sunstroke"). Another example is 天气/氣 *tiānqì* ("weather"): 天 on its own means "sky" or "heaven," and 气 could mean "air," but when combined as a single word, it means something quite different.

Not only are some words two-syllable words even from early times, others especially modern ones are even multi-syllabic, three or four are not uncommon. The same technique is used for creating these. Examples of three-syllable words are: 高射炮 *gāoshèpào* ("anti-aircraft gun"); 吃不开/開 *chī·bukāi* ("be unpopular"). Examples of four-syllable ones are: 一五一十 *yì wǔ yì shí* ("in every detail"); a more colorful one is 酒囊饭/飯袋 *jiǔ náng fàn dài* ("a good-for-nothing," literally "someone whose sole purpose in life is to eat and drink, to act as receptacle for food and wine").

We next draw your attention to another matter which may surprise you. Take a look at these two characters: 蝴 *hú* and 蝶 *dié*. These two characters together do indeed constitute, like some of the previous examples, a two-syllable word meaning "butterfly," but with a difference. The first character (*hu*) on its own appears to have no meaning, and hence cannot count as a word in its own right. However, the second character (*die*) on its own actually means "butterfly." So why then bother to add another character (with no meaning of its own) to one which already is a word meaning "butterfly"? We could perhaps venture to say that this seemingly curious example shows that the Chinese language displays a tendency towards two-syllabic words. This tendency already existed, albeit in an embryonic form, even in classical Chinese (as we shall see in a moment), but did not get underway until later in the evolution of the language. This particular example is of special interest as it precisely illustrates the early burgeoning of this tendency – the two-syllabic *hudie* is found in as early a text as the philosophical Daoist book called the *Zhuangzi*, whose supposed author is said to be Zhuangzi himself, living at the time of the Warring States Period (403 – 221 BCE) but born a century after Confucius. When the text itself first appeared is not so certain; however, the precise scholarship of this book is not a problem from our point of view. Let us simply say that it is a relatively early text, and is probably at least 2000 years old. This well-known philosophically playful text tells us that one day Zhuangzi woke up wondering whether it was really himself who had dreamed of being a butterfly or whether it was a butterfly that was now dreaming of being a philosopher. For our purpose, the importance of this tale is that the term *hudie* occurs seven times in the story, always with the two characters together, never with only one. We can infer two things from this example. First, it is possible to have a two-syllable (meaningful) word made from one meaningful and one other meaningless character, just as one can create a two-syllable word from two meaningful characters, each with a different meaning (but in this latter case giving the new word a new meaning). Second, this technique, already in use in the *Zhuangzi*, means that it has existed for at least 2000 years, if not more.

Let us conclude by way of a small summary of the main points made. We can clarify the relationship between the term "character" and that of "word" in the light of the above discussion in this way: all words involve characters but not all characters are words. A character may or may not on its own stand for a word, although the overwhelming majority does. It is a word only if it has a meaning. However, every character has a sound with a particular tone attached to it; in other words, one may regard a character as standing always for a syllable. It follows that there are two types of characters: the first represents a sound, standing only as a syllable, such as 蝴; the second has both meaning and sound, yielding a mono-syllabic word such as 蝶. Characters in classical Chinese tend to fall into this category, while the majority of modern Chinese words tend to be a combination of two (or more) characters (each with their respective meanings, unlike the 蝴蝶 *húdié* example) giving a new meaning altogether as in 中国/國 *Zhōngguó* , 中暑 *zhòngshǔ*, or 天气/氣 *tiānqì.* Alternatively, this technique of combining two characters may also incorporate two characters/words each with similar meanings to produce a new two-syllabic word with reinforced meaning. Such an example is 休息 *xiū·xī* meaning "to stop" or "to rest," as the two respective characters/words each means "to stop" or "to rest."

The examples of *hudie* and *xiuxi* may also perhaps be used to illustrate the creative powers at work of two of the six traditional principles or categories of use and classification (*liushu*), namely, the *xingsheng* and *huiyi* principles, but this time, applied not at the level of character construction but at that of two-syllable word construction. The *hudie* two-syllable word is an instance of the former at work – *hu* as a mere character appears to have been introduced for the sake of sound (*sheng*), but to supplement the sound of the word *die* rather than supply a tone for it, while *die* is the character/word with meaning (analogous to *xing*). The *xiuxi* two-syllable word is, by analogy, an instance of the *huiyi* principle at work, as normally that principle is used to generate a new character/word with a new meaning based on components each with different meanings, rather than similar ones.

If you always bear in mind these important techniques for creating Chinese words, you would not be too far wrong in understanding the nature of Chinese writing through the ages. The most fruitful technique for creating new mono-syllabic words is to rely on Xu Shen's principle of the semantic-phonetic compound (*xingsheng*) as well as (although to a lesser extent) that of his meaning compound (*huiyi*). The technique for creating multi-syllabic words is simply to put two or more characters together. Sometimes, both the *xingsheng* and the *huiyi* principles can even be seen to be at work in the creation of certain two-syllable words.

Brief account of archaic Chinese writing: the oracle-bone script

Until 1899, Chinese scholars through the ages had nothing earlier to rely on than texts which could be dated to the Zhou Dynasty (周代, ca. 11th century – 221 BCE). The earliest major kind of writing known up to then was 金文 *jīnwén* or the Bronze script, the form of writing used to make inscriptions on Zhou bronze vessels. Scholars also knew other scripts including 小篆 *xiǎozhuàn* or Lesser Seal script which Xu Shen mainly relied on in late Han times when he constructed his dictionary. Another script was 大篆 *dàzhuàn* or the Greater Seal script. Since 1899, great progress has indeed been made in the last hundred years in understanding the origins of Chinese writing which went beyond Zhou times, to the dynasty which preceded it, the Shang Dynasty. It turned out that the Zhou had so successfully overthrown the Shang that hardly any trace of that earlier dynasty was left. Its artifacts and other relics which survived destruction lay, in the main, deeply buried underground for three millennia or more until its fabulous bronzes (even more fabulous than the Zhou ones) were unearthed during the excavations (between 1928 and 1937) after Shang writing itself had been accidentally discovered towards the very end of the nineteenth century in 1899.

The bronze vessels together with the writing provided evidence beyond doubt that the Shang Dynasty was not only a truly historical dynasty but also an impressively advanced civilization. Here is one of these magnificent objects. Up to then, some historians had doubts about its existence, claiming that the reference to it in the great work of the Han historian Sima Qian (司马迁/馬遷, 145–85 BCE) commonly known in the West as *Records of the Grand Historian* or more simply *Historic Records* (史记/記) of the Han Dynasty, was probably based on legendary hearsay handed down the ages rather than historically grounded. However, the evidence produced by the excavations in the capital of the late Shang Dynasty in Anyang (安阳/陽), Henan Province, shows that Sima Qian's account of the Shang dynastic history was correct and accurate.

This Shang writing is 甲骨文 *jiǎgǔwén*, commonly known in the West as the Oracle-bone script. Its accidental discovery only just over a hundred years ago involves an interesting story. A high-ranking mandarin, called Wang Yirong (王懿荣/榮) in Beijing (called Pekin then) during the late Qing (清) Dynasty (1644 – 1911 CE) fell prey to a bout of malaria. His friend, Liu E (刘/劉鹗/鶚), a noted novelist, went to a traditional Chinese pharmacy to get medicine on his behalf. One of the ingredients in the prescription was something which people called 龙/龍骨 *lónggǔ*, dragon bone, believed to be fossil animal bones possessing medicinal properties. Liu saw the shop assistant crush a piece of the dragon bone into powder. He noticed that the bone seemed to have marks on it looking like some form of writing. When Wang recovered from the fever, he and Liu were determined to get to the bottom of this curious observation. Wang bought from the herbal shop whatever pieces of dragon bone it had in stock. On examining these, it struck Liu, who was also an expert of the Bronze script (*jinwen*) that these markings bore remarkable similarity to *jinwen*. Indeed, he was soon able to make out a few characters, such as those which stood for "fire," "water," "rain." Thus was established for the first time that there was an older script which had preceded the Bronze script. Wang continued to buy up as many pieces as he could lay his hands on. Unfortunately, in 1900, he committed suicide because of political events associated with the Boxer Rebellion, one of numerous disturbances, which led eventually to the collapse of the Qing Dynasty in 1911. Fortunately Liu was able to buy the collection from the family to continue his research. In 1903, he published a volume consisting mainly of rubbings of these inscriptions, making them readily accessible for the first time to the world of scholarship.

Other scholars soon joined in as well. The location of these dragon bones was kept a deadly secret by those who sold them as medicine or as antiques. But eventually it was identified as near a village called Xiaotun (小屯) in the county of Anyang in Henan (河南) Province. It has since been established through carbon-dating techniques that these dragon bones were not fossil bones at all, but shells of tortoises or turtles and the shoulder blades of ox, animals killed in more recent times, geologically speaking. In Shang times, that part of China enjoyed a wetter climate than today, supporting marshes and swamps, congenial as habitat for tortoises and turtles. Peasants turning the soil came up with them. The story went that a local barber in the nineteenth century suffered from a bad open sore for which he had no money to get proper medical treatment. He ground up some pieces of shell or bone and applied it to the sore. To his great relief he found that the ground up stuff got rid of the pus and the sore started to heal. Word spread, demand grew. Entrepreneurial peasants collected the stuff and took it to sell to the herbal shops in the city. Irrespective of whether this tale is true, there is no doubt that these "dragon bones" have been part of traditional Chinese pharmacopoeia since 600 BCE. It is said that the pharmacies for some unspecified reason preferred those pieces without markings. Some peasants filed off the writing and polished smooth the pieces. The practice of using them as part of

Chinese medicine over the centuries could well have destroyed some important evidence relevant to the scholarship of archaic Chinese writing.

It turned out that Anyang was a late Shang capital, and the site was where the Shang palaces and archives must have been. Systematic excavations first began in 1928, and in spite of wars and upheavals, were conducted sporadically in the numerous decades that followed. These have yielded a rich harvest, although over the years since the location of the site became known, a not insignificant amount had been pillaged. In 1976 a little to the north of the village, some Shang royal tombs were discovered. One belonging to the consort of King Wu Ding (武丁) referred to as Wife Hao (妇/婦好), has already been excavated. This produced a magnificent crop of artifacts. We shall be returning to the story of Fu Hao later in the book (***What is it to be a woman?***) to show why she was honored in death by such a sumptuous array of tomb goods – was it for her beauty? We can only wait with bated breathe for the day when archaeologists feel themselves ready to open another tomb found next to that of the consort. Scholars are pretty confident that it belongs to King Wu Ding himself. The tomb goods would very likely be even more sumptuous than those already excavated from his consort's tomb, which include more than 200 ritual bronze vessels, about 250 other bronze objects, more than 100 stone and semi-precious stone carvings, more than 560 bone carvings, some 750 jades, 3 ivory goblets, 11 ceramics and more.

Foreign scholars also got interested in *jiaguwen*. Today, Japan, unsurprisingly, has a large collection, but it is perhaps more surprising to learn that Canada has the second largest collection in the world of these bones and shells. As early as 1914, a Canadian missionary got to the site and simply helped himself to cart-loads of them. To his credit, he did some work on the material, publishing a volume in 1917 in Shanghai through one of the Western publishers there at the time. When the Japanese invasion of China began in 1937, he had to leave most of his collection behind, burying them in the campus of a university in Shandong province. He did not recover them until 1952, by which time, unfortunately, the greater part had perished. So readers, if you are Canadian, and would like to carry on this Canadian tradition of research into *jiaguwen*, the resources are on your very own door step.

Those of you who do not already know the story of *jiaguwen* would of course wonder why in English, it is called the Oracle-bone script (*jiaguwen* simply means "the kind of archaic writing found on shells and bones"), and even more puzzlingly, why inscriptions should be found on some of these tortoise shells and shoulder blades of large mammals, primarily ox. The English name gives the clue away. Yes, the writing is there precisely because these animal parts were used in a divination ritual during Shang times.

The Shang kings used divination for all sorts of important as well as relatively trivial events, from matters of state such as whether it would be auspicious to raise an army against an enemy, to matters of agriculture such as harvests, to royal pleasure pursuits like hunting which, all the same, was of state significance, to astronomy and the weather, to interpretation of dreams, to matters of illness and health (including even toothaches), births, etc. Evidence recovered from the shells and bones also showed that the aristocracy was permitted to indulge in this shamanistic practice, conducted by priests who not merely acted as scribes, but who were also assumed to have powers of communicating with gods and ancestors.

Shang life for the king and his aristocracy was overwhelmingly governed by divination because ancestors must be honored and their approval for actions sought and ascertained through divination. The year was divided into regular periods, with a cycle of sixty days. On every tenth day of each cycle, one must find out what events might take place in the next ten days.

The ritual involved the following procedure: first, one must prepare the shells and bones, cleaning and polishing them. Then a series of holes, as if making up rows of deep grooves, were carefully drilled on the inside of the flat underneath shell covering the stomach of the turtle. This drilling involved great skill, as the holes must penetrate the plate deep enough but not so deep as to go through to the outer side. The pictures below show these holes, which allowed cracks to appear more readily when the shell was later heated. As divination was based on reading such cracks, it is obvious that drilling them must be expertly done.

Preparations over, the ritual proper would begin. The priest as diviner would loudly proclaim the question the king had posed, at the same time applying heat to it, which produced crackling sounds. This was regarded as the shells "speaking," as if in response to the question asked. From the cracks produced by the heating, the priest would "read" the answer. Sometimes, the king himself would interpret them. The divination would then be recorded. The inscription – made using a knife on the outside of the shell where the cracks appeared – consisted of four parts, of which the first two were obligatory and the rest optional. The first consists of a kind of preface, stating the date of the divination as well as the person performing it. The second records the question posed. The third is the prognostication itself. The fourth is the so-called verification, giving an account of what actually happened. Although the convention governing the recording of the date of the divination gives only minimal, imprecise information, it is possible sometimes in conjunction with the recorded name of the diviner plus other evidence to infer a more accurate dating as in the case of solar eclipses recorded in the reign of Wu Ding.

Below are pictures of the inner and outer sides of the plate.

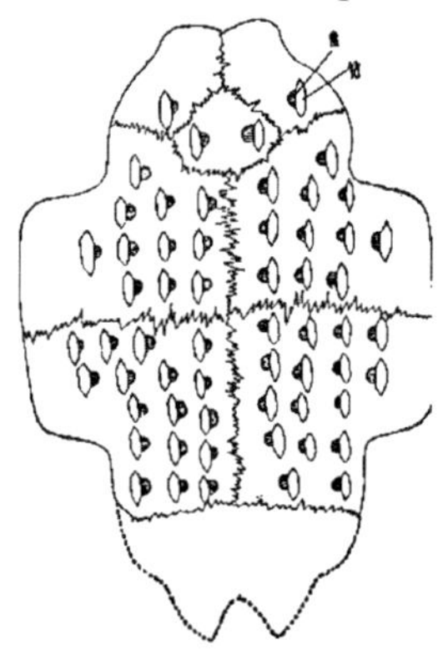

This shows the preparations made on the inside of the plate for the divination, displaying the rows of holes drilled.

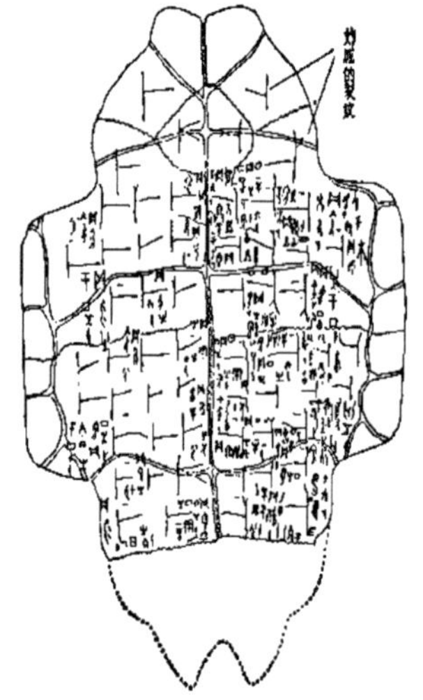

This shows the carved inscriptions, following the divination, on the outside of the plate. Note the cracks produced. The character for "divination" is a pictograph of these cracks. Today we write it as 卜 *bǔ*. There are numerous forms of the character in the Oracle-bone script, which are obviously simple copies of the various types of cracks:

Here are two recorded instances of divination. The first concerns Wife Hao who was about to give birth. King Wu Ding would like to know whether his favorite consort would be bringing him the gift of a son and heir. The inscription mentioned the date of the divination which was the Twenty-first Day (in a cycle of 60 days) and that the diviner was one called Ge. The king posed the question: Will it be a happy event? The king himself read the cracks: should the birth take place on certain specified days, the event would be a happy one. If it occurred on other specified dates, then it would be very auspicious. But should it take place at some other specified day, the event would be neither happy nor auspicious. According to the verification part of the inscription, Hao gave birth, three weeks and a day after the divination; it was a girl, and so was not a happy event.

The second goes like this: On the Thirty-third Day, the king asked: In the next ten days will any disaster happen? The diviner, studying the cracks said: Yes, news of something which will cause great unease will arrive. Five days later, indeed, from the west came the disquieting news that the Tufang (土方) tribe had encircled our territory on the eastern frontier, having already attacked two villages. On the western frontier, they had pillaged the countryside.

At first, it was thought that with the overthrow of the Shang Dynasty, the Zhou Dynasty straightaway abandoned the practice of divination. Excavated evidence now exists to show that this was not so.

As you can imagine, it is not easy to decipher the Oracle-bone writing. For a start, such archaic writing had its own conventions which, however, did not coincide entirely with those which had evolved since its time – the *jiaguwen* characters were “all over the place” to people used to reading Chinese characters each written within an imagined square space with equal distances between them as in printed books using *kaishu*. This convention had been observed for nearly two thousand years by the time the Oracle-bone script was discovered. However, *jiaguwen* had already laid down the convention of writing vertically from right to left, a convention which had been observed until the recent introduction of writing horizontally from left to right. Even after nearly a century of scholarship, scholars are today able to decipher only about 2000 out of the 4500 different characters found inscribed on the shells and bones.

When scholars first deciphered the Oracle-bone script, they realized that the writing was a mature, complete system, even bearing out in retrospect Xu Shen's six principles of classification. This led them to speculate that, although the earliest Shang piece of writing could be dated only to 1200 BCE, such maturity implies that its origin could be much earlier. Nearly a century later, this hypothesis, as we have seen earlier, may now have found confirmation in both the Neolithic painted pottery specimens as well as the rock paintings found in Damaidi cliffs, pushing the date of Chinese writing to about 8000 years ago.

Why not study this piece of divination in some detail. It could be fun.

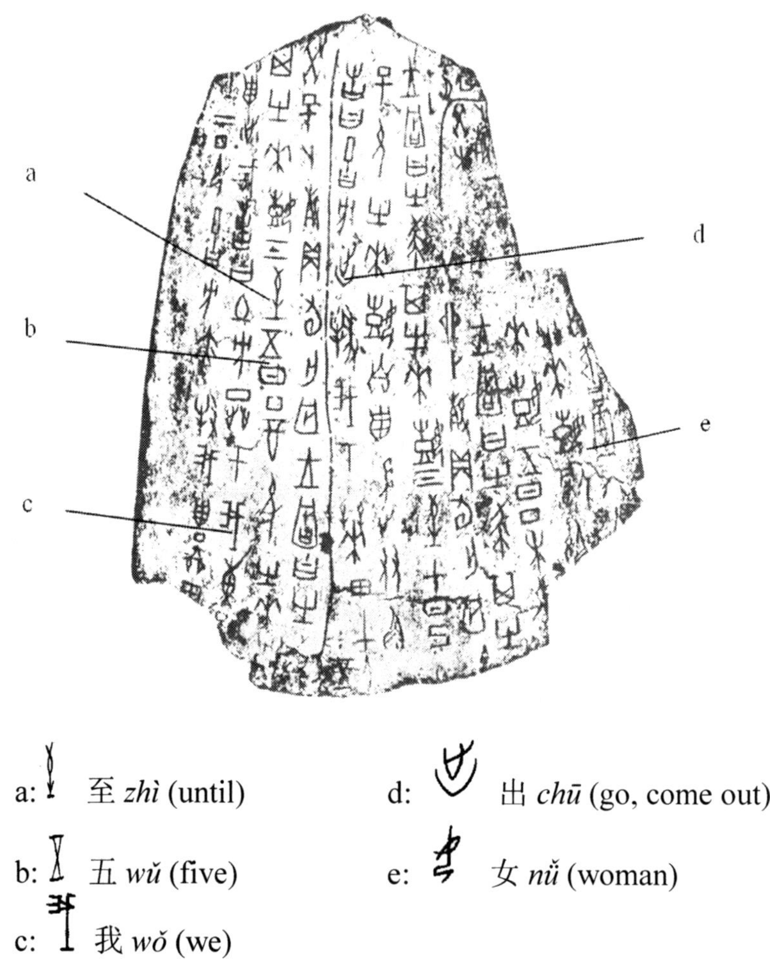

a: 至 *zhì* (until)

b: 五 *wǔ* (five)

c: 我 *wǒ* (we)

d: 出 *chū* (go, come out)

e: 女 *nǚ* (woman)

Now look hard at the plate above, and see how many more of the same characters you can spot.

Forms and reforms of Chinese writing throughout the ages

We need to talk a little about the relationship between the Oracle-bone script, *jiaguwen* and another we have also mentioned, the Bronze script, *jinwen* (金文). During the Song Dynasty in particular, scholars had started to collect Zhou Dynasty bronze vessels and to study the inscriptions on them which were written in that script. As the script was used for engraving on bronze vessels, it is called by such a name. As a matter of fact, the script was used not only on ritual bronze vessels for offerings in ceremonies to honor the ancestors, but also on jade artifacts.

It is commonly thought that *jinwen* is later than *jiaguwen*. Those who think so might have been influenced by certain historical facts. Shang sacrificial bronzes were only incidentally uncovered in excavations between 1928 and 1937. Shang bronzes were, in the main, not available then, only Zhou ones. Shang (in quantities) and more Zhou bronzes were discovered in fact during the last century. Shang bronze vessels bear minimal inscriptions, mentioning the name and clan, while Zhou ones are in general slightly more informative, indicating the person who had commissioned the artifact together with the event which it commemorated. Obviously even these do not yield as much information as those found on divination pieces. However, one exceptional Western Zhou piece, discovered in 1850, has 499 characters engraved on it. Today China itself has about 8000 Shang and Zhou bronze vessels; scholars reckon that there are more than 3000 different characters among the inscriptions, of which nearly 2000 are recognisable.

From such evidence, one could perhaps also infer that both *jiaguwen* and *jinwen* were contemporaneous or near contemporaneous in Shang times. If so, *jinwen* may not necessarily be too much later than *jiaguwen*.

It may also be a surprise to learn that some of the pictographs in *jiaguwen* are less "pictographic" so to speak than their equivalents in *jinwen* since in comparison, they are simpler, more abstract and stylised, and therefore can be said to look less archaic than *jinwen*. This has prompted at least one leading scholar to maintain that *jinwen* could even have preceded *jiaguwen*. Before we rush to agree with this interpretation, we should bear in mind other pieces of historical evidence which could explain why *jiaguwen* may look less "pictographic" than *jinwen*.

First, *jiaguwen* and *jinwen* played very different social roles – the former was used in divination, the latter in a different kind of ceremony where the vessels played probably an aesthetic as well as a functional role in honoring ancestors. Second, the difference between the two scripts may lie simply in the difference in techniques when executing them. The knife was used to carve *jiaguwen* on the shells and bones, whereas in *jinwen* (on bronze vessels at least), the inscription was first written on a mold, then carved with a kind of scoop, before the mold was used for casting the bronze vessel. It would obviously be more difficult to carve the equivalent of a character in the style of the Bronze script on shell and bone. Different techniques permit differences in style. The technique employed in *jinwen* enabled it the better to conform to the nature of pictographs (*xiangxing*) than its counterpart, *jiaguwen*. For instance, take a look at this picture of a pig, a wild pig painted on a Neolithic Yangshao earthern pot.

The beast portrayed looks fearsome, which it is. Next compare the picture of it above with representations of it as a pictograph under the various styles of writing below.

1 2 3 4

Let us play a guessing game. Which of these four looks to you to be the most "pictographic"? (In the case of 1 and 2, you must mentally turn the page anti-clockwise away from you in order to see it as a horizontal figure.) The answer to this is almost certainly 2 as it appears to possess more details which correspond to that of the actual wild pig. Next, place all four along a scale of "pictographic-ness." Here readers may disagree. Some may say: 2, 1, 3, 4; more controversially, others may even say: 2, 3, 4, 1 on the grounds, frankly, that 1 looks so abstract, so stylised that it must be a late development, and on the assumption that the more abstract and stylised, the more it departs from "pictographic-ness." Well, we are not going to adjudicate on this matter but simply tell you the truth that, in reality, 1 is *jiaguwen,* 2 is *jinwen*, 3 is *xiaozhuan* (the script relied on primarily by Xu Shen in his dictionary in the Han Dynasty and 4 is *lishu* (a script which we have not yet mentioned so far). The character for "pig" 豕 *shǐ* has evolved just as the wild pig in real life over the millennia has also changed in shape and form, to become the domesticated pig we know today, looking no longer fearsome but even cuddly. The wild pig, painted on the Neolithic Yangshao pot, still exists in endangered small numbers in parts of northern China, such as the forests of Heilongjiang province. (One can also find it in certain parts of Europe, such as in rural France.) It has evolved to become, at least, for English children, the lovable pig (dressed in human clothes) as illustrated by Beatrix Potter in her much-loved books for children. We shall, in Part III (***Happiness is piggy-shaped***), be following the story of the pig in Chinese culture, a story which, of course, is very different from that in English culture. However, we shall leave the pig for now.

After a while, the Zhou gave up the Shang practice of divination but not that of casting bronze vessels. Hence *jinwen* continued to flourish during the whole of the Zhou Dynasty (and even beyond to the Han). Given such a long period, the script itself was bound to change, and some of the later *jinwen* characters would no longer be quite so "pictographic." Such detailed developments do not concern us here.

The first great reform

We next turn our attention to *xiaozhuan* (Lesser Seal Script) in this story of the first great reform during the short-lived Qin Dynasty (221 – 207 BCE) which followed the end of the Zhou. *Xiaozhuan* enjoyed an exceptionally high status as it was associated in particular with a very powerful man, the prime minister or chancellor of the first Qin Emperor, called Li Si (李斯, ca. 280 – 208 BCE). When the king of the Qin state defeated the rival states, he unified China, declaring himself Emperor. To hold this newly acquired territory together as a coherent whole, he realized that he had to introduce major reforms, which included standardising weights and measures, the currency, and indeed the language itself. Li Si carried out these edicts with zeal. As far as orthodox scholarship itself was concerned, this meant very bad news, as the new regime did not favor Confucianism with its emphasis on morality rather than law to govern the people, but preferred to rely on laws to regulate their conduct. When the Confucian scholars protested, Li Si caused some 480 to be burnt alive in 214 BCE; he also burned the books about the philosophy they professed. As one can imagine, he was a much hated man. Eventually he himself also met with a grisly end, being cut in half alive, in public, in 208 BCE.

While Li Si and his master ruthlessly suppressed dissenting ideologies, they allowed various competing scripts (there were eight) to flourish, although vigorously promoting their favored style. Li Si used his own calligraphy in *xiaozhuan* when writing the Emperor's edicts as well as in engraving inscriptions on monuments.

Here is a reputed specimen of Li Si's calligraphy in *xiaozhuan* engraved on stone on the occasion when his master, Qin Shihuangdi visited Taishan (泰山), in Shandong Province, in North China.

The Emperor declared *xiaozhuan* to be the imperial standard, the script for the new unified China. However, Li Si did not himself invent the script; it emerged during the Warring States Period in the Zhou Dynasty, having evolved from *dazhuan*, the Greater Seal script. But he collated and edited what he found; what he found was confused and variable. Each of the previously independent states employed its own preferred style; furthermore, the same character in each style could be written in several different ways. In late Zhou times, there was a saying:言语异声，文字异形 /言語異聲，文字異形 *yányǔ yì shēng, wénzì yì xíng*). Loosely translated, it is: The languages sound different, their characters are also differently written. Writing, therefore, had to be standardised, assuming the form called *xiaozhuan*. Textbooks for schools were published in this script to ensure that it would be universally taught and propagated through the empire. When the short-lived Qin Dynasty gave way to the Han Dynasty, it did not immediately disappear with the death of Li Si, the man most associated with it, but continued to be popularly used during the early Western Han Period (206 BCE – 8CE). *Xiaozhuan* plays an important role in the development of Chinese writing, acting as a bridge between the archaic and the later more "modern" writing styles.

While *xiaozhuan* was consolidated during Qin times, a brand new script had evolved and begun to emerge. The basis of this development lay in the fact that running a unified China, covering an area which was the size of at least six previous other states put together meant that a larger and more efficient bureaucracy had to be put in place. Bureaucrats had to draw up memoranda, collate data, write reports; but lower level bureaucrats had physically to copy and write them out clearly, and do these things fast. A new style of writing therefore began to emerge from such a context; for good reason, it is called the Clerical script in English, 隶书/隸書 *lìshū* in Chinese. Here is an example of the difference between *jinwen*, *xiaozhuan* and *lishu* for the character "book" (书 /書 *shū*).

In the middle is *xiaozhuan*; note how complicated it is compared with *lishu* (on the right) as well as that *lishu* is identical to the traditional (*kaishu*) script still used primarily in Taiwan today.

The official credit for establishing, if not inventing, *lishu* goes to one called Cheng Miao (程邈), who had the misfortune, earlier in his life, of displeasing Qin Shihuangdi. As a result, he was thrown into prison where he remained for ten years. He did not waste his time while imprisoned. As a scholar, he was very interested in the written aspects of the language. He studied *dazhuan* (Greater Seal script) in particular, and for a decade experimented with simplifying and rationalising it. News of his academic pursuit reached the Emperor's ears. His studies found imperial approval, whereupon, the Emperor ordered his release and appointed him to research the project of language reform. He looked at the various styles of writing available at the time; he picked on one of them, collated the data on it, and put order into them. This system then was issued officially in its standardised form as *lishu*.

In ancient Chinese culture, the original use of writing was strictly speaking confined to the king when he discharged his duties in ceremonies honoring Heaven and ancestors, and when he issued edicts in their names. It followed that he had the exclusive privileged use of the written language. But during the Warring States Period when the Zhou mandate to rule disintegrated, writing also lost the unique, near sacred, respect it used to command. Aristocratic and other upstarts set themselves up as kings and legitimised themselves by engaging in ceremonies similar to those practiced by the Zhou king including the use of the written language. However, when *lishu* was established, the first Qin emperor decreed that *xiaozhuan* would be for his exclusive use while *lishu* would be for the use of his officials. In this way, Qin Shihuangdi attempted to restore, to an extent, the ancient custom of the king's exclusive use of writing. This amounted to a new way of marking the distinction not simply between king and people, but also between king and officials. The Qin emperor found not only could he not dispense with officials in the running of government and administration but also that he had to have even more of them, given the increase of bureaucracy due the enlargement of territory and economic developments in a unified China. "Clerical script" is indeed an appropriate way of translating the term *lishu*; its use became confined especially to minor bureaucrats or clerks in the vast administrative machine. The term, 隶/隸 *lì*, refers to a lowly post in the feudal China of the period, that of a court runner or policeman. The difference in use then between *xiaozhuan* and *lishu* marked a distinction between the Emperor at the very top of the hierarchy and those in his lowly employment at the bottom end of his administration, the scribes or clerks.

草书/書 *cǎoshū* or the Cursive script arose during the third century BCE in connection with the emerging *lishu*. Unlike the latter, it was used in informal personal communication outside of the public bureaucratic domain. The Cursive style has no particular detailed structure, focusing only on the overall shape and form of the character. It also led to 行书/書 *xíngshū*, called the Running script.

The last of the major scripts we are going to talk about is *kaishu* or the Standard script. It, too, evolved from *lishu*; and by late Han times (25 CE – 220 CE) or at the latest by the Three Kingdoms Period (220 CE – 280 CE), it had emerged. It is rigorously structured, every stroke and every character must be carefully written. For such reasons, it has been called "The True One" or just simply "The One." It is the script that has always been used in teaching children to write for almost two thousand years. It is the Gold Standard in education.

There is a lovely legend told about the supposed beginnings of this script. We know that the first Qin emperor was very keen on writing reform and was on the look out for talent. He heard that a certain person called Wang Cichong (王次沖) was developing a new script, *kaishu*. The Emperor summoned him to court, three times, but each time Wang Cichong ignored the summons. He had no time for any thing other than to perfect his new system day and night. The

Emperor flew into a rage and ordered that he be bound and caged in a cart and brought to the palace. A strange thing happened on the way. His head suddenly tumbled from the cart, fell on the road, then transformed itself into a bird and soared skywards. As the bird flew a long way away, it deposited its wings on two hill tops; as a result, the people called one the Big Wing and the other the Little Wing Summits. The guards escorting the prisoner picked up the two wings and presented them to the Qin emperor. Behind this legend stands a historical figure called by that name, who lived during the Han Dynasty and whose valuable contribution to the creation of *kaishu* is acknowledged by other scholars.

<u>The second great reform</u>
For nearly two millenia, after the Qin/Han reforms, Chinese writing settled down. The Gold Standard in education was/is *kaishu*, and when printing was invented, books were printed using the script. Calligraphy, however, was done in the various scripts available, depending on the preferred style of the individual calligrapher.

The next major reform occurred after the establishment of the People's Republic of China in 1949 when the Simplified script (简体/簡體 *jiǎntǐ*) replaced to an extent the Traditional script (繁体/體 *fántǐ*), whose use is increasingly confined to Taiwan, today, although Hong Kong and Macau also subscribe to it. One should note that both are written in *kaishu*; their differences lie elsewhere. However, as we shall also see, there was another root-and-branch project for reforming the language which has since been shelved.

Chinese is somewhat like English regarding some of the problems which arise from the ways they are written respectively. Both languages sport champions for their reform. Comparable to the Qin reform, English spelling was standardised by Samuel Johnson (1709 – 1784) in his *Dictionary of the English Language* published in 1755. Since then, those who claim that the peculiarities of English spelling are an educational time-waster and a distinct drawback to the battle against illiteracy want further reform to make spelling as phonetic as it is possible to be. Any one learning English, whether native or foreign, is bound to be frustrated by the fact that certain words in their written forms look alike, leading one to think that they, therefore, ought to be pronounced alike. Yet they turn out not to be so. For instance, the poor old student must painfully learn that "ough" in "cough" is pronounced as "off" while "ough" in "bough" (a branch of a tree) is perversely pronounced differently as in "bow" (the front part of a ship or the movement made bending the upper part of the body such as in "he bowed low and deeply"), but not as in "bow" meaning "a bit of ribbon tied up in a certain way" (as in "she has a bow in her bonnet"), a part of a weapon as in "bow and arrow" or what one uses to play a string instrument (a violin bow) where the "ow" is pronounced as in the exclamation "oh"! If the long suffering student knows how "cough" is pronounced, she might be sorely tempted to spell it as "koff," but no marks would be given for such ingenuity.

George Bernard Shaw, the famous playwright and social critic (1856 – 1950) was passionate about promoting the reform of English spelling to make it into a rational system, reflecting how English is actually pronounced. However, do pause and ponder. The key question is: as pronounced by whom? By BBC announcers? (Today, as a matter of fact, BBC announcers speak in a variety of accents; they no longer uniformly speak what used to be called "received pronunciation.") By those in Liverpool who speak "Scouse"? By those who live in south-east England and speak "Estuary English"? By those in Glasgow who speak Glaswegian or by those who live in Edinburgh who speak something else? (The political history and context of the UK are very different from those in the PRC which could promote *putonghua* as Standard Speech for the whole of China.) Shaw left part of his fortune which was considerable at the time he drew up his will, to further this project of reform. Unfortunately, upon his death, there was not too much left in his estates. However, the funds for the project perked up healthily when the musical *My Fair Lady* based on his play, *Pygmalion*, turned out to be a hit. Unfortunately again, Shaw was posthumously frustrated as the Public Trustee challenged the will; as a result of this challenge, an out-of-court settlement was reached, with only a small sum allocated to the project. Should you fancy taking it forward, do please apply to the trustees for a grant!

A similar tale of woe holds for learners of the French language. For instance, "il parle" and "ils parlent" are pronounced exactly the same, but they are differently spelled. Furthermore, "ils ont" are pronounced differently from the way they are spelled because there is a liaison between the "s" of "ils" and the "o" of "ont," such that one carries the sound of the consonant "s" to the vowel "o" next door. Furthermore, "ils sont" may look a bit like "ils ont" and given the liaison just mentioned in the case of the latter, you may think that they are pronounced the same. But you would be wrong; they are pronounced differently to reflect the difference in spelling, meaning as well as grammar of the two phrases. As we have already mentioned, a person who can understand and even speak fluently a language would not necessarily know how to read and write in that language unless taught to do so – the written words would be "gobble-de-gook" and mean nothing. This holds in any language whether it is written alphabetically or not. As Chinese is non alphabetic, it appears to make it easier for people to grasp that a foreigner long resident in China may even speak fluent Chinese but is not expected to be able to read Chinese, once it is known that the foreigner has never learned to read and write the language. However, they find it hard to grasp that the same thing happens in the case of English or French. Unfortunately, alphabets do not automatically grant immunity against illiteracy in the language.

The points just made should not be misunderstood to mean that the writing/spelling of English, French or, any other language have never changed through the ages. Of course, they have, but proposals to eliminate different competing spellings for the same word such as those introduced by Samuel Johnson are not attempts to create a so-called "rational" system of spelling as advocated by Shaw and those who think like him, as such a system is a fantasy and an illusion – the sounds of a language alter over time, and the same sounds carried by migrants to another part of the world soon alter. The Pilgrim Fathers set out from Plymouth in 1620 for North America, naturally, speaking the same tongue as their friends and relatives left behind in England. Yet American English soon diverted from the inherited English sounds, vocabulary, and indeed other linguistic features, too.

In a good many languages, a wide gap exists between the sounds and the written signs representing them. In some cases, such as Italian, Finnish, or German, the gap, by comparison, may be minimal, and are closest to the dream of reformers such as GB Shaw, for a "rational" system of writing where the signs by and large reflect the sounds they bear.

Having set out briefly this comparative framework, we can return to the second reform of Chinese writing in the twentieth century. China went through very rough patches in its history for more than two centuries, having first been humiliated by Europeans and later, also by Japanese. As a result, Chinese intellectuals agonised over the nation's sad fate and quite a few became convinced that one major, if not the sole cause, which prevented China from modernizing itself was its language. It might be somewhat unfair to portray their reasoning in such a simplistic fashion, but it might not be too far from the truth. European nations were successful. European nations are nations whose languages are alphabetical, primarily using the Latin alphabet. They also had a much higher literacy rate in their countries than in China. These observations were all true, of course, but did they justify the inference that should China wish to be successfully modernized, then it must change its system of writing and drastically adopt an alphabetic one, to have a Latinized script? One of China's intellectual giants of the twentieth century Lu Xun (鲁迅, 1886 – 1936) appeared to have reasoned thus, and thought so. He vigorously proposed and promoted the Latinization of Chinese.

Is such reasoning sound? Not necessarily. Take Japan, a country which has so successfully transformed itself that, in the twentieth century, Japanese were regarded as "honorary whites" in apartheid South Africa after the Second World War. Japan, since its recovery after its defeat in the Second World War, is regarded as belonging to the "modern Western world," the so-called First World, an elitist, exclusive club consisting of mature advanced industrialised economies. Lu Xun did not live that long to see this exceptional status granted to China's neighbor in the second half of the twentieth century. Lu Xun studied in Japan, and was suitably impressed by the success then of the Japanese economy and society. Literacy rate was low, and today it remains true that Japan has one of the highest literacy rates in the world. Rather curiously, it appeared that Lu Xun and others had overlooked the fact that Japanese writing was and is still one of the most complicated in the world, as it operates with three different scripts: *kanji*, borrowed from Chinese, was introduced in fifth or sixth century CE, supplemented by two phonetic scripts, *hiragana* and *katakana*. By contrast, Japan's neighbor, Korea had developed an efficient alphabet of its own since the mid-fifteenth century. Korea did not race ahead in developing its economy during the nineteenth century, in spite of its alphabetic script, whilst Japan did. Instead, Korea, or at least South Korea started to become a major player on the world's economic stage only after the Second World War, but because of complicated political reasons, which we cannot go into detail here.

When Lu Xun died in 1936, his friend and fellow advocate of Latinization, Guo Moruo (郭沫若, 1892 – 1978) another very distinguished intellectual, sent a couplet for his funeral. The irony was that Guo Moruo did not send it in alphabetic form. Instead he sent it in the traditional form of writing couplets. The couplet, as a matter of fact, paid tribute to Lu Xun's literary achievements, in particular, his masterpiece, the *Story of Ah Q*, while at the same time praising his promotion of Latinization as his greatest lifework.

The situation in reality is much more complicated than perhaps portrayed in the kind of thesis endorsed by Lu Xun's generation, even including, originally, Mao Zedong himself. How successful a country is in making its people literate is itself a very complex matter. The Nordic countries in Europe are highly successful, but they are also more equal societies with relatively very small populations, whereas the UK is not so successful in comparison, though more successful than the USA where inequalities are even more pronounced. All these countries use the Latin alphabet. Chinese is not alphabetic, of course. However, one must be careful when comparing one country's illiteracy rate with that of another, as the figures must be read against a relevant background of information. For instance, let us take the USA and China. The former has twentieth of the world's population, is acknowledged to be the richest in the world in terms of its GDP with a per capita income which is one of the highest, if not the highest, in the world today, while China has a sixth of the world's population, is acknowledged to be a developing nation with a per capita income which is low compared with that of the USA. It is reported that nearly half of America's adults are functionally illiterate, if not illiterate; 20% of adults read far below a level needed to earn a living wage. According to China's Census of 2000, there were 80 million illiterates aged fifteen or above. In September 2006, the Ministry of Education announced that there were 114 million illiterates, the majority of them concentrating in poor areas, in regions where the Minority peoples live as well as in remote areas. Adult illiteracy is said to be 9.08% while that at world level is 20.3% and the figure for the Asia-Pacific region is 8.3%. We need not pursue this matter further here. We leave you to work out for yourselves the relevant significance of such statistics as well as the complexities involved in the issue of illiteracy in general.

Mao Zedong, in the 1930s, long before the Chinese Communist Party showed any promising signs of being able to assume power in China, had accepted the line of argument laid down by the Chinese intellectuals associated with a social and political movement called the May Fourth Movement which began on 4th May 1919, when the Versailles Treaty ending World War I was announced. This movement tried to galvanise the Chinese people to save their country and themselves and cut across the left/right divide. Nationalists as well as

Communists supported it. Chinese intellectuals in general were convinced that its long feudal past, in every aspect, including its ancient writing system, must be swept away if the country were ever to become strong like Japan and the West. In 1936, Mao, told the American journalist, Edgar Snow, that Latinization would be an effective instrument for overcoming illiteracy, laying the basis for progress: "Chinese characters are so difficult to learn that even the best system of rudimentary characters, or simplified teaching, does not equip the people with a really efficient and rich vocabulary. Sooner or later, we believe, we will have to abandon characters altogether if we are to create a new social culture in which the masses fully participate."

Mao might have thought about such a reform as a good thing in principle, but he did not personally put it into practice. For a start, he was passionate about calligraphy. As a calligrapher, he was in demand when he was alive, no doubt, owing to his political status. Below is a specimen of his calligraphy, the masthead for the People's Daily, which is still in use today.

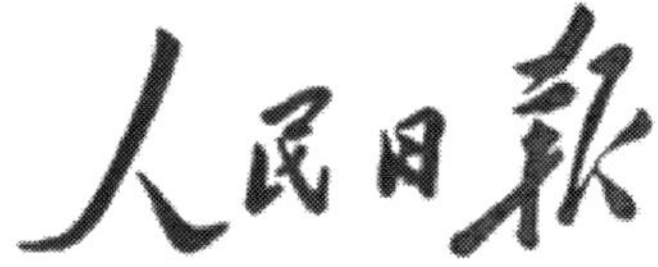

The Communist Party and its followers undertook the Long March – from October 1934 to October 1935 – when they retreated from their besieged locations in South-east China to Yan'an (延安) in Shaanxi (陕西) Province, to the already established commune there amidst the caves of the loess plateau in North China. On this trek, about 9000 kilometers (6000 miles) long, and which lasted 368 days, the Party developed a very different strategy from that of Latinization to teach illiterate comrades to read. Obviously on such a hazardous march, the hazards being both man-made (dodging bombs and bullets) and natural (crossing fierce torrents, climbing snow-clad mountains or sinking into bogs and swamps, often on empty or near empty stomachs), there would be no time for formal lessons. Instead the instructors each day would write a character, very large, and pin it on the backs of the comrades, so that as they marched they could absorb and learn what was in front of them. Indeed, by such and other ingenious methods, at the end of the epic trek, many who began illiterate had learned to read and even to write when they finally got to Yan'an.

When the PRC was established in 1949, it soon became obvious that the project of Latinization was not realistic and was as good as shelved. Zhou Enlai in 1958 signalled the abandonment of the goal of replacing characters with Roman letters, although the legal proclamation of the project of out-and-out Latinization has probably never been formally withdrawn. Instead, *pinyin* (a form of romanisation) is taught in schools, but simply as an aid to help children learn to speak *putonghua*, as well as to enable foreigners to read names of town and cities, streets etc. Since the IT revolution, *pinyin* also has become a handy means of raising Chinese characters electronically on the computer. It is not the only method of electronic input; other methods exist which some Chinese prefer to the *pinyin* technique, as a matter of practicality. So the fear that the nature of Chinese writing may be an obstacle to progress appears finally to have been laid to rest.

During the Cultural Revolution (1966 – 1976), the Red Guards campaigned against Latinization on the grounds that it would be a symbol of subservience to foreign culture. In 1966, the People's Daily even left out the *pinyin* under the characters making up its masthead. How the nature of national pride had altered over five or more decades. When Lu Xun and his colleagues campaigned for romanisation, this too was in the name of national pride – China must abandon the traditional form of its written language as it constituted an unacceptable emblem of feudalism, which had kept China weak and helpless. Today, no doubt, many former Red Guards are now captains of industry in China, and advocates of Lu Xun's ultimate goal of language reform, the replacement of characters by phonetic spelling, are few in Chinese-speaking lands, and even non-existent in China itself. However, one very prominent (Western) sinologist, like George Bernard Shaw with regard to English writing, continues to bemoan its abandonment.

One powerful impulse for resisting the project lies in aesthetics, a very important aspect of Chinese culture, let us not forget. Romanisation means the abandonment of calligraphy. Of all the fine arts, calligraphy (书/書法 *shūfǎ*) constitutes the highest aesthetic expression, above landscape painting (山水画/畫 *shānshuǐhuà*). Of course, calligraphy historically was an activity pursued by feudal elites. Getting rid of feudalism also meant, in the first half of the twentieth century, getting rid of characters and, therefore, also of calligraphy. This would mean throwing the baby out with the bathwater. Such a move was resisted, helped by the fact that many of the senior members of the Communist Party from Mao Zedong downwards were passionate about calligraphy and practiced it fervently. Today, calligraphy is, of course, no longer an elitist activity – many, young and old, throughout China, practice it and enthusiastically take part in calligraphic competitions. The essential aesthetics of the characters as expressed in the various styles of calligraphy, we shall leave to the eloquence of a noted Western historian of Chinese art, William Willets (1918 – 1995) who wrote in 1981:

> The basic units out of which Western writing is composed, the letters of the alphabet, are phonetic symbols and as such are simple in form, strictly limited in number, and relatively unchanging in appearance. Words are not more than linear combinations of these continually recurring basic elements; it follows that words cannot hold any inherent visual interest, since their forms are determined not by principles of structural design, but by the amount and nature of the phonetic material they have to carry. Each Chinese character, on the other hand, is organized within the boundaries of a square, and is conceived of and executed as an organic whole. Notwithstanding, therefore, that the elements out of which it is composed – the brush stroke – must take an intelligible pattern, and notwithstanding that certain combinations of brush-strokes do recur from one character to another, each separate character in fact constituted a fresh problem in structural dynamics, an "adventure of movement" whose successful resolution is a triumph of artistic management. And this, I maintain, is not a difference in degree, but an absolute difference in kind.

The intimate connection between calligraphy and Chinese writing is not merely a general, but also, a specific one between calligraphy and the various scripts invented in the history of Chinese writing. Calligraphers have their own preferences, and are reputed for their work in their chosen style. For instance, a very famous calligrapher in the annals of calligraphy who lived in the Jin Dynasty (晋代, 265 – 420 CE), 王羲之 (Wang Xizhi, 303 – 361CE) is revered, indeed "canonised," for his calligraphy. He was particularly famed for his brush work in the Cursive and Running scripts as well as in *kaishu*. (See chart at the end of the chapter for examples of these different styles of writing.) However, what may not be so obvious to those outside the tradition is that there is also an intimate connection between these on the one hand and painting on the other; it is almost as if the painter is painting within a particular school of calligraphy. To illustrate this point, we have chosen to use as subject the horse but we need first to say something very briefly about the role played by the animal in the history of Chinese culture.

The horse, everywhere in the world, has been used as a mode of transportation, as a traction animal, as well as in warfare. In some cultures, as in English culture, the horse is also an important subject in painting – George Stubbs (1724-1806) who is regarded as the greatest English painter of horses and even perhaps as the greatest painter of horses in European art, immediately springs to mind. You can see, for example, his famous "Whistlejacket" (1762) at the National gallery in London. The Chinese have always been equally devoted to the horse as an object of art and study. To perfect his painting, one painter commissioned by the emperor to paint the horse, spent every minute of the day and night in the imperial stable, living and breathing horse until he got every detail right, having absorbed the spirit of the animal. Such was his devotion to the object of his study that the emperor, not finding him in his studio, finally located him in the stable. The emperor had told him to study with another horse master painter, which he did. After a while, he realized that there was no better master to teach him than the animal itself. He decamped to the imperial stable.

What is unique about the Chinese is that calligraphy, written scripts and painting, all three are inextricably linked. Let us now take a look at the various forms of the character for "horse" (马/馬 *mǎ*) shown in the order of *jiaguwen*, *jinwen*, *xiaozhuan*, *lishu*, *kaishu* below:

Here is a painting of a galloping horse by a very famous painter of the last century called Xu Beihong (徐悲鸿/鴻, 1895 – 1953). You can find the painting hanging in the museum in Beijing dedicated to his works, the Xu Beihong Museum. Study carefully this painting in conjunction with the written scripts of the character for "horse" above. Decide which of the latter reflects best the galloping horse of the painting. We think it is *xiaozhuan*, but, of course, you may disagree.

Here is a painting, called "Walking the Horse," by the famous painter of horses, 韩幹/韓幹 *Hán Gān* (?-780AD) in the Tang Dynasty who was the painter in the story recounted earlier. Study it in conjunction with the forms of the character above. Which goes best with this composition of the more staid and majestic-looking horses? We suggest *lishu*.

Another type of reform of the language took shape instead of Latinization. It is to simplify the complicated writing of some commonly used characters by reducing the number of strokes required to write them. This much more limited reform also had roots which went back to the 1920s and 1930s, also cutting across the right left divide. In 1934 the Chinese Nationalist Party (国/國民党/黨) spearheaded it, publishing a list of 324 simplified characters, intended to be compulsorily implemented. However, it raised such a storm of protest that the government quickly dropped it. When the PRC was established, this project was resumed. That is why today, the simplified characters called 简体/簡體 *jiǎntǐ* are used in mainland China and the traditional characters called 繁体 /體 *fántǐ* in Taiwan, Hong Kong and Macau today, as well as in certain publications in the diaspora (this term is used for lack of a convenient alternative). However, increasingly, *jianti* as a script would predominate, edging *fanti* to a marginal status, especially as the UN has recently decided to adopt *jianti* in all its official documents and publications in Chinese.

The Government's Language Reform Committee formally issued altogether three lists of simplified characters: the first was in 1956 with 2,236 characters, the second in 1977 but rescinded in 1986 (its simplifications met with resistance as they were considered to be too radical), and the third in 1986 which, in reality, was the 1956 with some very minor adjustments resulting in 2,235 as the total number of simplified characters. In a vocabulary list of 3500 commonly used characters, *jianti* characters number just under a third, at 1116. The Committee itself, in the main, did not invent these forms, many of which were widely known and used down the ages. The Committee collected and collated these. They are culled from three main sources. The first is trade and commerce which the intellectuals used to look down their nose, regarding them as vulgar. The second is elitist in origin, characters evolved in the Cursive script favored by the literati in their own calligraphy and personal manuscripts – the simplified character for "horse" 马 *mǎ* (as opposed to *fanti* 馬), for "door" 门 *mén* (as opposed to *fanti* 門), "book/calligraphy" 书 *shū* (as opposed to *fanti* 書) are all instances from this particular source. Indeed, Mao Zedong himself urged the Committee to rely more on these elite Cursive forms. Ironically, the Committee was able to co-opt from Lu Xun's own manuscripts a rich cull of such simplifications. The third source is even more surprising: some of the simplified characters are merely reversions to archaic forms already in use more than 3000 years ago. For instance, the character for "cloud" in *jianti* looks like this: 云 *yún* ; that for *fanti* like this:雲.The so-called traditional *fanti* has an additional character added on top of it, 雨 *yǔ*, meaning "rain." The *jianti* has lost this component, reverting to the plainer ancient form, in particular of *jinwen* which it has directly copied. The additional component was added only in *lishu* (which emerged during the Qin Dynasty), as you can see below (*jiaguwen*, *jinwen*, *xiaozhuan*, *lishu*, *kaishu*):

Recall that *jinwen* existed as early as the Zhou, indeed, if not earlier, during the Shang Dynasty. The change in form occurred because the character 云 was borrowed as *jiajie*, a phonetic loan word to stand for "to say"; as a result, it was necessary to add a component to the original 云 to avoid ambiguity. This additional component is the character 雨 *yǔ*, meaning "rain," which as you can see clearly is actually *xiangxing*, a pictograph. Such addition is very logical as clouds are, in reality, no more than droplets of water which fall to earth eventually as rain. Indeed, this shows that the ancient Chinese had correctly understood the physics of clouds and rain.

The Chinese Government seems to think that simplification has gone far enough and appears to have no other obvious plans to further the process. Supporters of *jianti* disappointingly point out that so far simplification has been very limited. It might look impressive on the surface, having produced a total of 2,235 simplified characters. But do not be fooled, they say. Quite a few of these alterations concern the radicals. Take, for instance, the "metal" radical 钅/釒 *jīn*. By reducing the number of strokes from 8 to 5, one has, at a stroke, simplified over a 100 characters, those bearing that radical as part of their structure.

Jianti attracts critics both inside and outside China. Some bemoan the loss of meaning and historical cultural baggage carried by *fanti*. This may be true but such critics seem also to have overlooked the fact that some of the simplified characters are resurrections of ancient forms. Well, whatever the pros and cons, the matter rests with *jianti* as it stands today.

Conclusion

Below is a chart illustrating two characters written in accordance with the various major scripts mentioned in this brief history of Chinese writing.

Period	**Script**	***Pinyin***	**English**	**fish** *yú*	**woman** *nǚ*
ca. 6000 – 1000 BCE?	甲骨文	*jiǎgǔwén*	Oracle-bone script	魚	女
ca. 1600 – 300 BCE?	金文	*jīnwén*	Bronze script	魚	女
ca. 700 – 200 BCE	篆书/書 大篆 小篆	*zhuànshū* *dàzhuàn* *xiǎozhuàn*	Seal script Greater Lesser	魚	女
ca. 200 BCE	隶书/隸書	*lìshū*	Clerical script	魚	女
ca. 200 BCE	草书/書	*cǎoshū*	Cursive script	魚	女
	行书/書	*xíngshū*	Running script	魚	女
ca. 200 CE	楷书/書	*kǎishū*	Standard script	魚	女
Present	繁体/體楷书/書	*fántǐ kǎishū*	Traditional Standard script	魚	女
Present since 1956	简体/簡體楷书/書	*jiǎntǐ kǎishū*	Simplified Standard script	鱼	女

Exploring Themes: Words Tell Fascinating Tales

Surviving and living* 衣食住行 *yī shí zhù xíng

We are all curious about the past, the past of one's own culture as well as that of other peoples. We wonder how the Chinese, at each stage of their long history, lived and survived – what they wore (衣), what they ate (食), what their houses or furniture looked like (住), how they moved about (行). To get some idea, we cannot do worse than to look at some of the characters which refer to certain essential objects in their daily lives.

Food and drink

China is a huge land mass. Its various regions have very different climates and, of course, different geographical features. In the main, by historical times, northern China – north of the Yangzi River (the Chinese always call it 长江 *Chángjiāng*, the long river which flows into the sea) – grows wheat and its people eat a lot of bread or buns, while southern China grows rice and its people eat rice. One should not take it that, in very ancient times, rice could not have grown even in north China as the climate had undergone changes over the many millennia. Neither should one assume that in historical times that northerners never ate rice and southerners never ate bread, although to be more accurate, some southerners, especially the Cantonese, prefer not to have their buns plain but with rich fillings, whether savory or sweet.

Through the ages, the Chinese constantly talk about the "five grains" (五谷/穀 *wŭ gŭ*) forming part of their staple diet which include wheat (麦/麥 *mài*) and rice (稻 *dào*). Strictly speaking *mài* is a general term which refers not only to wheat but also to other cereals such as barley. Wheat, today, is called 小麦/麥 (*xiăomài*).

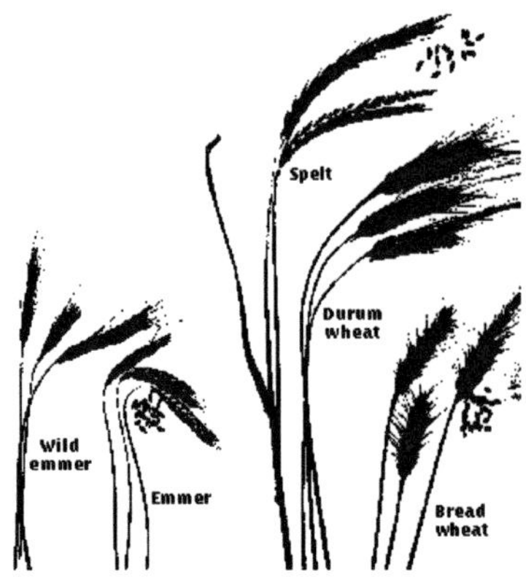

Here is a picture of various kinds of wheat during its long cultivation from wild emmer to durum wheat (for making pasta) to bread wheat. Wheat is not native to China as it has been domesticated from its forebear, the wild einkorn, in the Fertile Crescent (that part which is now south-east Turkey), nearly 9000 years ago.

For us there are several things of interest to note with regard to the various evolutions of the character *mài*.

The Oracle-bone (*jiaguwen*) version is clearly a pictograph, as it looks very much like an attempt to represent a stalk of barley or wheat with a beard. From it, the Clerical (*lishu*) and the Standard script (*kaishu*) forms (麦) have evolved, becoming more stylised and less pictographic in the process. However, according to certain experts, a curious mistake had been made regarding *mài* by scribes and scholars for more than 2000 years, who had confused it with the character 来/來 *lái* ("to come"). This is because the two characters in the earliest scripts looked very similar. We reproduce the various forms (*jiaguwen*, *jinwen*, *xiaozhuan*, *kaishu*) for the two characters below:

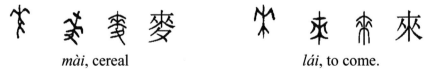

mài, cereal　　　　*lái*, to come.

Compare the first character at the beginning of each of the two sets above. They are both *jiaguwen*. See how similar they look. The *jiaguwen* character for "to come" looks remarkably like an attempt to capture what a wheat plant looks like with the bottom bit standing for the roots, the vertical line for the stem, the rest for the leaves. However, one must bear in mind that *jiaguwen* was not known to the ancient scribes. So what are relevant are the *jinwen* versions (second from the left of each set above) of the two characters – these, too, look remarkably alike. Originally, *lái* was used to talk about the grains on an ear of wheat, while *mài* means "come." We see that their similarity in form has led to their meanings being transposed, such that *mài* has come to mean "cereal" while *lái* to mean "come."

Another interpretation about *mài* and *lái* goes like this: it is said that the Zhou(周)people believed that wheat was a gift to humans from the god of the heavens who ordered the Divine Bird to carry it to Earth. This legend could mean that people during the early part of the Zhou period (ca. 11th century – 221 BCE) first started to cultivate wheat. As wheat was something coming from the heavens, the character "to come" was modelled closely on that for "wheat." This interpretation, however, may not stand up to critical scrutiny as we now know that in *jiaguwen*, the characters for "wheat" and "to come" both exist. A somewhat bold but not implausible alternative account for the character "to come" goes as follows: look closely at the Traditional *kaishu* form of the character *lái*, 來, the last on the right above, and you would notice that this character has two components looking like two people （人） standing under a big tree (木). One must bear in mind that there was little or no shade usually in areas devoted to cultivating crops. When people needed to rest or talk for a longish period, they would probably walk beyond their tilled patches toward the edge of the forest and congregating under a tree for shade. On this view, the characters for "to come" and for "wheat," looking alike, was just a coincidence.

Whatever the controversies amongst scholars regarding these two characters, there is no controversy that they both occur in *jiaguwen*. As domesticated wheat came into China from the Fertile Crescent, the *jiaguwen* character for "wheat" bears witness to the fact that wheat itself must have been introduced into China at least 4000 years ago, by Shang times (ca. 16th – 11th century BCE) if not earlier.

What about rice? It was held for a long time that rice, too, was an introduced crop, this time coming from India some 3000 years BCE. More recent scholarship has established that this is not so. According to studies using the techniques of DNA genetic engineering, scientists have established that in the world today, there are two cultivated species of rice: *Oryza sativa*, domesticated in south Asia at least 10,000 years ago, and *Oryza glabberima*, domesticated in the Niger delta in West Africa between about 1500 BCE and 800 BCE. The Asian species, as a matter of fact, has been domesticated twice, once in India or Indonesia as *O. sativa indica*, and the other as *O. sativa japonica* which happened in south China (the Yangzi valley). Both the Indian and the Chinese cultivars came from the same wild forebears. Experts believe that rice cultivation at an early date was in the form of dryland farming and that wetland cultivation, rice paddies, were not developed until about 2500 BCE.

Radiocarbon techniques have established that the Chinese domesticated plant can be dated to about 10,000 – 9000 years BCE. The most convincing evidence comes from the sediment deposits in a cave called Diaotonghuan, near Poyang Lake in the Yangzi river valley, in Wannian county, Jiangxi Province (江西万/萬年吊桶环/環洞), excavated during field work, conducted there between 1993 and 1995. By about 7,000 years ago, the so-called *japonica* species had spread throughout the Yangzi valley. There is some even earlier evidence found in Hunan Province which can be dated between twelve thousand and fourteen thousand years ago. Even if one were to dismiss these claims as too extravagant, there is a general consensus that it would be uncontroversial to say that rice was domesticated in China by 7500 BCE, and this would mean that rice had been grown there since ten thousand years ago. It is not a wonder that rice is so much a part and parcel of Chinese culture and civilization.

Rice paddy will only grow in areas with plenty of water available. As a result, they are planted where rivers could supply the water with the help of irrigation canals. Amongst its varieties is one which is very hardy, doing well under less water and poorer soil conditions. It also takes a shorter period to mature, between fifty and hundred days instead of nearly six months as was the case with the more usual type. This meant that farmers could have two harvests a year. By the mid-nineteenth century, farmers had further improved its performance and perfected the art of its cultivation such that it was capable of three harvests per annum. During a period of drought in the eleventh century CE, the emperor issued an edict that this variety, originating from what today is Vietnam, be planted. Given its different characteristics, new areas could be colonised in south China, as terraced cultivation. These developments led to new wealth and population growth. The landscape of a considerable part of south China has thus been transformed for a millennium or so with contoured terrace upon terrace of green growth – an inspiring and beautiful sight to behold, should you, for example, ever take the train from Chengdu, Sichuan Province to Guangzhou, Guangdong Province.

Rice as uncooked grains is called *mǐ* and this character has been written like this down the ages (*jiaguwen*, *jinwen*, *xiaozhuan*, *lishu*):

You can see that the character has evolved to assume a form which has been stable for at least 2000 years. In *lishu*, it is obvious that its radical is 木 indicating that the object referred to is a kind of plant, with the two dots representing rice grains. In *jiaguwen*, it is obviously a pictograph, *xiangxing zi*. But what exactly is it a picture of? Experts appear to differ in their opinion. Some maintain that the horizontal line represents the paddy stalk and the dots the rice grains. Others disagree and say that the horizontal line represents a sort of device for separating the grain from the stalk. However, we ourselves have nothing more to add to this on-going controversy.

Chinese distinguishes between the cooked and the raw in the case of rice. Uncooked rice is 米 *mǐ*; cooked rice is 饭/飯 *fàn*. One goes to the grocer to get a bag of 米 *mǐ*, not a bag of 饭/飯 *fàn*. One eats a bowl of 饭/飯 *fàn* but not a bowl of 米 *mǐ*. 饭/飯 is obviously *xingsheng zi*, a semantic-phonetic compound. It has for radical 饣/飠 *shí* ("food" or "meal"); as such, the radical is self-explanatory. Its sound component is borrowed from the character 反 *fǎn*, although in its borrowed form, note that the tone has altered from third to fourth.

Scholars have pondered why this particular character has been chosen for pronouncing the character for "cooked rice." Some have imagined the following scene, a meeting of four different experts convened to discuss the matter. Expert No. 1, a linguistician, gives the straightforward explanation that 饭/飯 *fàn* is simply *xingsheng zi*, a semantic-phonetic compound. It just happens that 反 *fǎn* had been chosen to represent its sound – obviously, if the ancients had been so minded, they could have chosen some other character with some other sound. Let us not create a controversy where none exists, he says. The other three disagree, pointing out that one must not forget that the sound component of *xingsheng zi* may also donate meaning. One should try to work out the possible meaning(s) of 反 *fǎn*, especially when it is a pretty curious character to choose for rendering the sound of "cooked rice."

Expert No. 2, a nutritionist, offers the view that one should always chew one's food properly before swallowing in order to derive the most benefit from it. Rice is a staple. It is very important to emphasize that people should chew and bite on their rice, again and again, before swallowing. Hence 反 *fǎn,* as in the expression 反复 *fǎnfù*, meaning "over and over again."

Expert No. 3, the Confucian scholar and philosopher, volunteers the explanation that Confucius has said that while one is eating, one cannot be talking at the same time, just as when one is asleep, one cannot be talking either (talking in one's sleep obviously does not count as real talking). However, even when one cannot talk while eating, this does not mean that one cannot be thinking while eating. 反 *fǎn* in the character 饭/飯 *fàn* refers to the expression 反思 *fǎnsī*, meaning "to turn one's thoughts over and over again in the mind." We eat three times a day, so there are three opportunities daily for profound reflection. Furthermore, each time we reflect, we must bear in mind the three virtues demanded of us in our behavior to others: to help to our utmost others in need, to be sincere and loyal to friends as well as constantly to revise and absorb what our teachers have taught us.

Expert No. 4, a political theorist or activist, holds that it contains a fundamental political insight, namely, that empty stomachs lead to revolution, as 反 *fǎn* can also mean "oppose," "to be against." The people throughout Chinese history have held that paradise is a place where food is plentiful: 民以食为/為天 *mín yǐ shí wéi tiān*. If you were to examine Chinese history through the ages, you would find that whenever people had no rice to eat, they had risen up against their ruler. Marie-Antoinette (at the time of the French Revolution in 1789), according to one story, proclaimed: "Let them eat cake instead." The Chinese emperors did not do that; instead, they knew they had to do something quick to ease the hunger and solve the problem, or Heaven would soon be withdrawing its mandate from them.

We leave it to you to work out which is the most plausible of these rival accounts. We shall here limit ourselves to the small observation that the linguistician's view may be inadequate or too bland in one respect: it does not explain why the ancients had not chosen some other character to represent the sound, one which has only positive and no negative connotations? For instance, why not borrow the character 香 *xiāng*, meaning "fragrant"? Then we could have "fragrant rice." Chinese people, after all, constantly dream up expressions and characters with auspicious associations. But they did not in this instance. The departure from the norm is perhaps significant, and the political theorist could well have a point. The character for "cooked rice" is, therefore, not merely a semantic-phonetic compound but also *huiyi zi*, a meaning compound.

We have already mentioned that northern Chinese eat a lot of buns and bread, while southern Chinese eat a lot more rice. A very well-known type of bun commonly eaten in north China is the 馒头/饅頭 *mán·tou*. The origin of this word has an interesting history. Shang China or earlier used the heads of humans on altars as sacrifice. These heads belonged to prisoners-of-war captured from marauding neighboring tribes. The Chinese had called such invading tribes, who harassed and ravaged their homelands, barbarians 野蛮/蠻人 *yěmán rén.* Their decapitated heads were therefore 蛮头/蠻頭 *mán tóu*, "heads of barbarians." This gruesome and barbaric custom was eventually dropped. Instead, heads made of flour became a substitute for real human heads in sacrificial rites. Then the practice also grew of eating these buns, which, however, continued to be called 蛮头 *mán tóu*, as if each time one ate a bun, one was eating the head of a barbarian (at least it seems plausible to think so)! After another while, it was felt that even this practice was not entirely "politically correct." Someone then dreamed up the word 馒头 /饅頭 *mán·tou*, with only a slight change in the sounds, but with a more acceptable as well as more accurate meaning to refer to the steam bun. 馒/饅 has the "food" radical and the sound borrowed from 曼 *màn*, meaning "graceful," although the tone has been changed from fourth to second for the purpose in hand. From the sense of "gruesome head of a barbarian," it was transformed into "graceful head which was good to eat"! This invention is a distinctive kind of two-syllable word, as one of its components alone, 馒 *mán*, is not used ever on its own, as on its own it does not refer to any thing. It is like the 蝴蝶 *húdié* ("butterfly") example of a similar two-syllable word, which we have seen in Part II, can already be found in the *Zhuangzi*. However, their difference lies in this: while *die* is used as short for *hudie* (*hu* on its own is not a word but only a character standing for a syllable), neither *man* nor *tou* can be used as abbreviation for *mantou*. *Tou* simply means "head," "while *man* is never used on its own, but only as the first character in the two-syllable word *mantou*, which means "bun," referring to a specific form of pastry. In other words, *man* has meaning but strangely, on its own, does not refer to any thing. You cannot say that you had just eaten a *man*; you must say you had just eaten a *mantou*. Should you say that you had just eaten a *tou*, people would wonder what sort of a head it was that you had eaten – was it a pig's head, a fish head? This is in contrast to *hu* in the *hudie* example, where *hu*, on its own, neither means nor refers to any thing.

According to the Qing Dynasty (1644 – 1911 CE) *Kangxi Dictionary*, the term 馒头 /饅頭 *mán·tou* dates from the Three Kingdoms Period (三国/國时/時代, 220 – 265 CE), when one of its famous heroes who was a brilliant military strategist, political thinker as well as scholar, 诸/諸葛亮 *Zhūgě Liàng*, led his army to cross a river in south China. There he found that the ancient Shang practice of decapitating heads as sacrifice still very much alive. He ordered that sheep and pigs as well as flour buns with heads painted on them be substituted. As far as one knows, there is no documentary evidence that Zhuge Liang himself invented the word 馒头 /饅頭, but it is not implausible to think that it might have come from him. That is the story of the plain bun. There is another story about the stuffed bun, which also goes back to Zhuge Liang's southern campaign. When he led his army to a swampy and unwholesome region, his troops fell prey to diarrhea and similar ills. He instructed that they be fed with steam buns but this time stuffed with meat or sweet fillings.

The next time you eat a Chinese steam bun, whether plain or stuffed, you would know that you are also metaphorically "eating" quite a large chunk of Chinese history. In our opinion, it involves a very critical point in the development of Chinese civilization. With the collapse of the Shang Dynasty and the rise of the Zhou Dynasty, one could even make a case for calling the change from human sacrifices, live burials or making slaves of prisoners-of-war to certain Zhou values, culminating in Confucian values of later Zhou times, the Chinese Enlightenment. It was an extremely big advance in moral thinking to stop making defeated peoples slaves, or to make live human sacrifices of them. This change amounted to extending "respect for persons" or "human rights" to outsiders, people who were not of your own kind. Of course, the ancient Chinese did not use the terms "human rights" or "respect for persons" but what they did was tantamount to implementing the notions these modern terms stand for. The scale of such victims could be judged by certain figures given by experts of *jiaguwen*: one inscription about a particular divination recorded the capture of thirty thousand prisoners-of-war who were either used in sacrificial rites to honor gods and ancestors or buried alive with the dead to serve their needs.

Scholars, however, point out that the term "slavery" as understood in Western history when applied to archaic China is problematic, as the institutional arrangements in the two contexts were different. The Shangs, for instance, did not have chattel slavery; slaves were more like servants and retainers whose prime duty in life was to serve their masters both in this world and in the next. As short-hand, one could perhaps say that the Shangs did not practice full-blown slavery, only a half-hearted attempt. But whether the lower orders buried alive with their dead masters were slaves or not in the technical sense is immaterial from the moral point of view, as such an arrangement appeared to have offended the moral sensibility of the Zhou and later Chinese people.

The British Museum recently – from autumn 2007 to spring 2008 – mounted an exhibition of the terra-cotta army of Qin Shihuangdi (秦始皇帝) No matter how tyrannical and megalomaniacal the first emperor of the very short-lived Qin Dynasty (221 – 207 BCE) was, he did not slaughter thousands of men to accompany him to the next world. He only caused earthen figures of them to be made. In this respect, it was significant that he did not challenge the moral universe introduced by the Zhou, reverting to the barbarism of the Shang Dynasty, although he did not see eye-to-eye with the Confucian ideal of relying more on morals rather than law in ruling his newly minted empire. In the history of the Chinese people and of humankind, that is a great moral stride forward. The Chinese intellectuals by then also felt that, at best, the after life was a mere possibility, not a certainty. Measured against the nebulous goal of serving the great and the good in such a nebulous existence, live burials would be morally out of all proportion, to say the least. It would be better just to make a gesture by making earthen images of human servants. Later on, even that practice gave way to making mere paper servants, carriages, houses, money, etc to ensure that the lives of the dead, who were rich and powerful, could continue in the luxury to which they had become accustomed. Furthermore, such paper goods also amounted to a form of democratisation, as relatively poor people could afford them in catering for the needs of their departed relatives.

Beans – 豆 *dòu* – are another ever-present item in the Chinese diet and forms part of the five grains. However, it could not play the role of being a staple food in the same way that rice and wheat could, for good reasons. In modern scientific terms, we say that rice and wheat contain more carbohydrates than other nutritional items, whereas beans contain far less carbohydrates in comparison. It is also because beans and pulses present problems to human digestion if eaten in any substantial amount. They are fart-making foods. Should one overdo it, the poor old stomach will become a little biogas processing facility, producing an ample supply of methane! They are like cabbages, except for the Chinese variety which causes no farts. Yet, Chinese civilization and culture would not have lasted as long as it had done but for beans, in particular, the soya bean. Mao Zedong was reputed to have said that Chinese civilization was built on excrement, human and animal. This is because the only available fertilisers for millennia (apart from growing nitrogen-fixers such as clover, but this would mean taking land out of cultivation for the usual crops) and indeed, the only truly sustainable fertilisers, are urine and feces. Night-soil and night-soil handlers are the true heroes of history; and so were Chinese peasants in Chinese history. Mao Zedong was most certainly right, but only partially so. If peasants had only grown rice and wheat with the help of human and animal manure, the Chinese people would not have flourished. Indeed, man does not live by bread or rice alone; man, at least, the Chinese kind, lived also on soya.

Chinese civilization was and still is to a great extent built on the soya bean. Soya with everything and soya in a thousand and one different forms and guises could be said to be an apt motto for ordinary Chinese home cooking. For example, take soya sauces – in the West, people are in the main familiar with the light variety, but in reality, there are numerous different kinds. Soya sauce is a liquid, is salty and looks brown. Soya milk, on the other hand, is not brown, is neither salty nor sweet but to which you may add a pinch of salt or sugar, and it looks like cow's milk. (But note: soya milk bears no resemblance to the adulterated specimen one can today buy in cartons from supermarkets and for which one is charged an exorbitant price for an item, which contains mostly water. In the West, should you want the genuine article, make it yourself. It is easy, but, of course, a little time-consuming.) A favorite traditional Chinese breakfast consists of a bowl of hot soya milk with a touch of salt, which you can buy from a stall in the streets of Chinese towns, accompanying it with a length of deep-fried pastry (a Chinese baguette) which, in *putonghua*, is called 油条/條 *yóutiáo*, while in Cantonese, it goes under a more colorful description which may be translated as "deep-fried devils."

You may also enjoy a bowl of soya custard as a snack or as dessert – as custard, it is neither liquid nor perfectly solid but a kind of very wobbly, smooth, jelly – it is the perfect "comfort food." In solid form, you can have soya in squares, as sheets, wet or dried, mashed up or in its original shape.

The traditional peasant diet consisted, as previously pointed out, of rice or buns in the main, accompanied by a relatively large amount of vegetables which were supplemented by soya products in one form or other. In bad times, one would be lucky to have simply rice with a touch of soya sauce. In better times, or at the New Year, one might have some meat. Of course, this is a very generalised picture of peasant existence which is not incompatible with enormous variations between rich and poor peasants, between those who lived in fertile regions (near lakes, rivers, the coast, where fish could be caught or if not caught wild, farmed) and those in dry zones with poor soil. Now you might wonder how people could survive on such a "protein-less" diet. In general, in the West, people consider only meat contains proteins, and some even seem to think that only beef is "proper" meat, that chicken or pork are not even meat in their estimation. They fail to notice that vegetarians thrive very well even without the benefit of fish and dairy products. Pulses and beans contain proteins. The soya is one of those beans which are very high in protein content, though not as high as some lesser consumed beans in the world. However, although the soya is admirable in providing the much needed protein in an otherwise meat-free diet, it remains the case, that the Chinese people would not have survived through the ages but for their discovery of the fermentation process and of the fermented soya bean, a process which we shall discuss in more detail later when we look at wines and spirits.

The human body needs twenty amino-acids to function properly. Soya bean in its simple cooked state provides only eighteen of the twenty amino-acids required; the two missing ones, which animal protein contains, the body cannot make. Where can these be found then if one relies mainly on vegetable proteins? The trick is to ferment the soya. In the process of fermentation, the missing two amino-acids are then produced. So the Chinese peasant depended not simply on the soya but also on fermented soya products. One particular form is called 腐乳 *fŭrŭ* which usually comes today packed in a bottle, little one-inch squares, soft and squishy. The majority of foreigners, when exposed to it, usually cannot stomach it, finding it disgusting in every way. May be, the French palate would take to it more readily than the

Anglo-Saxon one, as it can plausibly be described as the Chinese equivalent of their Roquefort cheese. Such strong pungent stuff like Roquefort cheese and *furu*, you either adore or hate. An extraordinary billionaire in Hong Kong, one who is listed in *Forbes Magazine* as one of the world's ten richest men, is reputed to eat three times a day, a bowl of gruel with some *furu*. There you are – the secret of business acumen and success lies in the eating of *furu*! In the annals of the late Han Dynasty is recorded a story about the Guangwu emperor (光武, 25 – 57 CE) who, before he successfully got on the throne, went through very rough times, when he was very hungry and very cold. He would have died but for the fact that a very ordinary and humble person felt sorry for him and fed him daily with a bowl of gruel with beans in it. It turned out that he never forgot this act of kindness. Later, as emperor, he showered his former savior and benefactor with pearls and other precious objects. As a result of this true, heartening tale, there is an expression 豆粥之恩, which can be translated as: the kindness of a bowlful of gruel with beans.

The character for 豆 *dòu* may be seen below (*jiaguwen*, *jinwen*, *xiaozhuan*, *lishu*):

Curiously enough, the character is based on the visual form of a sacrificial vessel (called *dou*), used to hold meat. Here is a picture of one on your left, although it is not a Shang but a later Zhou one, belonging to the Warring States Period (475 – 221 BCE). Look closely at the most "pictographic" version in *jiaguwen* and compare it with the picture: the top component of the character, the horizontal line, corresponds to the lid of the pot. The middle component is the body of the pot; and the horizontal line inside it shows that the vessel contains food. The third component, the two bits looking like legs correspond to the stem of the vessel. The fourth component, the bottom horizontal line represents the base. Status determined how many of these one was entitled to use.

Later, the word *dou* became a measure word: in the 礼记/禮記 *Lǐ Jì*, the *Book of Rites*, one of ancient China's revered classics, is found a rule which laid down how much liquor a person in a village was permitted depending on age: a person over sixty was allowed three *dou*, one over seventy four, an octogenarian five and if you made it to ninety, you were permitted six.

We shall now turn our attention to drink. In Part II, we have seen that even in Neolithic times (ca. 8000 – 2000 BCE), the early Chinese people had earthen wine vessels which they would have used in offerings to their gods. This shows clearly that they knew how to make wine, which involves yeast and fermentation. Peoples the world over probably stumbled upon fermentation by chance rather than deliberate experimentation initially. Apparently, even some ape-men got drunk from a pile of fruit which they might have gathered and which might have fermented, producing fruit wine – Chinese archaeologists have uncovered the fossil remains of such a drunken group by Lake Hongze, Huaiyin, Jiangsu Province (江苏淮阴洪泽/江蘇淮陰洪澤). About fifty thousand years ago, this lot was making merry, when suddenly either a volcanic eruption or earthquake occurred, which killed and fossilised them.

In 1985, archaeologists excavated a Shang site, Gaocheng (藁城), where they found a structure which was unmistakably a kind of wine-making factory. In a jar, they found a desiccated piece of grayish white substance which was the remains of some yeast. Uncovered were numerous jars; some of them had broad necks, suitable for fermenting grain or fruit. (The very ancient Chinese did not have grapes which were a later import; but by the Tang Dynasty, although grape wine had appeared, the Chinese people did not take to it in a big way.) More recently, in 2004, an international team of scholars using the most up to date scientific techniques has confirmed that nine thousand years ago, the Neolithic people (in a village called Jiahu in Henan Province, 河南贾湖) had made alcoholic beverages from fermenting rice, honey and fruit.

The character for "wine" or "alcohol" is 酒 *jiǔ*, consisting of two components: the water radical, 氵 for the obvious reason that wine is a liquid, but the other part is the character 酉 *yǒu*, to talk about spirits made from newly ripe millet in the eighth month of the year. The character for "wine" – *huiyi zi*, a meaning compound – shows that for the ancient Chinese, wine is a liquid with alcoholic content. The various versions (*jiaguwen*, *xiaozhuan*, *lishu*) are shown below:

The character 酉 *yǒu*, however, referred not only to the millet-derived wine but also to the sacrificial vessel which contained the liquor. It looks like *xiangxing zi*, a pictograph. It is obvious what it is a picture of, in particular, the *jiaguwen* version of a wine vessel. Here are the various forms (*jiaguwen*, *jinwen*, *xiaozhuan*, *lishu*) of the character:

However, this interpretation is not unproblematic as the *jiaguwen* and *jinwen* versions of the character bear no resemblance to the actual sacrificial Shang bronze 酉 *yǒu* vessels so far excavated. Below are some examples:

You can see that the vessel has loop handles and its shape can be long and slender (the first on the left which is a Shang artifact) or dumpy (the second on the left which is either late Shang or early Western Zhou, ca. 1027 – 900 BCE). It can also be cast in the shape of an animal, such as owl (second from the right) or tiger (first on the right). The most one can say is that the dumpy ones seem to correspond more to the *xiaozhuan* version of the character.

The question then arises: what vessel could the character 酉 *yǒu* be a pictograph of, if it is not the pictograph of the sacrificial vessel itself called by that name? We suggest that it could be the pictograph of the vessel in which the millet wine was brewed rather than the sacrificial vessel into which the wine was poured as offering on the altar. Take a look at these pots shown below:

These pots are not Shang artifacts but Neolithic ones. They are reproduced here just as a suggestive hint that by Shang times, some of the shapes of Neolithic earthenware pots could have influenced the way in which the *jiaguwen* or the *jinwen* character for 酉 *yǒu* was written. These two versions look remarkably like the first two pots above – the first flask belongs to the Yangshao Culture (5000 – 3000 BCE) and is dated ca. 4000 BCE, while the second flask belongs to the later Majiayao Culture (ca. 3300 – p 2050 BCE). The third is a jar belonging to the Yangshao Culture but dated towards the end of the period. It is shown here to indicate that Neolithic pots came in numerous different shapes and sizes, not only that of an amphora, and to suggest that some of these could have inspired the way the character was written in the earlier scripts, including *xiaozhuan*. By *lishu*, however, Chinese writing had opted definitively for the square look. It seemed very likely that earthenware vessels would have been used to make the wine, and not the bronze vessels which were used to contain the wine as sacrificial offering.

We next look at some characters involving 酉 *yǒu* as radical: 酿/釀 *niáng* ("to make by fermentation"); 酵 *jiào* ("yeast"); 酱/醬 *jiàng* ("sauce made from soya beans"); 醋 *cù* ("vinegar)." Here, 酉 *yǒu* appears to have the derivative meaning of "things to do with yeast and the process of fermentation." Soya sauce is indeed based on the fermentation of the soya bean; so does the production of vinegar involve fermentation. This shows that the Chinese, at least from Shang times, if not earlier, appeared to have grasped what exactly happened in the production of 酉 *yǒu*, the spirits made from millet, and extrapolated from it the more general notion of the process of fermentation itself, that yeast was required to start the process, and that many different substances subjected to the process of fermentation could yield very different products – wines/spirits are very different from soya sauces and these again are very different from vinegar. In other words, far from it being the case that radicals yield a system of classification which is inherently cumbersome, trivial at best, arbitrary at worst, one would wish to argue that in instances such as these, radicals give very informative insights into a lot of things and processes about which the ancient Chinese were knowledgeable. Here, they appeared to have a pretty good grasp of biochemistry. Of course, this is not to say that they were Pasteurs, but what they knew is entirely compatible with the knowledge given by modern science, based on Pasteur's experiments on fermentation. Nor is it to say that they had constructed formulae in terms of the molecular structure of those substances and their biochemical transformation as we understand these today. What one can say is that the ancient Chinese by Zhou, if not Shang times, had tumbled to the general idea of fermentation as a process which governed the transformation of the properties of certain substances under a specific set of circumstances. Otherwise, why should they have used the same radical 酉 *yǒu* with regard to so many different things?

An alternative explanation to the hypothesis just given is that common to all the different characters involving fermentation mentioned above (characters with the radical 酉 *yǒu*) is merely the use of the vessel called 酉. That sounds plausible on the surface but upon further scrutiny runs into problems. We have already seen that the Shang bronze sacrificial 酉 *yǒu* in its various known shapes do not match the *jiaguwen* or *jinwen* version of the character. We have pointed out just now that it might be necessary to distinguish the sacrificial bronze vessel itself containing the alcohol to be placed on the altar from the earthenware pot in which the grain was brewed to make the alcohol. This clarification makes the alternative explanation even more problematic as it seems to involve certain counter-intuitive assumptions, such as, that an amphora-shaped container was the most suitable and convenient for making a whole range of different products from vinegar (which seemed most likely) to soya sauce (which seemed least likely). It also overlooks the fact that the radical is also used as component of the character for "process of fermentation" (酿/釀 *niáng*) as well as with the character for "yeast" (酵 *jiào*). It seems to imply that the ancient Chinese believed that the fermentation process would occur only if one used the vessel 酉, no matter what shape it had, but no other type of container. However, fermentation itself is a process which can take place (when the right conditions obtain) whatever the exact shape or size of the container. While it might be suitable to use a certain shape or size vessel in fermenting millet grains for wine, that same type of vessel might not be convenient for fermenting soya beans to make soya sauce. Furthermore, even if the vessel for brewing the millet liquor was practical for fermenting other substances, why would the ancient Chinese use such a vessel, associated with a sacred rite, to ferment something quite so mundane or profane as soya sauce and vinegar? By comparison, the hypothesis that the ancient Chinese might have grasped the fundamental nature of the fermentation process seems more elegant and simpler in conception as well as having greater explanatory scope than its rival.

There is a legend about the origin of vinegar and the character for it in ancient China. In the Xia Dynasty (ca. 21st – 16th century BCE), a person wandered from the north to Jiangsu (江苏/蘇) Province in the south-east of China to open a wine shop or factory at a place called Zhenjiang (镇/鎮江). The process of brewing took three weeks. At the end of one such period, when he opened up the jar or vat, his nose was assailed by a smell which was both pungent and astringent. He knew the product was not the usual wine or spirits but something else. He tasted it and found it was good. He could not think of a name for this new product until it hit him that he could create a new character 醋 *cù*: for radical, it would have the character 酉 *yǒu,* as its production involved a process similar to that in making spirits from millet. He also thought it appropriate for a second reason, as 酉 also referred to a period of time in the day, five to seven in the evening. As second component, he thought the character 昔 *xī* would be most apt, as it means "former times"; in this context, *xi* would refer to the fact that the fermentation process took twenty one days. It was exactly on the twenty-first day in the evening, some time between 5pm and 7pm that he opened the jar and discovered that he had a wonderful new product on his hand. So in a fit of marketing genius, he put these two characters together to create a brand new character/word for his brand new product. Ever since then, Zhenjiang vinegar has remained a top brand. This example, though a legend, shows yet again that many Chinese words carry a lot of cultural baggage.

Wine is something which nearly all cultures and civilizations indulged in. But tea (茶 *chá*) is another matter, and seems peculiar to the Chinese. The Chinese tell a lovely story about its origin. A figure called Shennong (神农/農 literally meaning "Divine Agriculturist"), who lived ca. 3000 BCE, is said to have given the Chinese the secrets of agriculture, medicine, and tea. (There is a famous work on Chinese medicinal herbs called 神农/農本草经/經 *Shénnóng Běn Cǎo Jīng*.) In ancient times, people fell ill after swallowing what might have been toxic or what might contain what we, today, call germs. Shennong was determined to work out methodically as to what was safe and good to eat and what was bad and dangerous. He conducted experiments upon himself, as clearly he had not bothered to breed armies of white mice as experimental subjects. He would pop something into his mouth, study its effects, and if these were fine, he would pop a sample of it into a bag slung over his left shoulder. Things which produced ill effects, he would pop them into another bag slung over his right shoulder. He would then instruct the people in accordance with the results of his systematic investigations, and with the help of the samples he had distinguished and collected. Of course, today, you could say he was not doing "science" as his method does not conform to the gold standard of the Randomised Controlled Trial and he certainly did not submit his findings to be "peer-reviewed," nor did he publish them in a "diamond list journal" such as the equivalent of *The Lancet* or *The New England Journal of Medicine*! Such criticisms of his "scientific" method would be neither here nor there. His experimental work was greatly aided by the fact that he was no ordinary man – his innards were transparent, and he could see (without sophisticated machines such as PET, TOM, or whatever other very expensive high tech our medical experts today use to look at our insides) and follow precisely the path the substances he had swallowed would take as they journeyed through the body, and what they would do as a result to various bits of it. For instance, he could see that alcohol eventually got to the liver and the damage it could cause that organ. One day, so the story goes, he swallowed some young leaves, from what we later call the tea plant, and he found that they produced beneficial effects, such as dissolving built-up grease and fat in the stomach, scrubbing it squeaky clean. So he prescribed tea as a medicine in certain cases.

Shennong did not use the character 茶 *chá,* but another, 查 *chá*. Indeed, 茶 appeared quite late in Chinese history. Some time after Shennong (as recorded in *The Book of Songs* 诗经/詩經 *Shī Jīng*, an early ancient text) the character for "tea" was written 荼, as the tea leaves were bitter just like the leaves of another bitter but edible plant – the sow-thistle – called 荼 *tú*. If you look very carefully you would notice that 茶 *chá* and 荼 *tú* differ only by a stroke. In the Tang Dynasty, 茶 *chá* finally emerged in its present form for good when scholars and scribes removed the extra horizontal line, distinguishing it definitively from the original 荼 *tú*. It appeared for the first time in the world's first treatise on tea written during the Tang period, borrowing as sound Shennong's character for "tea": 查 *chá*.

Have you ever wondered why in English, the word is "tea" and in French, it is "thé"? These come from the pronunciation of 荼 *tú* above, by way of a south Chinese regional speech 闽/閩南话/話 *mǐnnánhuà* (more commonly known in English as Hokkien) which pronounces the word as "te." However, in Russian and Indian languages, the word is "chai" which obviously comes from "cha." In any case, these pronunciations, whether "tea," "thé," or "chai", ultimately could be traced back to the different early versions of the term in Chinese history.

The uses of tea in its long history in China ranged from its early use as medicine, as sacrificial offering, and finally as ordinary drink by early Shang times. The way in which it was processed as well as made (in the sense of making a cup or a bowl of tea) also altered through time. In the earlier days, tea was cooked together with other ingredients and drunk as soup. However, by Tang times, the other herbs and stuff were left out so that tea became the sole ingredient. In that period, we know that the process involved steaming the leaves, then grinding them into a powder, next compressing them into cakes, and finally drying these. Whenever you wanted to make a drink, you would break off whatever amount desired and then boil it.

In the Tang Dynasty, tea drinking spread widely, from south to north China, for two reasons. The imperial court showed great enthusiasm demanding tribute in the form of tea, as well as organizing tea ceremonies and tea parties. Tea was associated with Buddhism, which also got firmly established with the translation of the sutras brought back from India.

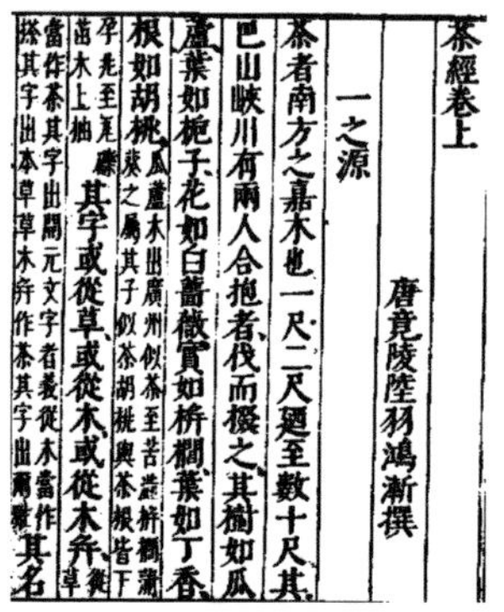
茶經卷上
唐竟陵陸羽鴻漸撰
一之源
茶者南方之嘉木也一尺二尺迺至數十尺其
巴山峽川有兩人合抱者伐而掇之其樹如瓜
蘆葉如梔子花如白薔薇實如栟櫚葉如丁香
根如胡桃瓜蘆木出廣州似茶至苦澀栟櫚蒲葵之屬其子似茶胡桃與茶根皆下孕兆至瓦礫苗木上抽
其字或從草或從木或從木幷從草當作茶其字出開元文字音義從木當作梌其字出本草草木幷作茶其字出爾雅
其名

The first tea classic in the world was written by Lu Yu (陆/陸羽, 733 – 804 CE). It is not surprising that such a work was written by someone steeped in the Buddhist way of life. As an abandoned child, he was adopted by a Buddhist monk and associated with people and other monks who had expert knowledge of the subject. He wandered to tea areas and so became even more steeped in the knowledge and know-how about tea. His book consisted of ten chapters, dealing with the origin, the history, the growing, the manufacturing, the method of making tea, the various kinds of tea and their individual favors as well as the utensils used. Here is the first page of his *Tea Classic*.

The book shifted the emphasis from the processing and cooking of tea to the tasting of it. The tea ceremony which first began to become popular in the Tang Dynasty was taken during that period together with (Chan or Zen) Buddhism to Japan, which explains why tea and the tea drinking ceremony continue to be so much part of Japanese culture even today.

In the Song Dynasty (960 – 1279 CE), craftsmen in tea-processing produced what were called the dragon-phoenix tea balls, with a picture stamped on them which you can see on your right.

The Song Dynasty introduced a change not so much in the manufacturing process itself, but more in the making and serving up of the drink. One no longer cooked the ground tea, but simply put a bit in a cup or bowl, poured some just-off-the-boil water on it, and let it infuse. Here is a painting: you can see a person with the kettle, pouring the water from it into the cup, and other persons drinking or sipping the tea from the cup.

Another major radical change occurred in the Ming Dynasty (1368 – 1644 CE), this time in the manufacturing process itself. In the twenty-fourth year of his reign (1391 AD), the Hongwu (洪武) emperor issued a decree that ground tea was no longer acceptable as tribute, only loose tea leaves were. This meant that the cakes or dragon-phoenix balls rapidly fell out of fashion. Instead, the best tea leaves were picked, spring water was heated and then used to infuse them. Indeed the ordinary people would not be drinking the best in the way just described, but the emperor would. The rarest and the best through the ages was reputed to be white tea, grown in secret gardens, delicately picked in early spring by damsels with dainty gold scissors. Such tea could not be bought for all the silver and all the gold of this world. Some people believe that such secret gardens still exist and that though the leaves may not be picked by damsels with gold scissors, white tea is still made from them. We leave it to your imagination to decide who may be the lucky recipients of such a gift, that is, if the secret gardens still do exist.

Tea drinking was not only associated with Buddhist practices but also played a big role in the form of tea-tasting together with wine drinking, poetry-making and calligraphy-writing in the lifestyle of China's literati since the Tang Dynasty. Scholars and their friends would gather and engage in such refined activities. Here is a painting of one such scene of tea taking and tasting.

In the Qing Dynasty (1644 – 1911 CE), tea drinking was no longer so much a literati past-time as something which entered the lives of ordinary people, with tea houses appearing. Tea became part of normal commerce. Tea firms and companies doing wholesale business as well as tea shops doing retail trade sprang up everywhere. Today, tea commerce in all its aspects remains just as lively.

Clothing

In Neolithic times, people used pelts as clothing. The character for "clothing made from pelts" is 裘 *qiú* and its evolved forms (*jiaguwen*, *jinwen*, *xiaozhuan*, *lishu* and *kaishu*) look like these:

The *jiaguwen* form does bear out the claim that the pelt was worn with the fury side out, as you can see. In *xiaozhuan*, the *lishu* and *kaishu* forms seem, more or less, already in place. This is *xingsheng zi* (semantic-phonetic compound) as the radical is 衣 *yī* and the component 求 *qiú* on top gives it the sound.

In 1973, major excavations of three second century BCE Han tombs took place at Mawangdui (马/馬王堆), now just a suburb of Changsha (長沙), the capital of Hunan (湖南) Province. The best preserved of the three family tombs belonged to the Marchioness Dai. Hers contained a rich hoard of artifacts including silk garments, silk banners and even silk manuscripts. One of her extremely well-preserved garments looks like this:

Experts have said that if one were to detach the collar and the borders, that garment would only weigh 49 gms (or about an ounce and a half), and if folded up could be stuffed comfortably into a match box, so fine is the texture and so light in weight of the silk used in that garment.

If you study the shape of the garment above, and imagine yourself following the lines of its cut, you could almost see that shape being replicated in the various forms (*jiaguwen*, *jinwen*, *xiaozhuan*, *lishu*) of the character 衣 presented below:

The character is indeed *xiangxing zi*, a pictograph, as it seems to capture in outline what an ancient upper garment looks like (upper in the sense of what covered the top half of the body, not in the sense of being the top layer of clothing).

Not every one wore silk, only those with the appropriate rank could wear and use it. Of course, the emperor and the nobility wore silk but the scholar-official class was also entitled to do so. Naturally there were silk garments and silk garments – how grand and elaborate were a matter of rank and status. What then did ordinary folk wear? After they left the Neolithic Age and pelts behind, they primarily wore hemp – 麻 *má*. Hemp is native to China. Impressed on some Neolithic pots could be seen the woven pattern of hemp. Archaeological records show that hemp was grown and used since five to six thousand years ago. The oldest agricultural treatise ca. the sixteenth century BCE mentioned hemp as one of the earliest crops grown. The character in *jinwen* looks like this:

Another material was also used, the bark from the stalk of a plant called 葛 *gě*, the kudzu vine. (This is a marvellous plant as nearly every part of it is useful: its young leaves could be used in salads or battered and then deep fried, its tubers can be eaten as food and also used in medicine. Not only that, but also as a nitrogen-fixer, it can enrich the soil, its deep tuberous roots can raise minerals from the deeper layers to the top soil, as well as act as control against soil erosion.) The cloth derived from this plant, however, was coarse and yellowish in color. It was used to make summer wear.

The cotton called 棉花 *mián·hua* was introduced into China in the Han Dynasty (206 BCE – 220 CE) from India. It did not seem to have taken off as a substitute for hemp on a large scale until in the Yuan Dynasty (1279 – 1368 CE). This was because the Mongol invaders had destroyed a lot of mulberry trees whose leaves are used to feed the silkworms, and the new Mongol rulers sought to fill the economic gap with cotton production. However, this woven cloth did not become readily available till the seventeenth century when it finally replaced hemp as the major fabric for clothing. Whether clothed in hemp, in *ge*-cloth, in cotton or other lesser fabrics, such people were referred to as 布衣 *bùyī*, "people of the cloth," "common people."

Let us examine more closely the character for "cotton":

棉

Its radical is 木 ("tree or word"). Its second component is the character 帛 *bó*, meaning "silk." The sound of 棉 is borrowed from another existing character 綿 *mián* ("silk floss"). So this is quite an unusual character as it seems to wish to suggest that it stands for a fabric which is both like and yet unlike silk. Cotton and silk are radically different in terms of their biological origins, their social status, their textures, such as what they feel like when they touch the skin. Cotton, however, does not have to be coarse like hemp or *ge*-cloth; it can be soft and fine, even if it does not quite have the feel of silk. As fabrics, they are different, yet could be said in a limited aspect to be alike. Perhaps, it is fitting that the character 棉 be constructed in this complex manner.

<u>Housing</u>

The earliest shelter that humans used was the cave; and so it was with the Chinese people in Neolithic times. The character for "cave" is 穴 *xué* . It can also mean "den" or "lair," as such caves were also used by animals and indeed, in some cases, probably shared by both humans and animals, such as the dog which they domesticated. Later, when the Neolithic peoples started to build shelters rather than simply looked for suitable caves, they were known to have built them half buried in the ground. They made a hole at the top called 窗 *chuāng* which was a kind of open-to-the-sky skylight, the original window. Apparently, these Neolithic and even later forebears used to spend most of the summer growing season away from such shelters but would return after the harvest to spend the winter. The first thing they did was to repair, clean and tidy the place, in particular chasing out the mice and the rats which would have colonised, without let or hindrance, the undisturbed house during the long absence of its human occupants. Next, they would seal up the window as well as plaster the door with mud to make the whole dwelling as warm and as tightly secured as it was possible against the fearsomely cold blasts in north China.

The *Book of Songs* (*Shi Jing*, 诗经/詩經) is, as we have seen, a rich source of information about life in ancient China. It is a compilation of anonymous songs or poems dated, according to scholars, to 1000 BCE, if not earlier. Later Confucius is said to have had a hand in editing it. A particular poem in it describes daily activities in the course of the year, as the seasons changed. Below is a passage which tells us about such details during late autumn and at the onset of winter. (The translation is by James Legge, a nineteenth century Scottish missionary and sinologist):

In the tenth month , the cricket
Enters under our beds .
Chinks are filled up , and rats are smoked out ;
The windows that face [the north] are stopped up ;
And the doors are plastered .
' Ah ! our wives and children ,
' Changing the year requires this :
Enter here and dwell . '

十月蟋蟀、入我床下。
穹室熏鼠。
塞向墐戶。
嗟我妇/婦子、曰为改岁/歲、入此室处/處。

The origin of windows in caves and cave dwellings shows why the character 窗 for "window" has as radical 穴 ("cave"). Even today in six provinces of north central China on the loess plateau, people live in cave-dwellings called 窑洞 *yáodòng*. The older ones are carved out of the mountain side, while others are half-dug-in, rather like some Neolithic ones, but more recent ones are even free-standing. What they have in common is the arched front. A family dwelling typically has three arched openings, the center one is the living-cum-kitchen area, with sleeping quarters on either side. Here is a picture of one. Note that this one sensibly has a solar water heater

installed on the roof, as such an environmentally friendly device suits admirably the local climate.

Let us now return to earlier times to see what the character 穴 *xué* looks like in *xiaozhuan*. It looks like this, not all that different from the Standard script of today:

We next see what 窗 *chuāng*, "window," looks like in *jinwen*: and *xiaozhuan*: . By *xiaozhuan*, architecture had long left Neolithic times behind, of course, and one can see more clearly that the window in the cave which was a mere hole in the wall or the roof of a cave had been transformed into an elegant architectural structure, looking very much like one of the designs (the middle one on the left) of traditional Chinese windows reproduced here. As shown in *jinwen*, it was already looking decorative.

Any house, no matter how basic or elaborate, must have a roof, the topmost part of the structure. The character for it is written: 宀 ("roof"). It refers specifically to the roof but, in reality, the whole dwelling, as no roof can exist without walls, not to mention the foundation, etc. on which it is built. As a radical, it enters into a good many characters whose meanings are associated with the notion of house as a physical construction, for example, in terms of its rooms 室 *shì*, spaces providing shelter and rest (where one might find peace or tranquillity:宁/寧 *níng*; where one can lay down one's weary head to sleep: 寢/*qǐn*, or where one can find refuge against cold: 寒 *hán*). It is also a component for "house as home" in 家 *jiā*. We shall select only one of these examples for detailed comment here, the case of 寒 *hán* ("cold"), shown below with *jinwen* in the first line, and *xiaozhuan*, *lishu* in the second:

Let us concentrate on the *jinwen* form. Its "roof" radical extends nearly the whole length of the character, as if suggesting that for a house to keep out the cold effectively, the whole place should be enclosed as much as possible. The space under the roof represents the space inside the house. In the middle of that space is a person, who appears to be standing on two blocks of ice, represented by two short horizontal lines, almost looking like two large dots, suggesting that the cold is seeping up the body from the ground through the feet. You see this: 艹 which is the grass radical. The bundles of dried grass surrounding the cold shivering person indicate the fuel for making a fire to keep warm. The character is obviously *huiyi zi*, a meaning compound. It encapsulates most vividly and graphically the idea of bitter cold in the winter, and how to survive it. Looking at the *jinwen* form of the character alone is enough to make one shiver in spite of the bundles of dried grass in the hut, so meager that they could at best just take a little chill out of the glacial air. Those, who live in centrally heated houses today, find it difficult to imagine what the winter would be truly like for earlier peoples. Curiously, contrary to expectation, the most graphic characters in Chinese are not the *xiangxing zi*, the pictographs, but instances of *huiyi zi*, meaning compounds, in our opinion.

The character for "cold" also hints at the ancient Chinese understanding of the nature of water and its various forms, from being liquid as flowing water to being solid as a lump of ice. In the *jinwen* version, we have noted that the person inside the house is standing on two slabs of ice, which are represented by two short lines. When ice functions as a radical, it is represented not by two short lines, but by two dots, like this: 冫. On the other hand, the radical for "water" is represented by three dots: 氵 . The difference in writing the two radicals reflects the understanding that the ancient Chinese had about the nature of water, on the one hand, and that of ice, on the other. Although water and ice look entirely different as substances and possess very different properties such as that one is liquid and the other solid, nevertheless, they are essentially the same matter. One is transformed to become the other when the weather got really cold, while the process would be reversed when the weather got warmer. In other words, it would not be entirely far from the mark for us to infer from the difference in the conceptualisation of water and ice as reflected in their radicals, that the ancient Chinese had some grasp of physics, even if they did not formulate that knowledge in terms of H_2O.

Let us next look at the character for "water," which is pronounced *shuǐ*. It is *xiangxing zi*, a pictograph, looking like this respectively in *jiaguwen, jinwen, xiaozhuan, lishu*:

The *jiaguwen* and the *xiaozhuan* forms are the most pictographic – they attempt to capture a flowing stream of water. This is liquid water in its most common and basic form. You can then use it as radical (氵) to construct new characters such as 河 *hé* ("river") or 海 *hǎi* ("sea").

We turn our attention next to the character for "ice" which is 冰 *bīng*. Its forms in *jinwen, xiaozhuan, lishu* are:

Unlike the character for "water," it is not *xiangxing zi*, a pictograph but *huiyi zi*, a meaning compound. Its radical ensures this. At the same time, it demonstrates that the ancient Chinese understood that ice is water but in a different state from that of liquid water.

To complete our account of ancient Chinese perception of the physics of water, let us look at the character for "evaporate or steam." It is 蒸 *zhēng*. We wonder if you have ever used a Chinese steamer to steam food. It is a bamboo basket. This probably explains why the character for "steam" itself sports the "grass" radical 艹. What is of more interest to us here is not so much the material out of which a steamer is made, but the process of steaming itself. This is indicated by the four dots at the bottom of the character *zheng*, looking like this 灬; it is a radical for the character "fire," 火 *huǒ*. Heat or fire is required for water to evaporate or to steam something. The sun evaporates the water for us when we dry wet things outside in the sunlight. When we want to cook something using water vapor, we have to use direct heat such as fire or indirect heat such as electricity to boil the water. The character *zheng* reflects the understanding that vapor is but yet another form of water, caused by applying heat to it.

We now turn our attention to the character 宫 *gōng* ("palace"). However, we shall see in a moment, that all is not what it seems. But first let us see what it looks like in *jiaguwen* and *jinwen*, of which there are numerous forms, but only two of each are reproduced below:

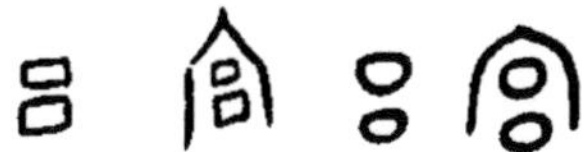

In *xiaozhuan*, it is:

The respective simpler version in both *jiaguwen* and *jinwen* looks remarkably like the cave dwelling of Neolithic times, with two "rooms" inside a cave. The more elaborate forms with the "roof" radical suggest a house, with the squares or squares with roundish corners inside the space under the roof representing rooms. *Xiaozhuan* is similar in design except for a slight change, as it seems to show that there is a passage linking the rooms in a house.

Up to the time of the first Qin emperor, houses were called 宫, as borne out by ancient texts, whether these were the humble dwellings of ordinary folks or the grand constructions of the noble or the rich. However, Qin Shihuangdi had the habit of magnifying himself in more ways than one. We have already seen in Part II that he decreed *xiaozhuan* to be the imperial script, leaving *lishu* to those mortals lesser than himself. Similarly, he sought to glorify himself by decreeing that 宫 *gōng* should henceforth only be used to refer to (his) palaces and administrative quarters. At the stroke of his pen, or rather of Li Si's brush (remember his all-serving, all-powerful chancellor), he ordained that ordinary folks dwelled in what are called 室 *shì*, while he, naturally, lived in palaces. He built numerous sumptuous palaces, such as the Palace of Everlasting Joy; little did he know then that, alas, that joy for his dynasty would be very short-lived, indeed. Today when you tour the Forbidden City in Beijing, you are visiting 故宫 *gùgōng*, literally "former palace," as it is now a museum. Being the most important of the imperial palaces (of both the Ming and Qing Dynasties), it has acquired the honor of simply being referred to as *gugong* without the implication, however, that it is the one and only former palace which still exists in China today. Amongst other former Qing palaces is the one in Chengde, north-east of Beijing, where the Manchu rulers used to retreat from the oppressive heat of the capital in the summer, while not forgetting Shenyang, the original Manchu capital before the capture of Beijing and its establishment as the capital of the new Qing Dynasty.

Palaces, naturally, are sumptuous constructions. So in the imagination of ordinary people, a palace became a place somewhere in the sky where the gods and immortals dwelt as in 天宫 *tiāngōng* or a place in the depth of the ocean where the king of the seas dwelt as in 龙宫 *lónggōng*. However, post 1949, the word 宫 *gōng* has undergone another reversal of fortune after just over two thousand years of imperial usurpation. Today, there are public buildings such as the Palace for Youth, for Children, for Labor, for the Arts, (folk and fine), etc. The people have re-appropriated but also at the same time re-furbished the meaning of that ancient word. This latest meaning combines the original meaning of a "dwelling of ordinary people" with the post Qin Shihuangdi (221 BCE – 1949 CE) meaning of the "grandness of an imperial palace" – a very apt innovation indeed.

In the 宫 *gōng* – those richly decorated imperial palaces filled with luxury objects – did the emperor sit on gilded chairs? You might have thought so. In reality this was not the case. Chairs were a late innovation in Chinese culture. Indeed, it was not even an entirely Chinese invention in one sense, in terms of its origin, as the Chinese had borrowed its predecessor from the nomadic peoples, such as the Mongols who constantly raided and marauded Chinese territory. The Mongols had stools which they could pack with them as part of their tent and its furnishings. The Chinese took over the stool and developed from it the chair. The conception of design and craftsmanship of chairs, cabinets and tables reached its apogee in the Ming Dynasty. The eighteenth century English style of furniture, as represented by Thomas Chippendale (1718 – 1779) as well as the Glasgow School of Art headed by Charles Rennie Mackintosh (1868 – 1928), has been greatly influenced by the Ming conception of furniture, or at least the Chinese influence was one of the strands.

Chairs first began to make an appearance in the Tang Dynasty but probably were only found initially in certain elite households. However, by Song times, they were a universal item, at least in towns and cities. No chairs then for the likes of even emperors till probably late Tang times. So how did they manage? They sat in two positions, the kneeling and the kneeling/sitting. The former involved both legs kneeling on the floor, with the trunk upright. The latter was more normal and involved first kneeling, then lowering the body in such a way that the buttocks eventually rested on the heels. If you have visited Japan and stayed at one of the traditional inns called *ryokans*, you would have sat in that way. Japanese (and Korean) people, except for the ultra modern ones, continue to sit thus today in the privacy of their homes. This is because the Japanese imported Chinese culture in a big way into Japan during the Tang Dynasty – the Tangs sat in that fashion, hence did and still do the Japanese. The former sat on a mat called 席 *xí* ; the Japanese sit on a similar mat which they call a *tatami*.

Take a look at the various (*jiaguwen*, *jinwen*, *xiaozhuan*, *lishu*) forms of the character 坐 *zuò* ("to sit"):

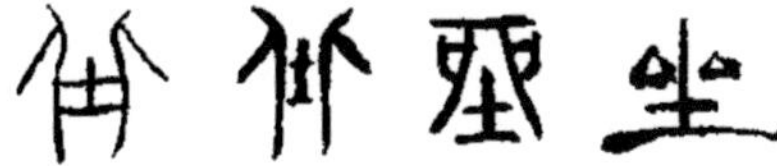

All versions are basically the same: the radical is 土 *tǔ* ("ground") and upon the ground two people (人 *rén*) sit, facing each other. Their form is very graphic, but the character is not merely *xiangxing zi*, a pictograph but *huiyi zi*, a meaning-compound. From its deconstruction, it becomes absolutely clear that the ancient Chinese till probably late Tang times had no chairs and also no tables of matching height to sit at. Instead, they sat at low tables which were called 几/機 *jǐ* which look like our coffee tables today.

Why did the Chinese, for so long, appeared content to sit on floor mats at low tables? We have already given the straightforward explanation that they happened not to have adapted the stool from the Mongols until relatively late in their history. There is, however, another less mundane explanation which holds that there was a close relationship between the seated posture and the influence of Daoism. This philosophy emphasized the cultivation of *qi* (气/氣) through breathing techniques, which could be practiced more readily seated on the floor than on a chair. Scholars, as calligraphers and painters, would run through such breathing exercises before lifting the brush. The arrival of high furniture may be regarded as marking the decline of Daoist culture.

<u>Transport</u>

The earliest form of transport for humankind the world over would have been animals, used for riding or for pulling carts. In ancient China, the ox played such a role. It is said that the philosopher Laozi rode on an ox, as he wandered through the land, after he got tired of politics and public affairs which he considered, in the end, to be ephemeral. Instead, as he jogged slowly along, he philosophised. Unfortunately, in all societies, not only in Chinese history, philosophers were few and far between. Instead, rulers and men of affairs preferred to rush about and for that purpose an ox was of little use. One must ride a horse. The faster a horse, the more valued it was. Chinese rulers desperately coveted "barbarian" horses as these were much faster than the native breed. Barbarians, riding their swift steed, raided Chinese territory, and even conquered the country because of their superior animals.

Horses drew carts and carriages in civilian life, but war wagons or chariots in the military. So we must take a look at these, in particular the latter. The character is 车/車, pronounced as *jū* in ancient Chinese but as *chē* today. (However, when it is used to refer to a piece in Chinese chess and not a vehicle, it is pronounced *jū*.) So important was this mode of transportation and warfare in ancient times that experts of *jiaguwen* have discovered that there are more than 400 different forms of the character in the script. Here are a few of them.

Below on the left is a model of a simple fighting wagon recreated with the help of material and data from the excavation at a Shang site, which the picture on the right shows very clearly.

As you can see from the characters which reflect them, these fighting wagons vary from the simplest such as plain carts to the left, to ones with an umbrella or awnings over them, to one with a box. The most elaborate on the far right might not, however, have reflected the most elaborate construction, as it could be a cart drawn by humans rather than by horses. But basically, these Shang carts and carriages were two-wheelers, primarily horse-drawn. One can make out the shaft, the yoke, the axle and in some instances even the lynch-pin of the wheel.

Today, the military prowess of a country is judged by the number of weapons of mass destruction in its arsenal. So it was in ancient times, except that military might, then, was judged by the quantity of fighting wagons or war chariots it possessed. A country was graded in terms of thousand, ten thousand war chariots. If yours fell into the latter category, then you would be the superpower of the time.

The honor of having invented the fighting wagon is commonly accorded to the Yellow Emperor (said by Sima Qian in *The Historical Records* (*Shi Ji* 史记/記) to have reigned from 2697 – 2598 BCE, although regarded by other scholars as a legendary figure), who had been credited with having given the Chinese people a good many inventions and discoveries.

By the Han Dynasty, the fighting wagon was no longer simple like the Shang one shown earlier; it would be more appropriately called "war chariots." Here is a picture of one engraved on a Han Dynasty brick.

Ancient large civilizations had the habit of being built along the banks or at the delta of large rivers – the Egyptian one was at the mouth of the Nile, the Fertile Crescent one was by the Tigris and the Euphrates, and the Chinese alongside the middle and lower reaches of the Yellow River. Negotiating a river means one thing: the need to build boats. Boats in Shang times were the major mode of transportation, especially for heavy goods. *Jiaguwen* and *jinwen* (the first three on the left are *jiaguwen* and the remaining two are *jinwen*) show many variations of writing the character:

On top of the three shown above, *jiaguwen* also sports some other forms such as these:

These obviously are meant to show different sorts of boats, passenger boats such as the one on the left, passenger-with-goods boat, as on the right, and in the middle a boat with punts. The *jiaguwen* characters are clearly *xiangxing zi*, pictographs. However, by *xiaozhuan* , the character was on the way to looking like today's version: 舟 *zhōu.*

Ancient Chinese boats were basically of two types in structure: squarish bow and flat-bottomed, or pointy bow and up-turned bottom. One variety belonging to the first category was noted for its sturdiness while another belonging to the second category was noted for its speed. By the time of the Spring and Autumn Period (770 – 476 BCE), boats had been used on a big scale in warfare, plying the Yangzi River, for instance. Chinese ship-building reached its height during the Ming Dynasty, culminating in the great fleet of Admiral Zheng He (郑和/鄭和, 1371 – 1433 CE) who made seven voyages to thirty different countries between 1405 and 1433 CE. His boats were called treasure boats for the simple reason that they actually did contain treasures, meant as gifts to impress the rulers of the various states visited, of the magnificence and munificence of Chinese power under the new Ming Dynasty. (It is important to bear in mind that these fleets were not ships of conquests, but bearers of Chinese diplomacy, a form of diplomacy which the Western mind sometimes find hard to grasp.) The main vessels were about 120 meters long and 50 meters wide, although modern scholarship claims they could not have been that long but at most were between 59 and 84 meters long. But such ambitious adventures came to a rapid end owing to certain unexpected turns in the political and economic situation in China during the period of the voyages. A little later, European nations took to exploring the world by sea and colonising most parts of it – thus began the long epoch of European world ascendancy.

末

Let the elephant take the strain

The ancient Chinese, certainly, by Shang times (ca. 1600 – 1027 BCE) if not much earlier, even in Neolithic times (ca. 8000 – 2000 BCE), had domesticated the sheep, the ox, the pig, the dog, the horse, the donkey as well as the chicken.

The character for "chicken" (鸡/鷄 *jī*), from its various forms in *jiaguwen*, to *jinwen*, *xiaochuan*, reflects the very different stages of domesticating the wild bird. Below are three *jiaguwen* forms:

The earliest of the *jiaguwen* versions, on the right, is simply the drawing of the bird itself – a character cannot get more pictographic than that. The other two versions reflect a further stage in the process of domestication itself. At the same time, the characters themselves are no longer pictographs, but *huiyi zi*, meaning compounds. Each is shown with two components. Note that there is a difference between them – the version shown in the middle exhibits clearly the following features: the right component is the general character for "bird" which today is written as 鸟/鳥 *niăo*. The left component 奚 itself has three bits to it: 爫 stands for "claws" (chickens have clawed feet), then 大 ("big"), and then something in the middle which looks like this 幺 (for "silken threads or ropes"). 幺 is pictographically shown as twisted silken strands. A wild chicken would fly away, so it had to be tied up should one wish to retain it. Tying it up and then feeding it regularly as well as cross breeding those with certain desirable characteristics, such as tasting good or being a good egg layer, would eventually domesticate it. The third *jiaguwen* version has even left out 爫; may be by then, the clawed feet were no longer quite so sharp and large that they need be represented in the character.

Below, in *jinwen*, *xiaozhuan*, *lishu*, the character looks this:

The *jinwen* version shows a cock in all its splendor, *xiangxing zi*, a pictograph. *xiaozhuan* restores the claws, but uses another component instead of 鳥 *niăo* to create an alternative way of writing the character for "chicken" 雞, also pronounced *jī* , which is the version used in *lishu*. However, today, on the whole, *fanti* uses 鷄 and *jianti* 鸡 both with 鸟/鳥 *niăo* as the radical.

The chicken or, more probably, the cock stands for the following characteristics: martial spirit as it fights, courage as it fights bravely, co-operation as it cackles when food appears so that others would know that dinner is being served, reliability as it crows at the appropriate moment of the day.

The dog is said definitely to have been domesticated during Neolithic times for hunting. In China, to date, the earliest remains, found at the excavation site at Hemudu, Zhejiang Province (浙江河姆渡), have been dated to 7000 years ago, whereas in Persia, it is said that the dog has been domesticated more than 11,000 years ago. As for the character for "dog," it has been in existence for more than 3000 years as it exists in *jiaguwen*, and also in more than one form. Below are the forms in *jiaguwen*, *jinwen*, *xiaozhuan*, *lishu*:

Note that the *jiaguwen* version presented here looks remarkably like the *jiaguwen* for "pig" presented in Part II. The difference lies in the tail. The pig's droops while the dog's curls up. (Remember that to see the *jiaguwen* form properly, you must turn the page anti-clockwise, until the graph is horizontal.) There are two different characters in Chinese for "dog": 犬 and 狗. The former today is pronounced *quǎn* and the latter *gǒu*; however, scholars hold that they were both pronounced *gǒu* originally. Today, 狗 *gǒu* is more commonly used although 犬 *quǎn* is still used. In any case, it is useful to be familiar with this term, as it enters into the character for "barking": 吠, pronounced *fèi* – the "mouth" radical together with the character for "dog" stands for the "barking of a dog," *huiyi zi*, a meaning compound.

The Chinese obviously valued the dog as a hunting companion, for rounding up sheep, guarding the house, raising alarm at the sight of possible trespassers. However, unlike European culture, Chinese culture does not perceive the dog only in flattering terms. For instance, 狗东/東西 *gǒudōngxī* means "son of a bitch" and 苟 *gǒu*, means "careless," "indifferent to right or wrong." In ancient times, the dog got a bad name because it could be a nuisance to ordinary folk with it barking at them, charging at them, etc. The animal was owned, in the main, by the rich and the powerful, it was not greatly loved as such, as it was regarded as an instrument used by its owner to hassle them. Following this line of thought, 狗仗人势/勢 *gǒu zhàng rén shì* means "bully with a powerful backer"; 狗眼看人低 *gǒu yǎn kàn rén dī* refers to an awful snob (literally, "they with their dog eyes look down on others"); 狗腿子 *gǒutuǐ·zi* equals "henchmen" (literally, "dog legs"); 走狗 *zǒugǒu* is "lackey."

The character for "raising an animal" 养/養 *yǎng* (although it is also used in the context of raising children) is interesting as it seems to have gone through different stages of evolution in parallel probably to the different stages in the ecological/economic development of society. The various (*jiaguwen*, *jinwen*, *xiaozhuan*, *lishu*) forms are shown below:

Both *jiaguwen* and *jinwen* (the first two above) show a hand holding a whip (the bottom right) against a sheep (the upper left) – this indicates a shepherd herding sheep on open pasture. By *xiaozhuan* and *lishu* (the third and fourth above), while the "sheep" radical is still there (top component), the whip has been replaced by 食 *shí* (bottom component), meaning "food" or "nourishment in general." This could indicate that conditions of pasturage had altered and that sheep might have been penned in and have to be fed at certain times of the year, such as the severe winter months, or even that there were fewer pastures for them to graze in.

Unlike the other animals mentioned, no one has ever succeeded in domesticating the elephant. Today, in some countries elephants may live in camps, but these animals are not domesticated in the proper sense of the term. This does not mean that humans have not succeeded in training some elephants to do work for them, important work such as felling trees, performed even today, and fighting in wars in the past. The last Shang emperor, 纣 *Zhòu* led his troops into battle on elephant-back.

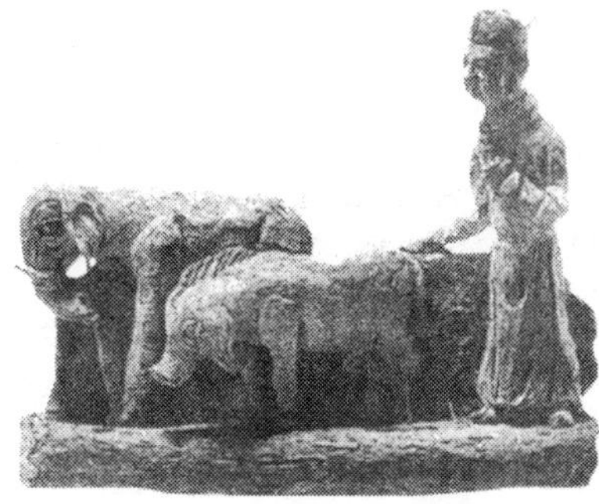

An excavation of a site in Shanxi Province (山西巍山马村 *Shānxī, Wēishān, Mǎcūn*) revealed a Jin Dynasty (金代, 1115 – 1234 CE) brick showing that in the Xia Dynasty, elephants were used for farming. The elephant played a key role in Shang and earlier Chinese history, one reason being that elephants were plentiful in those days.

Obviously the ancient Chinese had succeeded in this project of exploiting elephants so well that the idea and image of the elephant performing chores for them became the character 为/為 *wéi*, meaning "to help another to do something." Take a good look at the two *jiaguwen* forms of it below:

They clearly show a hand with a rope leading the elephant by the trunk. However, as shown below in *jinwen* (the first two) and *xiaozhuan* (third), although the hand remains more or less clear, the animal has become stylised. By *lishu* (fourth), the entire character is stylised and abstract, with none of the pictographic vividness of the original *jiaguwen*:

未

What makes us human?

Animals have mouths, just as humans do. Mouths are for eating. The character for "mouth" is 口 *kǒu*. In *jiaguwen*, *jinwen* and *xiaozhuan*, it looks like this:

Human mouths have to be fed; hence from the demographic as well as economic points of view, the term 人口 *rénkǒu* ("number of people in a household or a population") is highly significant. It is a two-syllable word, made out of two characters each with its own meaning to yield a new word with a different meaning from those of its components.

The mouth contains a very sensitive organ, namely, the tongue. With the tongue, one experiences tastes, such as sweet, sour, salty, bitter, pungent, the five tastes which Chinese medicine talks about. Let us take a look then at the character for "taste," pronounced *wèi* which in *xiaozhuan* and *lishu* are presented below:

咊 味

The *xiaozhuan* variant is interesting as the "mouth" radical has an extra horizontal stroke. (This feature will become clear a little later.) As taste is experienced in the mouth, it is very fitting that the radical should be the "mouth" radical. The second component supplies the sound for the word. However, in this instance, it appears to do more than that, as on its own, 未 (same tone) in Chinese cosmology, means something very distinctive. In that framework, spatial and temporal orientations are identified within a system of co-ordinates called "the ten heavenly stems and twelve earthly branches" (天干地支 *tiāngān dìzhī* or *gānzhī* for short). 未 *wèi* is the eighth position along the earthly branches co-ordinate. In terms of a day, it refers to that period of the afternoon between 1pm – 3pm; in terms of a year, it refers to high summer. In terms of spatial orientation, it points to the south-west; in terms of the five internal organs (五脏/五臟 *wǔzàng*) which Chinese medicine talks about, it is associated with the spleen whose "opening" is the mouth. This amounts to saying that taste is governed by the spleen. High summer is precisely the time when things grow, including the food that we eat. One could say then that the taste of a certain food in our mouth when we eat it after the harvest captures the goodness of the high summer. Furthermore, the geography of China is such that in the south-west of the country is Sichuan Province (四川), containing some of the most fertile soil, capable of growing the most diverse and delicious foods. All in all, you can see that the word 味 *wèi*, embodies these numerous, different but related aspects of Chinese cosmology, Chinese medicine, Chinese geography and Chinese gastronomy. It would be a gross over-simplification to label it as mere *xingsheng zi*, a semantic-phonetic compound, with the "mouth" radical alone carrying meaning while the second component simply donating the sound. It is obviously also *huiyi zi*, a meaning compound, with 未 *wèi* bringing to the word an extremely rich, multi-dimensional cultural heritage.

The word 甘 *gān* in the different scripts (*jiaguwen, xiaozhuan, lishu*) looks like this:

It is often translated as "sweet." This is a mistake. In Chinese, its basic meaning refers to a taste experience which is more generalised than sweet. It is about something which tastes delicious, so delicious that you want it to linger in the mouth, to savor it, not to swallow it straightaway. The Chinese call this 美味 *měiwèi* , literally meaning "fresh and lovely tasting" or "yummy." This desire to enjoy a particular food to the full in terms of its taste is reflected in the way the character is written. Note that inside the space standing for the mouth is a horizontal stroke; it represents the food which is being savored fondly by the tongue in the mouth. In Shang China (ca. 16th – 11th century BCE), the food considered to possess this quality most of all would have been lamb. So it was probable that the ancient Chinese had this in mind when they constructed the word. This meaning is found metaphorically in the expression 同甘共苦 *tóng gān gòng kǔ*, literally together "savoring the good things of life as well as suffering its slings and arrows," the equivalent of "for better for worse, for richer for poorer, in sickness and in health," which forms part of the wedding vows according to the Book of Common Prayer in a traditional Church of England or Episcopal ceremony.

Unlike the mouth of an animal, that of the human is for both eating and talking. To the ancient Chinese, this constitutes the radical difference between humans and animals. Humans speak, animals cannot. The character for "speak," pronounced *yán,* in its various written forms (*jiaguwen, jinwen, xiaozhuan, lishu*) looks like this:

The *jiaguwen* version shows very clearly that it is *xiangxing zi*, a pictograph – the top bit representing the tongue and the bottom bit the mouth. Without the tongue, one simply cannot speak; hence it emphasizes the important role of this organ for speech. 言 *yán* basically is a verb, meaning "to speak," but it can also be used as a noun to refer simply to any utterance, whether well-ordered or illogical. In this sense, speech is also considered to be "the voice of the heart." (This curious function of the heart will be discussed under a later theme: ***The heart has reasons which reason knows not of***.) Your thoughts "in the heart" are hidden, inaccessible to another until you care to divulge them through speech. The success of communication via speech is dependent on telling what "the heart really thinks," that is, the truth. If every one were to tell falsehoods instead of truths nearly all the time, communication would break down, and we, human beings, would no longer be able to use effectively that unique endowment which nature has given us, the ability to speak.

In modern Chinese today, in general, one uses 说/說 *shuō* instead of 言 *yán* as a verb. Modern Chinese uses different words to refer to different utterances in different contexts, as whatever is said is usually said under so many different circumstances that a single word may not be too helpful. For instance, if the words are uttered by someone in a position to give orders such as a sergeant-major in the army, then you call that kind of speech 号令 *hàolìng*; if it is the government proclaiming decrees, then it is 政令 *zhènglìng*; if it is at the end of a summit conference and the countries, forming the alliance, issue a declaration, then it is 盟约 *méngyuē*.

Another important distinguishing mark between animals and humans emphasized in ancient Chinese writing is the character for "hand," 手 *shǒu*. It looks like this in *jinwen, xiaozhuan, lishu*:

In the process of becoming bipeds, the original front two legs and feet of humans evolved as arms and hands. With our two hands, we could set about transforming nature around us much more efficiently than could other animals. We could forge tools with our hands, so that our hands wielding tools, such as an axe, could chop down a tree, which we would not be able to do with our bare hands (except for those martial arts practitioners who have achieved an extraordinary level of expertise). *Jiaguwen* and *jinwen* distinguish between the left from the right hand thus:

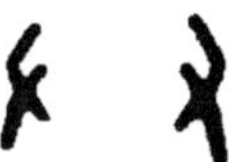

These hands appear to have only three fingers; as *xiangxing zi*, pictographs, the words seem misleadingly to portray a hand. However, to the ancient Chinese, three stands for several, more than just three, and so might be said to include five. These two words represent the hand from a side view whereas the front view in *jinwen* and *xiaozhuan* – – actually shows five fingers.

Next is a very significant word in Chinese history, that of "ruler," *jūn* . It looks like this (*jiaguwen, jinwen, xiaozhuan, lishu*):

The lower part is a mouth, which indicates that a ruler must issue commands, proclamations, and decrees. But a ruler was not then and is not now, simply some one who gives verbal orders. Commands must be backed up by brute force in the very old days, but as civilization progresses, commands are backed up by law, although law in turn is ultimately backed up by force. Hence one must look at the rest of the character. It consists of a hand, the right hand holding something which could be a large stick or probably an axe, originally fashioned from stone (in Neolithic times), but later (by Shang times) from metal. In the old days, kings as rulers must be able to wield a weapon, fight, lead men into battle to subdue rebellions, repel invaders or invade others. This character/word, too, is very graphic, but again it is not merely *xiangxing zi*, a pictograph but *huiyi zi*, a meaning-compound. In this context, the word is understood in the original sense of a ruler and not in the later sense of gentleman, someone imbued with Confucian virtues.

Note also that the *jinwen* and *xiaozhuan* versions show very clearly that it is the right hand which is used in wielding the weapon. The significance of this feature will be made obvious in the discussion of the theme which immediately follows.

末

The left wields the axe or brush; the right speaks with tongues

The words "left" and "right" are indeed innocuous. Yet behind their deconstruction lies perhaps an interesting surprise for us. The character for "left" pronounced *zuǒ*, and for right pronounced *yòu*, in *jinwen, xiaozhuan, lishu* look respectively like this:

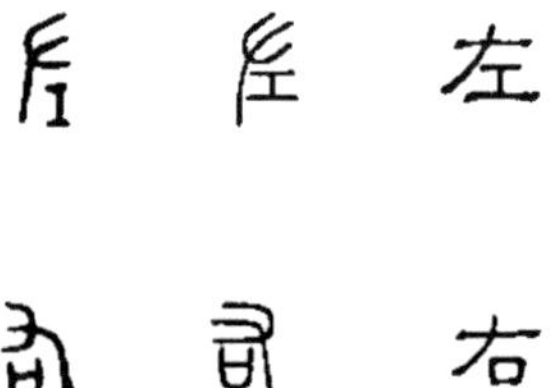

We must examine closely *jinwen* and *xiaozhuan* as in these two versions, the construction of the two characters shows up most clearly their peculiarities. Each consists of two components of which the first is the character for "hand." But as you can see, the hand that is used in the character for "left" is the left hand and that used for "right" is the right hand. The second component differs in the two characters – for "left," the radical is 工 *gōng* standing for "work," whereas for "right," the component is 口 *kǒu* ("mouth"). In *lishu* (and also *kaishu*), the word for "hand" used in either case, whether left or right, is simply the left hand form, 𠂇.

There are several interpretations on offer why in *jinwen* and *xiaozhuan* they are constructed in such a way. One view is that using hands alone is insufficient – we need sometimes tools to help us, sometimes words. Hence left is associated with work and implements, while right is associated with language or spoken words as represented by the word for "mouth." This seems fine as far as it goes, but there remains a puzzle: are the distinction and the distribution of labor between left and right, so to speak, arbitrary? This is to raise the question whether the ancient Chinese could just as easily have associated work and implements with right and mouth and language with left. According to this account, the answer would be: it just happened that they did not. And did they not do so even when they would have observed, just as we can today, that the majority of people in a population are right-handed rather than left-handed? Why make the majority of people who are right-handed wield tools with their left hand or make them use their left hand instead of their right to lift a heavy tree trunk? It seems a very perverse and silly thing to do, surely. A straightforward approach to left and right would simply do a swap in the construction of the two characters, unless the distribution of left-handedness and right-handedness amongst the ancient Chinese was distinctly out of line. But as we have no evidence that this was the case, one is left with the puzzle originally posed.

To solve this, we need to think of another hypothesis, a bold one, namely, that the ancient Chinese had noticed something which only very recently has become obvious to us via sophisticated scientific investigation. The left is linked to the right hemisphere of the brain which controls the grasp of spatial orientation, of shapes and patterns, while the right is linked to the left hemisphere of the brain which controls the grasp of language. Such an interpretation credits the ancient Chinese with having anticipated a twentieth century piece of neuroscience. This may sound over the top, but if we did not postulate the hypothesis, we would be smearing the ancient Chinese for being extremely silly, indeed. The smear in itself is neither here nor there. The important thing is that it cannot solve the puzzle which exists, why the ancient Chinese had constructed the two characters in precisely that way, which is clearly born out in both the *jinwen* and the *xiaozhuan* versions of writing them. We must give credit where credit is due, no matter how improbable it may seem at first sight.

In Chinese history and culture, right has not consistently been associated with the position of greater honor and left with lesser honor or even disgrace. On the contrary, there are numerous instances of evidence to the contrary. For instance, traditionally males walked on the left, females on the right. Laozi held that good things are associated with left and bad things with right. It is also said that the left eye spots wealth but the right disaster. Ancient custom demanded that the honored guest sit on the left in a carriage. However, different dynasties seemed to have arbitrarily selected one of the two to be the position of honor. The Warring States Period (475 – 221 BCE), the Qin (221 – 207 BCE) and the Han (206 BCE – 220 CE) Dynasties chose right over left. Later dynasties changed and chopped. People used to sit with their back to the north, facing south; as a result east is to their left and west to their right. The Chinese believed that west was where the immortals lived; hence right, according to this line of thinking, is superior to left. Traditionally, Chinese writing was right to left. A Chinese couplet is hung often on either side of a door; you read the right hand hanging before the left. So you could say right takes priority over left.

末

The heart has reasons which reason knows not of

A very important organ in the body is the heart. The word is pronounced *xīn*; its form in the various scripts (*jiaguwen, jinwen, xiaozhuan, lishu*) is shown below:

It is *xiangxing zi*, a pictograph; *jiaguwen* is obviously at its most pictographic, as the heart pictured by the character looks more or less like the organ itself. Indeed, another version of it in *jiaguwen* even shows some cavities inside the heart. Today, we are told by science that the heart has four cavities, two upper and two lower ventricles. Now, the question might occur to you as you read this: how would the ancient Chinese know what the heart looks like, especially the inside, that it is primarily hollow and has four cavities? The explanation is very simple. The Chinese like everybody else would have killed large or largish mammals for food. But animals are not humans. Why infer from their hearts that the human one would be similar, or indeed that humans even had a heart at all? Well, the real explanation lies in the grim fact that the ancient Chinese engaged in a lot of warfare. In Part II, we saw that according to one Shang (ca. 16th – 11th century BCE) divination, on one occasion, Shang troops had captured thirty thousand prisoners-of-war. Such a large number entailed that an awful lot of people, soldiers and probably the population at large, would have been killed. In those days, armies did not possess an air force with so-called precision bombing from above, to blast one's enemies to smithereens even without having the disagreeable experience of confronting them. They did not even have cannons, never mind, bombs dropped from a plane. It was face-to-face and hand-to-hand combat, wielding swords, axes and such like fearsome weapons. So there must have been an immense amount of disembowelling. The ancient Chinese made their observations and learned their anatomy on the battlefield, not in a pathology lab which the Europeans did from the seventeenth century onwards. European history is also full of killing and destruction on battlefields, but it appeared that the Europeans down the ages, unlike the ancient Chinese, did not do their science in real-life situations, but resorted to deliberate experiments conducted specifically under laboratory conditions, beginning four centuries ago.

Some scholars in the West might admit that the ancient Chinese could have got the anatomy of the heart right, given the explanation above. But what would they know about the function of that organ? As a matter of fact, they knew quite a lot; for instance, they knew that the heart pumped blood round the body. They might then be said to have scored a brownie point or two over William Harvey's discovery in 1616 CE of the circulation of blood, although one must quickly add that the ancient Chinese did not demonstrate blood circulation in quite the way that Harvey did in the seventeenth century. But then, they blotted their copy book because, perversely, in addition, they believed that the heart was the seat of thought. This belief discredits them in the eyes of modern science. Thought itself is written 思 *sī*. Numerous expressions exist attributing that characteristic to the organ, such as: 心里想 *xīn·li xiǎng* ("in my heart I was thinking"), or 心里盘算 *xīn·li pán·suan*, ("in my heart I was calculating"). Actually the first of the two expressions also exists in English ("in her heart of hearts, she did not believe it," or "in his heart, he thought otherwise"), and also in French. Blaise Pascal

(1623 – 1662 CE), the distinguished French seventeenth century mathematician and thinker famously said: "The heart has reasons which reason knows not of" (*Le coeur a ses raisons que la raison ne connaît pas*). So the ancient Chinese were not the only ones who credited the heart as the organ which thinks. One could argue that these are all metaphorical uses of language; indeed, they could not but be metaphors as they make no sense otherwise in the light of modern understanding about the function of the heart, which is that of a pump. If these people really believed that the heart is the seat of thought, then they were just plain wrong. Modern science tells us that the organ which thinks is the brain, not the heart. The English, the French as well as the Chinese were equally benighted regarding this point. But were they? Let us put another "spin" on the story.

We grant that the brain has to do with thought and memory which involve the synapses and their complicated neurological pathways. It is true that the brain is the place where the mechanism for storing thought and memory resides. In other words, it is a storage place, indeed a very intricate storage place with lots of nooks and crannies, *culs-de-sac*, tunnels, but all the same only a store-house. Does a storehouse possess the key to unlock itself? Who has the key? Of course, it is the owner of the storehouse. Which organ in the body is the analog of the owner and the key? The ancient Chinese said it was the heart.

They also believed that the heart was the seat of the emotions. Again this belief is by no means unique to the Chinese, ancient or modern. A lot of other peoples share it. In many languages, including English, French and Chinese, one says: "the heart aches," "the heart is broken," "the news fills one's heart with joy, anxiety, fear," etc. You could, of course, say that language lags behind science; even though science might have a long while ago discredited such beliefs, people are so attached to certain expressions that they refuse to give them up out of habit and nostalgia. Some words do embody out-moded theories about phenomena in the world – for instance, the word "influenza" used to refer to a theory about miasma (poisonous vapors arising out of swamps) as the cause of certain illnesses. Today we retain the word, but we have ditched the old theory in favor of the one which says that a virus is the cause of flu. However, on this particular belief about the intimate relation between the heart and the emotions, even modern science appears to have come up with data which are compatible with it. After all, people have been known to die instantaneously, their heart stopping to beat, upon receiving very bad news. The heart beat alters depending on whether the news is expected and neutral or whether it is unexpected and extreme. Indeed, on occasions, people have been known to die of joy on receiving unexpected good news. Add to this, the other belief which the ancient Chinese also held, that the heart governed thought and memory. These two beliefs together could explain why it is that people can suffer amnesia for traumatic events. Traumatic events are precisely those which affect the victims overwhelmingly, causing them immense sorrow and pain, and are of such an emotionally disturbing nature that the person could no longer contemplate them and their consequences. Freudians would say that these events have been banished to the unconscious, to be recalled only under psychoanalysis or perhaps hypnosis. In other words, to put it quite simply, what the heart does not want to know or could no longer bear to know, the brain would have no (conscious) memory of it.

A compelling example of the heart, controlling the brain, is women and child birth. To give birth is a painful as well as perilous process, even today. (Of all the branches of medicine, gynaecology attracts the highest premium in medical insurance against litigation – that is how dangerous childbirth is.) The pregnant mother, in English, is said "to go into labor," something which can last many hours, even days. Yet, in general, it is not known that women remember much of the pain during that prolonged period – the moment the bundle of joy emerges and they hold the new-born in their arms, all pain is banished, banished by joy. Today, of course, the experience of childbirth could vary – an epidural removes the pain.

Another telling example is forgetting what we have spent many years of sweaty labor and burning the midnight oil to learn. The moment the exams are over, at the school gate, we feel so liberated from those hateful lessons that we promptly forget everything we have learned. There is nothing wrong with the brain, as such a brain continues to work marvellously efficiently, carrying an enormous amount of data about a whole range of things, such as who exactly played in what football or cricket matches in the last fifty years, who scored what in which match, etc., etc., things which appear to delight a lot of people, usually male.

This analysis is borne out by deconstructing the character 忘 *wàng* ("to forget"). You can see the various forms (*jinwen, xiaozhuan, lishu*) for it below:

Like a majority of Chinese words, it has two characters as components, the radical giving the meaning and the second which in this case gives it sound as well as meaning. So one can say it is both *xingsheng zi*, a semantic-phonetic compound and *huiyi zi*, a meaning compound. The radical is the word for "heart" 心 *xīn*, and the second top component is 亡 *wáng* ("to lose, to perish, to die"). The character/word is really telling us this: what we remember or fail to remember is controlled by the heart. We forget what the heart chooses to forget, and we remember what the heart chooses to remember. It is the heart which instructs the brain what to forget, what to remember. This function of the heart is so important that the character for "heart," which functions as the radical, occurs here in its full, unabridged form, and not in its edited form, either 忄 (on the right-hand side of a character as in 忙 *máng*, meaning "busy") or ⺗ (at the bottom as in 恭 *gōng*, meaning "respectful"). This is the case with characters/words indicating strong emotions such as anger 怒 *nù*, anxiety 虑/慮 *lǜ*, fear or dread 忌 *jì*.

The heart, as mentioned earlier, is hollow inside but divided into four cavities. Of the five internal organs (五脏/臟 *wǔzàng*) dealt with in Chinese medicine, with exception of the heart, the other four – liver, spleen, lungs, kidney – all share the same radical, the character for "flesh," 肉 *ròu*, but when it functions as radical it takes the form 月 (this should, however, not be confused with the character for "moon"). This is said to be in recognition of the fact that the heart, unlike the other four, is hollow inside. In Chinese medicine, too, the heart is considered to be the ruling organ (not merely in the more limited sense discussed above as the organ telling the brain what to remember, what to forget) but in the more fundamental sense that it is the controller of the body. (Aristotle, too, held that the heart was the controlling organ.) For instance, when something is wrong with the body, the person feels pain. This is explained in Chinese medical terms by saying that the heart is functioning properly, being able to pick up such signals of distress, just as a properly functioning ruler in political terms would be able to pick up signals of dissatisfaction and unrest amongst certain sections of the population. A heart which is not doing its job properly would fail to detect the distress signals in the form of pain, just as the political ruler who neglects his official duties, leading a life of corrupt decadence, would fail to notice the rot spreading in the land.

Chinese medicine is greatly affected by Daoism, the classic of which is the *Daode Jing* 道德经/經. The author is said to be the philosopher Laozi (老子), a sage, equal in status to Confucius. He lived in the sixth century BCE, a senior contemporary of Confucius (although in the opinion of some scholars such a person never existed historically). It looks as if Laozi himself might have known, too, that the heart is a hollow organ and also, in his opinion, that it is the ruling organ in the body. These two beliefs could have led him to enunciate the famous fundamental tenet of his philosophy that everything which is comes from that which is not – the myriad things under Heaven come from what is full or solid, but what is full or solid comes from what is not full or solid but empty or hollow – something comes from nothing (天下万/萬物生于有, 有生于无/無 *tiānxià wànwù shēng yú yǒu, yǒu shēng yú wú*).

We cheekily suggest to the world's neuro-scientists to begin a new research program to investigate the link between the heart and the brain especially in the matter of the heart controlling emotions and memories.

末

In health, sickness, and wealth

Let us first look at a very basic word (in *xiaozhuan, lishu*) pronounced *huó*, meaning "alive":

As you can see it has the water radical 氵; its second component is the character for "tongue" – 舌 *shé* – shown in various forms (*jiaguwen, jinwen, xiaozhuan, lishu*) below:

The new character/word created by the combination of "water" and "tongue" has a new meaning altogether, and is, therefore *huiyi zi*, a meaning-compound. You may wonder why the ancient Chinese have chosen precisely those two components? What has the tongue to do with water, for a start? The "water" radical can be readily understood once you recall that the living human body is roughly 90 % water; that although one could survive many more days without solid food, one would be hard put to survive without water or liquid beyond three days. To put things quite bluntly: lack of water equals death. But the tongue? To grasp this, one must talk a little about Chinese medicine. Water in association with tongue means saliva in the mouth, as shown most vividly above in the *jiaguwen* and *jinwen* versions of 舌 *shé*, where one can see drops of saliva surrounding the tongue in the mouth. If one were alive, the body would be producing saliva all the time. Furthermore, Chinese medicine also holds that one can tell a lot about the state of health of the individual by looking at the nature of the saliva produced in the mouth. If the person is healthy, the saliva would flow freely as silken threads, looking clear like water, and smelling fresh. If the person is run-down or ill, then the saliva would no longer taste fresh, but bitter, and the mouth feel sticky and it might also be dry. In consultations, the physician would always look at the tongue; from its state, he would be able to diagnose what could be wrong with the patient.

Ancient Chinese distinguishes between being not so seriously and seriously ill, using two different characters/words. Let us first look at the character for "serious illness," pronounced *bìng*, which appears in *jiaguwen* (first line), *xiaozhuan*, *lishu* (second line) as:

Lishu shows clearly that the character has as radical the component 疒, and 丙 as its second component. However, *jiaguwen* (the first) and *xiaozhuan* (the second) seem to give a different picture as they do not use the radical 疒. So we need first to pay them close attention.

The story *jiaguwen* is trying to tell us is this: a person who is seriously ill is someone who would find it difficult to stand up, to move or run about, and would be greatly in need of leaning on something but preferably lying down. If you turn the page anti-clockwise till the word appears horizontal, you would see quite clearly that it consists of someone lying down on a bench or a simple bed made up of a plank over two supports. The *jiaguwen* version is *xiangxing zi*, a pictograph.

Xiaozhuan only shows the bench or the bed, but no longer the person lying on it. The simple bed found in both *jiaguwen* and *xiaozhuan* has evolved to 爿, the radical for the character "bed." Although *xiaozhuan* does not share with *lishu* the radical 疒, it does share with it the second component, 丙. 丙, standing as a character/word in its own right is pronounced *bǐng*. It gives the sound to the word for illness, although it does not also donate the tone. Are the two forms merely *xingsheng zi*, a semantic-phonetic compound? No, because 丙 does a lot more work than stand for the sound. What additional content and meaning are donated? First, we need to clarify what meaning it has in its own right as an independent word. We must again refer very briefly to Chinese cosmology in terms of the system of co-ordinates called "the ten heavenly stems and twelve earthly branches" (天干地支). 丙 *bǐng* is position number three in the heavenly stem category. This position is highly significant; together with its complement, the fourth position 丁 *dīng*, they signify the south. In terms of another dimension of Chinese cosmology, south relates to fire or heat (while east goes with wood, west with metal, north with water, and center with earth). In terms of the natural environment, Earth's heat comes from the Sun. The "epicenter" of Chinese civilization, in its origins, is in the middle and lower reaches of the Yellow River, and therefore has a northerly climate. The south side is, therefore, the sunny side and the northern side is the side where the cold blasts come from. Furthermore, for regions north of the Tropic of Cancer, the Summer Solstice marks the point when the sun reaches its zenith, after which, as we all know, the sunlight hours get increasingly shorter and its heat gets less intense. The human body and being, in terms of Chinese cosmology and Chinese medicine, have evolved and lives in accordance with the rhythms of the natural environment of which it is a part. However, although the sun's seasonal great outburst of heat and light is good for the natural environment as it enables things to grow and flourish, Chinese medicine, nevertheless, considers too much heat in the human body a very bad thing, as it upsets the balance between *yin* and *yang* (fire or heat being *yang*). Indeed according to it, the majority of illnesses is caused ultimately by an excess of *yang* over *yin*. Hence it is very fitting that 丙 *bǐng* be incorporated into the meaning of 病 *bìng*; it is there not merely as a phonetic marker, but also as the bearer of an exceedingly rich cultural load. This example as well as others we have already come across, should remind us that in certain cases to categorise a character simply as *xingsheng zi*, a semantic-phonetic compound, can be seriously misleading. It is also a *huiyi zi*, a meaning compound.

In ancient Chinese, what is the character/word for "not so serious illnesses"? It is pronounced *jí*; its forms in the various scripts are shown below with *jiaguwen* and *jinwen* on the first line and *xiaozhuan* and *lishu* on the second:

Jiaguwen and *jinwen* look very much alike; each shows a man being hit by what appears to be an arrow. *Xiaozhuan* shows what happens to a man wounded by an arrow – he would be ill, lying in bed, and so it uses the "bed" radical. *Lishu* uses 疒 as radical and its second component – the character for "arrow" (pronounced *shǐ*) – has become stylised, no longer looking like an arrow, but like this: 矢.

In *jiaguwen*, *jinwen*, and even *xiaozhuan*, the arrow looks very much like an arrow, and so, their versions of the arrow are *xiangxing zi*, pictographs. Their forms are shown below, with the first line showing three *jiaguwen* versions, the second four *jinwen* versions, and the third one *xiaozhuan* version:

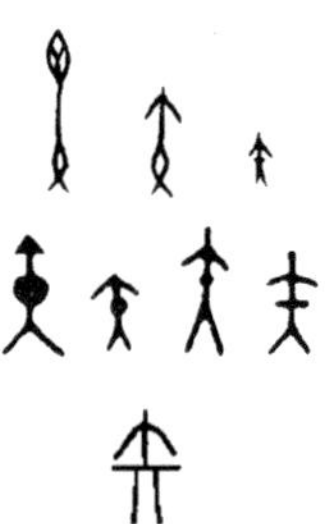

There are so many versions of this word in *jiaguwen* and even *jinwen*, probably because, as we have already mentioned more than once, China of the late Shang period (ca. 16th – 11th century BCE) was very violent, with plenty of killing. Lots of men presumably were wounded by arrows, a very important war weapon. In cases where the arrow did not immediately kill the victim, and the victim survived, then the chances of his recovery would be pretty good, given that those requisitioned to fight would, on the whole, be healthy men. At least the experience of the time would have borne this out. Those who suffered from 病 *bìng*, on the other hand, were not people who were healthy but for a wound; the cause of their illness was much more complex. So experience taught the ancient Chinese that their chances of recovery were probably on the whole much slimmer than those of the merely wounded. Hence, 病 *bìng* was used to talk about serious illness and 疾 *jí*, the less serious kind. Modern Chinese combines the two characters into one word, to become a two-syllable word 疾病 *jíbìng*, for "illness or disease."

When one falls ill, one needs a doctor and one needs medicine. What then is the character/word for "diagnosing and treating those who have fallen ill"? It is 医/醫 *yī* shown below in its various forms (*jiaguwen, jinwen, xiaozhuan, lishu*):

Let us first note that the *jianti* version (医) looks like the archaic *jiaguwen* form. This then raises the thorny issue how "traditional" is Traditional *fanti*, and how "untraditional" is the new-fangled *jianti*, a subject which, however, is beyond the remit of this book to pursue. The really embellished form did not appear till later, in *xiaozhuan* and *lishu*.

All the versions show a box. The box has three sides to it: 匚. What is the box doing here? It probably is the equivalent of the doctor's bag which the doctor carries on home visits. What is inside the box? There seem to be two views. One view holds that the box reveals an arrow; yet other scholars maintain that the box would probably have contained acupuncture needles (针/針 *zhēn*) and moxa sticks for moxibustion 灸 *jiǔ*. Moxa is a herb with therapeutic properties, the Chinese mugwort, called 艾 *ài* which, when matured, dried, pulverised and then rolled up like a cigar, burns at an intensely high temperature. The burning of *ai* is a kind of heat therapy. Often the two therapies are used together: 针/針灸, *acumoxa* in English. That is why it is said that the pointy thing you see inside the box is really not an arrow but an acupuncture needle. This view is plausible but only up to a point, as it assumes that, down the ages, scholars had mistaken the pointy thing inside the box to be an arrow when it was actually a needle. However, we can, perhaps, reconcile the two interpretations by admitting that the pointy thing may be an arrow or an acupuncture needle, which stands for why a doctor is needed as someone has fallen ill. The doctor carries with him a box containing some tools, such as acupuncture needles. There is no need to specify in the composition of the character what the tool kit is, as the only tools a Chinese doctor would ever use, as a matter of routine, in treating patients, down the millennia are acupuncture needles. We can take that as read. If this deconstruction is plausible, then acupuncture could be said to exist since Shang times (ca. 16th – 11th century BCE), constituting an important and distinctive part of Chinese medicine even then.

The significant additional component to the embellished form of the character is the character 酉 *yǒu,* a word we have come across in an earlier theme (***Surviving and Living***). The word in this context would refer to alcohol in general. Alcohol has always been an important ingredient of Chinese medicine which holds that it has numerous medicinal properties which include banishing damp and cold from the body, livening blood circulation, thereby speeding up the recovery process of wounds and other injuries, acting as an anaesthetic as well as an anti-septic in dressing wounds, improving the speed of absorption by the body when medicine is taken with it. Amongst the *jiaguwen* inscriptions recovered is one recording a prescription and a recipe for making a particular type of alcohol, used originally as altar wine, but also as a medicine to keep the brain and mind alert as well as to detoxify the body. The ancient Chinese believed that by infusing medicinal herbs in alcohol and then drinking the infusion increased therapeutic efficacy; this practice still holds today in Chinese medicine.

In 1973, at Mawangdui, Changsha, Henan Province three second century BCE Han tombs were excavated; amongst the silk manuscripts recovered, was one devoted to prescriptions. Of the fifty two prescriptions recorded, more than half mention the use of alcohol in their preparation. This is the earliest excavated book of prescriptions so far. Down the ages, texts on medicine talk about the role of alcohol in therapy. One Ming (1368 – 1644 CE) text lists nearly eighty different kinds of alcohol-related medicines; by Qing times (1644 – 1911 CE), such texts list nearly a thousand such prescriptions. So much was the reliance on alcohol in the preparation of medicines that there was a saying to the effect that no physician would be without alcohol, or that a practitioner who did not resort to alcohol could not be considered a proper physician (无/無酒不成医/醫 *wú jiǔ bù chéng yī*).

The link between alcohol and Chinese medicine is probably as old as the history of Chinese medicine itself. This is to say a history of at least 3000 years, dating back to the Shang Dynasty, as we have just seen. Prior to the emergence of Chinese medicine was another type of doctor, the shamanic doctor. The word for shamanic doctor differs from that for the physician who practiced rational, material-based medicine. The difference lies in the bottom half of the two respective characters. Instead of the word 酉 *yǒu*, the other has the word 巫 *wū*, meaning "shaman" or "wizard." This seems to say that instead of using medicinal herbs and alcohol in therapeutic treatment, the shamanic doctor used primarily spells and other supernatural means of curing.

We have done health and sickness, what about wealth in the larger sense of the term as well-being? Life would be perfect for most people if they have good health and a reasonable amount of material comfort. This conception is reflected in the character 裕 *yù* meaning "simple abundance," that is to say, "what adequately meets basic needs." A deconstruction in terms of its two components makes the meaning very clear – for radical, it is has 衤 which is the radical for "clothing," 衣 *yī*; its second component is 谷 *gǔ* meaning "grain" or "cereal." In other words, if one has clothes for protection against the weather, and if one has food to eat so that one never has to feel the pangs of hunger, then one is well-off, which is precisely what this Chinese expression says: 丰/豐衣足食 *fēng yī zú shí*.

However, it could be that things no more stood still for the ancient Chinese than they do for us today. The conception of being well-off might have changed with a parallel change in the economy. Sufficiency might no longer count as good enough. The next word that we look at seems to bear this out. The character is pronounced 富 *fù* ; below are its various forms (*jinwen, xiaozhuan, lishu*):

We have come across its radical before, 宀 ("roof or roof top"), standing for "house." Inside, the house is full of "goodies" which constitute wealth. Its second component 畐 *fú*, literally means "to fill." The *jinwen* version shows a wine jar, representing luxury and, therefore, wealth. Note that the second component donates both meaning and sound to the word.

末

What is it to be a man?

To understand what it is to be a man in traditional Chinese culture, one must bear in mind that Chinese society was primarily agriculture-based. This fact is reflected in the very construction of the character for "man," pronounced *nán*. Here are the different versions of the word (*jiaguwen, jinwen, xiaozhuan, lishu*):

The radical is 田 *tián* (“cultivated fields"). The second component, 力 *lì*, today, means "strength," "power," or "ability." The combination of the two yields a new word with a new meaning; as such it is *huiyi zi*, a meaning compound.

Cultivation – of cereals primarily – is an activity which requires strength as it involves plowing the soil. Plows in ancient times were not power-operated machines as we know them today. Manipulating a plow would require varying degrees of strength, depending on the type of plow involved and whether it was helped along by an ox. In very ancient times, the most primitive of plows, naturally, were initially used, to be replaced by more developed ones, as the implement evolved and improved. What would these look like? We have some idea by looking at the two forms of the character for "plow" in *jiaguwen*, as shown below:

The more primitive of the two is on the left which looks like a stick with a pointed or sharp end with which to poke into the soil and turn it over. It is called 力 *lì*. The second, called 耒 *lěi*, is more developed; attached to the handle is a two-pronged piece. You can see immediately that productivity would have increased a hundred-fold by using it, as the farmer would be able to turn over an area of soil twice as large in one single operation. Its invention has been attributed to two legendary figures, 炎帝 *Yándì* and 神农/農 *Shénnóng*, who gave the Chinese people agriculture. This kind of plow, since its invention, had remained in use throughout the long history of Chinese agriculture, in general until only a few decades ago; but probably even today, they remain in use in mountainous areas (usually also poor regions) where big machinery is neither appropriate nor financially affordable.

The character for 力 *lì* itself has evolved from that for the initial primitive plow in *jiaguwen* to something more stylised in *lishu*. The various forms (*jiaguwen, jinwen, xiaozhuan, lishu*) are shown below:

Corresponding to the evolution of the plow itself is the parallel evolution of the character for "man" in *jiaguwen*:

In the version on the left, the farmer uses the more primitive plow, 力 *lì*, while in that on the right, the farmer is pressing down hard with his foot on the horizontal wooden board to get the plow into the ground, then moving the implement forward, thereby creating a groove of upturned soil, ready for planting. This plow is the 耒 *lěi*.

These two versions of 男 in *jiaguwen* emphasize that the notion of being male is intimately bound up with physical strength plus skill in manipulating the plow. This in turn highlights the high value which an agriculture-based society placed on the expertise and strength possessed by men in the production of cereals for food. The high status of the male and his labor were thus guaranteed given that without staple food there could be no survival.

Surviving because there was food security was one thing; another kind of security was equally important, and that is, security from invasion and trespass upon one's territory, one's cultivation in particular. For this, one needed men to be soldiers. Not any male would do but, ideally, spirited men capable of courage in the face of danger in mortal combat with the invader. So we next need to look at another word which goes to define the high status of the male in ancient Chinese society. It is 勇 *yǒng*, appearing for the first time in *jinwen*. The various forms (*jinwen, xiaozhuan, lishu*) of the character are shown below:

It has two components: 力 *lì* is the radical and the other is 甬 *yǒng*, giving it the sound (as well as the tone). It stands for being brave; today, we speak of 勇气/氣 *yǒngqì*. In this context, 气 *qì* is spirit surging through the body while 力 *lì* refers to muscle power. 勇 or 勇气

combines both physical prowess with spirit, such that someone with 勇气 is one who dares to do what is required without flinching or hesitation. 勇 is *xingsheng z*i, a semantic-phonetic compound. However, although daring to do what others would run away from is a highly desirable quality, possessing it alone is not enough. Blind courage might lead to success but might also just as likely court disaster. There is an expression – 有勇无谋/無謀 *yǒu yǒng wú móu* – which says precisely that in any important undertaking, boldness and derring-do in the absence of clear strategy is flawed. The word as a noun stands for "soldiers," not so much the officers as the other ranks. In Plato's *Republic*, Plato (considered by many to be the greatest Western philosopher who ever lived) divided the soul into three parts of which the spirited element equalled the martial spirit, which he assigned to animals and soldiers. The early Chinese seemed to have thought the same.

There is a nice story recorded in a third century BCE text, which goes like this: a nobleman once set out in his carriage on a hunting trip. As he was about to climb into it, he saw an insect attacking the wheels of the vehicle, as if to stop the carriage moving forward. He did not know what it was and so asked his driver, who told him that it was a mantis. This insect, when confronting what it perceived to be its enemy, would always attack, irrespective whether its own strength was equal to the task. In other words, it was full of blind courage. The nobleman, upon hearing such an account, thought that the insect embodied the spirit of the soldier. He ordered his driver to spare its life, not to run the carriage over it. From this incident came the expression 勇虫/蟲 *yǒng chóng*, literally "spirited or courageous insect" but, figuratively, "someone who lacks judgment about his own strength or ability in boldly taking on an opponent."

A third character/word worth looking at is 夫 *fū*. Its various forms (*jiaguwen, jinwen, xiaozhuan, lishu*) are shown below:

Basically this character is constructed from 大 *dà* ("big") with an additional horizontal stroke across the top. It means "grown-up male or a young adult." In ancient China, childhood for males stopped at the age of 20. He would then be eligible to participate fully in labor of various kinds, hence the expressions 船夫 *chuánfū* (boatman), 漁夫 *yúfū* (fisherman), etc. When fully grown, a male is said to reach a 丈

zhàng. (However, it is not easy to determine what a *zhang* amounts to in modern measurement. According to one proposed conversion, it would be more than two meters; according to another, it would be 1.84 meters or about six feet. The latter calculation would still refer to the tall end of the scale, and might represent the desired rather than the average height.) 丈夫 *zhàngfū* is a term which literally means "a big man," but stands for "husband," as on reaching adulthood and full height, a male should and would marry.

The word 夫 *fū* does not only refer to male adults in general but is also used to refer to those who have exceptional talents, especially literary ones. According to this perspective, the word is deconstructed differently. The basic character is 人 *rén* ("human being" or "person"). The person represented by the character spreads his hands wide open, thus forming 大 *dà* ("big"). Nothing in the universe could be higher or more exalted than Heaven, 天, the character for which is formed by adding a horizontal stroke to 大. Yet 夫 is constructed in such a way as to burst through the limits laid down by 天, so to speak. This character/word then stands for the idea of truly exceptional talents.

末

What is it to be a woman?

We have seen the high status of the male in an agriculture-based society. But what of the female? Here things get more complicated. To unravel some of the main strands, we need to look at the character for "woman," 女 *nü* especially in its *jiaguwen* form:

In our earlier exploration (***Surviving and living***) of how the ancient Chinese lived, we drew your attention to the fact that the chair did not come into existence until probably towards the latter part of the Tang Dynasty (618 – 907 CE), and that people, from the emperor to the peasant, all sat on a mat on the ground or on a raised platform. As we have already explained what this kind of "sitting" amounts to, there is no need to go into details here. The *jiaguwen* form of the woman captures precisely that form of "sitting." Sitting implies being indoors, inside a house, the home. That is why some scholars say that the word gives the impression that the female is waiting for the males in the household to return from hunting or working in the fields. Some even say that she could be doing the cooking. This seems to imply that, by Shang times (ca. 16th – 11th century BCE), the role of the woman and her activities were generally confined to the home. Yet in late Shang history lived one powerful female, whose tomb was excavated in the 1970s – she was the consort called Fu Hao (Woman Hao) of the king, Wu Ding. She master-minded military campaigns and led incredibly large armies into battle. She did not sit at home waiting for the king to return from battles and wars. Her military prowess and victories earned her a special status and affection in the heart of the king. For this reason, she was handsomely honored in death, buried with a rich array of tomb goods. One could, of course, argue that she was an exception that proved the rule about the female role with its activities being mainly confined to the house. Another instance of a similarly exceptional female, much later in Chinese history, was the wife of the founder of the Ming Dynasty (1368 – 1644 CE) who, too, helped him to subdue his rivals on the battlefield. These two women led men into war without having to disguise themselves as men. Another well-known female warrior in the late Ming Dynasty (shortly before its collapse) is Qin Liangyu (秦良玉) from an aristocratic family, well versed in both the literary as well as the martial arts, who successfully fought a fearsome battle, fending off the Manchu assault on Peking, the seat of Ming imperial power. For this and other military exploits, she was given the title of Grand Protector of the Prince (太子太保). As such, she is regarded as one of the highest ranking female generals in Chinese history. She married a commander in her native Sichuan but when he died, she assumed his role and rank. She is the subject of novels and films. One other famous woman warrior is said to be Mulan (木兰/蘭), who would have existed during the Northern Wei Dynasty (386 – 534 BCE, part of Northern and Southern Dynasties), if she were, indeed, a historical figure. She had to disguise herself as a man. Her story is endearing to the Chinese people, not only because she was a brave and successful female warrior, but also because she was a filial daughter, as she volunteered to take the place of her own sick father, when he was summoned to perform military duties. After helping to gain victory against the enemy, she declined the offer of a post from the emperor, but hastened home to her family. When her ex comrades-in-arms visited her, they were shocked to discover that their brave colleague was a beautiful young woman. Whether she actually lived is immaterial; the figure, ever since she appeared in a musical ballad during the Northern Wei Dynasty, has captivated the imagination and the heart of the Chinese peoples down the centuries.

It bears repeating that late Shang times were not exactly peaceful and calm. There seemed to be many battles and vicious fighting. In such wars, the defeated males, captured as prisoners-of-war were later slaughtered, while the females were retained as slaves. This was a continuing source of slaves in Shang society. Now let us look at the *jiaguwen* form of the character for "slaves," 奴 *nú*:

One would be hard put to distinguish this character from that for "woman" shown earlier. It, too, is *xiangxing* zi, a pictograph. That is why some scholars have argued that the two characters are identical. The sitting woman is no more than the slave captured to serve the needs of the households of the winning tribe. (As already observed in *Surviving and Living*, Shang slaves should not be regarded simplistically as slaves in the Western sense of the term.) Furthermore, in ancient Chinese, the two words sounded alike.

The *jiaguwen* form is very different from that in *jinwen*, *xiaozhuan* and *lishu* as can be seen below:

All three forms above are constructed in a similar way, each with two components: the left is the radical and the right adds to the meaning. In other words, each is *huiyi zi*, a meaning compound. The *jinwen* and *xiaozhuan* forms show clearly the relationship between the two components which make up the character – the left hand component looks a bit like the *jiaguwen* form for woman except that she appears to stand rather than sit. The second component on the right uses the *jiaguwen* version of the character for "right hand." The woman plus the hand support the interpretation that a slave was a woman who was captured in war. This explains why the woman appears to be standing up, as the women were herded together and marched off to the homeland of the victors. In other words, one could say that the *jiaguwen* version of the character expresses their new status as slaves in households, whereas the *jinwen* and *xiaozhuan* encapture the very process of their being made slaves. (*Lishu* uses the stylised radical for "woman," 女 *nǚ*, and for the right hand component, the stylised character for "hand" which is: 又; it appears by and large to convey the same information though more skimpily.)

Jiaguwen did not have the actual character 妇/婦 *fù* which also means "woman." (Today, there is the expression 夫妇/婦 *fū fù*, meaning "husband and wife.") Instead, it made do with the character/word 帚 *zhǒu*, meaning "broom" – a slave, invariably a woman, as we know, had to keep the household clean, hence the broom would stand for the person wielding it. The "woman" radical was only added later – you could perhaps say that it was an attempt to humanise or add a little dignity to the person wielding the broom. The word came to represent the domestic role played by the woman in the household as well as the status she occupied, subordinating herself to the will of the male head of family, be this father, husband or son. The subservient role which women had to endure for millennia has been swept away since 1911 onwards, and especially after 1949. According to certain commentators, this momentous change is captured by the *jianti* form, 妇: its right hand component shows a mountain lying on its side ⺕ which signifies that the new Chinese woman belongs to the sex which can move mountains.

We next look at a more controversial issue. Some scholars in studying *jiaguwen* have arrived at the conclusion that Shang society seemed to have features which were consistent with matriarchy. One telling piece of evidence comes from the fact that some surnames bear the woman radical, such as **嬴, 姬, 姒, 姜**. Indeed, these ancient surnames exist today. Furthermore, there is the curious fact that the very character for "surname" – 姓 *xìng* – carries the woman radical, even today after several millennia of patriarchal history in China. Its second component is pronounced *shēng* ("to sprout" or "give birth"); its various forms (*jiaguwen, jinwen, xiaozhuan, lishu*) are as follows:

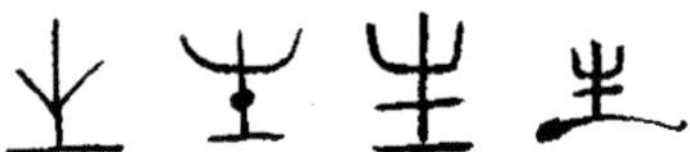

In *jiaguwen*, its pictographic nature is most obvious – the horizontal line at the bottom represents the soil or ground, the vertical line is the grass, or stem with leaves on either side. A woman, so to speak, grows a child inside her womb and eventually gives birth to it; she, too, sprouts forth something. When a child is born, it is obvious from whose womb the child comes, that of the birth mother. But who the father is, it is not obvious at all. Under such a set of circumstances, especially in a matriarchy, it would be natural to build into the character for "surname," the idea of the biological act of giving birth. As females alone could give birth, the radical for "surname" would naturally be that for "woman."

This, too, would explain why the character/word for "beginning," 始 *shǐ*, has the woman radical, with the second component donating the sound. This character first appeared in *jinwen*. You could say that the ancient Chinese held this "credo": in the beginning were women. For them, it was obvious that woman was the indispensable sex as it was the sex which gave birth.

If you were to take a cursory look at a standard Chinese dictionary, you would find a lot of characters/words with the woman radical, many of which refer to personality attributes. The attributes we looked at earlier about the male are all on the whole very flattering – the male is the sex with strength, power, ability, talents, etc. However those with the "woman" radical are mixed, yielding a more complicated picture – some of these are very flattering but others not. Let us first examine two very positive ones.

The first is 安 *ān* ("peaceful, tranquil, safe"). Here are the various forms (*jiaguwen, jinwen, xiaozhuan, lishu*):

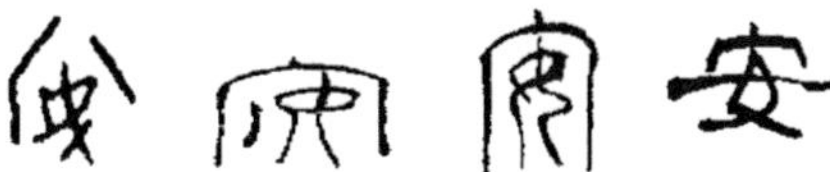

They all have for radical 宀, which represents the roof which in turn stands for a house. In the house is a woman. This is *huiyi zi*, a meaning-compound. A house as a physical building may stand for wealth or possession but it is without warmth, nurturing and family life. A house with a woman in it stands for a stable, peaceful existence, with nothing to disrupt the calm of family life and the economic activities of a household.

The word 好 *hǎo* (good, fine) equally gives women the most positive association possible. Its various forms (*jiaguwen, jinwen, xiaozhuan, lishu*) can be seen below:

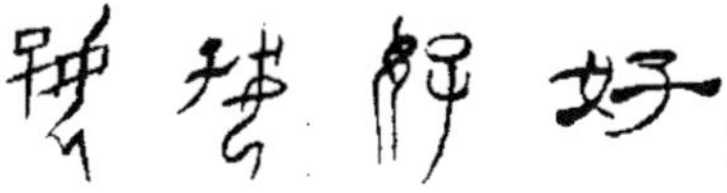

This is *huiyi zi*, a meaning-compound. Its original meaning refers to the physical appearance of a woman, that she is beautiful, and not to her moral qualities. Later, the word was extended to mean "good things or situations." Yet another later development turns it into a verb, "to like, to be fond of"; this use is accompanied by a change in the tone of the word from third to fourth tone as in 好吃 *hào chī*, "to love or be fond of food."

Its second component is the word 子 *zǐ*, and it looks like this in *jiaguwen, jinwen, xiaozhuan and lishu*:

The above *xiangxing zi* or pictographs could refer to a variety of things. It could represent a new-born babe with a tuft of hair on the head (as in *jiaguwen* shown above) or a child as in *jinwen* and *xiaozhuan*. According to this sense of 子 *zǐ*, the word 好 *hǎo* seems to imply that the idea that what is good is made up of two things: a woman/wife and children. Such a combination conjures up the idea of the close loving bond between mother and child, presenting that as paradigm of what is good. The Shang consort, Fu Hao was called "good woman" because she gave birth to many children, although we know that at least one of them was a disappointment to the king as she was a girl, according to the inscription recorded of the divination, mentioned in Part II.

However, the word 子 *zǐ* as it stands in ancient texts simply refers to children whether male or female – an unmarried daughter is 子. Another interpretation of 好 *hǎo* regards 子 *zǐ* as referring only to a man; hence the word 好 represents the man-and-woman relationship as part of the idea of what is good.

Other flattering attributes include 妙 *miào* ("wonderful, excellent, fine"); 嫺 *xián* ("refined," "skilled"); 妍 *yán* ("enchanting," "beautiful"). Now, for some negative attributes which include 妒 *dù* ("to envy"); 嫉 *jí* ("to hate"); 奻 *nuán* ("quarrelsome"). The last mentioned is self-evidently unflattering, as if to imply that when two or more women gather together, they are bound to quarrel. The second instance cited 嫉 *jí* looks a vicious one – it appears to say that women are singularly prone to something very bad, as bad as an illness, and that hatred is analogous to illness, as the second component 疾 which also gives the sound means "illness." But the worst example is this: 奸 /姦 *jiān* ("wicked," "evil," "treacherous" as well as "illicit sexual intercourse"). It is shown below in *jinwen* and *xiaozhuan*:

It seems to portray women as depraved – not only can women be adulterous but also treacherous. Today, the *jianti* version (奸) is keen to distance itself from such a politically incorrect view, and hence it is totally unrecognisable from the Traditional *fanti* version (姦).

In our opinion, there is an alternative interpretation which could plausibly explain why the word is traditionally written as such. Think for a moment back to something which we have been harping on, the frequency of warfare in ancient China, especially in the late Shang Dynasty. We have already referred to the fact that women belonging to the defeated tribe were captured and retained as slaves, while their men-folk were captured and slaughtered. From time immemorial, victorious soldiers, in whatever culture anywhere in the world, have been known to rape women whose men they have defeated. Worse, they gang rape them. Hence the word consisting of three women (three stands for a lot) is nothing more than a realistic attempt to re-enact such events in linguistic terms. The word, then, stands not for the depravity of women; instead, it stands for the depravity of men when war which, as we all know, is a totally brutalizing experience, has removed the veneer of civilization. Later, the word is also used to refer to illicit sexual intercourse in general.

A traitor is 汉奸 / 漢姦 *hànjiān*. In line with the preceding interpretation, we offer the following: we shall see in a later theme (***To be Chinese: is it to be a beautiful flower?***) how the Chinese have come to call themselves the Han people (汉/漢人 *Hànrén*). We have just mentioned that standing behind 姦 could be gang rape. When inter-tribal and inter-states feuding more or less calmed down with the unification of China, the Chinese people now unified had to continue to fight other tribes whom they called barbarians. From the Han point of view, to have Han women raped by victorious barbarians would be an appalling thing (and vice versa, one would assume). Hence, for a Han to betray fellow Hans, one's compatriots, would be comparable to a Han raping a woman or a group of Hans gang-raping their own women-folk. The country, China, is analogous to a Han woman; a traitor is therefore someone who performs a rape upon his own country. Of course, today, the word 汉奸/漢姦 *hànjiān* is the general word for "traitor" and has lost its original more specific significance of Hans betraying the Han people, of a Han performing a symbolic rape upon his own country.

末

Nothing's more boring than personal pronouns

Talking about personal pronouns is guaranteed to produce a big yawn. We hope, however, to convince you that the Chinese version is fascinating rather than boring.

Let us start with the first person pronoun 我 *wǒ* ("I"). Its various forms (*jiaguwen, jinwen, xiaozhuan, lishu*) are shown below:

This character had been hotly debated throughout the long history of Chinese scholarship, but no satisfying thesis emerged until the appearance of *jiaguwen* in the last century. Scholars are now convinced that the character, as shown clearly in the *jiaguwen* version, has something to do with weapons. The weapon in question appears below in *jiaguwen, jinwen, xiaozhuan and lishu*:

It is *gē* and, in its modern appearance written as 戈, it can be found already very clearly in *lishu*, as shown above. It is a long pole at the end of which is attached a dagger-axe. However, scholars point out that the weapon shown may be more elaborate than the simple *ge*. For instance, the bit on the left of the word for 我 *wǒ* in the *jiaguwen* version seems to picture something even more lethal than the *ge* on its own. It shows a blade with a jagged, toothed edge. In 1975, in an excavation of a Western Zhou (ca. 11th century – 770 BCE) tomb in Shaanxi (陕西) Province, archaeologists unearthed precisely such a blade (with no handle as it had presumably perished). In another excavation in 1978, this time in Henan Province, a weapon of the Spring and Autumn Period (770 – 476 BCE) was discovered, looking like this and called 戟 *jǐ*:

May be, the weapon might have been a combination of the *ge* and the *ji*.

However, other scholars have noticed something else about the evolution of the character. While the *jiaguwen* version supports the interpretation just given, other versions seem to suggest another possibility. Look at the *xiaozhuan* and *lishu* versions of 我 *wǒ*. They have two components but although the one on the right is the *ge*, the one on the left is not a weapon. It looks remarkably like the character 禾 *hé* ("cereal or grain"). The various forms (*jiaguwen, jinwen, xiaozhuan, lishu*) for the food crop are given below:

What then is the relationship between the two components? Cultivation of grain requires labor. John Locke (a famous English political philosopher, 1632 – 1704 CE) says if someone gathers firewood or cultivates a field, as he has put in work, he is morally entitled to the fruit of his labor. So in the same way, the ancient Chinese seemed to say that whatever grain you had grown, belonged to you. Unfortunately, others might covet your grain and would try to seize it from you, usually with weapons. In turn, you would have to protect your cultivation and possession with weapons, such as the *ge* or the *ji*. In other words, 我 *wǒ* is originally a legal/moral term indicating legitimate possession by the person who asserts through word and deed his entitlement. It says: I planted this crop, the crop belongs to me, I am its owner.

Property and possession in ancient China, during the Shang Dynasty (ca. 16th – 11th century BCE), was communal, in the name of the tribe, and not in the name of the individual. Given such a system of ownership, it is not surprising that the word 我 *wǒ* in *jiaguwen* was used in the plural, as "we," and not as "I." In speech the distinction between "I" and "we" might have already appeared but not in writing. In formal writing, that distinction did not appear till the Western Zhou Dynasty (ca. 11th century – 770 BCE). Today in modern Chinese, "I" is 我 *wǒ* and "we" is 我们/們 *wǒ·men* (in the context which excludes the hearer from the reference of "we.")

Another pronoun of interest is 自 *zì* ("oneself"). You will, no doubt, be surprised to hear that, originally, this character stands for "nose." Look at the various forms (*jiaguwen, jinwen, xiaozhuan, lishu*) as shown below:

It is *xiangxing zi*, a pictograph; in *jiaguwen*, you can see the shape of the nose clearly with bridge and two nostrils. In *xiaozhuan*, the bridge is less obvious, and the nostrils have become two horizontal lines. Why should the nose be used to stand for oneself? Scholars have two ways of looking at the matter. One is to say that it arose through the ancient custom on the part of the speaker to point to his own nose for emphasis whenever he is talking about himself. This practice, apparently, is still observed today in some rural parts of China. Another view says that 自 *zì* is *jiajie zi*, a phonetic-loan. When the word for "nose" was borrowed and taken over to mean "oneself," for a period of time, the same word was then used to mean both "nose" and "oneself." As this could be confusing, a new word for "nose" had to be devised. This new word is pronounced *bí* and it looks like this in *jinwen, xiaozhuan and lishu*:

鼻 鼻 鼻

The top component is the old character 自 but added to it at the bottom is another character 畀 with the sound *bì* – it is *xingsheng zi*, a semantic-phonetic compound.

The next pronoun we look at is equally surprising. It is written as 她 ("she"), and is modelled on 他 ("he"). The pronunciation proposed is also the same, *tā*. While 他 can be found as early as *jinwen*, 她 is a 'janie-come-lately', if we may coin a word, as it made an appearance only in the early 1920s. However, do not get us wrong; ancient Chinese did have other expressions for referring to the third person which given the context would make it clear whether it was he or she being talked about. What did not come into existence was only this word 她, so that 他 would no longer be gender neutral. We have already mentioned (Part II) that the first few decades of the twentieth century were a period of great intellectual angst and ferment in China, with intellectuals trying to come to terms with the might as well as learning from the west. It is obvious that European languages in general have genders, some with two such as French, others with three such as German. English has no genders yet it does distinguish between "he" and "she." The proposal then to invent the equivalent of "she" in Chinese seemed to come from the European model. The honor of creating it went to one eminent expert of the Chinese language called Liu Bannong (刘/劉半农/農) who played a big role in the reform movement of the time In 1920, he visited Britain and while there wrote back home to a journal to suggest it. It provoked a lot of opposition, in principle, from the more conservative quarters of Chinese scholarship, but in spite of that, the word took root.

For obvious reason, it has the "woman" radical. The controversial bit is the second component on the right hand side. Some scholars simply regard it as *xingsheng zi*, a semantic-phonetic compound, the sound being borrowed from 他, as we have seen. However, other scholars have a more interesting explanation, which would turn the word also into *huiyi zi*, a meaning-compound. They say that 也 in ancient Chinese refers to the female genitals and its parts, citing Xu Shen, the Han scholar of the Chinese language in support. In *xiaozhuan*, it appears like this:

If Xu Shen's account is right, then this could imply that the original word 他 would have been constructed with the female in mind. This would accord with the view that Shang society or even earlier in Neolithic times (ca. 8000 – 2000 BCE) had certain characteristics which showed the dominance of woman even if it might not have been a full-blown matriarchy.

During the same period when 她 was invented, another word was also proposed, this time to use in connection with animals. The word put forward was 牠 (with the "ox" radical on the right), with the same pronunciation as 他 and 她. Although it was used for some time, it seemed to have faded out, perhaps for the good reason that the very ancient word 它 also pronounced *tā* exists, and whose various forms (*jiaguwen, jinwen, xiaozhuan, lishu*) are shown below:

Jiaguwen, apart from the one shown above, has other versions of the character. It is *xiangxing zi*, a pictograph, depicting the head of a snake, moreover, that of a venomous snake. A single bite could be fatal. Such snakes, unfortunately, were a common occurrence in those days. A rare form of the character in *jiaguwen* seems to show not only the snake but also the character for "foot" – this version (not shown) embodied the fear which people had of stepping on it. Indeed, a common form of greeting, of inquiring about the well-being of friends and relatives in those times was to ask whether snakes had appeared, hoping that none had. The literal equivalent greeting of later times in China is: have you eaten rice? A snake is an animal, an animal is a kind of thing; as a result it was used as the pronoun for not only animals but more generally a thing (derived perhaps from "that dreaded thing, called a snake"). To avoid confusion, the character for "snake" was then written as 蛇 with the radical for "worm" or "insect"; it is pronounced *shé*.

The snake is a very ancient item in Chinese culture. While the above account showed how much venomous snakes were dreaded, the snake in general was a totem animal. Two figures in Chinese mythology 伏羲 *Fú Xī* and 女娲 *Nǚ Wā* were half human, half snake – their upper half was human, their lower was snake as one can see in the picture below.

This pair, said to be siblings as well as husband and wife, lived in the Kunlun Mountains (in Xinjiang Province). Fu Xi is credited with inventing fishing nets, breeding silk worms, domesticating animals, music, and most importantly the eight trigrams (八卦 *bāguà*), which are not only involved with Chinese writing but also with the *yinyang* principle. His alleged dates were 2952 – 2836 BCE. These dates predated the Xia Dynasty (ca. 21st – 16th century BCE); if Fu Xi were not entirely mythological then he would be someone who could have belonged to the Neolithic cultures, which would explain the account that he led the Chinese people out of the Stone Age. So far no archaeological evidence has been uncovered to cast light on the matter. Nu Wa is associated with marriage and fertility and is the goddess with overall charge of sexual intercourse. When she wanted to marry her brother, she was overcome with shyness. So brother led her to the mountain top and prayed to the heavens: should Heaven approve of the marriage, let clouds gather, should it disapprove, let the clouds scatter. The clouds duly gathered, shielding the pair while their act of copulation took place as husband and wife. Hence in Chinese literature, expressions about sexual intercourse are couched in terms of clouds.

Nü Wa is also credited with other very important achievements. First she created humans. There was beauty all around her, enchanting animals, plants, water, rocks, yet she felt lonely. So she decided to create humans to keep her company. She took some mud and crafted a human figure. The figure came to life; she made more and more. Soon she got bored and decided to go in for mass production instead. She dipped a rope into the mud and swung it round and round, splashing the mud about. Her hand-crafted ones became the nobility and the powerful, while the mass products became the common people. Next, the god of water fought the god of fire. The latter won but his "weapon of mass destruction" produced a disaster – half the sky collapsed. Nü Wa repaired the damage. She got hold of a turtle, killed it and used its four feet to hold up the restored sky. She burnt a lot of reeds, the ashes of which she used to mend cracks in dams to prevent floods.

*

Ancestors, kith and kin

Ancestor worship was an integral part of traditional Chinese culture. Of course, the ancestors worshipped were one's male forebears, and such worship went hand in hand with patriarchy. Yet, we have seen in the preceding discussion that some *jiaguwen* words seem to have features which might be compatible with some form of matriarchal ideas and arrangements. Admittedly, there were plenty of other features of Shang society which firmly showed that it was patriarchal in character, including the worship of male ancestors. May be those features of Shang (ca. 16th – 11th century BCE) society consistent with matriarchy are trace elements left behind by earlier times, such as the Neolithic Period (ca. 8000 – 2000 BCE)? Would archaeology be able to throw light on this matter? In the first three decades or so after the establishment of the PRC (1949), archaeologists were of the opinion that their excavations of certain Neolithic sites provided sufficient, if not absolutely conclusive evidence to say yes: Neolithic society was matriarchal. However, this consensus no longer holds – the evidence available is not judged sufficient to draw any reliable conclusion. Some single-sex communal graves have been uncovered which seem to point to matriarchy. On the whole, scholars now feel they cannot be sure whether a particular Neolithic culture (and there are several of them) was definitively matriarchal or patriarchal. The matter rests for now.

Even if future archaeological finds were to be supportive of the view that some Neolithic cultures were matriarchal, it remains true that patriarchy replaced it after the end of the Neolithic Period. The change-over occurred probably over 4000 years ago. We have mentioned earlier that the rise of agriculture, based on grains and cereals, requiring men as the main form of productive labor, raised the status of men, side-lining women. Perhaps that is not the whole story. Could it be that the whole story might include the growth in knowledge, in grasping the facts of reproductive life on the part of the ancient Chinese people? As long as the only significant thing they knew about reproduction was the biological phenomenon of birth itself, in which women alone were involved, and they remained hazy about the role played by the male, the more prominent role of women (even if not full-blown matriarchy) could not be so readily undermined even by the rise of agriculture. Patriarchy could only take firm root once people had a clearer picture of the part played by the male in the reproductive process. In other words, paternity grounds patriarchy which in turn led to male ancestor worship, with all three elements interlocking and reinforcing the rising dominant male role in agriculture. By late Shang times (the period for which we now have good evidence from *jiaguwen*), patriarchy appeared to have been established.

The word for "ancestor," 祖 *zǔ*, embodies this very tale of enlightenment or of darkness (depending on whether the standpoint is "male chauvinist pig" or feminist). The right hand component, 礻, is the radical for 示 *shì*, meaning "rites of worship of gods and ancestors." The right hand component is the really crucial bit as it shows in no uncertain terms the sex of the ancestors for whom the rites and rituals of sacrifice and worship were performed in order to obtain blessings from them on the part of their posterity. It stands for "phallus"; as written in *jiaguwen, jinwen, xiaozhuan*, the character looks like this:

The *jiaguwen* version is absolutely pictographic, and calls for no further comment. The character for "ancestor" is like this in *jiaguwen, jinwen, xiaozhuan*:

Note that in *jiaguwen*, the character "ancestor" is the same as that in *jiaguwen* for "phallus." The radical for "ritual worship" was added to the character for "phallus" in *jinwen* to make clear that ancestor worship had fully emerged as the worship of male forebears.

The phallic symbol made of stone or wood could be dated back to much earlier than late Shang times. Indeed, even today, there are a few ethnic minority groups in China who still conduct ceremonies centered on the phallus. For instance, a group of people – 傣 *dǎi* – in Xishuangbanna, Yunnan Province (云南西双/雙版納), still make bamboo phalluses, looking exactly like what is depicted in the *jiaguwen* version for penis, as part of their rituals. However, one could argue that honoring the phallus is not quite equivalent to ancestor worship; the latter notion only emerged with the emergence of the idea of blood relationship on the paternal side, which entitled a group of individuals thus related to worship at the same ancestral shrine, as descendants of the same male ancestor. Logically speaking, this emergence must have been accompanied by the side-lining of the previous view of reproduction, namely, that it had to do only with women, as they alone were involved with pregnancy and birth. The new view emphasized the crucial contribution of the male, so crucial that the female reproductive organs were now downgraded to an auxiliary role, that of being no more than a place to nurture the development of new life. The imagery implied seemed to be that the male seeds, or in today's language, the sperms were analogous to the seeds of a plant; these were cultivated in hospitable soil, the uterus, which nurtures the growth of the seed to develop into a new human being. This change also probably meant that the offspring no longer took the mother's surname but the father's.

In patriarchy, the father's role is supreme in the family. Under it, the destiny of women was dictated by the iron rule: obey father as a child, obey husband when married, obey son when widowed. So let us take a look at the character for "father," 父 *fù*, in *jiaguwen, jinwen, xiaozhuan, lishu*:

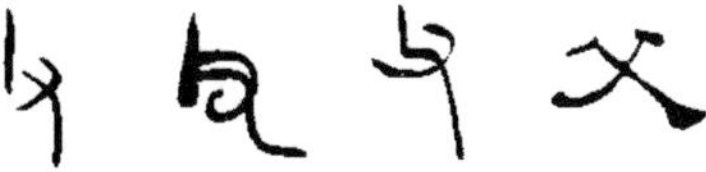

In *jiaguwen*, you see clearly a hand holding probably either a stone axe or a large stick, as represented by the vertical line. An axe is 斧 *fǔ* . It is shown in *jinwen* and *xiaozhuan* below:

In *xiaozhuan*, you can see very clearly the hand (on the right) carrying the axe. This character "axe" then donates the sound (but with the tone changing from third to fourth), but at the same time, it reinforces the meaning of the word for "father." Consequently the word "father" means two things. The father is the male who protected family and home from trespassers of one kind or another by (symbolically) wielding an axe. The father in the family is the disciplinarian. Traditionally, the Chinese family employs a division of labor between the two parents – the father does the big stick, metaphorically and also, literally, to instil and enforce core values as well as discipline, while the mother does the loving and the caressing. The Chinese expression 严/嚴父慈母 *yán fù cí mǔ* expresses precisely this sentiment and policy.

What does the character 母 *mǔ* ("mother") look like? Here are its forms in *jiaguwen, jinwen, xiaozhuan, lishu*:

It is *xiangxing zi*, a pictograph. The *jiaguwen* form shows this very clearly – the picture is of a woman with two breasts or nipples (represented by the two dots), emphasising her role as nurturer. The original *jiaguwen* representation of the sitting woman is preserved in *xiaozhuan* but lost in the other forms which have evolved. But all versions have either retained the two dots representing the breasts or nipples or replaced them with two horizontal lines as in the case of *lishu*.

In the traditional system of classification of relatives, any person who belongs to your mother's generation is called *mu*. You then distinguish between the different kinds of *mu* – your own mother is 母亲/親 *mǔ·qīn*, your father's sister is 姑母 *gūmǔ* (aunt on father's side), your mother's sister is 姨母 *yímǔ* (aunt on mother's side), etc. No-one today would address their mother directly as *mu·qin* (except perhaps in a playful manner to pull her leg) – she is either 妈/媽 *mā* or 娘 *niáng*.

亲/親 *qīn* refers to close bonds. The closest bond is between child and parents. That is why parents are called 父亲/親 *fù·qīn* and 母亲/親

mǔ·qīn. Relatives are also people with whom one has close bonds, though not as close as those with parents. Close bonds are created, too, via marriage. Matters relating to marriage are described as 成亲/親 *chéng qīn*, 定亲/親 *dìng qīn*, 亲/親事 *qīn·shi*. As part of the traditional wedding ceremony, the bride's relatives (of her generation) accompany her on her journey from her birth home to her new home – that is called 送亲/親 *sòng qīn* ("sending off a relative"). The groom's family forms a similar party to meet and receive the bridal party and that is 迎亲/親 *yíng qīn* ("welcoming new relatives"). Marriage creates a new set of close bonds between the two families.

Not only is the word 亲/親 *qīn* used in the family context, but also in a political context. One standard way of diffusing tension and creating closer relationships between two tribes or countries, was to create bonds through marriage alliances. (European history is also full of such arrangements.) For example, there is the famous story of the beautiful, much loved, Han consort during the Eastern Han Dynasty (25 CE – 220 CE) being married off to the chief of the Xiongnu tribe in order to decrease conflict and cement friendly relationships between the two groups – this was called 和亲/親 *héqīn*.

末

To be Chinese: is it to be a beautiful flower?

The Chinese refer to themselves in numerous ways. One of the earliest is 华/華夏 *Huáxià* as in the expression 华/華人 *huárén* ('the flower people' or 'the beautiful people'). We need first to say something briefly about the relation between the character for "flower" which is 花 *huā*, and that for "beautiful" which is 华/華 *huá* in modern Chinese. The former is a late arrival, appearing, as far as its meaning is concerned, only by the time of the Northern and Southern Dynasties (420 – 589 CE); the latter can be found in *jiaguwen*. For nearly two thousand years, the character for "flower" was not 花 *huā* but 华/華 *huá*. The meaning of 华/華 *huá* as "beautiful" is a derivative meaning, as flowers are naturally beautiful things. 花 *huā* is constructed from the "grass radical" 艹 plus 化 *huà* to give the sound, making its appearance in *lishu*, as *xingsheng zi*, a semantic-phonetic compound. The various evolutions in form (*jiaguwen, jinwen, xiaozhuan, lishu*) of 华/華 to 花 are presented below:

The older character 华/華 is not *xingsheng zi* but *xiangxing zi*, a pictograph, as it clearly is an attempt to show stem, leaves as well as buds. The flowers especially appreciated by the ancient Chinese included the peony. The Emperor Wu Zetian (625 – 705 CE) of the Tang Dynasty, it is said, loved this "king of the flowers" so much that in the end she ordered it to be eradicated from her imperial gardens! She wanted the delicious experience of seeing all the flowers in her gardens bloom at the same time, even though normally and naturally they would not do so. She gave orders that they must. Her gardeners managed to satisfy her tall order. She was absolutely delighted until she realized that the only flower which did not oblige was the peony, upon which she threw an imperial tantrum, ordered its elimination from her gardens and its destruction. Fortunately, her gardeners disobeyed her command and spirited the plant from her imperial Changan where she resided to the other imperial city, Luoyang, some seven hundred kilometers away. In Luoyang, the flower flourished even better and thus was preserved the beautiful peony. From this story, it is obvious who the true lovers of flowers were; they most certainly did not include the over-powerful, over-wheening Wu Zetian.

Why did the ancient Chinese pick on 华/華 to refer to themselves? The explanation is not so much that the Chinese regarded themselves as beautiful people, in the sense of being handsome to look at, but more that they had an aesthetic sensibility, the ability to appreciate beautiful things such as flowers. So one can perhaps say that integral to Chinese culture and civilization is a sense of the aesthetic, for which the people were and are indeed very proud, as is testified in their various artistic expressions across the millenia from calligraphy to painting, to embroidery, to ceramics, just to name a few.

Today, one of the meanings of the character 夏 *xià* is "summer." However, that has not always been so, as we shall see in a later theme (***To know astronomy and geography is to know all***) about the seasons in Chinese culture and history. Its original meaning is "big." The various forms in *jinwen*, *xiaozhuan*, and *lishu* are:

The character, at least in *xiaozhuan*, is clearly *xiangxing zi,* a pictograph, showing the figure of a man, looking strong and imposing, with the head held high, the body big and firm, and the feet apart, confidently planted on the ground. In *xiaozhuan*, the character is constructed in a very complex way with numerous components including the following: 页 (representing the head), 臼 (representing the body) and 夊 (representing the feet). By *lishu*, one can see that the character has been simplified, retaining only the head and the feet. This figure of the ancient Chinese male was taken to represent the people of 中原 *Zhōngyuán*, the Central Plains. As the figure is imposing, the character/word gives rise to the meaning of "big and imposing in size."

The word might also have derived force from the existence of the Xia Dynasty (ca. 21st – 16th century BCE) which preceded the Shang (ca. 16th – 11th century BCE). One of the China's cultural heroes, the Great Yu successfully engineered flood control. He was upheld throughout Chinese history as a model person with an impeccable sense of duty and determination in carrying out the task entrusted to him. Yu was so great that his greatness might have been transferred to the dynasty of which he was considered to be the founder. The Chinese people, after him, appeared to have incorporated this aspect of their appreciation of his heroic qualities into the construction of their identity.

Indeed, the two characters, 华/華夏 *Huáxià,* were also the name of the tribe which founded the Xia Dynasty. The name has been used by the Chinese to refer to themselves. China came to be known as *Zhongyuan* or *Zhongtu*. That is why the Chinese also refer to themselves as *Zhonghua*, 中华/華. The People's Republic of China is 中华人民共和国 *Zhōnghuá Rénmín Gònghé Guó*. The juxtaposition, *Zhonghua*, is clear indication that the image which the Chinese have of themselves and their history is a proud and positive one, that they consider their culture and civilization to be great and splendid – according to one scholar, Chinese civilization is great because it possesses the concepts of right and righteousness; it is splendid because it creates, possesses and appreciates beautiful things.

The Chinese also claim descent from two figures who could be regarded as legendary if not mythical, namely, 炎 and 黄; they call themselves their posterity: 炎黄子孙 *Yán-Huáng zǐsūn*. These two belonged to that cluster of personages referred to as Three Sovereigns and Five Emperors 三皇五帝 *Sān Huáng Wǔ Dì*. The Yan Emperor was credited with having discovered fire, his great gift to the Chinese people. He also taught them to burn off the vegetation before planting to ensure a good crop. He contributed, in other words, greatly to the development of agriculture. Naturally, he was called 炎 *yán* (scorching). Note that this is made up of two of the same character/word 火 *huǒ* ("fire"). Some scholars speculate that this figure could be traced to the people of the Neolithic Yangshao (仰韶) culture (ca. 5000 – 3000 BCE).

The Yellow Emperor, on the other hand, was said to have fought and vanquished the Yan Emperor, calling on the Dragon which controlled water to help him. Later, another legend came to be associated with him, that he was responsible for one of the classics in Chinese medicine, *The Yellow Emperor's Canon of Internal Medicine* 黄帝内经/經 *Huángdì Nèi Jīng*. He was also credited with having invented boats, not to mention chariots, bows and arrows, shoes, mirrors, divination as well as writing. We have earlier (***Surviving and Living***) mentioned that Chinese medicine was heavily influenced by Daoism and that the Yellow Emperor was associated with Daoism.

It is obvious that without the legendary achievements of Yan and Huang, there would have been no Chinese civilization and culture. It is not a wonder, then, that the Chinese people call themselves their descendants. However, you may wonder why two such legendary heroes are portrayed as having fought a fierce battle in which the Yellow Emperor defeated the Yan Emperor with the aid of the Dragon from the ocean depths. This myth can be seen as part of the *yinyang* principle, the fundamental basis of Chinese philosophy (especially Daoism) and cosmology. *Yin* must balance *yang*. Fire is *yang*, but *yang*, unchecked, as we have already seen (***In health, sickness, and wealth***), is not a good thing. It must then be controlled by water to restore balance. It follows from this principle that excess of *yin* is also a bad thing. Nothing, no matter how desirable or good, is good in itself, without limits; one can obviously have too much of a good thing. Good outcomes depend on the right proportion in the composition of things and their interactions, never on extremes in absolute terms. Everything depends on right balance between polarised characteristics.

The myth talks about the Dragon, the controller of water. Dragon is 龙/龍 *lóng*. The dragon is also the totem animal of the 华/華夏

Huáxià tribe. The various forms (*jiaguwen, jinwen, xiaozhuan, lishu*) of the character can be seen below:

龍

One can see straight away, it is *xiangxing zi*, a pictograph, trying to capture the essential attributes not so much of a real animal but a mythical one. The dragon is capable of causing clouds to form and hence rain to fall, of producing storms at sea and whipping up the waters of a river into frenzy. However, it also incarnates wisdom and intelligence manifesting in diverse situations and forms. It is both great and good. Legend has it that *Huangdi* was even the Dragon himself in human form. Hence, emperors in Chinese history had been keen to appropriate this mantle of succession for themselves and called their throne the Dragon Throne, their imperial garb Dragon robes. Not only did Chinese emperors lay claim to such august descent and lineage, the Chinese people, especially those of the diaspora, also thought of themselves as Dragon people.

The Chinese also have a less august expression to refer to themselves and, that is the Han people, 汉/漢人 *Hànrén or* 汉/漢族 *Hànzú* . Well, if history had dealt Qin Shihuangdi, the first Qin emperor, a different hand, for all we know, the Chinese might have called themselves the Qin people. As things turned out, the Han Dynasty (206 BCE – 220 CE) which succeeded the short-lived Qin Dynasty (221 – 207 BCE), stabilised the China which had just been unified, and this unification has more or less endured intact (with lots of ups and downs, naturally) till today. Hence the expression, the Han people, has appeared. The Confucianisation of Chinese culture also took place during the Han Dynasty which created a dominant philosophy and ideology with which China has become imbued for over two thousand years. The term owes its currency both to the establishment of the Han Dynasty as well as to the name of a river called Hanshui (汉/漢水) or Hanjiang today (汉/漢江), which rises in Shaanxi Province, flowing through that part of Zhongyuan from which hailed the founder of the Han Dynasty, Liu Bang (刘/ 劉邦). It eventually becomes a tributary of the Yangzi River.

Yet another source of the term came not so much from the Chinese themselves but from China's neighbors. During the Han Dynasty, the tribes invading China, particularly the 匈奴 *Xiōngnú*, began to call the Chinese soldiers 汉/漢子 *hàn·zi*, Han fellows, or even 好汉/漢 *hǎohàn*, admirable Han fellows. (The term has come to mean "hero.") Perhaps these were perceived by their enemies to be worthy opponents, not only well equipped but also having fighting spirit. Anyway, the term was taken over by the Chinese, perhaps because of such favorable connotations, to refer to themselves. The word Han when borrowed by the Hans in this sense was no longer used in regard only to soldiers as was the case with the *Xiongnu* people, but was extended in general to cover all males. Mao Zedong has "immortalized" the expression 好汉/漢 in the line of poetry: 不到长/長城非好汉/漢 *búdào chángchéng fēi hǎohàn*. Loosely translated, it means: No honorable men (heroes) are we unless we reach the Great Wall.

Some of you might wonder why the Chinese in the diaspora often call themselves "Tang people," 唐人, and why what in English is called "Chinatown," in Chinese is 唐人 街 *Tángrén jiē*, "Tang People Street." This is because the expansion of the Han people into the southern parts of China took place more systematically and on a larger scale during the Tang Dynasty (618 – 907 CE) rather the Han Dynasty. Secondly, the early migrations of Chinese into South-east Asia, and then, the much later migrations during the nineteenth century to Western countries (America, Australia, and elsewhere) came from the people of South China who tended to think of themselves as Tang rather than Han people.

末

A virtue uniquely Chinese

The outside world perceives a core set of values distinctive and peculiar to Chinese culture, and that is the set associated with Confucianism which is the philosophy and ideology built upon the key moral ideas taught by Confucius (551 – 479 BCE). These notions are systematically inter-related. Here is a very brief and simplistic account of that moral, social and political philosophy. At its heart is the notion of 仁 *rén*, which is best translated as "co-humanity" because the character has two components, one which is the radical (on the left) 亻, standing for humans and the other, on the right, for the number two (二). In other words, the notion involves one human being recognising and treating another as a fellow human being. At the center of Confucian political philosophy is the notion of 君子 *jūn·zi*; this notion is to be distinguished from the earlier one we have deconstructed (***What makes us human?***) in which the ruler was depicted merely as the person issuing orders backed up by force. The Confucian *jun·zi*, on the contrary, is a ruler who exerts moral force (德 *dé*), exercised according to the notion of 义/義 *yì*, doing what is morally, socially and aesthetically proper, what is fitting, right or righteous. In so doing, the Confucian ruler manifests the virtue of co-humanity, *ren*, within a hierarchical inter-dependent universe presided over by 天 *tian*, the Heavens. *Yi* may be further understood in terms of 忠 *zhōng*, and 恕 *shù*. The former stands for loyalty, in particular, loyalty to the ruler on the part of a minister. However, in Confucian thought, it means more than that, as it also includes the notion of any person realizing himself to the fullest in all inter-personal relationships whether these are with people below or above one's social standing. Loyalty, in this sense, is not meant to be blind, but only owed to those who deserve it – in the case of the ruler, one owes loyalty to him only if he acts in accordance with the precept of *yi* and as one who embodies in himself *ren*. *Shu* is "reciprocity," which may be understood as the Confucian version of the Golden Rule: what you do not want done to yourself, do not do to another. (*The Analects* say: 己所不欲，勿施/于人 *jǐ suǒ bù yù，wù shī yú rén*.) 礼/禮 *li* , often translated as "rites and rituals or ceremonial rules of behavior." However, such rules should not be understood merely to mean adhering to conventional forms of conduct as a morally empty gesture towards mere conformity to social norms. One is required to act in accordance with them as a means of demonstrating *ren* and yi, and in so doing, one would exercise *de* in a manner befitting the *jun·zi*, whether the *jun·zi* is the ruler or simply some one who aspires to serious moral conduct.

We would not like to give the impression that we challenge the above as distinctive and unique to Chinese culture in so far as it is a highly structured ensemble of moral ideas. However, we would like to draw attention to another virtue which could be said to be peculiar, and in that sense, unique to it: there seems nothing comparable in other cultures, as far as we know. One could argue that each of the various virtues forming the complicated inter-related system of Confucian moral thought can be found in other moral philosophies. For instance, the Golden Rule in one form or other can be found in the Bible, in Aristotle (384 – 322 BCE, one of the great proponents of classical Greek philosophy, living roughly two centuries after Confucius) as well as in Immanuel Kant (1724 – 1804 CE), a great philosopher of the German Enlightenment. So, too, the notions of loyalty, benevolence, the virtuous person (*de*), or that of conforming to clearly laid down rules of conduct appropriate to the status of the person (such as in the rules of medieval chivalry).

What, then, is that peculiar virtue? It is 忍 *rěn*. The character for it looks like this in *jinwen, xiaozhuan, lishu*:

As you can see very clearly in *xiaozhuan* and *lishu*, the radical is the "heart" radical (at the bottom), and the second component on the top is what gives it the sound, making it out to be *xingsheng zi*, a semantic-phonetic component. But as we shall soon see, it is more than simply that. We have already (***The heart has reasons which reason knows not of***) discussed the character for "heart," so let us take a closer look at the so-called sound component. It is itself formed basically out of another character/word, meaning "knife," but with the addition of one small stroke. The character/word for "knife," pronounced *dāo*, looks in its various forms (*jiaguwen, jinwen, xiaozhuan, lishu*) like this:

It is obviously *xiangxing zi*, a pictograph with *jiaguwen* and *jinwen* leading the way. As you can see, *jiaguwen* looks like a slightly curved knife with a handle to it. *Jinwen* goes even one better, displaying vividly its blade.

However, when an extra stroke is added to the character, it alters the meaning, from being general to something more specific, namely, "the sharp edge of the blade of a knife." It is pronounced 刃 *rèn*; its various forms (*jinwen, xiaozhuan, lishu*) are presented below:

The various components added up, then, turn 忍 *rěn* into *huiyi zi*, a meaning-compound, not merely *xingsheng zi*, a semantic-phonetic compound. What does the character/word mean? It means "to endure," "to put up with," "to tolerate."

Now, it would be a mistake to understand its meaning in a negative fashion, as if it implies some kind of stereotypic oriental fatalism – however bad a situation, do not protest, but accept it as fate and destiny. On the contrary, it is a word which carries great moral courage, as we shall explain in a minute. But to see that it does, you must first appreciate the very nature of the character: as one scholar has commented, it is the most dramatic and spectacular in the whole of Chinese vocabulary. It conjures up this picture: some one who may be your outright enemy, your scheming rival, your sadistic tormentor with a (literal or metaphorical) sharp knife in the hand, stabbing it right into your very heart. What do you do? Return the violence? Or rest your grounds to confront the aggressor through patient endurance? Now you may think the latter kind of reaction stupid – meet force with force is the natural reaction. To overcome the instinct to meet violence with violence requires control, an inner moral strength which gives one the physical courage to stay one's ground when it may be dangerous to hang on.

That is one possible interpretation of 忍 *rěn.* Another also requires moral courage, and that is, to steel oneself to do what is normally regarded as morally repugnant a thing to do, such as even to kill, under exceptional circumstances. That explains, for instance, the admiration for the resistance workers against the Third Reich in Europe and against the Japanese in China in the Second World War.

The notion has an underlying Daoist dimension to it as shown by the following story. In the Tang Dynasty (618 – 907 CE) there was a scholar-official who was noted for his equable temperament, his dedication to the notion of 忍 *rěn*, so much so that the emperor came to hear about it. The emperor asked the official the reason for his devotion. He replied: "Things which are strong and stiff, contrary to expectation, break easily and do not last unlike things which are flexible, which can bend. So that is why in my way of dealing with people and affairs, I follow 忍." The emperor appreciated this response so much that he showered him with gifts. To the Daoist way of thinking, fighting hard with hard might not be the best strategy; it might be more effective to meet the hard with the soft. This is what *The Daode Jing* (道德经/經) has to say about the notion of yielding:

Nothing in the world is as soft and yielding as water,
Yet nothing can better overcome the hard and strong,

For they can neither control nor do away with it.

The soft overcomes the hard,
The yielding overcomes the strong;
Every person knows this,
But no one can practice it.

天下莫柔弱于水，而攻堅強者莫之能勝，以其無以易之。
弱之勝強，柔之勝剛，天下莫不知，莫能行。

This virtue of 忍 *rěn*, hence, emphasizes that direct confrontation is not the best mode of handling inter-personal relations, that confrontation tends to make matters worse, not better, that yielding and enduring might be both more efficacious and morally superior in handling conflicts at all levels. When people are caught up in hassle from members of the family or colleagues at work, friends would counsel 忍 *rěn*. This explains why you may find the word hanging in some offices.

However, the notion of 忍 *rěn,* above all, implies self-discipline. Nothing worthwhile in life is achieved without enduring inconvenience, discomfort, suffering and sacrifice to a greater or lesser degree. One, who gives up, runs away at the first sign of difficulties or problems, would not achieve lasting success in whatever field of endeavor s/he has chosen. Enduring success is based on endurance. That is why scholars traditionally had written the character/word and pinned it up on the wall of their study.

末

Happiness is piggy-shaped

There are two things which any parent would want for their children. These are embodied in the expression 成家立业/業 *chéng jiā lì yè*, that is, "to marry or set up home as well as to establish a career." Home is where happiness is. It is said that an Englishman's home is his castle. To the Chinese, what then is happiness in the home? We have seen while exploring an earlier theme (***What is it to be a woman?***) that peace and tranquillity come from the presence of a woman in the house. Well, that is fine. But something more is needed to complete one's happiness; home is also where the pigs are. The character for "home" is 家 *jiā*. It is *huiyi zi*, a meaning-compound. The radical is by now the familiar 宀 for "roof"; the second component is 豕 *shǐ*, meaning "pig." We have already come across the pig in Part II.

The word *jia* implies that marriage alone, no matter how loving the relationship between the couple is insufficient on its own to form a sustainable basis for a home. Marital and family happiness must also have a solid economic base, and that is where piggies come in. The character, in its various forms (*jiaguwen, jinwen, xiaozhuan, lishu*), are presented below:

Both the *jiaguwen* and *jinwen* versions show the pictographic pig under the roof. As you can observe, *jinwen* is even more pictographic than *jiaguwen* as its pig is drawn in detail rather than in mere outline. (To see the animal properly in these two versions, you have got to turn the page anti-clockwise until the picture is horizontal.) In the two other versions, the character for "pig" has been replaced by a more stylised pictograph of the animal but also showing the pig somewhat annoyed, according to some scholars.

The pig's wild forebear is a forest-dwelling animal, but piggy is very adaptable and so made itself very suitable for domestication. Pigs not only could thrive in an environment very different from the original one, they are also unfussy about what they eat, even if the food is not their beloved acorns but scraps from the household. Furthermore, pigs have a fantastic breeding record. The more pigs one has, the richer one is. Hence, the more pigs, the better. For all these reasons, the selection of the pig as the symbol for home is entirely reasonable and perfectly understandable.

In the very early days, humans and pigs would literally live under the same roof – humans and animals co-habited. Indeed, even in rural France up to not so very long ago (probably well into the early decades of the twentieth century), in a household, the animals would live on the ground floor and their owners on the floor above. Not only could they keep an eye on their livestock, but you must also bear in mind that in the absence of central heating, it would make a lot of sense to live above the animals, as warm air rises and their breath would keep people on the floor above warm. Such an arrangement is eminently sensible. Later, as things developed, the pigs, in a Chinese household, were kept in sheds, next door, or in the yard.

The pig played an equally important role historically in the economic life of the European household. In England, in the old days, every cottage would try to keep its own pig. Every autumn, when the animal was slaughtered, it was a big event in village life. Some of you who may have read Flora Thompson's marvellous book of rural life in England towards the end of the nineteenth century, *Lark Rise to Candleford*, might recall her account of such an occasion. Beatrice Potter's books are, of course, full of the doings of pigs. Many civilizations should be very grateful to the pig – without it, forebears from those parts of the world, would probably not have survived and flourished. The pig guarantees a safe supply of animal protein in the diet. Traditional English recipes speak of a hundred and one different ways of cooking, preserving every part of the animal, just as the Chinese recipes do. Of course, pork is taboo meat for religions such as Judaism and Islam, but that is another story altogether.

Today, the character for "pig" is not 豕 *shǐ* but 豬 in *fanti* and 猪 in *jianti*; both are pronounced *zhū*. *Fanti* retains the older word for "pig," 豕, as the radical, whereas *jianti* uses the "dog" radical 犭, which shows that *jianti* has gone back to a form of writing the character "pig" which first appeared during the Tang Dynasty (618 – 907 CE).

A variation of the *jiaguwen* form of writing the character is shown below:

Some scholars hold this as evidence that in Shang times (ca. 16th – 11th century BCE), while the domestication of the pig might be going on apace, nevertheless, the source of pork still came from hunting the wild pig. This interpretation might not be entirely correct; the fact that people still hunted the wild animal is not necessarily evidence that the domestication of the pig had not been completed. After all, men liked to hunt and if there was a ready supply out there in the wild, they would hunt. In France, even today, people hunt the wild pig and make a big event of it. A recent excavation in Zhejiang Province of the Hemudu Neolithic culture (5000 – 2500 BCE), dated from seven thousand to four thousand five hundred years ago (浙江余姚河姆渡) revealed certain pottery animals, looking exactly like the domesticated pig – this constitutes evidence that roughly five thousand years ago, if not earlier, the domestication of the pig was already in place.

You have family, you have solid economic means of sustaining family life. You should be perfectly happy. Are you, though? Not if you are Chinese. The picture of happiness would only be complete if you were to live to a ripe old age. Hence, the significance of 寿/壽 *shòu*, meaning "longevity" in Chinese culture. It appears below in *jiaguwen, jinwen, xiaozhuan, lishu*:

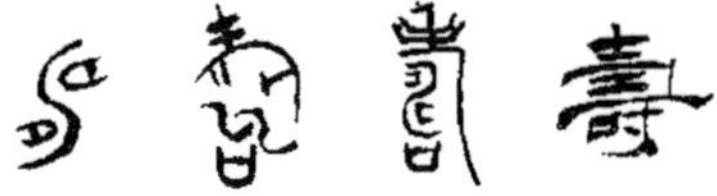

It could be understood as *xingsheng zi*, a semantic-phonetic compound as well as *huiyi zi*, a meaning component. According to the former, the top component stands for "old" while the bottom component gives the sound. Originally, the word meant "long lasting": *lishu* shows clearly that the bottom component refers to "time," 时; the middle component shows the word for "work" 工. The three components assembled – "old," "work," and "time" – imply a piece of handiwork so well made that it lasts a long time. Hence according to the latter understanding as *huiyi zi*, the top component standing for "old" and the bottom component standing for "time," would yield the derivative meaning of "longevity." Throughout its long history, it has numerous variations and forms, each to suit a different context of use.

In traditional Chinese culture, one does not celebrate children's birthdays; of course, many do today, but that is simply a concession to modern life. Only those who have lived several decades deserve to be congratulated on their birthdays, the more number of decades, the greater the celebration. In such a feast, one dish is compulsory and that is noodles, for the simple reason that they are long, and so are called "longevity noodles," 寿/壽面/麵 *shòumiàn.*

However, do be very careful with the use of *shou*, as it is an extremely slippery term. It is also used in certain contexts, not associated with the joys of living long and healthy lives but with death and funerals. For instance, a coffin is 寿/壽木 *shòumù*. In traditional Chinese culture, people chose their coffins, prepared for their funerals, and picked their burial spots well in advance of old age. Emperors and the aristocracy spent a lot of their time and energy planning their own burial. The site must have good *fengshui*, above all. Their elaborate tombs when excavated today provide us with a treasure trove of historical evidence. Unfortunately, over the millennia, tomb robbers had also been very active and some of the tombs have been ruined from the archaeological point of view. Anyway, should you ever be invited to a birthday celebration, whatever present you care to bring, please remember not to bring a present of a garment and call it 寿/壽衣 *shòuyī*. That would be a hideous *faux pas* to make, as *shouyi* means "burial suit."

While ordinary folks hope to live to a ripe old age, emperors and a few elites hoped to get hold of the elixir of life and to live forever. Innumerable stories are told of such a quest in Chinese literature. Indeed, some scholars even hold that Daoism cannot be explained except in terms of this quest with its preoccupation of alchemical experiments. One of China's greatest poets is 李白 *Lǐ Bái,* who lived in the Tang Dynasty. Li Bai had two main ambitions in life – one was to be the emperor's top minister or at least an important adviser on matters of state, and the other to find the elixir of life. Alas, he succeeded in neither. Regarding the first, the nearest he got to the seat of power was his appointment as poet resident to the emperor, a job he found so boring that he left just after a year or so. Upon his resignation, the emperor did give him a leaving present. The historical records as well as his own writings did not say exactly how much, but one could infer that it would be more than a trifle. As to his second aspiration, scholars think he probably died from it – in his alchemical concoctions, he used himself as the experimental subject. Over the years, imbibing such untried exotic drugs as well as the other more familiar and mundane one, that is, alcohol (for Li Bai loved his tipple), he fell victim to this lethal combination of poisons. However, he succeeded marvellously in another way, his poetry. He was like Mozart. With Mozart, heavenly music came from his quill; with Li Bai, exquisitely moving and elegant lines of poetry came, seemingly, effortlessly from his brush, whether sober or drunk, usually the latter. In his lifetime, wherever he went, people would queue to fête him and to enjoy his company. He is China's greatest romantic poet.

Now before we pour scorn on Li Bai and his fellow Daoists, let us not forget that alchemy (which is the forerunner of the science of chemistry) has a long and honorable history in many cultures. None other than Sir Isaac Newton (1642 – 1727), acknowledged as the greatest scientist of modern science, indulged in it, so much so that John Maynard Keynes (1883 – 1946, the famous Cambridge economist) wrote in his essay on Newton: "… Newton was not the first of the age of reason. He was the last of the magicians, the last of the Babylonians and Sumerians, the last great mind which looked out on the visible and intellectual world with the same eyes as those who began to build our intellectual inheritance rather less than 10,000 years ago." After Newton's death, it was found that his surviving manuscripts dealt more with alchemy than physics. So embarrassing was this discovery that the "offending" manuscripts were quickly suppressed and were so successfully suppressed that Newton's obsession with alchemy did not come to light until more than two centuries later, in 1936, when those papers were sold. Keynes was writing, if one may say so, entirely from the Eurocentric point of view; obviously, he did not know anything about Chinese culture and civilization. We can be sure that if he had, he would also have mentioned the Daoists and perhaps even Li Bai. Li Bai, in this respect, we could say, is in the company of the great, including Newton. Newton, like Li Bai, also conducted alchemical experiments.

We have already mentioned Qin Shihuangdi several times. He, of course, was greatly interested in longevity, if not immortality. He ordered his calligraphers to design the character for "longevity" especially for him, in the *xiaozhuan* style, which, if you recall (Part II), he had decreed to be the imperial script. Here it is, magnificently intricate and elaborate, incorporating birds as part of its design.

What else would make the Chinese happy? Music. The character is 乐/樂. In *jiaguwen, jinwen, xiaozhuan, lishu*, it looks like this:

Scholars agree that it seems to represent a musical instrument of some description, but disagree about which.

Some think it is a drum (like that on the left which is Shang bronze) and others that it is a kind of zither (like that on the right which is called *sè* – 瑟 – from the early Han Dynasty, 206 BCE – 24 CE). Those who hold the former view argue that the zither is said to have come into China later from the West, probably India but via the ancient Central Asian kingdoms, and therefore it could not have been the zither, unless one says that the zither arrived as early as the late Shang Dynasty, or that the instrument is, perhaps, even indigenous to China. Those, who argue that it is a plucking instrument, ask us to look at the character in the following way: the bottom bit is the character for 木 *mù*, representing the wooden stand upon which the instrument is placed; in *jiaguwen* form, the top part consists simply of two silken strands, standing for the strings. So how could the instrument be a drum? Furthermore, other versions of *jiaguwen* show that between the two strings is something which could be understood as the thing for plucking them.

For our purpose, it does not matter which interpretation is correct; what is significant is that the character 乐/樂 had two different sounds, *yue* (fourth tone) and *le* (fourth tone). Pronounced in the first way, it means "music," pronounced in the second way, it means "happiness." This is a rare instance of Xu Shen's sixth category in his system of classification – *zhuanzhu zi*, mutually interpretive. Which of these two meanings came first? Again, scholars disagree. But again, for us, this does not matter, as the important point to grasp is that for the Chinese, music makes them happy, that music is a very important part of their idea of happiness, so important that they use the same character to stand for two different words, to mean "music," on the one hand, and "happiness," on the other.

A particular musical instrument which the ancient Chinese loved is indeed the drum, so much so that the character for "joy," 喜 *xǐ* is represented by the drum. It appears below in *jiaguwen*, *jinwen, xiaozhuan, lishu*:

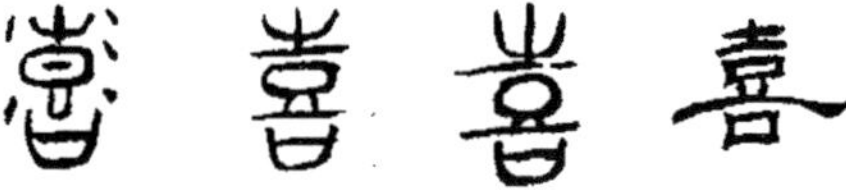

One can see, especially in the *jiaguwen* version, that the top bit is a drum and the bottom is a laughing mouth, implying that when one hears the drum, one is filled with joy. It is used then also to characterise any joyful event – for example, a wedding is a joyful matter, so it is 喜事 *xǐshì*. Another derived usage is 喜欢/歡 *xǐ·huan* ("to like, to love, be fond of").

The Chinese people love the word so much especially in the context of *xishi*, wedding, that they even put two instances of the word side by side, to create what is called "double happiness," *shuāngxǐ*. Here is the charming tale about its origin. A young scholar in the Song Dynasty (960 – 1279 CE) went up to the capital, where he stayed with his uncle (his mother's brother), to do his exams. One day, while out strolling, he saw hanging outside a large house a pair of lanterns. On one side was the first part of a couplet which he read with interest, and then exclaimed to himself: now it should not be too difficult to provide the second half to complete the couplet. He was overheard by a servant of the household, who promptly told him not to go away while he (the servant) went in to inform his master of the young man's comment. However, as the scholar was in a hurry, he did not bother to wait and went on his way. The next day, he duly presented himself for the exams which he did with ease. In an idle moment, he looked around him in the exams hall and saw a banner with some words on it. Suddenly, he was reminded of his experience outside the house with the lanterns, and thought to himself that what was on the banner would do nicely as the complement to the first half of that couplet. On his way back after the exams, he passed the house again. This time, the servant insisted that he go in to meet his master. He obliged.

The host told him why he had posted the lanterns plus the first half of a couplet on his front door. It transpired that he had a daughter, already twenty eight years old, yet unmarried. The worried father conceived of this scheme of attracting a talented scholar to become his son-in-law. Whoever provided the most elegant complement to the missing half of the couplet, he would give his daughter's hand in marriage. Hopeful suitors aplenty came and tried their luck, but their efforts were mediocre, and were sent away dejected. Upon hearing this tale, our young scholar took up the brush with great confidence and wrote down what he saw on the banner in the exams hall. His host was so delighted, he immediately arranged for the marriage to take place. Young man's uncle, when approached about the match, heartily approved of it, as the bride was known to be outstandingly beautiful and her family was well heeled. The day of the wedding arrived. During the celebrations, in came a delegation from the official quarters announcing the exams results, that the bridegroom had won top place. On hearing this news, the groom seized a brush and a sheet of red paper and wrote the character *xi*, then a second *xi*, side by side with the first. After all, he was the lucky recipient of two joys – he had won a bride as well as the first prize at the exams. His cup truly runneth over.

From then on, every wedding displays the *shuangxi*, "double-happiness" character, written in red color, or on red paper.

This practice has gone on for nearly a thousand years. But do you know that the character does not exist officially? You would not find it in any dictionary. We think it is about time that the Chinese Academy recognize it as a proper character in the Chinese vocabulary. Let us hope that the Academy would come round to the view that this is only just and fair. After all, the character has stood the test of time.

末

Sage and big ears

A sage is 圣/聖人 *shèngrén*. The character looks like this in *jiaguwen, jinwen, xiaozhuan, lishu*:

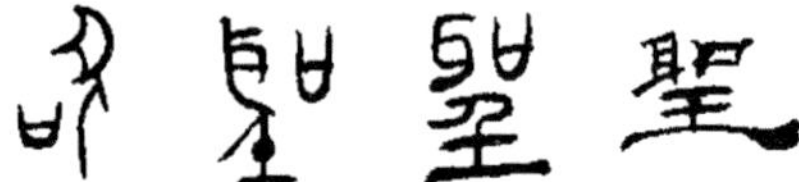

It is *huiyi zi*, a meaning-compound, with three components. In *jiaguwen* it is shown with "mouth" on the left, "person" on bottom right and "outsized ear" on top right. What do all these add up to? They add up to a person who has the capability of carefully listening to all that is said around him, understanding what he hears, and then expressing himself clearly and coherently with regard to what he has heard. In other words, the original sense of the character/word means "intelligence," which is 聪/聽 *cōng*. Note that this character, too, sports the "ear" radical 耳 ěr. Intelligence is also a two-syllable (*huiyi*) word, 聪/聰明 *cōng·míng* – the second character which we have already come across before (Part II), means "bright." In other words, intelligence amounts to being able to listen carefully to what is said, whilst seeing clearly what surrounds one. The two words "sage" and "intelligence" are intimately linked. There is an expression: 耳聪/聰目明 *ěr cōng mù míng* meaning literally and metaphorically "quick of hearing and being clear sighted." A person with such qualities could be said to be wise, if not exactly to qualify to be a proper sage.

The importance of large ears in a sage is borne out by tales about Laozi, who is acknowledged as one of the foremost sages by the Chinese people. His poor mother carried him in her pregnancy for 72 years! When he was born, he already had a crop of snow white hair. That is why people called him 老子, as *lao* means "old." His mother gave birth to him under a tree. As soon as he emerged, he pointed to the tree and told his mother to name him after the tree. That is why his surname is 李 *Lǐ*, as that was the name of the tree. Well, that accounted for his surname. What was his personal name? He was Big Ears. There are two explanations. Some people say that is because he had extraordinarily long ears. His mother, who was not capable of literary sophistication or refinement, took one look at him, then, simply said "Big Ears" would do. Others say, not exactly so, as he was also known as 聃 *dān*, meaning "ear without folds" or "flat ear," in other words. We have no means of adjudicating the merits of these two charming views. We like them both. Not only does Laozi have large, hanging ears, so do statues of the Buddha and his disciples – the next time you visit a Buddhist temple, look out for them. They are so long that they droop down to the shoulders. The Chinese say: 耳大有福 *ĕr dà yǒu fú*, "blessed are those with big ears." Do a spot of physiognomy the next time you say hello to a new-born babe – see if the little one has big or long ears. If the tell-tale sign is there, be sure to let the parents know!

However, over the centuries, the word has acquired additional meanings, both religious and political. 圣/聖人 *shèngrén* with religious overtones means "saint." Politically, the word 圣/聖 *shèng* had been appropriated by emperors to magnify themselves. For instance, their decrees were called 圣/聖旨 *shèngzhǐ* ("sacred orders"); their officials called them 圣/聖上 *shèngshàng* ("sacred or wise highness").

A sage – in the original sense of being wise and intelligent – for the Chinese cannot be divorced from 道 *dào*, usually translated as "way." A sage is someone who knows 道 *dào*, whether it be the *dao* of Confucianism or the *dao* of Daoism. Scholars of *jiaguwen*, to date, have not been able to find the character amongst the inscriptions so far excavated and studied. Its first appearance is in *jinwen*, inscribed on two Zhou bronze vessels. But all is not lost, as it turns out the *jinwen* version is based on putting together two separate characters which can be found in *jiaguwen* itself. The two characters in *jiaguwen* are: 行

xíng meaning, in early Chinese texts, "the way and distance traveled," which looks like this: , and 首 *shǒu* meaning "head," which looks like this: . *Jinwen* simply puts the "head" in between the passage in *jiaguwen*'s character for *xing*. Scholars have interpreted the head to represent a person. The implication of *dao* then amounts to this: someone walking along a path, and from this, one infers that *dao* is basically "path or way." A path is something clearly defined, with a beginning and an end. A person, who walks along it, walks with a destination and objective in mind. That is why another related meaning is 道理 *dào·lǐ*, meaning "reason" or "principle."

Other scholars have come up with an alternative interpretation which gives it a Daoist flavor, which would be a reasonable thing to do. Imagine the head moving through the path represented by the character . All this adds up to birth – the baby's head, which always appears first in a normal birth, coming through the birth canal. Hence, 道 *dào* can be understood in terms of giving birth, reproducing life, whether human or animal. This then would cast light on a famous passage in the Daoist Classic, the *Daode Jing* (道德经/經) in which Laozi said: *Dao* gave birth to one, one gave birth to two, two gave birth to three, three gave birth to the myriad things (道生一, 一生二, 二生三, 三生万/萬物). On this interpretation, *dao* embodied the whole of the cosmos including the relationship between Heaven, Earth and Humans.

末

Friends, comrades, fellow disciples

The characters nowadays, for "friend(s)" are 朋友 *péngyǒu* , to constitute a two-syllable word. Here is a simple allegorical tale about its origin. Once upon a time, there were two neighbors, one called Ah Peng, the other Ah You. They were as close as blood brothers; each cared for and helped the other. They gathered wood for a living. One day a storm blew down Ah Peng's shack. Ah You was deeply troubled. He invited the homeless Ah Peng to share his house, which fortunately had managed to withstand the weather better. He also used whatever he could spare from his meager earnings selling the wood he had gathered to help his neighbor to rebuild his house. Hence, *pengyou* stands for friends.

As a matter of fact, each of the two characters on its own historically has meant something different. 朋 refers to those who studied with the same master or teacher. The seventy two pupils of Confucius were all *peng*, as they all acknowledged Confucius to be their master, and Confucius had accepted them to be his students. *Peng*, in other words, means "fellow disciples."

The character 朋 in *jiaguwen, jinwen, xiaozhuan and lishu* looks this:

In *jiaguwen*, it appears as a necklace of jade pieces, according to some scholars. To other scholars, 朋 is a measure word – it refers to shells, used as a form of currency in ancient times. It represents two strings of shells, each string with five shells. In ancient China, jade and shells were equally precious. A string of jade pieces or two strings of shells suggest not only that the pieces are linked to one another but also that what are linked are precious. (We shall be exploring this further in ***Precious as the warp***.) Such is the relationship between the students of one master.

While 朋 refers to fellow disciples, 友 *yǒu* refers to comrades. The various forms for 友 *yǒu* in *jiaguwen*, *jinwen, xiaozhuan, lishu* are shown below:

In the first three, two right hands are involved. Ancient times were very violent and people always carried a weapon when they traveled. When travelers met and they meant no hostility, each would lay down their respective weapon, each putting their hands forward, with the hands always in the same direction. This would imply that they would have to stand side by side. This gesture would establish a friendly attitude. Naturally, the character/word, developed from this gesture, came to represent being friends with another. In turn, it lends plausibility to the interpretation that it means "people helping one another to achieve a common goal."

In *lishu*, although two hands are still involved, one hand has taken the form 𠂇which is the left hand, and the second hand the form 又, which is the right hand. It seems to stand for a gesture of greeting – when two people meet, they shake hands.

Here is a picture of such a greeting in a rubbing of a stone carving of the Han Dynasty (206 BCE – 220 CE), looking much like a modern handshake, but not quite, as the person seated on the left seems to be using his left hand and the person seated on the right his right hand, which is exactly what the *lishu* version says. (This is also the case with *kaishu*.)

However, the different forms, between them, yield the connotations of the word in terms of mutual help, warmth and goodwill.

A very popular story about friendship is found in an ancient text about two people, one called Xu Boya (徐伯牙), the other, (Zhong Ziqi) 钟/鐘子期. Xu Boya was a very accomplished musician especially playing the 古琴 *gǔqín* (a kind of zither). His friend Zhong Ziqi understood his playing perfectly and appreciated it in the only way a soul-mate could. Unfortunately, his friend died; he was heart-broken, and grieved so much that he could no longer bear to play the *guqin*. In his grief, he smashed his instrument to pieces, and never played music again. From then on the expression 知音 *zhī yīn*, literally meaning "understanding the notes of music and its sounds," has been used more generally to stand for a rare friend who truly understands oneself in all aspects, what may be called "soul-mate" in English.

The opposite of the phrase "to help each other in friendship" is "to compete, to strive, to contend against the other." The character/word for this is 争 *zhēng* or 争斗/爭鬥 *zhēngdòu*, a two-syllable word. Let us see what each of the characters looks like in the various scripts. 争/爭 *zhēng*, in *jiaguwen* looks like this: with two hands, like two horns, locked in combat, quite unlike the two hands put forward in friendship as shown earlier. 斗/鬥 *dòu* is shown in its various forms (*jiaguwen, xiaozhuan, lishu*) below:

One can see that as *xiangxing zi*, it is at its most pictographic in the *jiaguwen* version – it shows two people fighting each other. When people fight, they fight for some thing or for some objective; whoever wins the fight gets the prize, be it honor, women, money, property, power.

The sense of competing just discussed which invariably involves fighting, hurting the other in some way is not the only sense, as one can compete with others in a friendly spirit, or indeed, one can even compete against oneself. This sense is brought out by the character/word 比 *bǐ*, meaning "to compare." In this kind of competition, the competitors are simply judging or comparing their own qualities against those of others. Its various forms (*jiaguwen, jinwen, xiaozhuan, lishu*) look like this:

Jiaguwen, *jinwen* and *xiaozhuan* show clearly that two people are standing side by side both facing right. (If the two figures both face left, this is another word, 从/從 *cóng*, meaning "from," "pass by.") For instance, if two people were comparing their height, standing side by side would be an obvious thing to do. From this same image of two people standing side by side follows another meaning of 比 as in 比靠 *bǐ kào* or 比紧/緊 *bǐ jǐn*, "standing really close to another."

末

In the twilight snatch the bride

Every society has its own *rites de passage*, from childhood to adulthood, sometimes at puberty. Traditionally in China, for the aristocracy and the well-off, childhood officially ended for males at twenty (much later than puberty), and for females at fifteen (probably at puberty itself, as the onset of menstruation would not be as early as it is today). This meant that they could marry and start a family of their own. The ceremony of marking the passage to adulthood involved the hair, as Chinese tradition dictated that people did not cut their hair (there were no barbers) but let it grow long, as hair was regarded as a gift from one's parents at birth. Boys, then, till the age of twenty, wore their hair long, just like girls.

At fifteen, the girls then coiled up the hair, wearing it as a bun, decorated by elegant hairpins (called 笄 *jī*). Their ceremony was called 笄礼/禮 *jī lǐ*.

The boys, too, knotted up their hair but in a different style, covering the top knot with a piece of material which is the precursor of the hat. This is called 冠 *guàn* and the rite is the 冠礼/禮 *guàn lǐ*. (礼/禮 are rites and ceremonies.) Here, on your right is a picture which shows very clearly the *guan* on the head of an officer of Qin Shihuangdi's terra cotta army.

The *xiaozhuan* and *lishu* forms of *guan* are:

 冠

In *lishu*, one can see more clearly that the character has three components: 冖,元, 寸. The first refers to the fabric covering the knot, the second stands for a person, and the third for the position on the wrist represented by three fingers cross-wise, the position used when the Chinese physician takes the pulse. It is *huiyi zi*, a meaning compound.

At this ceremony, too, the young adult is given a second name which is 字 *zì*. The name given at birth is 名 *míng*. Actually it was only at three months old that a child was named; infant mortality was high and furthermore, it would be hubris to name a child the moment it was born. (Indeed, in order to avoid the evil eye, some families were fond of calling their sons Little Dog, Little Ox, something humble and insignificant so that no attention would be drawn to their existence, and they would be left to grow up in peace and health. As a matter of fact, common folk would only have 名 *míng*.) This explains why sometimes you may hear one Chinese asking another for his or her *mingzi*, not just the *ming*. Today, of course, nobody seriously would expect someone to have both, so the expression is only a manner of speaking. In the past, when a person was addressed by his 字 *zì*, this was a sign of respect.

Often the *zi* would be related by association or meaning to the *ming*. For instance, the philosopher the West refers to as Confucius is 孔丘 *kǒngqiū* – the surname is 孔, his *ming* is 丘. His *zi* is 仲尼 *Zhòngní*. *Qiu* literally, is "mound of earth or hill." A well-known story goes that so keen were his parents to have a son that they went up a mountain, called 尼丘 *níqiū* (by their ancestral village in Qufu, Shandong Province), to pray for one. As a result of that pilgrimage, Confucius was conceived and born. That his why his *ming* is *qiu* and his *zi* includes the word *ni* – he was named after the mountain.

An instance where the *ming* and *zi* are related by meaning rather than by association is that of Zhuge Liang, a distinguished figure in Chinese history, whom we have already mentioned in an earlier theme (***Surviving and Living***). His *zi* is *Kongming* (孔明) – *kong* is in honor of Confucius but 明 means "bright," which then matches in meaning with 亮 *liàng*, which also means "bright or well-lit," as in the expression 明亮 ("moonlight").

As 名 *míng* and 字 *zì* are related, the first leading to the second, this is considered metaphorically, as if 名 *míng* gives birth to 字 *zì*. This is analogous to 生子 *shēng zǐ*, that is, to a woman giving birth to a child. A child is 子 *zǐ*; that is why the name adopted at adulthood is 字 *zì* - both characters share the same sound but have different tones. However, we shall leave a more detailed discussion of this relationship to a later theme (***Words as zi: go forth and multiply***).

As we have mentioned above, the aristocratic male became an adult at twenty, the female at fifteen. The female at her 笄礼/禮 *jī lǐ* was also given a 字 *zì*, like her brother at his 冠礼/禮 *guàn lǐ*. While the adult male was ready to embark on a career (as well as to marry, if circumstances suited), the female would simply become eligible for marriage. In her case, the 字 acquired additional significance in view of the intimate relationship between 子 ("child") and 字 ("word") – her new status as the bearer of the latter meant that she had become a legitimate potential bearer of the former.

How did people in general marry in ancient China? To discover this, we need to deconstruct certain key characters, such as 娶 *qǔ* ("to get a wife"), 婚 *hūn* ("to marry" or "marriage").

娶 *qŭ* has two main parts to it: the bottom is the radical, the character for "female" 女 *nǚ* which we have already come across, and the top half is 取 *qŭ*, "to get or to obtain." So the whole character is *xingsheng zi*, a semantic-phonetic compound (as the top half donates the sound) as well as *huiyi zi*, a meaning compound, as the top half also contributes to the meaning of the word, namely, "to get hold of something."

The more interesting tale about marriage in archaic China would not emerge until we further deconstruct the character 取 *qŭ* itself, which turns out also to have two components. The one on the right (which is the radical) is the character 耳 *ĕr* ("ear"), which we have already come across in ***Sage and big ears***. The other component on the right stands for 手 *shŏu*, hand. A curious puzzle arises: what has the word "to get hold of," got to do with hand and ear? The hand bit is easily understood, as to get hold of something, one uses the hand to grasp the object in question. The ear? Why is it so desirable an object to get hold of? Indeed, someone appeared very keen to get hold of somebody else's ear. But who was that person, and whose ear was he so eager to grab and what did he do with it? To answer these questions, we need to look at the various forms of the character (*jiaguwen, jinwen, xiaozhuan, lishu*) as shown below:

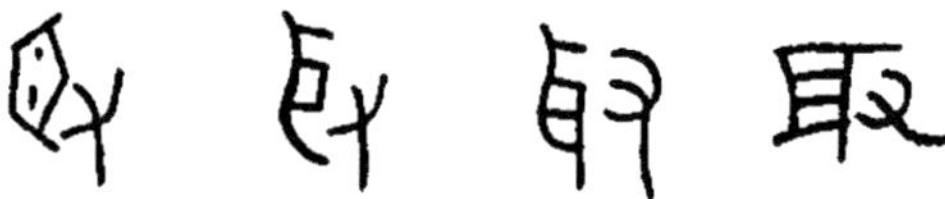

All the forms above show the right hand grabbing hold of the left ear. However, the sign for the hand itself has evolved from *jiaguwen* and *jinwen* to *xiaozhuan*, ending up with 又 in *lishu*, a form it has retained to this day in Standard *kaishu*. In any case, the hand was not simply pulling someone's ear as a bully might, but much worse, it was to cut it off. In Shang times (ca. 16th – 11th century BCE) and probably earlier, in a battle, the thing to do was to cut off the left ear of the enemy dead and of prisoners-of-war as proof and symbol of victory, and more importantly as evidence for rewards. It is equivalent, in other cultures, to decapitating the head, using the scalp as tally of the enemy killed. Cutting off the ear of your enemy is, indeed, an achievement; you have got what you set out to get. Hence, the meaning in general of the character/word is "to get" or "to obtain." The Zhou Dynasty (ca. 11th century – 221 BCE) which followed the

Shang found the practice of slicing off the ear morally repulsive and discouraged it; however, this is not to say that the custom did not continue, which it did, during the Warring States Period (475 – 221 BCE), until the short-lived Qin Dynasty (221 – 207 BCE). It had altered somewhat, however, by Qin times; in the Shang Dynasty and even during the Warring States Period, the victorious soldiers mutilated the corpses of the defeated dead, whereas the Qin soldiers confined themselves in the main to slicing off the ear of prisoners-of-war.

Having the left ear sliced off was the fate of the captured defeated male. Prisoners-of-war, however, were not meant to live long as it would be too costly and too dangerous to keep them alive; instead in Shang times (as mentioned in Part II), they were soon offered up as sacrifices to the gods and ancestors of the victors, or buried alive to accompany the nobility of the victorious dead as slave-servants to serve their needs in the next life. The fate of the defeated female, captured as prisoners-of-war was different – their lives were spared but they were made domestic slaves or servants. (An earlier theme – ***Surviving and living*** – has mentioned that the Zhou had discouraged slavery, although the practice would have persisted in spite of the new attitude.) Some were selected to be wives and concubines. Hence, originally, the word 取 *qǔ* was also used to mean "to get a wife." This was apt, as the women would have been the wives or daughters of the very men whose ears had been sliced off in defeat.

Xu Shen, in his dictionary, showed that in *xiaozhuan* the word, when used to mean "to get a wife," had acquired the radical 女 *nǚ* (meaning "woman"), so that it looks like this: 娶 *qǔ*. In this way, one has created a new character/word with a different, distinctive, specific meaning, differentiating it from the older one with the older meaning. It remained true that the old and the new shared some thing in common. What they had in common was this: just as the soldier in grabbing the ear of the enemy and slicing it off had got a trophy, snatching a woman for a wife from amongst the female prisoners-of-war was also getting a trophy. However, as the new character/word evolved in parallel with the evolution of society, an important difference between the older word 取 *qǔ* and the newer word 娶 *qǔ* lay in this: the former occurred in the context of war, of getting a wife as part of the war booty, whereas the latter occurred in the context, not of war, but of private rather than state war enterprise. To understand why this is so, we need to delve a little more into the history of archaic Chinese society.

Recall that in exploring an earlier theme (***Ancestors, kith and kin***), we talked briefly about the change from a Neolithic society where women played a more dominant role even if the society was not a matriarchal one during the Neolithic period (ca. 8000 – 2000 BCE), to one with an obviously patriarchal structure by Shang times. When the ancient Chinese grasped that men (via their sperm) played a key role in reproduction, and increasingly, too, as society became an agricultural one, relying on male labor, men became more and more powerful and women less and less so, until by feudal times (Zhou Dynasty onwards till 1911), women had come completely under the control of men, whether these be father, husband or son. Surnames were no longer those of mothers but of fathers only. Under patriarchy, women married out (as we saw in Part II) and became incorporated into the husbands' family structure. The word 娶 *qŭ* by *xiaozhuan* reflected this change in the social/social power structure of ancient Chinese society. We can say that the character was constructed from the male perspective – it represented the male getting hold of a female to be his wife from the outside and bringing her into his family. At the same time, male domination of females within the family in feudal times was such that the expressions commonly used to talk about the marriage of females were: 嫁女 *jià nǚ* ("to marry off a daughter") or 嫁妹 *jià mèi* ("to marry off a younger sister"). It was the duty of the patriarch in the family (the father or the older brother, should the father be dead) to marry off the young female members to whomever he judged to be suitable.

When the practice of snatching a female prisoner-of-war for a wife faded, males had to resort to private enterprise as a substitute for war booty. Hence he and his mates (clan members) mounted raiding parties to snatch a female whom he fancied in the neighborhood or district. Obviously, the best time to carry out such a raid would be twilight, not so dark that one could not see, and not so light that the party could be spotted miles away. In this context, the word 娶 *qŭ* retained its association with violence, though not the violence of war.

This "arrangement" of kidnap would also explain why the character for "marriage" was and is 婚 *hūn*. It is shown in its various (*jiaguwen, jinwen, xiaozhuan, lishu*) forms below:

Let us first look at the *xiaozhuan* and *lishu* versions (third and fourth from the left). Although they look different at a quick glance, actually they are identical in construction. They both have two components, the usual "woman" radical (*xiaozhuan*, unlike *lishu* uses the *jiaguwen* form of 女 *nǚ*, appearing thus: , which is what makes the entire character look so different from the *lishu* version) and 昏 *hūn*, meaning "twilight." This was precisely because marriage was something which was carried out during such a time of day. Again, at first, the character 昏 *hūn* stood for both "twilight" and "marriage"; by the time *xiaozhuan* emerged, it was felt better to create a new character to separate it from the old just to be clear, by adding the "woman" radical. 婚 *hūn*, therefore, is both *xingsheng zi*, a semantic-phonetic compound (昏 *hūn* gives the sound to the new word) as well as *huiyi zi*, a meaning compound (昏 *hūn* also contributes meaning).

If you now go back and look carefully at the *jiaguwen* version of the character for "marriage" above, you will find that it is the same as that for "twilight." It itself has two components: the bottom is "sun" (日 *rì*), the top is "low" (低 *dī*), as twilight or dusk is precisely the time of day when the sun is low on the horizon, so low that it is in danger of disappearing altogether, and also precisely that time of day when marriage was carried out.

The character/word 婚 *hūn*, embodying the notion of marriage-conducted-at-dusk reflected another change from the context in which the word 娶 *qǔ* was originally embedded. In the latter, we have just seen that there was violence, though not the violence of war. But it remained true that the raiding parties were bold affairs, conducted at any time of day, including broad daylight. Hence the violence would have been considerable and the exercise carried out with obvious hostility. By contrast, the raiding parties at dusk would be a much less violent affair, conducted more as stealth than open hostility. Over the millennia, the violence became less and less, so much so that today, the custom of mounting raiding parties at dusk, still practiced amongst some minority groups in China today, have nothing more than symbolic ceremonial significance – the bridal set is permitted to beat the raiding party with sticks, to claw the "raiders" etc., until they escape with the bride into the distance. 婚 *hūn* also evolved to mean not only "a man kidnapping a wife," but also in general to mean "marriage" as in 婚姻 *hūnyīn* or 结婚 *jié hūn* ("to get married"). However, today, there still remains a difference (to which we have already drawn attention in Part II) between the word 娶 *qǔ* and the word 嫁 *jià* – the former is only used in the case of a male marrying ("acquiring a wife") and the latter only in the case of a female marrying ("acquiring a husband" through being given away by or "snatched" from the bosom of her family).

末

How the butcher became the prime minister!

We have already talked briefly about ancestor worship and sacrifices to ancestors and gods in general (***Ancestors, kith and kin***), but now we briefly look at a character which is at the very center of the notion of sacrifice itself. This is 宰 *zǎi*, "to butcher" or "to slaughter." In its various forms (*jiaguwen, jinwen, xiaozhuan, lishu*) it looks like this:

The character has two components: the "roof" sign 宀 and under it, that for "a particular type of knife." It is *huiyi zi*, a meaning-compound. In a sacrifice, naturally, only the best that Earth could produce would be used. This included wine and meat. The former, we have already mentioned earlier (***Surviving and Living***); we must look now at the latter. Meat for sacrifice would include beef, pork and lamb. We know that the ancient Chinese loved the taste of lamb; the sheep obviously played a very important role in their economy, so that the more sheep one possessed, the greater was one's wealth.

Now, offerings of meat meant that animals must be slaughtered. The word which referred to sacrificial meats was 牺/犧牲 *xīshēng*, with the "ox" radical 牛. (This word today is used to mean simply "sacrifice.") If animals have to be slaughtered, and the meat then prepared, you need a butcher as well as a cook. As all these were carried out in aid of making sacrificial offerings, within a set of carefully ordained rules and rites, the person in charge would indeed be shouldering a great responsibility. The job was an immensely important one, as the success of the offerings depended upon its competent and correct discharge, which in turn would guarantee the stability and destiny of the kingdom itself. In Shang (ca. 16th – 11th century BCE) and Zhou (11th century – 221 BCE) times, sacrificial offerings were on a massive scale. According to one of the oracle-bone inscriptions, it was recorded that on a particular occasion, three hundred cattle were slaughtered. It stood to reason that such activities took place in something specially constructed, an abattoir – hence the character has "roof" for radical. The whole complicated procedure, from the selection of the beasts, to their actual proper slaughtering, the precise way of disjointing the carcass, the careful preparation of the meat for the sacrifice itself, etc. would come under the management of the royal kitchen. The official in charge of this whole domain of activity, as you can imagine, would enjoy extremely high standing and status. In the word's evolution, it is no surprise, then, that *zai* soon left the abattoir and the kitchen behind to form part of a new two-syllable word 宰相 *zǎixiàng*, with a new meaning, that is, "prime minister" or "chancellor," the highest office in the state.

The sheep – 羊 *yáng* – is seen as an animal fit for sacrifice in ancient Chinese culture but its related species, the goat, is similarly regarded in other civilizations. The Bible tells us that God told Abraham to sacrifice a kid instead of his son, Isaac. At the Greater Eid, a celebration which marks the end of the pilgrimage ceremonies during the month of *Dhul Hijjah*, Muslims slaughter a goat. Apart from being a sacrificial animal, the sheep enjoyed a high status amongst the ancient Chinese for several other reasons. It is likely that it was the totem animal of one of the tribes; some surnames still embody the character for it. The animal was regarded as possessing certain virtues, such as showing respect and gratitude to those to whom they are owed. The lamb, in sucking milk from its mother is said to do so kneeling down by her side. To the Chinese, this shows that the animal understands the over-arching moral notion of 礼/禮 *li*. Its behavior stands for filial piety.

There is also a tale which attributes a Solomon-like quality to an animal which looked remarkably like the sheep except that it had only one horn. This story is in a philosophical text entitled 墨子 *Mòzǐ*, said to be written by a near-contemporary (470 – 390 BCE) of Confucius. Once, two officials squabbled over something and took the matter to court. Even after three years of litigation, the court still could not decide which of the two parties had a case. The king then intervened, ordered the litigants to appear at a shrine where resided this wise animal, and each to put his own case before it. Its verdict would be final. The animal, after hearing out the two litigants, proceeded to leap upon one of them butting him, causing him to fall and break a leg. Every one then knew who the guilty party was.

Let us look at the *fanti* version of the character for "justice" or "fairness." It is written 義 *yì* (in *jianti*, it is 义) – the top component is 羊 *yáng* and the bottom component is 我 *wǒ* ("I"). Recall how we deconstructed this pronoun earlier (***Nothing's more boring than personal pronouns***); looking at the word *yi* in the light of that deconstruction suggests that the notion of fairness is about sorting out what is truly ours from what was truly thine. This seems to us to be a reasonable interpretation to advance. We can see that the ancient Chinese held that the sheep is the embodiment of justice and fairness.

This Solomon-like aspect of *yang* is also borne out by deconstructing the character 善 *shàn* ("morally good or virtuous"). Originally it was not written as just shown, but with *yang* as top component and under it is a character looking like this 誩. This character is itself made up of two identical 言 *yán*, which means, you might recall, "to speak" – the character 誩 implies two people talking but not necessarily agreeing. Hence *yang*, the sheep has to preside over the dispute to determine who is speaking truthfully and who falsely. Any one who possesses this ability to sift truth from falsehood, to distinguish the honest from the dishonest is indeed a morally good and virtuous person. You can see below its various forms (the first two on the left are *jinwen*, the next is *xiaozhuan*, the last is *lishu*):

Furthermore, the sheep is considered as an auspicious animal, so much so that the word 羊 *yáng* itself forms a component of the character 祥 *xiáng* meaning "auspicious"; its other component is 礻, which is the radical of 示 *shì* originally meaning "ceremony of honoring gods and ancestors." *Yang* enters into other characters with positive meanings, such as 美 *měi* ("beautiful" or "good") whose bottom component is 大 *dà* ("big").

For all these reasons, it is not surprising that the character for "sheep" 羊 *yáng* appears in so many different forms in *jiaguwen* itself. Some of these are shown below:

末

Justice is Solomon-like

In the theme above, we have seen how the Chinese people in the past used to believe that the sheep possessed the Solomon-like ability to distinguish just from unjust, right from wrong. This legend is, of course, revealing; but, nevertheless, it is only a legend. In reality, how did the ancient Chinese understand certain crucial notions, such as the important distinction which all societies must make, between the public domain, on the one hand and the private, on the other? How did they grasp the moral/legal idea of just distribution? To elucidate this cluster of themes, we need to look at and deconstruct a related set of characters: The character for "public" is 公 *gōng*; for "private" is 私 *sī*; for "divide" is 分 *fēn*; for "half" is 半 *bàn*.

These four characters, if you look closely at them, show that they have certain things in common as well as other aspects which are different. They bear what is sometimes called family resemblances, as in a family, members share certain features and yet differ in others in an intricately linked manner. *Gong* and *si* have this in common: 厶. *Gong*, *fen* and *ban* have this in common: 八. As 八 *bā* ("eight") is shared by three of the characters we are interested in, let us first take a good look at it. In *jiaguwen, jinwen, xiaozhuan, lishu*, it looks like this:

It is said that this character depicts exactly what you see if you were to do the following contortion with, say, your right hand. Let it hang down from the wrist, with the palm facing you, and three of your fingers folded towards the center of the palm, leaving the thumb and the little finger stretched out – you see 八. The two fingers stretched apart, however, imply the idea of separation. Some scholars hold that this is the original meaning of the character/word, although it was long lost, ever since it was taken over as *jiajie zi*, a phonetic-loan to stand for the number "eight." Other scholars also point out that the *xiaozhuan* version of the character looks somewhat like two people standing back to back – now when two people have their backs to each other, this means the parting of ways, going in opposite directions. This, too, implies separation.

Bearing this deconstruction of 八 in mind, let us now turn to 分 *fēn* meaning "divide." Beneath its radical 八, is the character 刀 *dāo* ("knife"). To divide something like a cake or fruit into two or more pieces, you need a knife. So it is *huiyi* zi, a meaning-compound. If you wish to demonstrate how to divide an object neatly into two exactly equal halves without resorting to cumbersome equipment of any kind, then dividing something with symmetrical halves, such as a chicken or an ox, would do the job nicely. We know that in Shang times (ca. 16th – 11th century BCE), people slaughtered a lot of oxen, especially for big sacrificial ceremonies. A butcher, who could cut up the animal expertly, would earn a lot of credit and admiration. Hence, what better way of representing the idea of dividing something into two equal portions than the character 半 *bàn*? The top bit, looking like this 丷 is another way of writing 八 (upside down) as radical; the second component is the character for "ox" 牛 *niú*. *Ba*, we have already seen, originally meant "to separate"; hence, an ox neatly divided or separated out into two equal halves is *ban*. One can see this clearly in the *jinwen, xiaozhuan, lishu* versions of the character:

Other things being equal, if something has to be shared between two or more people, then dividing them into equal portions would be the right and just thing to do. The Biblical story about Solomon is basically about this sense of justice as fairness. When he proposed that the two disputing mothers should each have an exact half of the disputed baby, he was adhering to this rule of equal shares. Of course, the twist of the story is that the baby is not a piece of cake or an ox; in other words, other things were not equal in this case. Solomon should be criticized for having failed to grasp this important point. But Solomon was not noted for his wisdom for no good reason; he was also relying on a piece of human psychology. He reckoned that the real mother of the baby would rather let another woman have her baby than see her baby cut into two halves in front of her very eyes. And, indeed, Solomon was right in his expectation.

The public domain may simply be defined as the opposite of the private domain. In Chinese, that definition is built into the very construction of the character 公 *gōng*. As already observed, it has the radical for "divide" or "separate" as its top component; the bottom component stands for "private." In other words, the public is that which excludes the private. Another compatible interpretation is based on the view mentioned earlier that in the *xiaozhuan* version of 八, two people are standing back to back, facing opposing directions – this implies the definition of the public as that which turns its back on and repudiates the private. The component, standing for private, is 厶. Scholars have interpreted this differently – some judging, by its *jiaguwen* and *jinwen* forms, have interpreted it to represent a mouth, and others, the most prominent bit of the nose. Every one has a mouth and a nose; hence, these parts of the body can be used to stake claims to what belongs to oneself, that is, what belongs to the private, not the public domain.

Later on, to 厶 was added another component 禾 *hé*, standing for "grain or cereal" (a word which we have come across before). The character, 私 *sī*, is *huiyi zi*, a meaning-compound; it implies that what I/we have cultivated with my/our own labor is mine/ours, that it belongs to me/us exclusively, hence, that it is private to me/us.

未

The elevated and the despised

Who were the political and social elites in China in its long history? Obviously the king and, later, the emperor were at the very top. Let us now explore a little further what is behind that role. Earlier, we have looked at the deconstruction of the character 君 *jūn*, originally meaning "chief of a tribe." We have also seen that such people with power were inclined to magnify themselves. Hence, they fancied even more august terms to refer to themselves. Qin Shihuangdi (the first emperor of unified China) crafted a new term 皇帝 *huángdì*, which emperors after him, for some 2000 years, used until the end of the Manchu Dynasty in 1911. Let us first take a look at 王 *wáng*, the most basic term for "king." In late *jiaguwen* and *jinwen*, it looks like this:

Scholars have noted that the character looks like the blade of an axe. In *jinwen*, the blade is even made more realistic, looking exactly like what the sharp edge of an axe is in reality. These two forms remind one in no uncertain terms that power is ultimately based on force – that is the nature of state power in all cultures, throughout all periods, no matter how long and complicated the intellectual and moral chain of justification between sovereign power, on the one hand, and force, on the other, which political theorists have constructed in justifying state power. (Recall, too, that 君 *jūn* also bore an axe.)

In *xiaozhuan* and *lishu*, the character had evolved as the character of sovereign power also evolved, such that it no longer looked like the sharp edge of an axe any more, as shown below:

The three horizontal strokes, with a vertical line linking them are now interpreted as the king or sovereign power uniting in himself the three essential elements of Chinese cosmology: 天 *tiān* , 地 *dì*, 人 *rén*: Heavens above, Earth, and Man below. Naked power has been transformed and given a cosmological as well as moral basis in this implied chain of intellectual development for the justification of state power. This means that the king was Heaven's representative on Earth; in other words, he had the Mandate of Heaven to rule. Since China became unified under Qin Shihuangdi, this line of justification took on an additional layer of meaning – all China must be united under one sovereign power. Just as there is only one sun up in the heavens, there must only be one source of sovereign power.

This attempt to aggrandise the attributes of kingship resulted in its appropriating the character 王 itself, which originally meant "jade." Now the Chinese people have always regarded jade to be not only beautiful and precious but also the symbol for certain virtues of which there are five:

- its being smooth and bright stands for 仁 *rén*, co-humanity
- its sharpness notwithstanding, it never hurts any one and this quality stands for 义/義 *yì*, doing what is right or righteous
- it can also be made to hang downwards and this quality stands for 礼/禮 *lǐ*, rites and rituals in which the ideally moral person would participate

- when struck, it emits a sound which travels far and this quality stands for 智 *zhì*, wisdom or intelligence
- its translucence, its purity, and its inability to hide its defects stand for 信 *xìn*, trust

Hence appropriating the character for "jade" would, for as long as people remembered its original meaning, also meant taking over its positive image. Jade, however, having been driven out of its linguistic home, had to find alternative accommodation – it became 玉 *yù*, that is 王 with an additional dot. Now, the last laugh could be on the powerful and the mighty who had deprived jade of its original character. Look at it this way. Amongst its various virtues, jade stands for trust, being unable to deceive by hiding its own defects. Is it then not appropriate that 玉 should now sport a dot, perhaps, representing a small imperfection? Does this then not imply that the king 王 in contrast is not capable of owning up to imperfections and, therefore, not trustworthy? The new character for "jade" could then be said to be a piece of disguised political subversion, at least according to our deconstruction.

To reinforce this interpretation, let us take a look at the different (*jiaguwen, jinwen, xiaozhuan, lishu*) evolutions of the character for "jade":

The *jiaguwen* version of "jade" shows a string or necklace of jade slivers or slices. In *jinwen*, the word has become stylised as three horizontal lines with a vertical one linking them through the middle. *Xiaozhuan* also has the same form. The change comes in *lishu*, with the extra dot then appearing. Recall from Part II that Qin Shihuangdi had ordained that *lishu* be the script of lowly bureaucrats and commoners; this shows that when *lishu* was formally established, the evolution of the character has ended with a dot added to its original form. Perhaps, this means that the process of glorifying the king by appropriating the original character for "jade" itself was initiated by Qin Shihuangdi. Furthermore, the piece of concealed subversion in the *lishu* form of the character for "jade" might have something to do with the person appointed by Qin Shihuangdi himself to oversee the formalisation of *lishu* – remember, he was someone called Cheng

Miao (程邈). If this inference is tenable, then Cheng Miao did have the last laugh at the newly minted emperor. Recall, too, that he was once cast into prison for ten years by that king, now turned emperor. He could be having his own quiet mockery at that well-known megalomaniac in world history. Well, that seems a plausible way of looking at the emergence of the new character for "jade" in *lishu*.

The character 皇 *huáng* ("emperor") first appeared in *jinwen* and looks like this: . Some scholars hold that it looks like a lamp – the bottom bit is the stand, the middle bit the oil well with oil in it, and the top little bit sticking out of the well, the burning wick. Like the sun, the *huang* shines, and gives forth light. Others maintain that the character looks very much like the king wearing the crown which is 冕 *miǎn*. In the Chinese tradition, the crown is more like a very special hat or headgear, rather than looking like a crown in the European image of a crown. In fact, it bears a remarkable resemblance to the mortar board which Bachelor degree graduates wear at their degree ceremony. We have seen (***In the twilight snatch the bride***) how in the aristocracy, the male became an adult at the age of twenty and the *rite de passage* is marked in a ceremony called 冠礼/禮 *guàn lǐ*, which involved the tying up of the hair into a knot, covered with a piece of material, called 冠 *guàn*.

冕 *miǎn* is then another kind of headgear which the emperor and other high officials and nobility were entitled to wear on top of the *guan*. You can see Qin Shihuangdi wearing it in this portrait traditionally said to be of him. The word coronation is 加冕 *jiā miǎn* ("adding the *mian* to the *guan*"). The *mian* as worn by the emperor (at least during Han times) had twelve tassels of jade pieces dangling from the ends of the board. (Their number and type of material used indicated the wearer's rank.) The whole headgear was secured by two lengths of silk ribbon which could be tied under the chin. What is of special interest here is that attached to the ribbon on either side was a pearl-shaped jade drop which passed in front of the ear, symbolically reminding the wearer, in particular, the emperor, that he should not listen to falsehoods or malicious tales. The expression 充耳不闻 *chōng ěr bú wén* "to turn a deaf ear to," is derived from this context. The pearl itself is called *chong er* (充耳), literally "ear plug." Similarly, the tassels also served symbolically to prevent the emperor from seeing evil – if one sees no evil, hears no evil, then one speaks no evil and does no evil. This arrangement reflects Confucius's four "thou shalt not" (四勿 *sìwù*) in *The Analects*: what is not in conformity with the ritual code of correct/upright behavior, do not look, do not listen, do not say (or repeat), do not do (非礼/禮 勿视/視，非礼/禮勿听/聽，非礼/禮勿言，非礼/禮勿动/動 *fēi lǐ wù shì*, *fēi lǐ wù tīng*, *fēi lǐ wù yán*, *fēi lǐ wù dòng*).

As usual, Qin Shihuangdi, appropriated for himself (and henceforth, after him, by all Chinese emperors) the word 皇 for personal use, to signify that he was, the king of kings, the ruler of all rulers. In other words, he was eager to surpass the ancient 三皇五帝 *Sān Huáng Wǔ Dì*, in power and glory. As a result, he also combined the two characters 皇 and 帝 into a single (two-syllable) word, 皇帝 *huángdì*, to refer to his new status as emperor of all unified China. After him, all Chinese emperors were *huangdi.*

The cosmological significance of the word 帝 *dì* in turn was added to the term. And what is that significance? The term 天帝 *tiāndì* or 上帝 *Shàngdì* refers to god in the heavens above or the highest divine being, who rules over nature. The character *di* comes from a depiction of the base of a fruit, which is written with the "grass" radical on top as 蔕 *dì*. The various forms (*jiaguwen,* then *jinwen, xiaozhuan, lishu*) of that character 帝 *dì* are shown below:

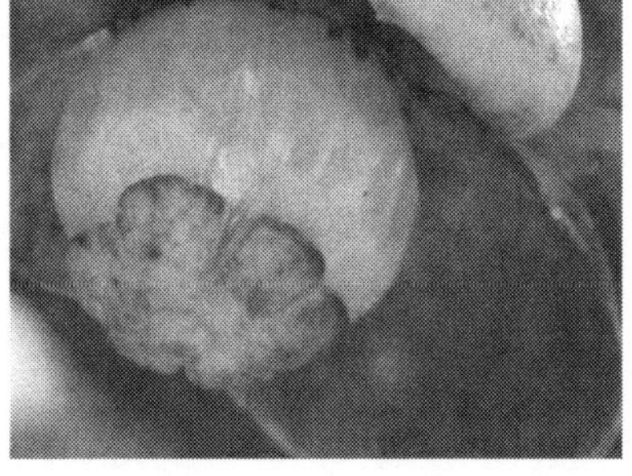

In the *jiaguwen* form, you can see very clearly that it is an attempt to replicate the structure of the base of a fruit. In the majority of cultivated fruits, one might not see this very clearly, but there is a tropical fruit called the mangosteen (山竹果 *shānzhúguǒ*) which displays it brilliantly. Here is a picture of an unripe mangosteen. The number of raised parts at the bottom of the fruit corresponds exactly to the number of segments inside the ripened fruit. Here is a tip for buying mangosteens should you ever come across them in your travels, and fancy tasting this very delicious fruit. Count the number of raised segments on the outside to determine the number inside – as a general rule, the fewer the segments, the larger the seed in the segment and the lesser the amount of the flesh which you can eat. Well, obviously, the ancient Chinese, as early as Shang times (ca. 16th – 11th century BCE), knew a thing or two about the reproductive development of fruiting plants and their botanical structure.

Throughout its long history since the Zhou Dynasty (ca. 11th century – 221 BCE), Chinese society had recognized four main classes: the scholar (士 *shì*), the peasant (农/農 *nóng*), the artisan (工 *gōng*) and the trader (商 *shāng*). These were ordered in a hierarchical fashion, with the literati being the highest and the commercial at the very bottom of the scale. The various forms (*jinwen, xiaozhuan, lishu*) of the character 士 *shì* look like this:

This character has attracted many interpretations, the most general of which says that any aristocratic male over the age of twenty after his *guan* ceremony qualifies to be 士 *shì*. A much more stringent interpretation holds that the character is constructed out of two characters: 一 *yī* ("one") and 十 *shí* ("ten"). One is the lowest digit, and ten the highest. (In the Chinese system of counting, any number after ten can be constructed out of one to ten until one reaches hundred, when a new word is introduced, which is 百 *bǎi*; hence, "eleven" is 十一 *shíyī*, "ninety nine" is 九十九 *jiǔshíjiǔ*.) In Chinese cosmological understanding, *yi* ("one") is where everything begins and *shi* ("ten") is where everything ends. That is why Xu Shen in his dictionary says that 士 *shì* means "someone whose knowledge of things is encyclopaedic and whose understanding of things is equally comprehensive." Judged by this account, the translation of the word as "scholar" seems inadequate; one might have to say "polymath," perhaps.

In political terms, the status of scholar varied – in Zhou, and even up to Han times, *shì* referred to the lowest rank in the aristocratic hierarchy. But as his rank did not entail property and taxation rights bestowed on him by the king, he was a kind of independent operator, an intellectual, as his chief asset was his store of knowledge, his understanding of affairs of state as well as his reputation for being a virtuous person. As a result, a scholar was not necessarily an official, nor was an official necessarily a scholar. A scholar was someone who generally aspired to be appointed an official, and sometimes did become one. Hence he occupied an intermediary position between the common people and those in office with power. To get an official appointment, the scholar must put himself through a very complicated, long drawn out process of examination, with three major levels; the majority of candidates failed. There were cases of families who bankrupted themselves putting their sons through the procedure, and there were also cases where the candidates did not succeed till well past their prime, even in their fiftys.

Even without either bureaucratic or political power, nevertheless, the scholar as a class occupied top rank in society, though after Han times, he was no longer part of the aristorocratic hierarchy. Li Bai never submitted himself to the official examinations, although this did not stop him from aspiring to an official appointment, as we have seen (***Happiness is piggy-shaped***). But we have also seen the high regard with which he was held as poet in particular, and as scholar and intellectual in general. We have mentioned a case of how a father thought of the scheme of advertising for a son-in-law who would be a talented scholar. Scholars were in demand whether as husband material, calligrapher, writer of elegant poetry or prose, as theorists of politics, morals. In contrast, the other three major classes of commoners in society could not carry a candle to the scholar class.

While the scholar was honored, the trader or business people were despised, at the very bottom of the social pyramid. Wealth, through commerce, meant nothing in the eyes of the social or political elite. Look at the ancient walled city of Pingyao (平遥) in Shanxi Province (山西), a foremost commercial city in Chinese history. Its origin could be dated back to Zhou times, but the city you see today when you visit it is, by and large, a city built in the Ming Dynasty (1368 – 1644 CE), being added to during the Qing Dynasty (1644 – 1911 CE). The town occupied a strategic position, half way between two imperial cities, Beijing and present-day Xi'an (西安), and was close to two military towns, Datong (大同) and Taiyuan (太原). Throughout its long history, it was very prosperous, as it was the commercial and banking center for the trade of the Silk Route. Indeed, the first modern bank in China appeared there in the early Qing Dynasty, introducing the check. Just outside Pingyao is a famous temple (first built in 963 CE), where you will find the calligraphy of a single character 魏 *wèi*, but curiously written without the slanting stroke at the top of the right-hand component of the character. The explanation for the missing stroke is that although commerce had brought great wealth to the city, alas, the wealth had not yet so far produced a top candidate in the country's highest exams – the day the city had the honor of one of its sons obtaining the top position of 状/狀元 *zhuàngyuán*, the missing stroke would be restored. Well, it looks as if Pingyao never achieved that distinction.

The word for "trade or commerce" is 商 *shāng*; it is the same character as the *shang* of the Shang Dynasty. A businessman is called 商人 *shāngrén*; the Shang people were also 商人 *Shāngrén*. It looks as if businessmen are called after the Shang people, yet all that we have so far mentioned about the Shang people seemed not to have anything to do with commerce. This is, of course, not to deny that trade took place in Shang times, but Shang culture was more noted for fierce fighting, for enslaving female prisoners-of-war, for divination and other religious rites, for its bronze technology than for its commercial activities. The clue lies in the end of the Shang Dynasty. The end of that dynasty is always presented by Chinese historians as decadent and debauched. Its last king, 紂 *Zhòu*, is, in Chinese history, a by-word for moral corruption and decadence. He was said to have conducted drunken orgies in his palaces – his courtiers, men and women, naked, would lap up wine from a specially built wine lake. So drunk were some that they simply fell into the pool and drowned. Are these stories exaggerated tales? This matter is not our real concern. What is critical is that the Shang ruler was defeated. It is also said that when the king led his men into battle against the Zhou (周) army, his men deserted him to join the Zhou forces, and he committed suicide. The Zhou Dynasty did not entirely annihilate the Shang people as it would not be practicable to do so, to say the least. In fact, the Shang king's brother was given a fiefdom under the new management, tucked away in an innocuous spot. Furthermore, for the smooth continuation of administration, the new regime had no choice but to retain the services of certain of the old officials. Nevertheless, the Zhou ruler did not entirely spare the rest of the Shang elites, especially the rich, the powerful and the noble; he took their lands from them and ordained that from then on, the only livelihood they were permitted to pursue was to engage in trade and commerce. (Well, perhaps, these should consider themselves lucky and be grateful that the Zhou people did not see eye to eye with the Shang practices either of slavery or of killing the living in order to accompany and serve the dead in the burial rites of the nobility. The Zhou victors appeared to have disapproved of such customs.) Hence, traders and businessmen were called 商人 *shāngrén*, and some of them, undoubtedly, even became immensely rich. (May be some of the Pingyao citizens were descendants of the original Shang nobility.) Obviously, even during Shang times, commerce did not particularly enjoy high status; the Zhou policy further ensured that traders remained at the bottom of the social pyramid, as from then on, the occupation became near identical with the defeated Shang people.

末

Words as zi: go forth and multiply

We saw in Part II how the Catholic missionaries from the sixteenth or seventeenth century had misunderstood the character of Chinese writing and, unwittingly, started the myth that Chinese is entirely a pictographic (or ideographic) language. This misunderstanding has since often been repeated even today. We have also remarked that if only these Europeans had been familiar with Xu Shen's dictionary (end of the first century CE), even ever so superficially, they would never have been misled by the "exotic," non-alphabetic nature of Chinese writing. The very title of Xu Shen's dictionary 说/說文解字 *Shuō wén jiě zì* should have alerted them to the fact that Chinese writing could not possibly be entirely pictographic. The title may loosely and inelegantly be translated as: *Discussing Wen and Explaining Zi*. In other words, Xu Shen distinguished between two types of written forms, 文 *wén* and 字 *zì*. What are these?

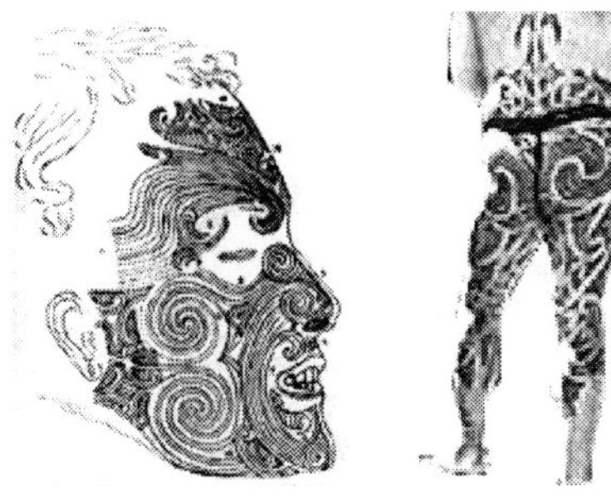

We take a look first at 文 *wén*. Scholars say that this word comes from 纹 *wén*, referring to lines, those lines and markings made on people's bodies, often of their totem animals. These markings would constitute a pattern, looking decorative and these are called 花纹 *huāwén*. Above are pictures of face and body tattoos practiced by the Maori people in New Zealand. Their patterns would bear resemblance to the 花纹 *huāwén* of the Chinese people in archaic times. The various forms (*jiaguwen*, *jinwen*, *xiaozhuan*, *lishu*) of 文 are reproduced below:

The *jiaguwen* version appears to depict a large man, standing straight and erect, shoulders pulled well back, chest jutting out, feet apart firmly planted on the ground. On the chest are markings, constituting a design. Those are 纹 *wén*. (One version of *jiaguwen* even shows a heart blazoned on the chest.)

The Chinese male practiced tattooing not only in archaic times during the Neolithic Age (ca. 8000 – 2000 BCE) but as late as the Han Dynasty (206 BCE – 220 CE). Some did it using a knife to carve patterns on the face or body, others used needles and yet others hot iron. In the days before writing, the marks made were of their totem animal; when writing was established, then the names of their clans or their title were tattooed.

Imagine the early Chinese people attempting to brand or tattoo their totem animal on their body. What they did would be an image of the animal. When writing evolved, and they needed a word to refer to their totem animal, it seemed likely that they would recycle their tattooed image of it. As a result, tattooed image and word would look much alike. If their totem animal were a sheep 羊 *yáng*, then both their tattoo and the word would be like one of the numerous versions of 羊 in *jiaguwen* which we have earlier reproduced (in ***Rites and rituals: how the butcher became the prime minister!***). In other words, what Xu Shen called 文 *wén* falls precisely into the category of 象形字, *xiangxing zi* or pictograph. Xu Shen grasped this without the benefit of knowing *jiaguwen* or indeed even of its existence, as *jiaguwen* was not re-discovered until nearly 1900 years after he published his dictionary. Xu Shen would not have been original in deploying the six categories of formation and use, as the classification was known to exist, as observed in Part II, since the Warring States Period (475 – 221 BCE). Anyway, what is important is that his dictionary has enshrined for later generations the crucial distinction between 文 *wén* and 字 *zì*. Whatever myths non-Chinese commentators might have propagated about the nature of Chinese writing, such as the Ideographic Myth, Chinese scholars would be quite clear that not all characters in their language are *xiangxing zi*, pictographs, and that *xiangxing zi* are 文 *wén* and not 字 *zì*. Of course, today, in general usage, as opposed to specialist publications about the nature of Chinese writing, words are just called 文字 *wénzì* , and no further distinction is made between them.

If 文 *wén* is primarily *xiangxing zi* or pictographs, then 字 *zì* would appear to refer to what Xu Shen called *xingsheng zi*, semantic-phonetic compounds, that category (out of the six) which is the most fruitful, accounting for the majority of characters in the language throughout the long history of Chinese writing. It would also cover the category of *huiyi zi*, meaning compounds, also inventive as a technique of character creation, though not quite so fruitful as *xingsheng zi*. We have also seen how the combined use of these two techniques is involved in the generation of a good many characters. What is even more fascinating is that the fruitfulness of these two techniques in generating new characters is built into the very construction and meaning of the character to refer to their products, 字 *zì*. First look at the various forms (*jinwen*, *xiaozhuan*, *lishu*) of the word shown below:

Some scholars hold that the top bit is 宀, the "roof" radical standing for a house, and that inside the house is a cheeky or frisky child 子(*zǐ*) romping about. Other scholars, focusing on the *jinwen* rather than the *xiaozhuan* or *lishu* version, argue that the top bit is not 宀, as it lacks a small stroke above the line. Instead, it looks remarkably like a woman in labor giving birth, with her legs apart and the baby being born. These are two very different interpretations but basically they share the same deconstruction, that the word 字 *zì* has something to do with reproduction – the second interpretation emphasizes the process of birth and the first the product of the reproductive process, a child. We saw in an earlier discussion (***What is it to be a woman?***) that to give birth to a child is 生子 *shēng zǐ*. (Today, more commonly, one says 生孩子 *shēng hái·zi*.) A new character (that is, one which the student or reader does not know and has yet to learn) is 生字 *shēngzì*. (An alternative term is 生词 *shēngcí*.) Humans procreate other humans, but of course, it is the female of the two sexes who actually gives birth to a child. When sperm meets egg, this encounter results eventually in a new human; when one existing word meets up with another existing word, you get a new word. In other words, the principles of character-creation at work are *xingsheng* and *huiyi*. Under the former, one component – the radical 部首 *bùshǒu* – gives the meaning, while the other component donates the sound, but also in many cases, brings meaning too. In the case of the latter, two characters each independently with very different meanings, together yield a brand new character with a brand new meaning when they are put together. Words multiply words just as humans multiply humans.

Every language needs to invent new words. So there is nothing unusual about character/word creation in itself in the Chinese language. However, what is interesting are the techniques it employs, especially the combined principles of *xingsheng* and *huiyi*. In Part II, we mentioned kenning, the Old English and the Old Norse technique of word-creation for poetic effects which appears to us to be an analog of the principle of *huiyi*. We have, there, also given examples from modern English as well as Arabic of this principle at work. If readers know of an analog of the principle of *xingsheng* in any living language, we would love to know of such examples.

末

Write on what, with what

Chinese writing conjures up for nearly everyone, even including many Chinese, brush, ink, ink stone and, of course, paper. While this image has a long and honorable history, so much so that it is almost part of Chinese cultural identity, it remains true to say that Chinese writing had not always been done with the kind of brush with which one is so familiar. Today the word "brush" is written: 笔/筆 b ǐ. Take a look below at the word for "writing implement" as conceived at different periods of the history of Chinese writing (*jiaguwen, jinwen, xiaozhuan, lishu*), and you will see straightaway the point just made:

Neither *jiaguwen* nor *jinwen* sport the "bamboo" radical 竹 *zhú*, which made an appearance only in *xiaozhuan* and *lishu*. This radical here indicates that the body of the implement is bamboo, of which, indeed, today's brush is generally made. However, some scholars hold that by the Zhou Dynasty (ca. 11th century – 221 BCE), bamboo was already used. Historically, depending on wealth and status, the body could be ivory, silver, gold, more expensive wood such as sandalwood, or even glass.

The hand which grasps the implement can be seen in all the forms: in *jiaguwen* and *jinwen*, it is to the right whereas in x*iaozhuan* and *lishu*, it is just under the bamboo radical. (In Chinese calligraphy, the brush is held like this; in Japanese calligraphy, it is held differently, more like holding a pen in the Western style.)

However, study carefully the actual bit of the implement which does the writing. In *jiaguwen*, *jinwen* and to an extent even in *xiaozhuan*, it seems to look like a three-pronged bit which has altered somewhat in appearance in *lishu*. All the four forms appear not so much to show animal hairs (which constitute the brush) as a stiffish object, like a stylus. That is why some scholars think that the earliest writing implement was probably a bit of stick, sharpened and then dipped in coloring material or ink. The writing bit, as something soft such as animal hairs, might have appeared later. From this point of view, the similarities as well as the differences between *jianti* and *fanti* of 笔/筆 *b ǐ* are very interesting and instructive. Both sport the "bamboo" radical; *fanti* is really based on *lishu* and *kaishu* (these two scripts are very similar in essence) and so retains the hand grasping the implement as well as the actual writing bit of the implement looking like a stylus, whereas *jianti* dispenses with the hand and uses 毛 *máo*, which is the character for "body hair." As a matter of fact, today's *jianti* is actually a throwback to a character of the word which first appeared during the Northern and Southern Dynasties (420 – 589 CE). This is yet another example of the peculiar complexities surrounding the relationship between *jianti* and *fanti*; the presumption that *fanti* is traditional while *jianti* is necessarily not so, may lead to problematic conclusions when simplistically applied across the board. As shown in this instance, both versions are, in one obvious sense, equally, authentically traditional. (This is in contrast to those instances where *jianti* has undoubtedly produced new-fangled versions of characters, such as the case of 国 *guó*, meaning "country," to replace 國 in *fanti*.) Perhaps, the appearance of this form of the word – 笔 – during the Northern and Southern Dynasties was in recognition that the standard design of the writing implement, since the early days of writing, had long generally assumed the form of the by now familiar calligraphic brush, and that both the implement as well as the material upon which the writing was carried out had altered over time. Today, 笔/筆 is a generic term for pen of which 毛笔/筆 *máobǐ*, the traditional calligraphic brush, is an example; others are 铅笔 *qiānbǐ* (pencil), 圆珠笔/筆 *yuánzhūbǐ* (ballpoint pen), 钢笔/鋼筆 *gāngbǐ* (fountain pen).

What the above discussion shows is this: that in the long history of Chinese writing, the writing implement took various forms, from something hard to something soft. Even amongst the brush forms, the type of animal hairs makes a difference to the type of writing implement and the kind of calligraphy which is the result. Harder hairs first emerged: from the wolf, tiger, deer, goat, pig (if it is a wild boar), chicken, duck, and rabbit. Even hairs from the rat have been used. Some brushes are also made from a combination of different types of hair, the harder variety inside and the softer one wrapped round it on the outside for greater and more subtle control of the writing implement.

No discussion of the writing implement really makes much sense without mention of the material upon which the writing was to be done. It is obviously useless to try to write on stone with an implement made of rabbit hair, just to cite an absurd example. To carve on stone you would need a knife; to write on the mold which eventually appears as *jinwen* on a bronze vessel, one would again need something like a scoop, not something soft. One must bear in mind that Chinese writing was done on a variety of media, ranging from ox bones, tortoise shells, rocks, stones, wood, bamboo, silk, paper made from silk, paper made from hemp, reeds, trees, etc. On the other hand, although the writing must in the end be carved with a knife on a stone tablet, nevertheless, a copy of the text with a writing implement would probably first be made to guide the carving. In *jiaguwen*, for instance, before carving (with knife) on the ox shoulder blade or the tortoise shell, the divining scribe had first written on the medium, sometimes in red, sometimes in black ink. We know this because, some of the writing in the end was not carved and their remains today still contain minute traces of their color. In any case, a writing implement was already used to make certain patterns and symbols on earthenware pots during Neolithic times; these pots, found at the Neolithic site of Banpo (半坡 belonging to the Yangshao Culture, ca. 5000 – 3000 BCE), were made around 4000 BCE.

Other surfaces, in particular, such as wood and bamboo also required that indispensable tool, the knife. Indeed, so great is its relevance and importance to all forms of calligraphy that the knife (刀 *dāo*) and the writing implement were linked together as 刀笔/筆 *dāobǐ*. This is because, when a mistake was made, it had to be scraped off and the word written again. Of course, when the surface was stone or rock, then the knife (or some chipping tool) acted not as an eraser but was the main implement for doing the job.

Ink, naturally, would be as old as the writing implement itself. The character for "ink" is 墨 *mò*, *huiyi zi*, meaning-compound, as the first component on top is the character for "black" and the second below is the character for "earth." Alternatively, you can read it as *xingsheng zi*, a semantic-phonetic compound, with the character for "black" donating the sound, and that for "earth" donating meaning. Either implies that the object referred to is black and is made from earth.

There is a tale about how the first ink came about in the Zhou Dynasty (ca. 11th century – 221 BCE). Someone was washing himself by a stream when he fished out a piece of charred wood. This object stained his hand. He took it home, made experiments with it: grinding the charred bits to a powder, mixing the powder with the sticky water in which rice was cooked as binding agent, rolling the mixture into a ball, drying the balls in the sun. And that was the first ink made for writing. Reality, however, was a little different: the first ink appeared to have been made from coal substances, including the coal we burn as a form of carbon fuel. Ink made from such a base continued to be produced even till the end of the Han Dynasty (206 BCE – 220 CE). The ancient Chinese also used an alternative method of making ink, using pine. The pine wood was lit but not allowed to burn right through; this way, the maximum amount of ash was produced. This ash became another base for ink production. Scientific analysis of some pieces of oracle-bones (upon which *jiaguwen* was written) shows that pine ash was, and has continued to be used, such that the coal-base method was ousted altogether.

In the Jin Dynasty (晋代 265 – 420 CE), people discovered that by adding an animal glue to the ash, the ink produced writing which was more lustrous and whose luster lasted a long time. Some specimens of Jin writing, now over 1600 years old, have preserved extremely well.

The best ink is said to be produced in what is now called 徽州 *Huīzhōu*, southern China. During a period of disturbance in the Tang Dynasty (618 – 907 CE), an expert ink maker fled the north with his family for safety. He got to 徽州 *Huīzhōu*, found that pine grew abundantly in the area. So he settled there and continued his manufacture of ink, improving its quality all the while. Ink from that place has, since then, enjoyed the status of producing the best ink in all China.

Although the word for "ink" incorporates the word for "black," and although it is true that the ink normally used for writing is black, we would like to remind the reader that Chinese ink is not only black in color. It comes in many colors which Chinese painting, in particular, uses. Furthermore, some writing was even done in vermillion. For instance, in the Ming (1368 – 1644 CE) and Qing (1644 – 1911 CE) Dynasties, in the state examinations, in order to preserve the maximum anonymity of the candidates, two sets of their examined work were involved. The original manuscripts submitted by the candidates themselves were written with the usual black ink. After submission, the portion of the scripts in which their names were written would be sealed up, and to prevent the examiners from recognising the handwriting of the candidates, a copy of their submitted work was written out by a set of scribes, this time, in red ink. It was this copy which the examiners read.

Until printing enjoyed great demand by the Tang Dynasty, everything written in Chinese up to that time was done by hand. But printing required paper in greater quantities than before; moreover, paper which could be economically produced. China, probably during the latter half of the Zhou Dynasty, had accidentally discovered how to make paper during the process of silk production, by sieving the tiny bits of silk fibers left in the water used in making silk floss. But silk was expensive. By the Western Han Dynasty (206 BCE – 24CE), less expensive material, such as bark, hemp fibers, even old recycled fishing nets, became available after experiments based on the careful analysis of the silk fibers used in silk paper production. These newer kinds of paper were called 蔡侯纸/紙 (Duke Cai paper), named after the inventor whose name was Cai Lun 蔡伦/倫 and who was ennobled, for his inventions.

Before cheaper paper was invented and before the printed book came into existence, Chinese books had since Shang times (ca. 16th – 11th century BCE) been primarily written by hand on wood (牍 *dú*) or bamboo slips (竹简/簡 *zhújiǎn*).

This is how the bamboo was treated for book production. The cane was cut into lengths, the shortest about ten cms (roughly six inches), the longest seventy cms. Next, these lengths were spliced into several portions, each a few mms wide. If you have ever looked at a fresh bamboo cane, you would have noticed that it usually has a green peel (the commonly used variety for this purpose), which had to be removed: the bamboo slips then had to be carefully heat-dried to remove all moisture as well as possible pests lurking in the woodwork, so to speak, before one could use the slips to write on. After that, the entire set of bamboo slips on which was written the report or essay were threaded together by silken or hempen threads, or even leather laces, which varied in number from three to five, even six, depending on the length of the slips.

Qin Shihuangdi was a very conscientious ruler; each day in his dispatch box, as it were, were large numbers of documents weighing nearly sixty kilos (one hundred and thirty two pounds) which he had to read. They weighed so much for the simple reason that they were made of bamboo or wood. Carts had to be used to transport such books. Books of any description have always been a problem from the point of view of their storage and their transportation – they are just heavy and take up a lot of space. May be e-books would finally solve these problems for us.

In Chinese, books made up of bamboo or wood slips are called 册 *cè*.

Here is one such book on the left – it is a contemporary reproduction of the edition commissioned by the emperor Qianlong of the Qing Dynasty (1644 – 1911 CE), of a very famous ancient book, *The Art of War*.

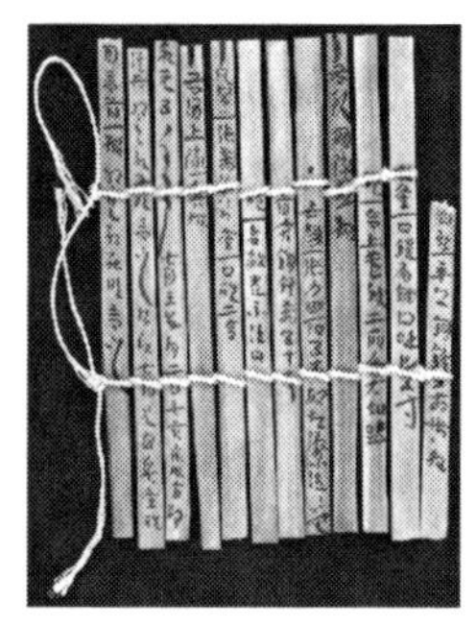

This is an example of ancient book-binding, with hempen rather than silken binding.

Now let us look at the various forms of the character for 册 *cè*:

On the left are two versions in *jiaguwen*; on the right, three in *jinwen*. All are *xiangxing zi*, pictographs. However, let us not forget that in ancient China, books before the use of paper, took forms other than this kind of tied-together wood or bamboo slips. For instance, one could even say that there were *jiaguwen* books – some of the oracle-bones and shells had holes drilled through them at a corner, presumably, so that they could be threaded together as one set, thereby constituting a single book – you can say each shell or ox blade is equivalent to a page.

Books may also take the form of a scroll: here is an eighth century Tang Dynasty scroll, called the *Gem Heap Sutra*, rolled up with its original roller and silk tie. This scroll, which consists of panels of paper glued together, was part of the Dunhuang Library Cave but which now lives in the British Library. The British Library also possesses the Diamond Sutra, the oldest complete printed book in the world which is dated – at the end of the scroll is a note which gives the Chinese calendar date equivalent to 11 May 868 CE. However, it is not the oldest printed book as the *Gem Heap Sutra* and other books had preceded it, when the technique of block-printing was invented earlier in the Tang Dynasty. When such scrolls were read, they were unrolled. As you can see from all the pictures of Chinese books shown here (until the reform in the 1950s), these books had always been written right to left, top to bottom, unlike the Western convention of left to right across the page.

末

The emperor's prerogative: words at their disposal

Books were precious things, and in particular, certain books were so revered that they became elevated to the status of classics. These were called 典 *diǎn*. You can see the various versions (*jiaguwen*, *jinwen*, *xiaozhuan*, *lishu*) of the character below:

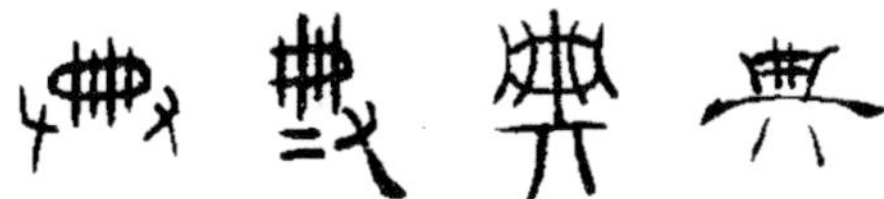

This is *huiyi zi*, a meaning-compound. In *jiaguwen*, you can see very clearly two hands holding a book between them. In *xiaozhuan*, the hands are missing but the book now seems to be resting on a stand. Xu Shen said that the word referred to the books of the legendary Five Emperors; in other words, books called *dian* are so revered that they are almost sacred. To put them on a stand would be like putting wine on the altar as offerings to gods and ancestors.

Down the ages, Chinese emperors had consistently recognized the importance of books and the great regard with which they were held in terms of scholarship. However, this attitude could manifest itself in one of two opposing ways. The first, we have already come across (Part II), in Qin Shihuangdi's decree to burn the books of Confucius and his followers, not to mention slaughter such scholars into the bargain. This was because of his disapproval and fear of the ideas contained in their books. The second, which similarly involved violence, was, however, born out of misguided sheer reverence for books. We have mentioned in Part II another important dictionary in the Qing Dynasty (1644 – 1911 CE), *The Kangxi Dictionary* (康熙字典), commissioned by the Kangxi emperor and published in 1717. During the reign of Kangxi's grandson, Qianlong, who was himself another distinguished Qing emperor, a certain scholar, on going through that dictionary carefully, had discovered numerous mistakes in it. He published his findings, upon which Qianlong ordered not only that the publication together with all his other works be destroyed but, also, that the scholar himself as well as his entire extended family be killed. Qianlong had probably done this for the following related reasons: the dictionary was commissioned by his grandfather whom he revered exceedingly; his grandfather had appointed the best scholars of his day to achieve that monumental task; his grandfather had considered that achievement to be one of the crowning glories of his reign. (Kangxi was emulating an earlier dictionary commissioned by one of the great emperors of the Ming Dynasty which had achieved the status of 典 *diǎn*. Unfortunately, only a tiny fraction of that work now exists.) After that harsh and tragic event, nobody, naturally, dared whisper any criticism against the dictionary. It was not until 1827 when, under the aegis of another Qing emperor, a descendant of Kangxi and Qianlong, that a publication listing 2588 mistakes appeared. Since then, other scholars had discovered further mistakes in that celebrated dictionary.

In China's long history, only one woman ever became emperor of China, not a mere empress, but an emperor in her own right. For this, she was vilified by the patriarchal ideologues. She lived during the Tang Dynasty (618 – 907 CE). She was known (posthumously) as Wu Zetian (武则天), Wu being her surname. She began life at court in a humble position, as a comcubine of the Taizong emperor, but occupying a rank low down even in the concubine pecking order. However, this did not discourage her from trying to climb the dangerous, greasy pole of power through a combination of sheer intelligence, determination, cunning, ruthlessness and luck, not to mention beauty, at least, in her youth – a cluster of characteristics which all successful emperors (bar female beauty, of course) had displayed down the ages. At first, she became the power behind the throne, ruling through first sickly, then weak emperors, such as husband, brother-in-law. When the Taizong emperor died in 649 CE, she married his son who became the Gaozong emperor (650-684 CE). Eventually, in 690 CE, she proclaimed her own dynasty (Zhou 周), and sat upon the Dragon Throne, declaring herself emperor.

Like many great kings and emperors in Chinese history, she showed dedication to the arts, especially calligraphy. Naturally, she was sensitive to words, their construction and their significance. Some of her courtiers, knowing her inclination, tried flattering her by devising special new words for her. One, in particular, crafted twelve. One of them, she chose as her 字 *zì* the word 曌 *zhào*, a word which had exactly the same sound as an existing word 照, "to illuminate." Wu Zetian's chosen name (字 *zì*) has two components: the one on top is 明 *míng*, "bright" and the one at the bottom is 空 *kōng*, "sky." So, her 曌 *zhào* is *huiyi zi*, a meaning compound – it was meant to highlight that the new emperor's brightness and light would shine upon her realm, just as the light from the heavens above shone upon the earth below.

She had noticed that the word 国/國 *guó*, "country," was problematic. Why? If you look at the *fanti* version (on the right) which would have been the one in use in her time, you would see it has two components, a big square which stands for the territory occupied by a country and inside that space is another word 或 *huò*. This second component resembled too much another word 惑 *huò* for her liking, as it means "to be puzzled" or "bewildered," "to mislead," or "delude." These meanings were in her eyes distinctly inauspicious or scurrilous. Surely, the country she ruled was not bewildered, and how could she be said to be misleading or befuddling the people. She decreed that the offending word inside the first word be replaced by 武, her own surname; that is to say that she, the emperor, born Wu (武), would ensure that the country would be safe in her hands and by her might (武 itself means "weapons," and so, derivatively, with "matters relating to war"), that it would endure. However, following that decree, it was then pointed out to her, that her invention was also inauspicious but in a different way – the space inside the square now occupied by none other than herself appeared to suggest that she was like a prisoner encaged. She devised yet another word, but before she could put that into effect, she was deposed and, indeed, was incarcerated in the "golden cage" of a side palace in the imperial compound by the next Tang emperor. Her Zhou Dynasty lasted from 690 – 705 CE.

Even in death, she defied convention. Today, should you visit the site of the eighteen Tang dynastic tombs (nearly all officially unexcavated), west of Xi'an, you would walk along a spirit way leading to the mausoleum of the Gaozong emperor. On the left stands a tall stele with inscription in his honor. However, opposite it on the other side, you would find another stele in front of the tomb of his step-mother and wife, none other than Wu Zetian herself, who had ordered that it should bear no inscription, in order to make the point that no word could express the supreme and unique power she exercised. Indeed, she had the last laugh.

Hers was a wonderfully impressive life, the Confucian assessment against her notwithstanding.

末

What hangs upon a name? A lot

Traditionally, the name of a sage, a (reigning) emperor, a grand official, one's immediate dead ancestors were regarded as almost sacred, and should not be invoked or mentioned. To do so would amount to an act of profanity. Every effort must be made to avoid such tabooed words.

The name of the great sage, Confucius, in Chinese, as we have already mentioned (***Rites and rituals: in the twilight snatch the bride***), is 孔丘 Kong Qiu. 丘 means "mound." There are many places in China with names which incorporate the word 丘. In the Song Dynasty (960 – 1279 CE), in 1100 CE, it was decreed that those places must change their names to something else. 丘 is also a fairly common surname; in the Qing Dynasty (1644 – 1911 CE), the Yongzheng emperor (雍正 1723 – 1735 CE), in the third year of his 13-year reign (1726), decreed that people with such a surname had to add the "ear" radical to the word on the right hand side, so that it would look like this: 邱. This decree was not rescinded till the early decades of the twentieth century, after the end of the Qing Dynasty in 1911.

This decree of Yongzheng, shortly after its proclamation, contributed to the settling of a law suit which involved two litigants, one named Wang (王), the other Qiu (邱). Wang claimed that ten years ago, he bought a two-room property from Qiu, but because he himself was not in urgent need of using it, he permitted the former owner to stay on until such time when he needed the accommodation. After a while, Qiu's daughter married and left home and as he, Wang, himself now needed the house, he requested Qiu to leave but who refused. Hence the litigation. When the judge asked for evidence of the original purchase, Wang claimed that the witness to the act had since died, but produced before the court a document containing the details of the transaction. The judge took one look at the piece of paper and declared it to be a forgery. Why? For two reasons: first the document recorded the purchase as having been made in the fifty-fifth year of the reign of Kangxi, the emperor Yongzheng's father (1716), and second, that Qiu, the vendor, was written 邱 with the ear radical. These were all tell-tales signs that the deed was not genuine, but recently forged by Wang. The judge found in favor of Qiu.

Xu Shen, the compiler of the Han dictionary, faced some thorny problems. The surname of the founding family of the Han Dynasty (206 BCE – 220 CE) is Liu, 刘/劉. The meaning of 刘/劉 is "to kill." To save his own head from being chopped off, he thought it wise to invent a new word altogether to stand for "to kill" in his dictionary. That, however, was not the end of his headaches – characters which entered into the construction of the names of the Han emperors had also to be left out to avoid committing the taboo of invoking their names. So you can appreciate that his dictionary is inherently incomplete, given the constraints under which he was working.

There was once a top ranking mandarin, during the Five Dynasties (907 – 960 CE), who served ten different emperors as prime minister for twenty years. His personal name was *Dao* (道). He was a great devotee of Laozi's philosophy, Daoism. He organized seminars, inviting scholars to discuss the *Daode Jing* (道德经/經). The scholars ran into a truly head-wracking problem – the classic is about the *dao*. To avoid the taboo word, whenever they came across it, they substituted "dare not say" (不敢说/說). For the famous opening line of the classic 道可道,非常道, the scholars read as: "what one dares not say, one dares not say, indeed, one is especially too terrified to say." And what was the reaction of the grand official? He laughed and he cried at this ludicrous display of reverence towards his name and his own person.

Another story is not quite so harmlessly amusing because of its dark underlying message. It happened in the Song Dynasty (960 – 1279 CE) about another official, not all that grand, but who thought himself very grand and acted so. His personal name was Deng (登 meaning "to ascend" or "mount"). He forbade people within his jurisdiction to have that name or use it in any other context. Worse, he also forbade any other word with the same sound as his personal name. Anyone caught trespassing upon his linguistic space, so to speak, would be punished with strokes of the cane, or even with some forms of mild torture. Unfortunately, the word for "light" or "lamp" has the same sound with the same tone as his name: 灯/燈 *dēng*. So the expression for "lighting lamps or candles" 点灯/點燈 *diǎn dēng* had to be altered to 点/點火 *diǎn huǒ*, meaning "to light a fire." On New

Year's Eve, when festive lanterns were lit, the expression 放花灯/燈 *fàng huādēng* was turned into 放火 *fàng huǒ*, meaning "to set fire to something," "to commit arson." His underlings would post up notices all over his jurisdiction to remind the people that they were permitted to commit arson for three days to celebrate the festival! As a result, there came into existence an expression to the effect that while the district official may commit arson, ordinary folks are not even permitted to light their candles or their lamps: 只许/許州官放火，不许/許百姓点灯/點燈. This expression has come to symbolise the arbitrary, corrupt ways of officialdom.

Within the family, the rule of avoiding this kind of taboo was clear – if parents were alive but grandparents were dead, then one should not utter the names of the deceased forebears; if the parents themselves were dead, then one should not utter their names. This practice was followed by none other than Confucius himself. His mother's name was 徵在. In *The Analects* (论语/論語), a famous classic, attributed to him, he went to great lengths to avoid using 徵在; he only ever used one of the two characters in any context, but never the two together.

Desperate efforts to avoid uttering the names of one's parents had led to some entertaining tales. There was once a scholar whose father was called 良臣 Liangchen, which literally means "pure, incorrupt official." In a classic, called the *Book of Mencius* (by a philosopher called 孟子 Mengzi, 371 – 289 BCE), the phrase 良臣, meaning "a good official," occurred. When the scholar came to read it, he uttered "father" instead, thereby producing ridiculous results as it had the effect of altering the meaning of the whole sentence of which the phrase was a part – the scholar's avoidance of the prohibition to utter the words resembling his father's name ended making all fathers into common thieves and robbers. The sentence, "What today we regard as good officials, the past regarded them as robbers of the common people" then became "What today we call our fathers, the past called them robbers of the common people."

In the Jin Dynasty (晋代 265 – 420 CE), a person invited the local big wig to a meal. The host realized that his honored guest had taken some medicine which meant that he should not drink cold or room temperature wine. So he ordered his servants to warm up the wine for the guest. Upon hearing this, the guest dissolved into tears which the host found bizarre. As he wiped away his tears, he explained that he was crying because his father's name was 温 Wen; when he heard his host ordering wine to be warmed up for his benefit, this meant he was participating in an act of profaning his father's name, as the expression for "warming up wine" was 温酒 *wēn jiŭ.*

末

Literary talents overcome all, win all

Chinese culture celebrates the word; it is almost unique in putting words and scholarship on such a high pedestal. To be a talented scholar, throughout China's long history, had been the highest ambition for the male amongst the elites. The scholar class was at the top of the pecking social order (not counting the aristocracy, of course), as we have seen (***The elevated and the despised***). Note that there is no mention of any warrior class. Of course Chinese history is full of warriors and great generals. However, to the Chinese, to be only good at fighting is to be unbalanced. You could say, it is to have too much *yang* and not enough *yin*. The *yin* component is missing. One must also strive to reach the highest peak of intellectual and moral development. The ideal man would have reached heights of perfection in both: 文武双/雙全 *wénwŭ shuāngquán*. However, if a son could not be both, then a parent would ardently pray that he would be a talented scholar. Traditionally, no Chinese parents would dream of imploring their ancestors to bless them with sons who were only good at fighting.

Such an outlook may be illustrated by a story about a famous historical figure during the Three Kingdoms Period (220 – 265 CE). He was the king of the State of Wei, a man of great distinction both as warrior and scholar, called 曹操 *Cáo Cāo*. Chinese succession was not determined simply by primogeniture, that is, the first born inheriting all, including power in the political realm. It was a much more complex affair. When faced with nominating the crown prince, Cao Cao made, from amongst his numerous sons, a short list of three (all coincidentally borne by his wife), considered to have the most positive characteristics. (Officially he had twenty five surviving sons, as he had seventeen concubines besides his wife.) The youngest was a brave and marvellous warrior, always returning from battles in triumph. The middle possessed truly exceptional literary talents, was a great poet and stylist. The eldest was an all rounder, good at the martial arts as well as in literary matters. One day, he took the youngest aside and told him that he ought to take in some book learning to turn himself into a more complete man, and issued him a reading list. But son had no interest in moldy classical tomes and complained to his mates about his old man foisting something on him which, in his opinion, was of no earthly use to him on the battle front. His father accepted his limitation but he then eliminated him from the short list, as military talents alone would not fit the job description. The king had a special affection for the middle son because of his great literary gifts, but in the end he, too, was struck off the short shortlist, leaving only the eldest in command of the field because it was obvious that the first born alone was gifted both in the literary and military spheres, unlike his middle brother who had less talent in the latter sphere. The king's choice of successor and the criteria he used, other things being equal, for selecting the most appropriate candidate embodied the following principles, at least towards the end of the Han Dynasty(206 BCE – 220 CE):

- sons of wife before sons of concubines and these before nephews
- the older before the younger
- the more talented before the less talented with
    - brush as well as sword
    - brush alone
    - sword alone

Affection as the principle of succession was considered to be unacceptable; hence Cao Cao's top mandarins, whose opinions he secretly sought, were not in favor of the middle son. Another criterion for selection was virtue, whether the short-listed candidate possessed virtues such as filial piety, humanitarianism and so on. One can cite Cao Cao's two sons to illustrate success relying on filial piety. Once, the king himself had to lead troops on a hard campaign. His family and court gathered at the gate to bid farewell on the morning of his departure. Second son delivered a superbly written address which every one could not help but praise and admire. Older brother knew that the younger rival would use just such an opportunity to display his literary talents. Good as he was with poetry and the brush, he knew that he could not outshine his brother's efforts in that field. He discussed the matter with one of his own advisers. This wily fellow agreed that he ought not to compete on that front. Instead he advised him to display filial piety. After the applause had died down for his younger brother's oration, he threw himself to the ground and started to wail about how much he would miss his father, how much he would worry about his safety, and so on. He was such a convincing actor that tears soon rolled down the cheeks of those gathered to say goodbye, but most importantly that his father should start to cry as well. Father was very touched by such a display of filial piety. Father eventually nominated him as crown prince. He got the throne through a strategically timed exhibition of a virtue which the Chinese have always held in high esteem.

An instance of success relying on a display of humanitarian sentiments happened in relatively more recent history, when in the Qing Dynasty (1644 – 1911 CE), the Daoguang emperor (道光, 1820 – 1850), had to choose between two eligible sons as crown prince, the older of which was not so talented and was also frail in health. One New Year, the emperor decided to lead a royal hunt. The older son knew that he was no match of younger brother as far as hunting was concerned. His tutor and counsellor advised him under no circumstances to lift his bow during the excursion. At the end of the hunt, every one gathered to show off their bags. Younger sibling proudly showed off his. Father was stunned to find that older son had nothing. When asked to explain himself, the young man delivered his well-prepared speech about how he felt it morally inappropriate to hunt and to kill animals at that time of year, when the animals were just about to mate, reproduce or nurture their young. The emperor and the court were so impressed by the young man's moral sensibility that he was soon endorsed as crown prince.

We have already seen how one could win a beautiful and rich bride through being talented with the brush. There are numerous other tales in which lives were saved, lost spouses regained, favors won from emperors, all because of this all-important quality called literary talents.

An emperor was surrounded by concubines, of different ranks, the majority of whom spent their entire lives in the palace without coming into the remotest contact with the emperor, or indeed without even catching a glimpse of his imperial majesty. Should a concubine want to be noticed by the emperor, possessing outstanding beauty helped. But she had better be truly outstandingly beautiful, as the majority of the concubines, if not all of them, had been chosen for their beauty, often, through competitive selection procedures conducted throughout the land to recruit them. One concubine springs to mind for having succeeded in luring the emperor's attention by her ability to soothe the emperor's nerves through her mastery of the art of mixing and burning perfumes. Another route to pursue was the literary one. Emperors had been known to fall for women with superb literary talents, women who could out-perform them in rapid repartee, in coming up with the second line of a couplet in the most elegant and exquisite form possible no sooner as their imperial majesties had finished uttering the first.

Although women could earn recognition via the literary route, feminists should not immediately rejoice, as the daughters of even the elite families were not necessarily those with such accomplishments. Many fathers had taken to heart the Confucian teaching that for daughters, virtue lay in not being formally educated in the way sons were, but in being submissive and self-sacrificing. As a result, the most talented, the most accomplished of females could be found more readily amongst the professional class of entertainers (the model for the Japanese *geisha*) who were not only beautiful but could play musical instruments, dance, compose poetry, etc., with ease and grace. Naturally, many scholars fell for them, but alas, as they were not compatible class-wise, it was best to forget them but as a faint memory of the pleasures of youth, and settle instead for the dull, sub-educated but worthy daughters of well-connected families in high society, who could act as their patron and clear their path to promotion in their career.

Here is a tale of a sorrowing wife long abandoned by her husband, posted far away to be a grand official but, who seemed to have forgotten even to write to her. This story happened during Western Han times (206 BCE – 24 CE). The scholar official first met the girl in Sichuan (四川) Province, the daughter of a very rich merchant. Having fallen madly for each other, they decided to elope to another city. However, he was poor as a church mouse, as he had just resigned from a post which he did not fancy. As a result, his bride was reduced to selling wine or doing other menial chores to earn enough to keep body and soul together, until her father heard about their plight and sent men to bring them back to his home. Not long after the rescue, suddenly, the scholar found that his writings had become the flavor of the month at court. The emperor summoned him back to Changan (长/長安), the capital (today's Xi'an). This time, he made good. However, he seemed to have suffered amnesia for the wife he had left behind in the province. She waited and waited but no word came from the husband. After five years or so, one day, she finally got a letter from him. She opened it and found to her amazement that it contained nothing more than these numbers: one to ten, then hundred, thousand, ten thousand (一, 二, 三, 四, 五, 六, 七, 八, 九, 十, 百, 千, 万/萬). It was not surprising that, at first, she could not make head or tail of it, but upon reflection, it occurred to her that he meant to tell her that their marriage was at an end, but was too cowardly to say so directly, and so had chosen this bizarre way of announcing his intention to abandon her. She understood him to say that no matter how long she waited for him, whether for one, ten, one hundred or ten thousand years, he would never return. (The figure "ten thousand" *wan* is used in this context not literally but to stand for the notion of forever.) She then sat down to compose a reply to it. In this composition, she used each of the thirteen numbers mentioned in the original letter. Loosely translated, in part, it reads like this: Once (一) separated, we two (二) thought it might only be for three or four (三, 四) months, but who knew that the parting would be five or six (五, 六) years. This sorrowing heart could not bear to pluck the seven- (七) stringed qin (zither), with no hope of getting even a letter of a mere eight (八) lines, thus severing a chain of nine (九) loops linking us together. At every stop, ten (十) li (roughly a kilometer or two-third of a mile) apart, from its pavilion, I look out in vain for you. My heart, in spite of myself, is hundred-fold (百) filled with regret, thousand-fold (千) with longing, ten-thousand-fold (万/萬) with blame for my spouse. Upon receiving her reply, and reading her elegantly composed response to his own wretched letter, the husband was overcome with shame. He read and re-read it, and the more he read, the greater his shame and remorse, so much so that he set out from Changan with the best carriage and the fastest horses his office could command to hasten back to Sichuan, and to bring his long abandoned wife back to the capital with him. Thus happily ended this tale, thanks to the wife's literary talents.

Literary talents could also save one's life. We have just told the story of Cao Cao eventually choosing his eldest son to succeed him. We have mentioned that the middle son was an exceptional scholar and poet. Even as a child he could write elegantly and maturely. His father at first thought that he must have plagiarised and got some one else to do it for him. When challenged, the boy denied that he had cheated and suggested that his father test him, which was duly done until there was no further doubt that the child had done all the compositions himself. We also know, Cao Cao was so impressed that he wanted to make him the heir apparent to the throne. When older brother came to know of his father's affection for the younger sibling, he became jealous and plotted to undermine him. Father once ordered the middle son to lead a battle.

Older brother got wind of the news and invited him to a farewell do, during which he made sure that his guest got very drunk. When father heard about his drunken state which prevented him from setting out to battle on time, father was naturally furious, and decided finally that such a son did not deserve to inherit the throne.

The king eventually died and eldest son succeeded. However, in spite of this elevation, he continued to be deeply jealous of his brother and sought an excuse to get rid of him. He soon found such an opportunity. When his mother heard the news as to what would happen, she pleaded with him to spare the brother's life. He relented but on one condition, that his brother compose a poem within seven strides that he would take. And should the poem be considered not up to the usual standard expected of him even if completed on time, the death penalty would be enforced. Younger brother was taken into his presence and told what was at stake. He proceeded to take the accorded seven steps in a measured fashion and duly completed the assignment. Older brother next ordered him to compose another, this time about fraternal relationship but without mentioning the word "brother." He uttered it almost immediately. This poem has four lines, of five words each. Loosely translated, it reads:

To stew beans, light one must the pot	煮豆燃豆萁
The beans a-crying in their cot	豆 在釜中泣
As they have come from the same pod	本是同根生
Why so eager to cook the lot?	相煎何太急

Even his jealous brother was touched, and thought it not merely excellent. Anyway, his literary talents won him reprieve from death. However, we feel we ought to record here our profound apologies to the poet (Cao Zhi 曹植) for having mangled his beautiful poem in this clumsy translation, and to generations of Chinese, for nearly two millennia, who have loved the poem and found it moving.

Such is the power of words in Chinese culture.

The scholar must not only be thoroughly grounded in the classical texts, 经/經典, able to write stylish prose in essays which also tested his analytical prowess, and to compose elegant poetry, he must, above all, have an excellent calligraphic hand. During certain periods, some emperors prized calligraphy even higher than the other skills. However, all imperial examinations would rate it extremely highly. Candidates, who excelled themselves assessed by all the other criteria, but failed to excel in terms of their calligraphy, would not be successful, no matter how high their level of excellence in the other fields examined. Scholars must never neglect to cultivate the brush. We have also seen that Chinese aesthetics regards calligraphy to be the highest art form, above even landscape painting. Those paintings which combine both calligraphy and landscape are the most appreciated – the calligraphy could be poetry by notable poets down the centuries, or the artist's own composition. Emperors aspired to leave their own calligraphic hand behind for posterity, preferably engraved on stone tablets or rock faces. Those whose hand was not so good got well-known calligraphers to write on their behalf. Even today, major political figures are expected to have a reasonable hand as part of their job description.

We have already mentioned in Part II an extremely revered calligrapher, the Jin Dynasty (晋代, 303 – 361 CE) 王羲之, Wang Xizhi. His calligraphy, today, exists only on carved stone tablets, but generations have made rubbings of his work to master the art. He was devoted to studying geese; he was said to derive inspiration for his calligraphy from such observations, and that his calligraphic style was influenced by the graceful movements of these birds, especially the way they turned their necks. These observations taught him how to move his wrist while writing with his brush. One day he passed by the dwelling of a Daoist monk with a splendid gaggle of geese swimming in the pond. He wanted the birds badly and asked the monk to sell them to him. The monk said no, since no amount of money would tempt him to be parted from his gaggle. The calligrapher was very disappointed. However, the monk added that should he be willing to do a copy of Laozi's *Daode Jing* in his own hand, he would be more than happy to do a swap. The calligrapher gladly accepted the bargain.

Well, the bargain turned the two parties into happy men – the monk got his copy of the Daoist canon written by none other than the great man himself, and the calligrapher got his geese. Today, there is an expression 以鹅换经/以鵝換經 *yǐ é huàn jīng*, meaning "to get something very precious in exchange for something with much less value," such as a classical text by a famous calligrapher for a gaggle of geese. The equivalent expression in English is: "to throw a sprat to catch a mackerel." Here is the great calligrapher's word for "goose" 鹅/鵝 *é*. Judge for yourself whether his calligraphy captures the spirit of the bird and whether the monk did get the better bargain.

末

Word superstitious, word magic

The Chinese people, apart from their reverence for words, have also through the ages been immensely superstitious about them. There are certain words one should not utter or have anything to do with, for fear they might bring disaster or misfortune, because their pronunciation or associations resemble other words which are not auspicious. The Cantonese, particularly those living in Hong Kong as well as in the diaspora, more so than any other group, are prone to this habit of regarding certain words as inauspicious. For instance, no Cantonese would buy a property whose address is "fourteen" or want a telephone or a car plate with that taboo number: "fourteen" is 十四 *shísì*. However, in Cantonese, the number sounds like the phrase, "bound to die." Who can blame them for avoiding it.

During the period of celebrating the New Year, should you break a plate or a bowl, you should never say 打碎 *dǎ suì* ("to break something"), but say 岁岁/歲歲平安 *suìsuì píngān* ("may there always be peace"). The *sui* of "to break" is replaced by the *sui* of "year." A year beginning with breaking things may well portend a year of home and country devastated by strife, violence and war; hence one should ward off such evil by uttering an incantation for perpetual peace instead.

One of the most auspicious words in the Chinese language could be said to be 福 *fú*, "blessings." Some of its various forms (*jiaguwen, jinwen, xiaozhuan, kaishu*) may be seen below:

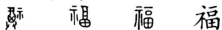

Jiaguwen shows very clearly what is involved: it is the ceremony of offering wine on the alter to gods and ancestors asking for their blessings – the bottom component of the character consists of two hands, holding up a wine vessel for sacrificial offering on the altar, as part of ceremonial display (示). By *jinwen*, the character 示 is replaced by the radical form of the word, 礻, the two hands are no longer there, although the wine vessel still looks recognisably like one. In *xiaozhuan*, the vessel is replaced by something looking like this: 畐 *fú*, which donates the sound as well as add to the meaning of the word, as it means "full." In other words, to be blessed is to lead a life which wants for nothing. Another interpretation of this component points out that it consists of the character "mouth" above that of "cultivated field"; this implies that any one who has land to grow food would not go hungry, and therefore, is blessed.

The word is considered to be so auspicious that it competes with another equally auspicious word (*shou*, "longevity") to spawn a large, if not the largest number of forms in writing them. In x*iaozhuan* alone, one is told that there are at least a hundred different ways of doing so. Here is a design, the *baifutu* (百福图/圖), in the form of a circle incorporating those hundred different versions.

People reckoned that the bigger the word was written, the greater the amount of blessings it would bring. One particularly large version recorded in the Song Dynasty (960 – 1279 CE) required a calligraphic brush as long as two Chinese feet, weighing the equivalent of ten pounds (about 4kgs). The person wielding the brush must have been super-human. According to one story, in the Qing Dynasty (1644 – 1911 CE), for the New Year celebrations, one prominent family had the word written extremely large to put on their door. The servant of the household, who was illiterate, was naturally confused, and hung the word upside down. When his master saw it, he was furious and would have ordered the man and those in charge to be severely punished. Fortunately, the equivalent of the head butler of the household, fearing implication in the affair, had a brilliant idea which saved the day. He explained that it was only too fitting that the blessings, which should naturally descend upon such an honorable family, had indeed already been bestowed. The master was duly appeased and every one was all smiles again. The trick was to pun upon the word 到 *dào* and 倒 *dǎo* (in 颠/顛倒 *diǎndǎo*) – the latter means "upside down" and the former "having arrived." In other words, 福 *fú*, the blessings, so much wished for, had already arrived. Ever since then by New Year's Eve or what is now commonly called the Spring Festival (since 1949 in China), people would have posted the word 福 *fú* upside down on their doors or windows.

As the language is tonal, the different tones combined with the way in which words are written, leave plenty of room for word play and word magic. This kind of game can be very simple or very complex. Take the word "bat" (referring to the animal, not the cricket bat), 蝠 with the "insect" radical, 虫; its sound is *fú*. As we have seen, the sound for "blessings" is also *fú*, with exactly the same tone, 福 *fú*. The bat then is a symbol for blessings. It is not so much the animal as such which brings blessings but the fact that the word, referring to the animal, shares the same sound as the word for "blessings." Other cultures make certain animals stand for certain qualities because the animal is said to possess the quality in question. In the USA, the national symbol is the bald eagle. This is because the bird, especially in flight, looks powerful and majestic, qualities which Americans believe their country to have. The Chinese construct symbols in that way too, but they are also very fond of using sounds as a way of creating them. The next time you happen to look at a Chinese painting or a Chinese bowl or dish, look out for the bat. The message the bats bear is: May your family or household be blessed or may your life be filled with happiness. When you think of bats, you may also think of them, not in full flight, but at rest and motionless. Bats hang from the walls of caves and nooks upside down. Seeing the word for blessings, 福 *fú*, hung upside down will certainly also call to mind the animal 蝠 *fú*, hanging upside down. So the image actually calls up two puns, not simply one. Sight and sound combine to make this kind of punning a very lively affair indeed.

Another story which explains the popular practice of pasting the word for blessings on doors dates from the beginning of the Ming Dynasty (1368 – 1644 CE) when the founding emperor set up his capital in the south, in Nanjing (Nanking). He was keen to inspect his domain in plain clothes. Once, on the fifteenth day of the New Year, as he was walking down a street, he saw a crowd gathered in front of a poster, laughing heartily away. On closer inspection, he saw that the poster was a barefoot woman carrying a large water melon. This was clearly a satirical reference to women from a certain region in China, whose feet were not sufficiently small and dainty. (The custom of foot-binding is said to have begun around the tenth century during the Song Dynasty.) The emperor was not amused as the poster mocked his own empress who, indeed, was someone from that region. Moreover, she was a singularly able woman who had led men into battle and helped her husband defeat his enemies and establish the new dynasty. She was known not to have dainty feet. Upon returning to the palace, the emperor sent his men to find out who were behind the poster, who were those gathered in front of it mocking and laughing. Of those not implicated, the emperor's men posted the word 福 *fú* on their doors. Two days later, they descended on the town, but this time, to arrest those whose doors were unadorned by that word and led them away to be dealt with suitably. After this, every household made sure that on New Year's Eve, the word was hung on its door. The practice, in any case, had already existed from Song times, but this incident reinforced it during the Ming Dynasty and made it even more popular.

Word superstition and word magic may also be seen vividly at play with regard to the word for chopsticks. Historically there are two words in Chinese for what we in the West call "chopsticks." One is the much older 箸; the other is 筷. Both share the "bamboo" radical, 竹, implying that generally chopsticks are made of bamboo, that is, the garden-or-common variety. (Historically, they have been made, and still are, of expensive materials such as ebony, ivory, gold, silver, etc.) They differ in their sounds: 箸 is pronounced *zhù*, while 筷 is *kuài*. Today, in general, Chinese people call chopsticks 筷子 *kuài·zi*. Sometimes the older word 箸 is used but in writing, and at other times, again in writing only, the two words are used together either as 箸筷 or as 筷箸. One reason why the older word 箸 fell eventually by the wayside is because of its sound – very unfortunately, *zhù* is the same for another word – 住 *zhù* – which means "stop," "arrest." The sound is also similar to yet another word – 蛀 *zhù* – meaning "to bore," as well as "that kind of worm which bores through wood," 蛀虫. Now it is said that in the Ming Dynasty, sailors and fishermen suddenly wanted nothing to do with anything that could remotely suggest that their boats might stop moving or that their ships might fall to bits because worms attacked them! So they hastily threw overboard, not the chopsticks, of course, but the names for chopsticks. Having got rid of such a potential bearer of ill luck, what on earth should one call these things? A Saatchi and Saatchi in their midst reminded people that there was already in existence an alternative name, not so often used, but sweet smelling and fragrant. This was 筷 *kuài* or better still 筷子 *kuài·zi*. The name *kuài* then suddenly became the new hot favorite. Its appeal lies in the second component of the word, underneath the "bamboo" radical. This bit on its own, written like this – 快 *kuài* – means "quick" or "quickly." The final component of the new name – 子 – means "child," but, in this context, "little fellow." The entire word *kuaizi* means "nimble (swift/speedy/nifty/quick) little fellow." When you talk about a pair of chopsticks, you're really talking about two swift-footed little fellows. So at a stroke or a few strokes of the brush and the use of the vocal chords, word magic has turned something with a dull and dreaded image into something colouful, cheerful and cheeky! A master stroke of spin and PR, sold successfully to the entire Chinese nation.

However, a puzzle remains: why suddenly in the early Ming Dynasty did the entire Chinese nation throw a collective superstitious fit over the name *zhu* for chopsticks when by and large they had not minded it too much till then? The explanation can, perhaps, be found in Chinese history itself. China is and has always been a great land mass, but it has a very long coastline. As early as the Qin (221 BCE – 207 BCE) and the Han (207 BCE – 220 CE) Dynasties, Chinese sailors had been sailing from her ports to explore the sea and other surrounding lands. These voyages became more common and systematic in the Tang (618 – 907 CE) and Song Dynasties, setting up, in one direction, a southerly trade route to South East Asia, India and Arabia, and in the other, a shorter, northerly one to Korea and Japan. But the real crowning glory of Chinese sea voyages and naval expeditions happened during the Ming Dynasty. Six hundred years ago, the Yongle emperor (永乐/樂) ordered his admiral, Zheng He (郑/鄭和, a Muslim, born in Yunnan belonging to what in China today is called the Hui ethnic group) to lead seven stupendous sea voyages, covering twenty eight years which, between them, visited about thirty countries, going as far as East Africa and the mouth of the Red Sea.

In 1405, a fleet of two hundred ships with a crew of as many as twenty seven thousand men (the first of several) left the port of Liujiagang 刘/劉家港 in Jiangsu (江苏/蘇) Province. (Today, Liujiagang is called Liu He 浏/瀏河. Shanghai is not too far away, though that mega-city, today, is not part of Jiangsu province.) Those men on board were sailing out into the great unknown, at least once their ships got beyond hugging the coast. If you had been one of them, would you, too, not be superstitious? Every ship in the fleet (and later fleets) had a small cabin dedicated to Ma Zu 妈祖 (also called "Tianhou," "the Empress of Heaven"), the Daoist goddess of the sea. It was not merely the common sailors on board the ships who prayed to her. It is said that even Zheng He, the admiral himself who was a Muslim, would call upon her for help whenever he was in a difficult spot, and she would respond immediately by causing a bright light to appear on the mast. With the passage of the "divine light," the danger would also pass away. Divine protection, of course, was fine, but one should have more than one string to the bow. That pesky name for chopsticks, 箸 *zhù*, a name which clearly bore no good omen, would bug the men. It would be best to get rid of it. That other word for chopsticks 筷 *kuài* would do the job perfectly. Its sound as well as meaning – as *xingsheng zi*, a semantic-phonetic compound as well as *huiyi zi*, a meaning-compound – performed the magic. Suddenly, twenty-seven thousand pairs of chopsticks on board instead of stopping the wind, so that the ships could not move, instead of thus encouraging worms to rot away the hulls, miraculously became twenty-seven thousand extra pairs of hands, those nimble cheeky little fellows, helping the ships to sail at an increased speed of knots. The sailors could sit back, happy and relaxed. At each meal, three times a day, as they used their chopsticks, they knew that they were adding speed and power to their ships or junks. For your amusement, we have dreamed up the following couplet which the men on board (and even women, for indeed, there were women in the fleet) might have done to add to the powers of their word magic:

筷速带来，一帆风/風迅
kuài sù dài lái, yī fān fēng xùn

We have turned it freely into a quatrain in English as follows:

Nimble of foot, swift of hand
Twice twenty-seven thousand
Chopsticks, coming and going
Fill the sails, wind a-blowing

末

Women's script

Chinese writing boasts of a women's script, 女书/書 *nǚshū*. In this respect, it appears to be unique. Nothing too much is yet known about it, the precise date of its emergence, for example, is not entirely clear, although its purpose seems clear enough. It was for women to record their thoughts about matters concerning them in their daily lives, even though these matters might appear relatively trivial compared with the great political and social events which, undoubtedly, determined and shaped their broader existence. It created a bond between mother and daughter, between female relatives as it was meant to be a secret code hidden from the prying eyes of male members of the family. Three days after the wedding, the woman would be given a book by her mother and other female relatives. In the first few pages, the mother would tell her daughter about her sense of loss. The rest of the book was left to the daughter to record her thoughts and feelings as she left one family to become part of another, of what would be in store for her in her new life. It seems to be confined primarily to a relatively specific small area in Hunan (湖南) Province, and is, therefore, dialect-based. One must remember that traditionally women were not taught to read and write; the women, who learned the women's script, as they sang and embroidered, would not know the Standard Chinese script, *Hanzi*. Through their own script, they had made themselves literate.

China and the world at large only officially knew of its existence in 1982. Earlier attempts to draw attention to it came to nought. For instance, in the early 1950s, during the period of language reform at which we looked in Part II, one story told that a woman from Hunan Province arrived one day in Beijing in 1958, speaking her local dialect and writing in a script which no one seemed to recognize. The Beijing Security Department sent her on to the National Language Reform Committee in Beijing which, also, could not make head or tail of what she was trying to say or what she wrote. In 1961, the Hunan Provincial Language Reform Committee tried again to submit some specimens to the National Language Reform Committee in Beijing, this time marking on the front of the folder: Women's script from Jiangyong County, Hunan Province (湖南江永). The experts on receiving it, took a look and concluded that it was probably a script of some non-Han ethnic minority group and, therefore, would not be of immediate relevance to their task in hand, which was language reform of the Han script. So they filed it away for later consideration.

In 1959, a member of the Hunan Cultural Department called Zhou Shuoyi (周硕沂) had a sample of the script, together with a brief introduction, published locally in a volume together with other material, in Jiangyong County. It turned out that Zhou Shuoyi, as a child, had remembered his own father possessing a volume containing certain verses, entitled Women's Script (although its original title was 训/訓女词/詞 *Verses to Educate Girls*). This volume had been written by a maternal ancestor traced back to six generations, who had brought it with her when she married and settled in her new home. As a result, Zhou Shuoyi was very interested in the subject and, when he was posted to the area in which that maternal ancestor had settled, he looked out for such material. In this work, he also came across elderly ladies who knew the script and eagerly helped him in his collection and research. Unfortunately, this activity on the part of Zhou and others was interrupted for more than a decade by the political upheavals of the Cultural Revolution during which they were declared to be "Rightists," and duly censored and silenced. By 1979 when life became normal, and people returned to their original posts, the work of getting the nation to recognize this unique linguistic phenomenon resumed. Zhou updated his earlier work and finally in 1982, a volume was published by the Hunan Cultural Department. The world finally got to know about it.

Here is a specimen of the script:

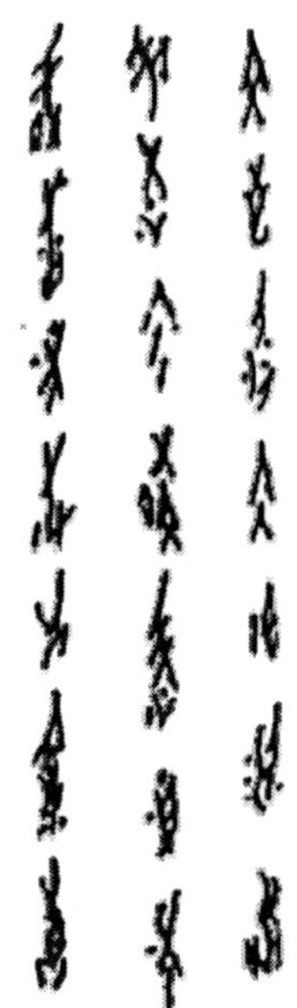

In the script, the lines are always written (as is the case traditionally with standard *Hanzi*) top to bottom, right to left. It uses no punctuation marks, makes no division by paragraphs. In total, it has one thousand two hundred words but often its practitioners use about eight hundred. It uses four different kinds of strokes: vertical (竖 *shù*), slanting (斜 *xié*), dots (点/點 diǎn) and arcs (弧 *hú*). As for the individual character, the right component is above the left; in its structure, it seems to follow that of *jiaguwen*. As a result, one speculation, concerning its ultimate origin, hypothesises that it could be even earlier than *jiaguwen*; another claims it might be contemporaneous with *jiaguwen* and *jinwen*; yet another, that it could be based on the Greater Seal script of Han times. It looks like an ancient script, but how ancient nobody really knows. Still others think that it is an "italic" version of *kaishu* (the Standard script), stretching and elongating the character. The translation in English of the passage cited runs roughly as follows: teach her to wear make-up and style the hair; in her hair to wear a hairpin of glistening pearls that she may sit resplendent, like Guanyin, on the altar. In Standard Chinese, it would read: 教她打扮便梳妆/妝, 头/頭插珍珠放豪光, 坐似观/觀音出佛堂.

There are at least three different legendary tales, in circulation about its origin. The first claims that in the village where Zhou Shuoyi's maternal ancestor settled upon marriage, a girl was born weighing nine pounds at birth, who grew up to be a talented woman. She could weave, embroider, sew but most importantly of all, she was very intelligent. Based on what she heard from her elders about the past, she created the script. Another tale said that long ago, a wonderfully intelligent and beautiful maiden was born, called Pan Qiao (盘/盤巧). Not only could she embroider, she could also sing. One day she was kidnapped by some officials. She had no means of communicating with her family. So she dreamed up a code. Every day in her embroidery, she would embroider the new word she had invented. In three years, she had embroidered one thousand and eighty new words. She then used this new script to communicate with her folks at home. The women of the village and the area sang her songs and learned the words she invented through them. The third story is set in the Song Dynasty (960 – 1279 CE). It tells of a girl as talented as she was beautiful. Her reputation spread so far and so wide that she was selected to enter the court as a concubine. At first she enjoyed the favors of the Song emperor but not for long. She wanted to let her family know of her sad fate, but such complaints would not get past the palace censors and would get her into deep trouble. So she had the bright idea of modifying the standard script to create a new one. She wrote on her handkerchief and told her relatives that the words must be read in a slanting direction. From this grew the women's script.

末

Domesticating foreign words

Things change, societies evolve and different cultures come into contact with others. New ideas are always in the air; new words are needed to talk about them. Every language faces the problem, at one time or other, of incorporating novel notions and foreign words into the vocabulary. English vocabulary is rich today because after the Norman Conquest of 1066, not only did French become the language of the ruling class and of the socially superior, but that, more importantly, long after the decline of French in English society, that language had left as legacy to English a good many words, which have since become so English that only specialists would recognize their "foreign" origin. Examples which spring to mind are "autumn," "joy," "beef." In other words, they have "gone native." As English and French use the same alphabet, the process of domestication was easy in one sense; just tweak the spelling a little and the word looks no longer like its original from across the Channel – *boeuf* becomes "beef," and *joie* becomes "joy" to reflect the change in pronunciation. Of course, in another respect, borrowing has given rise to certain problems which have plagued generations of English people learning French and *vice versa*. Today, the French Academy bitterly complains about the invasion of English (or, more realistically speaking, American) words: *le management*, *le parking* and such like are used in spite of the fact that French already has words for them.

Chinese, being non-alphabetic, cannot borrow foreign words in the way that, say, French and English have borrowed from one another. It can use one of three strategies: transliteration (translating by sounds), meaning equivalence, or a mixture of meaning and sound. It prefers the latter two and is not really keen on the first. Hong Kong, particularly during its existence as a British colony, adopted the lazy option of transliteration in a big way, not because there are no equivalent Chinese terms in existence, but that somehow, it was more "with it" to talk of the boss as 波士 *bosi*, and film as 菲林 *feilum*, just as the French do about "management" and "parking." Putonghua and Standard Chinese, sometimes, fall back on it as a first reaction, but later when a suitable term has been worked out in terms of meaning equivalence, the transliterated word would lapse – such was the case with "telephone." Originally, people called it *tie-le-feng*; eventually, the word is 电话/電話 *diànhuà*, literally meaning "electric talking," that is, "talking via electric lines or cables." In the same spirit, "computer" is rendered as 电脑/電腦 *diànnăo*, meaning "electronic brain," although the word did not first go through the stage of transliteration at all.

The strategy of mixing meaning and sound may be seen in the following three examples: "minibus," "gene," and "media." The first is rendered as 小巴 *xiǎobā* – *xiao* is "small" and *ba* is a half-hearted attempt at transliterating "bus." While this is a rather crude effort in applying the strategy, the other two examples are far more subtle and sophisticated. 基因 *jīyīn* is a serious effort to approximate to the sound of the word "gene" and at the same time an equally serious effort to embody the meaning of the term in the newly created two-syllable word. *Ji* implies something basic and foundational; *yin* is "cause" or "reason," and in certain contexts, "element" or "factor." *Jīyīn* amounts to "fundamental cause/reason," "basic element/factor." Indeed, genes are the basic stuff in the business of transmitting characteristics from parents to offspring. 媒体/體 *méitǐ* is equally effective in combining sound and meaning. As it stands, *meiti* almost sounds like plain transliteration but it is not. Look carefully at *mei*, how it is constructed. It means "go-between," "match-maker" (as match-makers traditionally have been women, the word has the "woman" radical 女). Look at *ti*; it means "body." *Meiti* is literally equivalent to "a match-making body or go-between." The media are the intermediary between two parties – the one which wants to say something in order to be heard by the public and the other, the public, which is keen to know what is said. Another excellent example is: 黑客 *hēikè* ("dark/invisible visitor"), 骇客 *hàikè* ("frightening visitor"), 海客 *hǎikè* ("visitor wandering freely about the world's oceans," like a pirate, except that in this context, such a visitor would be roaming cyberspace to commit mayhem as the spirit moves) which are all different versions of "hacker" in Chinese.

Chinese people in general would not regard the words 葡萄 *pútáo* ("grapes"), 胡同 *hútòng* ("narrow lanes in the older quarters of Beijing"), 幽默 *yōumò* ("humor"), 马/馬虎 *mǎ·hu* ("slap-dash, casual, passable"), to be foreign in origin. But they are. *Putao* is straightforward transliteration of the Persian word for "grapes," which shows that grapes were not indigenous to China proper but an imported plant, which today grows beautifully well in Xinjiang Province. So is *hutong*, a word from Mongolian imported during the Yuan Dynasty (1279 – 1368 CE), when the Mongols conquered and ruled China for about eighty years. 胡同 *hútòng* replaced the Han word for "narrow lane" which is 巷 *xiàng*, so much so that one invariably talks about the *hutong*, and never the *xiang* of Beijing. *Youmo* poses a bit of an issue. Is it plain transliteration or does it try to mix sound and meaning? *Yōu* is a stab at transliterating the first syllable of the English word. 幽, when describing a place, means "quiet," "secluded," and *mò* (默) means "silent." These two words together would, indeed, suggest a quiet sense of humor. However, humor is not necessarily always quiet and subtle; after all, some people have a loud or, indeed, vulgar sense of humor. May be the intellectuals of the time appreciated only the sophisticated sort. It entered the language in the 1920s, and in spite of the offers of several alternatives, it has held out against such competitors and has been firmly entrenched in the language for nearly a century.

马/馬虎 *mǎ·hu* is transliteration of the Sanskrit word (*mohu*), but it is also probably an attempt to combine sound and meaning – if one were to paint an animal which looks neither convincingly like a horse nor a tiger, but something which looks like a cross between the two, then the painter could not have done a good job at all. There was a competing term which was used in the Qing Dynasty (1644 – 1911 CE), 麻麻糊糊 *mámáhú·hu*, but that expression could also mean "seeing things in a bleary fashion." This seems to have lost out to 马马/馬馬虎虎 *mǎ · mǎhūhū* over the years. One satirical piece about the dire consequences of being slapdash to illustrate the expression goes as follows: fifty years or so ago, a cadre in Tianjin dashed off a quick memo ordering his underlings to go to a certain shop to buy fifty crates of the tiger-brand soap. He wrote instead: buy fifty monkeys from the said shop. The underlings were equally slapdash or perhaps they just adopted the attitude, theirs not to question why, and proceeded to get the number of monkeys mentioned in the memo. They first scoured the city, then the region, then, nearly half the country to make up the number of monkeys wanted. Suppliers responded to the demand. Crates full of monkeys soon arrived, creating pandemonium. The official, naturally, was someone called 马/馬大 哈 Ma Daha – it is obvious why his surname is Ma and his personal name Daha as it reflects the expression 哈哈大笑 *hā·ha dà xiào*, "to laugh one's head off." In other words, he is really Ma, the Laughing Stock.

There is another much older story about the expression, said to have originated in the Song Dynasty (960 – 1279 CE), concerning a fairly well-regarded painter who specialised in painting animals. One day, he had already finished doing the head of a tiger when some friends visited to watch him do the rest of the picture. He proceeded to add the body of a horse to the tiger's head. His friends were astonished and puzzled and asked him what sort of beast it was that he had painted. He laughed and said: 马马/馬馬虎虎 *mǎ · mǎhūhū*. He also told his eldest son that it was a tiger and his second son it was a horse. When these sons grew up, they went hunting. One day, the eldest saw a horse whose head was bent to the ground munching away at the grass. He thought it was a tiger and shot it dead. The owner of the horse was outraged and naturally demanded compensation for the dead animal. The second son, while wandering the countryside, had the misfortune to run into a tiger, but bearing his father's painting in mind, thought it to be a horse. The said "horse" proceeded to tear into him and claw him to death. The father, when he heard these two sets of doleful news, was beside himself with grief, and tore up the "horse-tiger" painting in a fit. After that, he wrote a poem about the whole sorry business, leaving it as a moral to posterity, that one should never do things in a *mamahuhu* manner.

There seems little point in finding meaning equivalents for certain foreign words, as they themselves are meaningless inventions to begin with; so the best strategy is plain transliteration. Examples are words from sub-atomic physics, such as "quarks," "gluons," "muons," etc. The scientists have just made them up as they discover such particles. "Quark" is simply 夸克 *kuākè* in Chinese. With regard to acronyms (words created using the first letter of each of the words in the name), the strategy adopted in certain instances is to use basically plain transliteration, but also to specify the kind of thing the acronyms stand for – this is so in the case of "AIDS" (**A**uto **I**mmune **D**eficiency **S**yndrome), which in one version is 艾滋病 *àizībìng*, *aizi* being the phonetic rendering of "AIDS" while *bing* indicates that it is an illness.

末

Precious as the warp

To the non-Chinese world, for centuries, the by-word for luxury has been silk, and silk came from China. Obviously, silk was precious, to the Chinese themselves as well as to foreigners. However, as we shall see, although silk was already in existence by Shang times (ca. 16th – 11th century BCE), the Shang people appeared then not to regard silk to be quite so precious. What then were precious to these ancient Chinese? Two things: jade and shells, possibly a third, not silk, but pots. It is not surprising to learn that jade was precious but sea-shells and pots being held as precious, that seems quite bizarre. But is it?

Any way, how do we learn that such mundane objects as sea-shells and pots were so highly regarded in those distant times? All we need to do is to look at the various forms (*jiaguwen, jinwen, xiaozhuan, lishu*) of the character for "precious," 宝/寶 *bǎo*:

All versions have the "roof" radical 宀, signifying "house." What precious things are inside the house? In *jiaguwen*, two things: sea-shells and jade. The top bit under the roof represents shells (a pictograph of the shape of a sea-shell), the bottom component, a string of jade pieces. We have come across the jade component before (***Friends, fellow disciples, comrades***) in the deconstruction of 朋 *péng*, fellow disciples. If you look at *jinwen* and *xiaozhuan*, you will notice that the string of jade has become simplified to look like this 王 (the original character for "jade" before Qin Shihuangdi appropriated it to stand for "king," as shown in ***The elevated and the despised***). The component for shells has been simplified to look, more or less, like this 貝 *bèi* and that, furthermore, it has been shifted to the bottom. Observe, too, that in the *xiaozhuan* and *lishu* versions, an extra component appears, looking something like this: 缶 which refers to earthenware pots in ancient times. There are two different interpretations of this additional component – one group of scholars hold that pots were not so readily available in those days and hence considered as precious, while another holds that the character serves to give the sound to the word for "precious," as in archaic Chinese pronunciation, the sounds for 缶 and 宝/寶 were very close. We think that these two interpretations are not necessarily incompatible. If so the character *bao* is both *xingsheng zi*, a semantic-phonetic compound as well as *huiyi zi*, a meaning compound.

Archaeological excavation in 1976 of a late Shang tomb, that of a Shang consort, Fu Hao, confirms two out of these three precious items – not only did her tomb goods include 755 jades as mentioned in Part II, they also include 4000 cowrie shells.

To begin to understand why the people of Shang times held sea-shells in such high esteem, one must bear the geography of the country in mind. The early Chinese people lived, as we have mentioned, in 中原 *Zhōngyuán*, the Central Plains. This region is miles from the coast. Given the difficulties of fast transportation, some four thousand to five thousand years ago, sea-shells would be rare and exotic items. Not only that, shellfish tastes good and their shells are beautiful objects. It is recorded that when the king of Zhou was once fighting against the last Shang king, he was captured by the enemy. One of his high officials thought of a scheme to rescue him, and that was to dispatch men to the coast to get shellfish, big ones, in order to bribe the Shang king to release his prisoner-of-war. The trick worked.

Initially, the shells were used as decorations as well as regarded as talismans. Indeed, it was said that a whole army of thirty thousand men were kitted out in uniforms with cowrie shells sewn on them with red thread. Economics tells us that when something is rare and in great demand, its price goes up, and people would want the object as part of their investment portfolio, so to speak. This happened to cowrie shells in those days. Furthermore, as people began to outgrow the barter trade, they needed a medium of exchange in their economic transactions with one another. The shells became Shang currency. The practice continued into the Zhou Dynasty (ca. 11th century – 221 BCE) and it was not until the Qin Dynasty (221 – 207 BCE) that it ceased to be legal tender, when Qin Shihuangdi undertook extensive currency reforms. The cowrie currency, in fact, lasted some one thousand eight hundred years. A string of ten cowrie shells was one 朋 *péng*.

You will find that numerous terms relating to trade and commerce include 貝 *bèi* as one of their components such as: "buying and selling"买卖/買賣 *mǎi·mai;* "trade"贸/貿 *mào*; "goods" 货/貨 *huò*. Let's take a quick look at 买/買 *mǎi* (to buy): the top component in the *fanti* version (right of the slash) is 罒, the "net" radical. If the legal tender was cowrie, then it stood to reason that you would put your money (strings of cowrie shells) in a net or string bag, and you would take this purse or wallet of yours to market. Hence the word is *huiyi zi*, a meaning-compound. In contrast, 货 / 貨 *huò* is *xingsheng zi*, a semantic-phonetic compound, as the top component 化 (today pronounced *huà*) gives it the sound.

The characters for "wealth" 财/財 *cái* and for being "poor" 貧 *pín* , too, incorporate 貝 *bèi* as a component. 财/財 *cái* is both *huiyi zi*, a meaning-compound as well as *xingsheng zi*, a semantic-phonetic compound: 才 *cái* gives it the sound as well as contributes meaning as the word on its own means "ability or talents." Obviously, he, who has the talent for making money, would be wealthy. What then does it take to be poor, 貧 *pín* which is *huiyi zi*, a meaning compound? Take a close look at the top component; it is 分 *fēn*. We have deconstructed it already (***Justice is Solomon-like***), so we would not repeat the details here. It means "to separate" or "to divide." In other words, if whatever there is (by way of material possessions such as money or land) is divided into further portions, the resulting portions would naturally be smaller than the original amount. The person now holding one of these reduced portions would be poorer than he was before the division, when he held the whole lot. If the resulting smaller portion were in turn to be subdivided into further portions, the original owner of the whole smaller portion would be even poorer, after this second round of division, and so on. On this account of what it is to be poor, it seems to imply that the distribution of goods results in diminishing the size of the portion and one ends up with very little. It seems to us that this could reflect a theory of inheritance in a society which traditionally did not recognize primogeniture, but simply regarded all sons in the family as eligible to inherit. European societies, by and large, was based on primogeniture – the eldest son took all, which explains why in aristocratic families down the ages, other sons in the family had to find careers in the church or in the army. Primogeniture continues even today through the male line in the British aristocracy as far as inheriting most titles and property are concerned. (On the other hand, the British monarchy sticks to primogeniture, though not necessarily of the male, regarding succession to the throne.)

Naturally, characters/words relating to value have 貝 *bèi* as part of their construction. "To be valuable" or "expensive" is 贵/貴 *guì* and "to have little value or worth" is 贱/賤 *jiàn*.

Let us now go back to the character for "precious" 宝/寶 *bǎo* and look a little more closely at the *jianti* version (to the left of the slash). Note that of the two or possibly three items held to be precious originally, the number is now reduced to one, namely, 玉 *yù*. The rationale appears sound. As the ultimate aim of *jianti* is to reduce the number of strokes in a character, it is reasonable to retain only the bare minimum of items to convey its meaning. Of the three, clearly jade wins on both counts – it is universally regarded by the Chinese people to be beautiful, precious and "virtuous." The word is truly simple to write.

Silk was obviously a precious item, and we have seen that only the rich and the powerful could afford to wear silk, or indeed, were permitted to wear it. When silk got to, what today is called, the Middle East and then to Europe, it produced a similar reaction. There were rules and regulations governing its use in both the Roman and then the Islamic and Christian worlds. Christianity argued that it was sinful for women to wear silk; it was both immodest and decadent. Silk should, however, be used to wrap the holiest of relics. On the other hand, Islam forbade only men to wear silk. While infidel males wore them in this world, Muslim males were exhorted to wait till the next before garbing themselves in the luxurious sensuous fabric. As early as 638 CE, it was said that Caliph Omar (the second caliph) made a point himself of wearing patched clothes made out of coarse material as an example to his generals in Jerusalem whom he had criticized for wearing silk garments.

We have observed that although silk did not appear to be part of the "formal" list of precious objects recognized traditionally by the character 宝/寶 *bǎo*, it has not been entirely overlooked. The character for "currency" –币/幣 *bì* – is based on a general silk product, which is called 帛 *bó*. The bottom bit 巾 indicates that it is a silk-related thing and the top component 白 (today, pronounced *bái*) donates the sound. So it is *xingsheng zi*, a semantic-phonetic compound as well as *huiyi zi*, a meaning compound. It looks like this in its various (*jiaguwen, jinwen, xiaozhuan, lishu*) forms:

As this character exists already in *jiaguwen*, we can take it that silk and silk production were already established by Shang times.

The character for "currency" did not appear in *jiaguwen* but it occurs in *xiaozhuan* as you can see below, to the left of the *lishu* form:

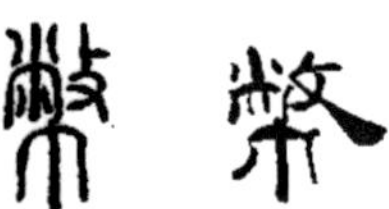

As already mentioned, Qin Shihuangdi abolished the currency based on cowrie shells and favored bronze coins, while silver ones became common in the Han Dynasty (206 BCE – 220 CE) which followed. As a matter of fact, gold as currency was already in existence well before the Qin and Han Dynasties, during the Warring States Period (475 – 221 BCE). By the Northern Song Dynasty (960 – 1127 CE), paper currency had appeared. However, the term 币/幣 *bì* originally did not mean "currency" but simply stood for precious objects (as it referred to silk products) which would make suitable offerings to gods and ancestors as well as gifts on especially grand occasions for very important people. So the use of the word to refer to currency is a derivative meaning.

To talk about silk, one must first talk about the silkworm and what it feeds on, the leaves from the mulberry tree. Silk, in zoological terms, is *Bombyx mori*. Today, the character for "silkworm" is 蚕/蠶 *cán*, but it already existed in *jiaguwen* as *xiangxing zi*, a pictograph. The *fanti* form (the version on the right of the slash) is based on the *xiaozhuan* version, and is *xingsheng zi*, a semantic-phonetic compound as well as *huiyi zi*, a meaning-compound The 虫 radical shows that the object referred to is a worm; the component above the two worms give the sound but also meaning, as it refers to the action of boring into something. In this context, it refers to the fact that these worms bury their heads into the mulberry leaves and chew away at them, first from the edge, munching their way towards the center of the leaves. In the history of the domestication of animals, the silk worm probably is one of the earliest, stretching back into the Neolithic period (ca. 8000 – 2000 BCE) in China.

The character for "mulberry plant" is 桑 *sāng*. Its various (*jiaguwen, xiaozhuan, lishu*) forms can be seen below:

In *jiaguwen*, it is *xiangxing zi*, a pictograph as it looks like a tree with roots, a trunk, branches, and leaves. In *xiaozhuan*, we can see three hands picking the mulberry leaves – it is *huiyi zi*, a meaning compound.

The picture on your left is an engraving from a Zhou bronze vessel illustrating the harvesting of the leaves. These leaves which the silkworms feed on are those of the white mulberry, a plant native to north China.

The long evolution of the characters relating to silk shows that, by Shang times, silk was already firmly established as an industry in the economy. Silk cultivation may even be traced further back into the

Neolithic Age itself – archaeological excavations in 1958 of a Neolithic site in Wuxing county, Zhejiang (浙江吴兴/吳興) Province uncovered a bamboo basket with the remains of a piece of raw silk fabric. This means that silk in China has a history of probably over five thousand years.

Naturally, such a long and distant history is bound to give rise to many legends about its origin. Here is one. Once upon a time, there was a widower with a young daughter who had a beautiful white horse. Unfortunately, he had to go away on business leaving her alone at home with only the horse for company. The girl longed for her father to return. In her loneliness, she talked to the horse and jokingly said to the animal that if it could bring her father back safely from distant parts, she would marry him. Upon hearing this promise, the horse bit loose the rope which tied him to the post and galloped off. Sure enough, a few days later, father came home on the horse. The animal, on seeing the girl, embraced her with joy. The father began to dislike the animal, and when daughter told him of her promise to marry the horse, he went into a rage, and struck the animal dead. He skinned it, laying the hide on the ground to dry. His daughter went to the field where the hide was. Suddenly the hide rolled itself up together with the girl in it and disappeared in a flash. The father could find no trace of them. Some time later, people found the hide with the girl still rolled up in it on a mulberry tree, munching the mulberry leaves and spewing forth silk threads, entwining the threads around themselves. "To entwine" or "to bind" is 缠/纏 *chán*; its sound is then given to the character for "silkworm" 蚕/蠶 *cán*. From then on, too, people regarded the mulberry as the tree of sorrow, as the love affair ended in sorrow. It is perhaps because mulberry is pronounced *sāng*, with the same sound as the character for "mourning the dead," 丧/喪 *sàng*. This is another instance of the Chinese passion for punning with words. The girl in the legend is called the Horse Head Maiden (马头/馬頭娘 *mǎ tóu niáng*). She is regarded in folklore as the goddess of silkworms, and every year offerings would be made to her.

Traditionally, women were in charge of the entire cottage industry in silk production, from the rearing of the worms, to the killing of the cocoons, the unravelling of the cocoon threads, to the spinning and the weaving of the threads finally into fabric. A single cocoon is capable of producing a continuous thread of up to nine hundred meters or three thousand feet long. Every stage of the process of production is arduous as well as requiring great skill in order to avoid spoiling.

The thread from the cocoon is no more than ten micrometers (or 1/2500 of an inch) in diameter. It is too fine for the purpose of weaving. Several of them have to be combined together to form a usable thread. It is this form of usable thread which is represented by the "silk" radical 纟/糸 ; you can see its various (the first three are *jiaguwen*, the next two *jinwen*, then *xiaozhuan, lishu*) forms below:

The character itself for "silk" is made up of two of these strands put together side by side; its various (the first two are *jiaguwen*, then *jinwen, xiaozhuan, lishu*) forms look like this:

They are all *xiangxing zi*, pictographs, except that in *lishu* the strand has become stylised.

What was the early model of a loom? Obviously, it was the simplest possible. It appears to be something that the weaver strapped round her waist at the top end in order to secure it, with the other end being put in place with her feet anchoring each side of the beam which held the warp, while her hands were busy with the shuttle. (The sketches below are from the Chinese translation of Cecelia Lindqvist's book, *Hanzi Wangguo*, 2007.)

This model is still used in certain remote parts of China today.

It seems curious to say that Chinese weaving is different in "philosophical" outlook from Western weaving. Of course, all weaving necessarily involves the warp which are the strands over and under which the other threads, that is, the weft (or woof) are passed when fabric is woven. Western weaving regards the weft to be more important as it determines the pattern ultimately produced in the material, while the warp is considered more like a kind of necessary but neutral backing, just as the canvass is the backing for tying the knots in rug-making. The Chinese perceive the matter differently. They regard the warp to be basic and foundational; the number of strands it constitutes must be determined and definitively settled at the start of the weaving. One cannot subtract or add a strand or two as one goes along, whereas in the case of the weft, there is some degree of flexibility for changing one's mind.

In Chinese, the warp is 经/經 *jīng* and the weft is 纬/緯 *wěi*. As you can see, *jing* is made up of the "silk" radical whose ancient forms we have already presented above, while its second component looks like this in *jinwen*:

The entire character for "warp" looks like this (also in *jinwen*):

This "philosophy" of weaving, which accords priority to the warp over the weft is transferred to other contexts, so that the word 经/經 *jīng* is used when something is considered as foundational and crucially important, to be revered and, therefore, precious such as in the case of canonical texts, the classics, which are 经书/經書 *jīngshū* – that is why Laozi's book about the *dao* is called by posterity 道德经/經 *Dàodé Jīng*, and why the *Book of Songs* is the 诗经/詩經 *Shī Jīng*. It is also used for religious texts or scriptures, and these are 圣经/聖經 *shèngjīng*.

As we have seen, for the Chinese, it is the warp which has to be rigorously adhered to. Hence, anything which is regular, invariably occurring is also 经/經, as in 经脉/經脈 *jīngmài*, which is a basic notion in Chinese medicine, referring to the system of pulse and blood as well as qi (气/氣) circulation in the body. Menstruation for healthy women of child-bearing age is as regular as the phases of the moon. That is why it is called 月经/經 *yuèjīng*, a matter to which we shall be returning in our exploration of another theme (***To know astronomy and geography is to know all***).

An interesting – much later – extension of the notions of warp and weft is to render "longitude" as 经/經度 *jīngdù* and "latitude" as 纬/緯度 *wĕidù*. The former reflects the north-south axis and the latter the east-west axis. The modern global system for determining longitude was established in 1884 by twenty five nations which agreed that the imaginary line drawn through Greenwich (outside London) would be the prime meridian. In other words, zero degree longitude starts at Greenwich; all other meridians are either to the east or the west of Greenwich, thereby dividing the globe into different longitudes and times zones. The sun rises in the east and sets in the west – hence times zones are established following the (apparent) passage of the sun from east to west. On the other hand, zero degree latitude begins at the equator with the other imagined latitudes either north or south of it. In the northern hemisphere, we know that when we face the sun, the east is to our left and the west is to our right. Imagine a weaver weaving silk, seated by the door, facing the sun, which would be the position occupied traditionally in China as the door of a house always opens to the south, to the sun – see ***To know astronomy and geography is to know all***. Naturally, it is also the place in the house which has the most light. Then the warp 经/經 *jīng* would be the threads running from north to south. The weft, in turn, would be the threads which run from east to west.

This book uses as metaphor the distinction between warp and weft to characterise the relationship between the Chinese language, in its written aspect, on the one hand, and Chinese culture and history, on the other. In one obvious sense, no such distinction can be made, as the language is embedded in and, therefore, part of the culture. Yet it does not appear absurd to insist upon the distinction. What justification is there then for saying that the written language is the warp, 经/經 *jīng* while the culture and the history constitute the weft, 纬/緯 *wĕi*? Why privilege the language, claiming that it is more fundamental than the culture and the history? Paradoxically, the justification lies in Chinese history itself. Like the weft, which introduces patterns and colors into the weaving, Chinese history and culture, since its earliest tribal beginnings in Neolithic times, are a rich mosaic of very different strands, each bringing its own stories, its own cultural specificities to contribute to what, today, we call Chinese history and culture. The whole is a veritable kaleidoscope of cultural and historical encounters which, over the millennia, have coalesced and become what looks, on the surface, to be a tightly woven fabric. However, it is not impossible to separate out and identify some of the different strands, even today, in spite of the passage of time. Indeed, sometimes archaeological finds throw up unexpected turns of which scholars attempt to make sense. In historical times, let us not forget that two major Chinese dynasties were non-Han in origin – the Yuan Dynasty (1279 – 1368 CE) which was relatively short-lived and the Qing Dynasty (1644 – 1911 CE) which lasted nearly two and a half centuries. The former was Mongol, the latter Manchu.

Yet in spite of all these different cultural and historical highways and byways, what remains constant is the written word. This, however, should not be interpreted to mean that there have been no changes to the written language. Part II has shown some of the major evolutions. Even though *jiaguwen* was lost to Chinese culture and history for more than three thousand years, yet, as we have seen, scholars have been able to make a good deal of sense of that earlier writing, and to show that it shares with later developments the same six principles of formation and use (六书/書 *liùshū*), which guided Xu Shen when he drew up his dictionary towards the end of the first century CE. When *jiaguwen* re-appeared right at the beginning of the twentieth century, scholars were able to decipher it in general (though not all the characters) only because of this underlying continuity. Without it, no sense could have been made.

However, it is important to point out that deciphering *jiaguwen* is not analogous to deciphering Egyptian hieroglyphs, engraved on the Rosetta Stone, by scholars such as Jean-François Champollion (1790 – 1832) in the early decades of the nineteenth century. By a quirk of bureaucratic history, the same text was carved in two different languages, Egyptian and Greek, and three different scripts: Greek (because it was the language of the ruling class in Egypt at the time the Stone was engraved in 196 BCE), Egyptian hieroglyphic (used for religious or important documents) as well as Egyptian demotic (used in common communication). Egyptian demotic first appeared about 650 BCE and survived as a spoken language till about 500 CE. However, it used not Egyptian hieroglyphs but a script not unlike the Arabic script. The Coptic language is a dialect or descendant of Egyptian demotic, although unlike its forebear, it is written in the Greek alphabet. Luckily, Champollion knew Greek and some Coptic.

This knowledge enabled him eventually to work back to the Egyptian hieroglyphs and the Egyptian demotic, finding equivalents between the various scripts and languages, aided by some inspired educated guesses. If Ptolemy V's decree had been carved only in Egyptian hieroglyphs, deciphering it would have then been impossible.

In the case of *jiaguwen*, unlike that of the Rosetta Stone, no help was available nor needed from external linguistic sources. What helped, as we have seen, was that scholars who knew *jinwen*, recognized straightaway certain characters in *jiaguwen*. It was primarily the continuity of the written tradition which enabled scholars to make sense of *jiaguwen*, and make it yield fascinating details about the history and cultural life in the late Shang Dynasty.

It seems, then, appropriate to privilege the written language over the culture and the history in this context, and to regard the former as the warp, 经/經 *jīng* and the latter as the weft, 纬/緯 *wěi*. Such a view, however, should not be taken to imply that the weft (Chinese history and culture) is not important. Warp and weft are both essential and integral to the weaving process and to its products – they are inextricably linked. It is just that without the continuity of the Chinese character/word, the Chinese people today would not be able to have as much access to their long history – cultural artifacts on their own without a text do give posterity some information but not perhaps as much as when they are accompanied by texts which could be deciphered and understood. For instance, scholars might speculate that the tortoise shells and the ox shoulder blades could have played a role in some religious ceremony in Shang times, but they would not be certain that they were used for divination in the absence of the *jiaguwen* text. Furthermore, without the characters/words carved on them, there would have been no way of knowing the contents of the divination, and hence, the details of existence in the late Shang court.

It is almost as if the Chinese people down the ages have an inherent fascination for the written word. Whenever an appropriate occasion arose, they would commit their sentiments and their thoughts as well as their accounts of selected events to writing, preferably using the most lasting media available to them, such as stone, rocks, shells and bones, metal. In the Song Dynasty, scholars were already worried that the stone text engravings of their ancestors might perish if they were not properly conserved – to this end, they collected as many of them as they could. Today, in Xi'an is the Stone Stelae Museum or the Museum of the Forest of Stone Tablets (part of the Provincial Museum of Shaanxi, 陕西) which is devoted entirely to such inscriptions. This collection has a history of nearly a thousand years, as its origin can be dated to 1087 in the Song Dynasty. The oldest items in the museum have a history of two thousand or more years, although the earliest core of the collection was Tang (618 – 907 CE) engravings, to which were added later Jin (265 – 420 CE), Song (960 – 1279 CE), Yuan, Ming (1368 – 1644 CE) and Qing stelae.

For the Chinese people, cultural transmission via the written word appears crucial, even obsessive, in contrast to some other cultures, such as Indian, which appear to value more the oral tradition. The Indo-Aryans crossed into India in 1700 BCE from Afghanistan but whose forebears were probably Persian in origin. They brought with them their Vedic (religious) hymns; some passages of the oldest Vedic literature might have been composed by 1700 BCE, but it was orally transmitted and was probably not written down till the first millennium CE in what today is called Vedic Sanskrit. However, the oldest surviving written Vedic texts are mostly from the second millennium CE. Of the two great (post Vedic) epics, the *Mahabharata* began to take shape orally between 400 and 300 BCE, but was not written down till several centuries later around 400 CE in post-Vedic Sanskrit. The *Ramayana*, the other epic, was composed later than the *Mahabharata*, between the second or third century CE and was not committed to writing till even later. The earlier Buddhist scriptures were written first in Pali, probably about four hundred years after the death of the Buddha himself; the consensus in recent scholarship on the death of the Buddha puts it twenty years either side of 400 BCE. These Pali texts were written, however, in Sri Lanka; the later scriptures were written in Sanskrit. However, Buddhism did not, in the end, maintain itself as a dominant religion in continental India, in spite of about one thousand five hundred years of presence, from its beginning in the middle of the first millennium BCE to the beginning of the second millennium CE. Pali, a vernacular, declined towards the latter part of the first millennium CE, with the decline of Buddhism itself. Sanskrit, an Indo-European language, appeared about 1500 BCE, becoming dominant after Panini, the great Sanskrit grammarian, produced his grammar of the language about 400 BCE. It reached its height as the language of the elite during the fifth and sixth century CE. However, as the emphasis was more on the oral tradition, Sanskrit could be written in almost any script available in India. There was just no one prescribed script for writing the Vedic hymns and stories, all depended on the scribes, using their own preferred regional scripts.

Before the arrival of the Indo-Aryans from today's Afghanistan, India had a Neolithic culture (from 7000 BCE, if not earlier) which eventually morphed into the Harappan civilization. This Indus valley civilization may be divided into two periods: early (ca. 3500 – 2600 BCE) and mature (ca. 2700 – 2400 BCE). Excavations have found some seals with inscriptions, which unfortunately, so far, remain undeciphered. As a result, scholars have not been able to tell us as much as we would like to know about the Harappan civilization.

In ancient India, there was no equivalent of a Qin Shihuangdi to unify the sub-continent, and then to impose linguistic uniformity. In more modern times, Mughul rule in India (1526 – 1858 CE) did introduce, for the first time, a single administrative language, but that was Persian, a foreign language. When British rule was later established (1757 – 1947), English (another foreign language) was used as the official language. India, today, has two official languages: Hindi and English. While the former is comfortably accepted in north India, this is not so in the rest of the country. On the other hand, English is happily endorsed by all the major linguistic groups, being seen to be neutral. Furthermore, given the recent history involving the partition of the sub-continent into India and Pakistan, Hindi and Urdu (the official language of Pakistan) are linguistically too uncomfortably similar for Hindi to be seen as a distinctive language of the new India. Ironically, then, English, the language of India's last colonial master, has become firmly established not merely as an official language, but also the language of choice of the elite and the educated.

In contrast, when the Manchus ruled China during the Qing Dynasty, Manchu and Chinese were officially used. Furthermore, the Qing emperors felt it politically imperative to school themselves thoroughly in the Chinese language, culture and history. This major period of foreign rule in China did not basically disrupt the continuity of the written Chinese language (indeed in any other aspects of the Han language) or undermine its status, in the long run, in the country, either socially or educationally. For instance, the traditional civil service examinations continued, based on the same canonical texts, on calligraphy and other aspects of Chinese literature, language and philosophy. In the Qing Dynasty, success in it remained a necessary requirement for Han candidates to be considered for official appointments, though not, however, for appointees of Manchu stock.

However, during the Yuan Dynasty, the Mongol rulers at first suppressed the traditional examinations and, when these were restored in 1315, they were no longer the only means to official appointments as they had been in the past. The Mongol rulers were suspicious of the Chinese scholar-officials class; they barred native Chinese from certain top positions in government service. All the same, Kubilai Khan (the grandson of Genghis Khan who ascended the Dragon throne), in the end, restored and adopted many traditional Chinese practices; he even educated his second son in the Confucian tradition. On the linguistic front, a Tibetan monk, who became the Khan's confidante and adviser, had developed an alphabetic script called *Basiba* (*Phags-Pa*, the name of the monk), 八思巴, which could be used not only to write Mongolian but also the very many different languages throughout the Mongol Empire, stretching from China in the east to parts of Europe in the west. For instance, in the case of Tibet, imperial decrees and seals were done in *Hanzi* as well as in Tibetan written in *Basiba*. However, in spite of imperial promotion, its use on a popular scale did not take off and was confined to official texts and documents.

This brief discussion of some major differences between the respective histories and cultures of India and China may justify the claim that the history of Chinese civilization might not have taken the route it did but for the continuity of the written tradition, even through the vicissitudes of two major periods of foreign rule. Furthermore, it survived the tumultuous events that China lived through in the last two hundred years and in spite of the various attempts in the first half of the twentieth century to "modernize" it through Latinization. China in the end did not go down that route which Turkey did in 1928 under Ataturk. Turkey, India, and China have each adopted different paths in response to the dominance of European and other powers in the nineteenth and twentieth centuries. For all these reasons, it is not unreasonable to suggest that the written character/word is the warp in the context of Chinese civilization and Chinese history.

The character for "silk," as we have shown earlier above, is 丝/絲, and is pronounced *sī*. This sound has given the word for "silk" to Latin, as *serica*, which later evolved to *soie* in French and then "silk" in English. *Serica* was also a term used in the past to refer to China, the land from which silk products came. Unfortunately, often, the ancient geographers and writers themselves were none too clear as to where and what exactly was the land from which silk products came. Imagine the long land route or sea route by which the goods had to travel before arriving finally in Rome and other parts of Europe. Furthermore, remember that the trade itself was not, in the main, conducted by the Chinese themselves but by middlemen who ranged from the peoples living in what today is the Gobi desert (their countries and cities had long disappeared into the sands only to be uncovered at the beginning of the last century by European adventure archaeologists such as Sir Aurel Stein), to Persians, Armenians, Arabs, Jews, and others. As a result, ancient references to China (no matter the terms used) might not always be to China and the Chinese who produced the commodity, but perhaps to the middlemen of one kind or other, along the long Silk Route.

There are many views about the name "China" itself in Western languages. One holds that the word comes from 秦 *Qín*, either after the short-lived Qin Dynasty when Qin Shihuangdi unified the country or even earlier, after the state of Qin itself, which had existed long before its ruler in 221 BCE swallowed the other five rival states to form a much larger unified empire. The sound *qín* became distorted to sound like "chin" in the southern European countries or "kin" in the northern European ones. In Swedish, for instance, China is Kina. From the Song, Yuan, Ming and Qing Dynasties, Chinese porcelain became greatly appreciated in the West. The Yuan Dynasty was part of the greater Mongol rule of the time which stretched from China right across Asia to what today we call the Middle East. The western end of this vast empire included Islamic countries which the Mongols had also conquered. Celadon or *longquan* ware was an extremely popular export, followed by the blue and white porcelain whose creation and manufacture as a distinctive kind of ware was made possible by the import of cobalt from the western end of the Mongol empire into China itself. The sultans of the Ottoman Empire (ca.1300 – 1923), for instance, throughout the dynasty, which overlapped the Yuan, Ming and Qing Dynasties of China, were such enthusiasts of Chinese ceramics that the Ottoman collection is said to be the largest in the world after that housed, today, in the National Museum in Taipei, Taiwan. The sultans, like other Islamic rulers, had ordered to their own specifications. Part of the collection is on display in the Topkapi Palace Museum in Istanbul. So great was the reputation of Chinese ceramics in the West and elsewhere that the English call the clay from which the porcelain is made, "china clay," and all cups and plates made from clay, “china.” In these convoluted ways, the word “china” has entered profoundly the English language.

We have discussed briefly some of the things which the Chinese people traditionally regarded as truly precious. If they were asked to name only two objects, perhaps, many might be tempted to mention, on the one hand, the classics in the various fields of knowledge and, on the other, jade. Why not put that question to your Chinese friends? It would be interesting to have their response.

末

To know astronomy and geography is to know all

There is an expression from the classical texts: 上 知天文,下知地理 *shàng zhī tiānwén, xià zhī dìlǐ*, which loosely translated, says that all human knowledge is encompassed within astronomy and geography. To know what there is to be known about what happens in the sky above and what happens on earth below is to know everything, especially if one also knows the relationship between astronomical phenomena, on the one hand, and terrestrial phenomena, on the other. Even more important, if one also knows the place of humans within this web of natural relationships between heaven and earth, then one would not simply be a walking encyclopedia but wise. This, in a nutshell, is Chinese cosmology and Chinese philosophy.

What did the ancient Chinese know about astronomy? Let us begin by telling you a story about China’s first astronomer 阏伯 E Bo and his observatory, the earliest in China, it is often claimed. He lived about four thousand years ago. It is said that he was born from an egg in the river in which his mother was bathing. He helped the great Yu (in the Xia Dynasty ca. 21st – 16th century BCE) to control the floods of the Yellow River. He established the first observatory in Henan Province, not to mention the lunar calendar to determine the times for planting and harvesting as well as the twenty four divisions of the year. (On the latter, there are more details later.) Upon his death, people honored him as a god. Today his temple (called E Bo Tai 阏/閼伯/台臺 or Huo Shen Miao 火神庙/廟) in Henan Province dates from the Yuan Dynasty (1279 – 1368 CE). Legend has it that he was buried in the site of the temple. Archaeologists recently have excavated it but they found no burial; however, they did find a lot of pot shards belonging to the Spring and Autumn Period (770 – 476 BCE of the Zhou Dynasty), which shows that the cult of honoring him had already begun, then if not earlier. He was guided by his study of the passage in the sky of the star, Antares (which the ancient Chinese called 大火星 *dàhuǒxīng*) in the Scorpio Constellation (心宿 *xīn xiǔ*), to help him draw up the lunar calendar and determine its main features.

Actually, according to archaeologists, the earliest observatory (for which there is material evidence) is probably not E Bo's. The honor of being China's oldest known astronomical observatory (and probably one of the world's earliest such sites) is a Neolithic burial site, first excavated in 1958, belonging to the late Neolithic Longshan Culture (龙/龍山文化, ca. 2300 – 1900 BCE) at Taosi in Shanxi Province (山西陶寺). However, in 2005, Chinese archaeologists announced that they have identified a structure on the site which points to it being a solar observatory. Another Neolithic burial and astronomical site is even dated earlier to about 4300 BCE, excavated in 1987 at Xishuipo, Puyang in Henan Province (河南濮阳/陽西水泼/潑), belonging to the Yangshao Culture (ca. 5000 – 3000 BCE). One of the graves, in particular, has preserved intact, details in the burial arrangement, which bear cosmological and astronomical significance.

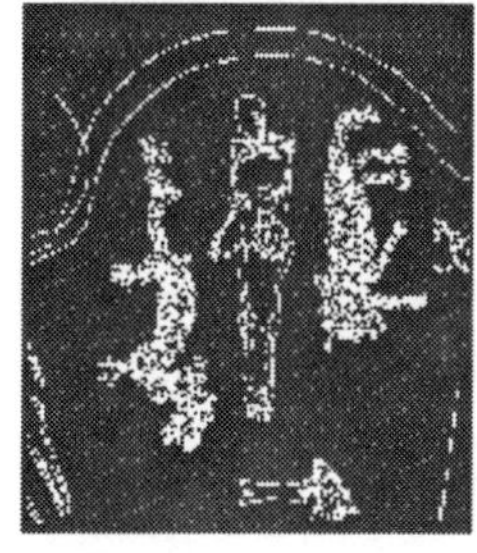

The body, probably that of a tribal chief or even shaman/astronomer, was laid out in such a way that the southern face above the head was round while the northern face at the foot of the body was square. This is entirely in conformity with Chinese cosmology which held that Heaven was round and Earth square. Flanking the body to the east is the outline in white mussel shells of the dragon, and to the west that of the tiger. These referred to constellations in the Chinese sky. The Northern Ladle or the Big Dipper (北斗星 *běidǒuxīng*) was represented, pointing towards the head of the dragon. After carbon 14 as well as tree ring date-testing, the consensus is that the tomb arrangement appears to be a representation of the Chinese sky at the time of the burial, nearly 6500 years ago. All this suggests that the Yangshao people were knowledgeable about astronomy, at least, to the extent that they were attempting to orientate the tomb in accordance with the annual revolution of the Big Dipper around the North Star.

The ancient Chinese did not tumble to the fact that the earth revolved around the sun, although it is said that an astronomer in the Han Dynasty (206 BCE – 220 CE) knew that the earth moves, but he said that people just do not feel it move: "they are as persons in a closed boat; when it proceeds they do not perceive it." All the same, they had a fairly good grasp of the relationship between Earth and Sun. This understanding can be seen in their notion of time. Time in the West is measured in terms of "something" which happens on earth – in biological terms, we are born, we grow, we mature, and finally we die. We "know" that time has passed because the last time we looked at ourselves in the mirror, our skin was taut and firm, our hair was brown, blonde, or black. Today what we see in the mirror is someone with wrinkles on the face, and strands of white hair on the head. Another measurement of time is in terms of cause – we light a candle at the beginning of the meal, but towards the end of the meal, we find either that the candle has burnt down to its stump or even died out completely. A lit candle does not grow longer as it burns but shorter.

The ancient Chinese measured, and therefore, understood time somewhat differently. For them, the passage of time is primarily an astronomical matter. It is about the (apparent) motion of the sun. We can see this very clearly in the *jiaguwen* version of the character for "time" shown below:

The bottom component is the character for "sun" 日; the top component is the character for 之 which means "moving about." The character/word then really refers to the (apparent) motion of the sun, or the sun's passage across the sky. Scholars hold this to be *xingsheng zi*, a semantic-phonetic compound (with the top component donating the sound, and the bottom giving the meaning) as well as *huiyi zi*, a meaning compound (the top component contributes also to the meaning as it implies movement).

In *xiaozhuan* (first below) and *lishu* (second), there has been a change in the construction of the character.

時 時

But in *jianti* today, it is simplified to: 时 *shí*.

In the account we are about to give, ignore the *jianti* version but concentrate on the other two versions given in *xiaozhuan* and *lishu*. There are two ways of looking at them. The first simply says that it is *xingsheng zi*, a semantic-phonetic compound. The radical for "sun" 日 *rì* on the left obviously shows that the word is connected with the sun and its activity. The second component on the right 寺 *sì* (which today means "temple," though not in ancient times) contributes the sound. The character/word refers basically then to ceremonies to mark the seasons – at each season, the king or emperor must perform certain rites to welcome the spring, to thank heaven for the harvest, etc.

However, there is another interpretation, a more interesting and complicated analysis. If you look again at those versions carefully, you will find that the character has three components, not two. These are: the "sun" radical 日 *rì* on the left; the top component on the right is the character for "earth or the ground" 土 *tŭ*; the bottom component on the right is for " unit of measurement," which refers to the Chinese inch, 寸 *cùn*. The use of the "sun" radical shows that the notion, like that of *jiaguwen*, has something to do with the sun – that much seems clear. But the two components on the right, what can they be telling us? What they are telling us is that time is measured (on earth) in terms of the motion of the sun (or in today's correct astronomical language after the Copernican Revolution, the apparent motion of the sun) in the course of the day as well as in the course of a year across the heavens. In other words, this new construction introduces two innovations: the character for "earth" or "ground" as well as that for "unit of measurement." These in turn bring out two further points: first that the notion of time since *jiaguwen* had come to be understood not simply as an astronomical matter (about the movement of the sun) but also an astronomical matter which involves the earth. That is to say, it is both an astronomical as well as a terrestrial matter, as the sun's (apparent) movements are related to the earth and could be ascertained on earth. Second, the new construction embodies a technique for measuring the motion of the sun. An early astronomical text 周髀算经/經 *Zhou Bi Suan Jing*, translated sometimes as *The Arithmetical Classic of the Zhou Gnomon and the Circular Paths of the Heavens,* dated ca. 100 BCE – 100 CE mentions, amongst other things, such a technique.

What then is this technique and what sort of instrument did the ancient Chinese use to measure the passage of time? The instrument is the gnomon, called 碑 *bēi* or 表 *biǎo*. In its simplest form, it is nothing but a long pole whose length varied from ten Chinese feet in the early period, then to eight over a very long period of more than a thousand years, before reverting to ten in the Qing Dynasty (1644 – 1911 CE) with the arrival of Jesuit astronomers at the Qing court. This was firmly planted in the ground. In setting up the gnomon, care must be taken to ensure that the pole was absolutely straight and that the ground was absolutely horizontal. To get the latter right, even before Han times, the astronomers looked at the level of water in a bowl. Before the Tang Dynasty (618 – 907 CE), they used to tie eight cords from the top of the pole forming four angles and stretching to four points on the ground, so that they faced one another exactly. In the course of the day, from sunrise to sunset as the sun shone on the pole, the ancient Chinese astronomers would notice that the pole cast a shadow on the ground. In *jiaguwen*, the gnomon looks like this:

It shows a hand holding what looks like a pole with the sun behind it. Other *jiaguwen* characters look like this:

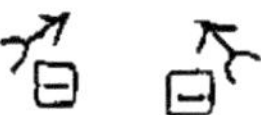

They show the sun and a person's shadow at different angles in the course of the day.

The shadow got shorter and shorter as the sun rose higher and higher in the heavens until at noon or round about noon, the shadow was at its shortest; but after the sun had reached the zenith at noon, the shadow would correspondingly get longer and longer as the afternoon wore on. At sunrise and at sunset, one would mark the shadows cast by the pole. If one were to join up the two markings, one would get the east-west direction. (Scholars have pointed out that the *Book of Songs* 诗经/詩經 *Shi Jing*, of the early or Western Zhou Dynasty, ca. 11th century – 770 BCE, already mentions how to determine the east-west direction.) If one drew the shortest line from the base of the pole to the east-west line, this would point to the north (in the northern hemisphere).

By measuring the length of the sun's shadow each day, in the course of the year, the ancient Chinese astronomers would also have noticed that the shadows measured differently, and were thus able to determine the solstices which by Shang times were called *zhì* (至). This shows that as early as the Shang Dynasty (ca. 16th – 11th century BCE), the ancient Chinese knew about the summer and winter solstices (夏至 *xiàzhì* and 冬至 *dōngzhì*). The ancient Chinese also worked out the spring equinox, 春分 *chūnfēn* (around 1100 BCE) and the autumn equinox, 秋分 *qiūfēn* (*fen*, in this context, refers to the fact that day and night are equally divided). In *The Spring and Autumn Annals and the Tradition of the Zuo Commentary* (*Chunqiu Zuo Zhuan*, a chronicle of events in the state of Lu, during the Spring and Autumn Period), there is a passage, which refers not only to the solstices, but also to the equinoxes.

To observe the shadow of the pole and to measure it, the Chinese used a measuring tablet called the 土圭 *tǔguī*. This device is as ancient as the gnomon, as it is also mentioned in the *Zhou Li* (周礼/禮 *The Rites of Zhou*, probably dated to the third century BCE) and the *Kao Gong Ji* (考工记/記, *The Manual of Crafts*, which was the first important official book detailing the arts and crafts industries, such as leatherwork, metalwork, dyes, carpentry, pottery, and scraping in ancient China, dated to the latter part of the Spring and Autumn Period). In reality, the ancient astronomers only measured the shadow for the summer solstice as it would be somewhat inconvenient to measure the much longer shadow in the winter. The astronomers simply calculated the date of the winter solstice rather than use observational data to determine it. The Chinese believed that the shadow of a gnomon of eight Chinese feet at the summer solstice would diminish by a (Chinese) inch for every thousand Chinese miles as one moved southwards, and that it increased by an inch for every thousand miles as one moved towards the north.

However, the *tugui* was a very imprecise instrument. Astronomers throughout the Han Dynasty were not too happy with it. By Eastern Han times (25 – 220 CE), it was no longer a serious astronomical instrument but a kind of ceremonial object, made of jade and worn as a marker of rank amongst the aristocracy, so that they could "play" at being astronomers.

Finally, by the end of the fifth or beginning of the sixth century CE, the idea of casting an instrument in bronze combining the *biao* with the *tugui* took shape, with the addition of a water-level device for ascertaining that the instrument be placed in an absolutely horizontal position on the ground – it was called 圭表 *guībiǎo*.

There is an expression which implicitly refers to the two solstices: 立竿见/見影 *lì gān jiàn yǐng*. At the summer solstice, the sun is at its zenith over the Tropic of Cancer, and that is why the northern hemisphere enjoys its longest hours of sunlight. The reverse obtains at the winter solstice when the sun is at its zenith over the Tropic of Capricorn, and that is why the northern hemisphere is exposed to the shortest hours of sunlight or daylight. At the summer solstice, at noon, the pole casts no shadows at the Tropic of Cancer, but at the winter solstice, the pole would cast the longest shadow in the northern hemisphere. The latter context serves as a metaphor which amounts to saying that a certain measure or action taken is immediately effective.

To understand the measurements, we need to give a very brief account of the three main units of measurement used here: 寸、尺、丈 *cùn, chǐ, zhàng*. Chinese measurements are based on parts of the body. To cut a long story short, the *cun* appears to be equivalent to the width of the second, lower joint of the middle finger of the (average male) hand, that is, about 23 mm or just under an inch (0.905). The *chi* is equivalent to ten *cun* (this is also sometimes given as eight *cun*, depending on the historical period); and the *zhang* to ten *chi*. As the exact conversion to today's equivalents can be problematic, we shall just leave the measurements in traditional Chinese units. In the course of the year, the shortest shadow is 一尺六寸 *yīchǐ liùcùn* (one *chi* and six cun), the longest shadow is 一丈三尺五寸 *yī zhàng sān chǐ wǔ cùn* (one *zhang*, three *chi* and five *cun*). It is obvious that the former would occur during the summer solstice, and the latter during the winter solstice. (Here is a very rough conversion guide: one *zhang* either equals just over 2 m or 6 feet thereabouts.)

The ancient Chinese understood the notions of day, month and year in the following ways. A day is marked primarily by the rising of the sun, then its setting until its next rising. "A day" is 一日 *yī rì*, *ri* being also a character/word for "sun." A month is based on the cycles of the moon – hence "month" is 月 *yuè*, *yue* being the character/word for "moon." A year is based on the passing of the seasons and the changes they bring such as the length and strength of the sunlight as well as on the observation and measurements of the sun's position at different times of the day and on different days of the year as discussed just above. The ancient Chinese did not divide the year into twelve months but twenty four different periods (二十四节气/節氣 *èr shí sì jié·qi*), each period roughly of fifteen days, reflecting changes in temperature, humidity, rainfall, in general, weather conditions which, in the main, dictated the rhythm of agricultural activities.

The ancient astronomers, it appears, began to construct a calendar based on the revolution of the moon around the earth, as long ago as the Xia Dynasty. They decided on a system of twelve lunar months. This system suited better the needs of an agricultural society. That is why the Chinese called their calendar 农历 / 農歷 *nónglì*, the agricultural calendar or 阴历/陰歷 *yīnlì*, the *yin* calendar, as according to *yinyang* philosophy, the moon is *yin* whereas the sun is *yang*. The start of the lunar year is based on the cycles of the moon. Each lunar month is 29.5 days. Such a year works out to have only 354 or 355 days. On the other hand, the ancient Chinese knew that the year has more days than the twelve lunar months, based on their observations and measurements of the sun's passage across the heavens, as we have indicated above. They already knew this by around 484 BCE during the Zhou Dynasty (ca. 11th century – 221 BCE).

By 104 BCE, the astronomers had calculated the year to be 365.2502 days. By 480 CE, the astronomer Zu Chongzhi 祖冲之(shown on the left) had further refined that calculation to 365.2428 days as compared to the modern value of 365.2422 days. This shows that the fifth century CE astronomer's calculation was out only by 53 seconds. Quite a feat, one must admit.

The known discrepancy between the number of days in the twelve lunar months and the number of days in the year, thus, presented a problem to the Chinese astronomers. Their solution lay in adding an extra month every two to three years, to have seven leap months within nineteen years, or another way of putting it, to have two hundred and thirty five lunar months in nineteen years. For this reason the traditional Chinese calendar is strictly speaking not a simple lunar calendar but what may be called a luni-solar one. The solar calendar which is in global use today adds an extra day to February in years evenly divisible by four (that is, as a general rule, every four years). Both calendars have leap months or days, but they work out differently in the two systems. (Regarding the Western calendar, it was Julius Caesar who first introduced in 46 CE the notion of the leap day. However, the Julian calendar chose to have two 24th February, with these two days counting as one single day legally speaking, instead of adding an extra day, 29th February, an arrangement, according to the Gregorian calendar, with which we are familiar.)

To some up, for the Chinese, time was measured in terms of the (apparent) motion of the sun as determined on earth. This explains, in the very construction of the character for "time," the presence of the respective characters *ri* for "sun," *tu* for "ground" as well as *cun* for "inch" (as every unit of difference in the length of the shadow constitutes a unit of the passage of time). We have seen that the ancient Chinese had divided the year not into twelve months but twenty four *jieqi*. The early astronomical text, *Zhou Bi Suan Jing* (周髀算经/經), mentioned above, had calculated that for every *jieqi* of fifteen days, the shadow cast by the gnomon of eight (Chinese) feet would have either lengthened (counting from the summer solstice) or shortened (counting from the winter solstice) by 九寸九分六分分之一, almost one Chinese foot.

There is a text, the *Liezi* 列子, which some scholars say contain material as early as the fifth to the first century BCE, but which was stitched together with other material towards the end of third century CE. Others, however, simply put it as a late text about the third century CE. It is Daoist in origin and inspiration with a tone generally mocking of Confucius and his teachings. It contains a charming story about Confucius and two small children regarding the perceived distance between the sun and the earth in the course of the day. One day, Confucius was traveling east, probably, to give lessons (he was always on the move, going to wherever his teaching would be welcomed by a receptive audience). On the way, he met two children sitting by the roadside, hotly disputing something between themselves. The subject of discussion centered on the question at what time of day the sun was nearest the earth and at what time it was furthest away. One child held that naturally the sun was nearest in the morning, but further away at noon, as in the early morning the sun looked so much bigger than later in the day. Surely, what was larger was nearer, while what was smaller was further away. The second child held the opposite. In the early morning, the sun was not as hot but at midday, it really burnt; surely, the hotter the sun, the nearer it must be. They saw this kindly looking sage coming along and approached him to arbitrate the matter. When Confucius heard the issue under dispute, he scratched his head, thought about it but could not pronounce a verdict. The children were not well pleased. They told him: you are supposed to be a learned man, a know-all. Why can't you answer our question as to who is right? Ah, so even you are ignorant about certain things. This story may be entirely apocryphal, but it meant to say that Confucius knew no astronomy and, more damningly, appeared not to be interested in the subject either. This tale is often cited to make the point that Confucius was too preoccupied with social and moral matters to bother much with the investigation of natural phenomena.

Today, "hour" in Chinese is 小时/時 *xiǎoshí*. *Shi* is just a unit of time – a smaller unit of time or a larger unit of time. Today, the 24-hours clock is used throughout the world, including China. However, traditionally in China, the day was divided into twelve different units or *shi*, each unit covered two hours of the 24-hours system. That is why in modern Chinese, an hour is *yi xiaoshi*; the emphasis is on *xiao*, meaning "small." As for *shi*, as a unit of time in the context of a whole year, the Chinese talk about 四时/時 *sìshí*; and here, *shi* refers to the four seasons – these are 春 *chūn* (spring), 夏 *xià* (summer), 秋 *qiū* (autumn), 冬 *dōng* (winter).

It may surprise the reader to learn that originally the Chinese – up to the Eastern or second half of the Zhou Dynasty (770 – 221 BCE) – officially named only two seasons, spring and autumn, not four. The other two were not formally labelled. This might not be as strange as it looks at first sight. In an agricultural society, the two really important times in the year are the time for planting and the time for harvesting – this would be spring time, and autumn time. If you did not plant at the right season, there would be little or no harvest. In between the sowing and the gathering in of what you have sown, nature, by and large, provided the conditions for crops to grow, courtesy of the greater heat and light from the sun at the onset of spring to the end of summer. In classical Chinese, the expression 春秋 *chūnqiū* literally meaning "spring and autumn," actually stands for a whole year – every spring which passes, every autumn which passes amounts to a year passing by. Hence, that famous classic called <春秋> *Chunqiu*, said to have been edited by Confucius, is actually the annals of the Lu state (鲁国/國), a country where Confucius found himself at that stage of his life. Chinese historians then referred to that period of Chinese history as the Spring and Autumn Period, 春秋时/時 代.

The various forms of the character 春 *chūn* ("spring") are shown below: the first two are *jiaguwen*, the third *jinwen*, followed by *xiaozhuan*, then *lishu*.

In the forms above, except for *lishu* which has become stylised, one can see the following components: “sun” in some form of 日 is common to them. In *jinwen* and *xiaozhuan*, one can see this symbol 屮, which stands for the very first small shoot breaking through the soil as if with considerable effort. Again in *jinwen* and *xiaozhuan*, one can see very clearly the sign 艸 which is the archaic radical for “grass” or “plant,” on the top of the character. It is obvious what the character/word 春 *chūn* is trying to convey. It is that spring is the season when the sun gets stronger, sunlight hours get longer, the general temperature rises, vegetation starts to stir and plants begin to grow.

The various (*jiaguwen, jinwen, xiaozhuan, lishu*) forms of the character for “autumn” 秋 *qiū* are shown below:

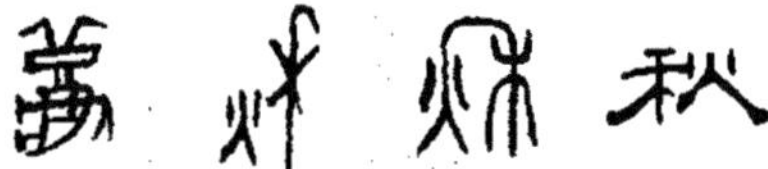

In *jiaguwen*, it is *xiangxing zi*, a pictograph of a cricket. Cricket, for the ancient Chinese, is an insect associated with autumn and the onset of winter. With the drop in temperature in October, as we have mentioned (***Surviving and living***), according to the *Book of Songs* (*Shi Jing*), the insect moved indoors. It also grows wings on its back, and develops an organ for making chirping noises which sound a bit like *qiu*. The character in *jinwen* and the other two versions, which follow, is written in a totally different way from *jiaguwen*: it has two components. In *jinwen* and *xiaozhuan*, on the left is the character for 火 *huǒ* (“fire”), while on the right, is that for 禾 *hé*, “cereal” (a character/word we have come across already). In *lishu* the two components have been swapped round, a form which remains to this day in *kaishu* or the Standard script. This new construction shows that the character is now *huiyi zi*, a meaning compound. There are various related ways of understanding it. The most obvious is that 火 *huǒ* refers to the sun’s heat which is required to ripen the cereal before they are ready for harvesting, and autumn is the harvest season – in fact harvesting used to start right at the beginning of autumn (called 立秋 *lìqiū* which, in the traditional calendar, is the seventh day of the eighth lunar month). The character/word also seems to refer to the fact that a field of ripening cereal makes a golden vista, as if the whole countryside is on fire. Yet another way of looking at the significance of 火 *huǒ* is to say that the beginning of autumn marks the peak in the amount of heat stored in the soil of the earth or in the atmosphere. It is not at the beginning of summer that heat is at its maximum; heat and its absorption take the whole summer to build up to a peak. If this is a plausible interpretation, it would mean that the ancient Chinese had a good grasp of the physics of heat in the general environment and its relationship to the strength and length of sunlight in the course of the year. This way of understanding the presence of the heat or fire component in the construction of the character is ultimately also related to how Chinese medicine understands the seasons.

If two seasons, 春 and 秋 *chūn* and *qiū*, spring and autumn, make up the year, let us next see what the character for "year" has in store for us – it is 年 *nián*. We have already said something about the notion above though not about the character itself. Its various (the first two are *jiaguwen*, the next two *jinwen*, followed by *xiaozhuan*, then *lishu*) forms may be seen below:

The *jiaguwen* and *jinwen* versions (first four from the left) have two components with the character for "cereal" 禾 *hé* on top and that for "human being" under it looking like this. It seems to depict an abundant harvest – the farmer being laden with the harvest, humping it all the way back to his home. If so, then it is *huiyi zi*, a meaning compound. In north China, there was only one harvest in very early times. So, one harvest was equivalent to one year. By *xiaozhuan*, the top component 禾 *hé* is retained, but the bottom component is changed to 千 which turns the character into *xingsheng zi*, a semantic-phonetic compound. By *lishu*, the character has become so stylised that the information contained in the earlier versions has got lost.

Traditionally, the Chinese year or the New Year begins at the planting season, that is, spring, as the old year would have ended. Today in China, though not necessarily everywhere in the world where Chinese people can be found, the New Year is no longer officially called 新年 *Xīn Nián*, but 春节/節 *Chūn Jié*, the Spring Festival. This is a return to an ancient custom and tradition, as the lunar New Year started at 立春 *lìchūn*, the beginning of spring. On the eve of this day, a ceremony would be performed at court in which an ox (used normally to pull the plow) would be brought into the palace and struck with a whip, to symbolise "whipping spring into shape." On the day itself, there would be banqueting as well as special foods for the occasion. Ordinary people would celebrate too in ways to be described in detail a little later. The practice of calling such a festival the New Year celebrations and no longer 春节/節 *Chūn Jié* festivities emerged just after the Northern and Southern Dynasties (南北朝, 420 – 589 CE).

On the eve of the Spring Festival, just as on Christmas Eve for people in the West, members of the family would gather together to celebrate the new year. That is why it is best to avoid traveling in China at that time of year as every one posted and working within the four corners of China would be hurrying home for the celebrations. In north, though not so much in south China, one particular food, which is an all-time favorite, assumes even greater importance for this occasion, forming an indispensable part of the celebrations. It is called 饺/餃子 *jiǎo·zi*, a kind of dumpling. The entire family would gather around a table to make them – making *jiaozi* is a communal activity with lots of conversation and laughter accompanying it.

However, at this special time of year, its significance goes beyond mere communal merry-making. To understand what that significance is, we need, as usual, to look at how the character is constructed. The radical is 饣/飠 *shí* ("food"); the second component is 交 *jiāo*. At first sight, then, it looks like a straightforward *xingsheng zi*, a semantic-phonetic compound, with the second component donating the sound (though not also the tone) to the character. But there is more than meets the eye. First, the character 交 *jiāo* may mean "to hand over" as in 交代 *jiāodài*. In this context, what exactly is being handed over? What is being handed over is the old year in exchange for the new. We have already quickly referred to the traditional 12-units clock, where each unit covers two hours in today's 24-hours clock system. The critical periods for this occasion are two. The first covers 9pm – 11pm in the 24-hours system. This unit in the traditional system is called 交时/時 *jiāoshí*, and is the last position in the 12-units system of time demarcation. In other words, it is the critical period of handing the old year over to the new. The period which follows is called 子时/時 *zǐshí*, the first position in the system, covering 11pm of the preceding night to 1am, the following morning; it is called that because 子 means "child" or "seed," thus indicating that it is the period in which a new year/a new day (like a new babe) is born. When the family eats *jiaozi*, the family, every family, hopes that the transition from one year to the next would be smooth, that the good fortunes of the old year would continue into the new. In other words, 饺/餃子 *jiǎo·zi* is not simply *xingsheng zi*, a semantic-phonetic compound but a profound *huiyi zi*, a meaning compound, embodying Chinese astronomy, as well as the Chinese passion for auspicious symbols and symbolic significance, the Chinese fondness for puns, not to mention food. You could almost say that the character/word itself is as good as any to stand as an encapsulation of Chinese culture.

In common folklore, the word "year" is amusingly explained as follows: 年 *nián* is the name of a mightily ferocious wild beast, which was bigger than a camel, which ran as fast as the wind and which roared like thunder. It ate humans and harmed other animals. When the god of the heavens eventually heard of its atrocious behavior, he confined the beast to the deep forest, permitting it to get out only once a year. On one such occasion, the beast got as far as the entrance of a village, where he met a small shepherd boy setting off fire crackers, which rather put it off its stride, and so it retreated. But it saw in the distance a sea of red (every house would have red paper stuck on its door on which New Year wishes were written and designs were drawn) which it also found upsetting. Finally it tried to find refuge under the eave of a house in the village, but lit candles and lanterns inside made such a dazzling sight that it could not stand the bright light. It had no choice but to return to the forest. People came to realize that the ferocious beast had three phobias: loud crackling noises, bright colors such as red, and dazzling light. This is the reason why, at every new year, when it is time for the beast to appear in their midst, they would set off fire crackers, decorate their houses with designs in red paper, wear bright clothes (the children and the women, at least) and light plenty of candles and lanterns.

We have seen the intimate link between the dumpling called 饺/餃子 *jiǎo·zi* and astronomy. Let us next say something quickly about another food, 馄饨/餛飩 *hún·tun*, ravioli. The "food" radical in the two characters is self-explanatory; but what about the other components? Are they there to give the sounds to the characters? Yes, but they also contribute meaning. Chinese cosmology may be said to subscribe to a kind of Big Bang theory about the beginning of the universe. Before the Big Bang, there was only chaos; after it, there was order in the universe and cosmos. Before order, there was 混沌 *hùndùn*, that is, chaos. The eating of the ravioli on the day of the winter solstice (which according to another Chinese tradition also marked the end of the old year and the beginning of the new) reminds us of the fact that chaos preceded order.

In Chinese, sky or heaven is 天 *tiān*. Here are two *jiaguwen* followed by two *jinwen* forms of the character:

The *xiaozhuan* and *lishu* versions are shown below:

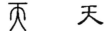

In the first version of *jiaguwen*, you see a square on top of the character for "large," 大 *dà* which is beneath it. The square represents the head of a person. Hence, the original basic meaning of 天 *tiān* is "the top of the head." *Jinwen* continues in the same way, making it even more obvious that it is talking about big man with a very big head that is being represented (except that the head is round). This meaning is preserved even today in Chinese medicine – a certain pill for headaches is called 正天丸 *zhèng tiān wán*, where 天 refers literally to the head. In *xiaozhuan*, there is a change – the head is now replaced by a line over the character 大 *dà* (a little bit like the second version of *jiaguwen* shown above). As a result, Xu Shen (remember that he was working with *xiaozhuan*) says 天 *tiān* not only stands for the opposite of earth but also derivatively for the notion, the highest, that for which nothing could be higher. In Chinese cosmological understanding, *tian* is supreme, and humans, no matter how grand or important they fancy themselves to be, are subject, nevertheless to the constraints of *tian*. *Tian* watches over us, and we pray to it to protect us. When we suffer injustices for which we get no redress from emperors, officials or neighbors, we hope that *tian* might dispense justice on our behalf. Not even the most mighty emperor would dare to put himself above *tian*: he humbly called himself "Son of Heaven" 天子 *tiānzǐ* and he ruled only by the grace of the Mandate of Heaven 天命 *tiānmìng*, a political concept of legitimation invented by the Zhou Dynasty, which followed the defeat of the last Shang king.

The compass points in the West are given as north, south, east, west. In China they are east (东/東 *dōng*), south (南 *nán*), west (西 *xī*), north (北 *běi*). The Chinese clockwise ordering of the points could be explained perhaps by the fact that the country is in that part of the world which Europeans called "Far East," and which the Chinese themselves simply call "East." East is, of course, where the sun rises; it is a place one associates with daylight and sunlight. Sunlight makes things grow; hence in *jiaguwen* and *jinwen* (the first two on the left below), the character looks like this:

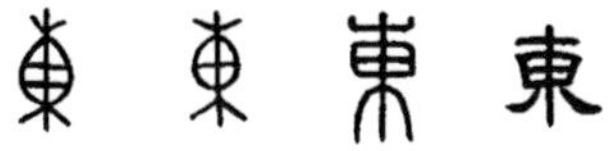

Jiaguwen seems to show an enlarged bulbous stem with leaves at the top and roots down below. By *xiaozhuan* and *lishu* (the two forms on the right), it is easy to see that the character has two components: one for "sun" 日 *rì* and the other for "wood" (derivatively "tree")木 *mù*, the one being superimposed on the other. The character created is obviously *huiyi zi*, a meaning compound. It suggests the sun coming through the trees in a forest; this is compatible with *jiaguwen*'s idea that where and when the sun rises, plants grow.

West is where the sun sets; and when the sun sets, the birds return to their nests, their resting place for the night. Hence in *jiaguwen*, *jinwen* forms of the character (the first two shown below), it looks like a bird's nest:

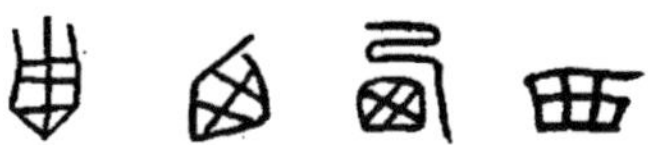

(To appreciate the image in *jiaguwen*, you have to turn the page anti-clockwise so that it is horizontal.) *Xiaozhuan* (third from the left) has an additional bit to the nest to show more explicitly that it is a bird's nest, the extra bit "hovering" over the nest represents the bird. By *lishu* (the last on the right), however, the character has become abstract and stylised, looking like today's writing of it, 西 *xī*.

There is the story that the Yellow Emperor was the inventor of the magnetic compass. In Chinese, the instrument is called 指南针/針 *zhǐnánzhēn*, "south-pointing needle." During a fierce battle, mentioned in various ancient texts such as the *Book of Rites* (礼记/禮記), the Yellow Emperor had mounted the device in the front of his war chariot, in such a way that the hand of the little wooden figure always pointed south. As a result, he knew where he was going whatever the fog and mist. In this way, he defeated his enemy and won the war. In its various forms (*jiaguwen, jinwen, xiaozhuan, lishu*), the character 南 *nán* looks like this:

Its *jiaguwen* form has given rise to different interpretations. Some scholars maintain that it is *xiangxing zi*, a pictograph, the front plate of a tortoise, but they have nothing to offer about why such a pictograph was used. Other scholars prefer to see the character as *jiajie zi*, a phonetic-loan, with no real hidden meaning. Yet another alternative makes it into *huiyi zi*, a meaning compound. The first component is the character for "door" and inside that is the character/word 幸 *xìng*, meaning "good fortune." In the history of Chinese architecture from time immemorial, the door faces south, in order to get the sun. To live facing south – enjoying the warmth of the sun, where things grow – is to enjoy good fortunes, which explains the construction of the character for "south."

The character for "north" – 北 *běi* – follows the logic of the explanation of "south" just given above. China is in the northern hemisphere. Therefore, the sunny position is the south-facing one with the north side being sunless, cold and dark. Hence, when one sits, one faces south, with the north to one's back. The character for "north" embodies this fact, as can be seen in its various (the first two are *jiaguwen*, then *jinwen*, *xiaozhuan, lishu*) forms below:

This is the opposite of how the character for 比 *bǐ* ("to compare") is constructed, which we have looked at (***Friends, comrades, fellow disciples***). We reproduce its various forms (*jiaguwen, jinwen, xiaozhuan, lishu*) here so that you can compare their respective forms:

Bi shows two people standing side by side whilst *bei* shows two people standing with their backs to each other. 北 *běi*' s original meaning is "to run counter" (showing two people going in opposite directions) and is related to the character/word 背 *bèi* , meaning "back," whose top component, as you can see, is 北 *běi*. In the context of the general environment as well as of architecture, north is the direction to which people turn their back, as that is the side from which the bitterly cold winds come sweeping from the Mongolian steppes.

In formal Chinese etiquette, the honored position is, therefore, the south-facing position, as it is the side which faces the sun. We have already mentioned that in traditional Chinese architecture, the door is always on the south side of the building to welcome in the sunlight. Hence, the honored position in a room would be the one facing the door, on the far side of a room. This position is then for the guest, while the host occupies the north-facing position, that is, the position nearest the door. The king or emperor was an exception – he always occupied the northern position, thus always facing south, to signify his supreme status. Be careful here in distinguishing the northern position as opposed to the north-facing position. The north itself is associated with dark and cold, but this is not to be confused with the position occupied by the emperor or the guest. That position is 坐北朝南 *zuò běi cháo nán*, sitting-north-but-facing-south, and it is the *yang* position, while the host's position, sitting-south-but-facing-north is the *yin* position, according to the fundamental principle of *yinyang* in Chinese philosophical thinking. In other words, to occupy the northern position is always to face south; to occupy the southern position is always to face north. In terms of protocol and etiquette, what is significant is that the most important person in the room sits facing south.

There is an expression for "playing host" which is 做东/東 *zuò dōng*. It comes from an incident during the Spring and Autumn Period which involved three different states – Zheng 郑/鄭, Qin 秦 and Jin 晋. Zheng was in the east, Qin in the west and Jin in the middle. Jin and Qin (the middle and western states) formed an alliance to annihilate Zheng (the eastern state). Zheng faced defeat and destruction with the combined might of the other two descending upon it. In desperation, its chief minister leaped over a wall and secretly stole into the camp of the Qin commander to make a case to save his country saying: My country undoubtedly faces certain defeat, as you know. Of course, this would be welcome news to your country. However, before you rejoice at such a prospect, pause and think of the geography of the three states. We are in the east, and you in the west. When we have been annihilated, what good would it do for your state of Qin? Having annexed us, Jin would be twice as big and twice as powerful as it is now. And what would such a more powerful neighbor do to a smaller neighbor such as your state? The next obvious step would be to annex you as well. Therefore, you would be far better off, breaking the present alliance with Jin. If Zheng were to continue to exist in the east, this would allow you to have a line to the east, and this new axis would benefit your state far more than your present alliance with Jin to annihilate us, the state of Zheng. This logic apparently convinced the Qin commander, and Zheng was saved. Zheng, far from facing defeat and destruction, happily played host instead to the Qin troops who were left behind in Zheng in order to help it build up defenses against the state of Jin. As the state of Zheng was in the east, the expression 做东/東 *zuò dōng* is used derivatively to mean "to play host," although its original meaning, arising from a political narrative, was "to act as master of the eastern region."

To understand the Chinese attitude towards the earth and to geography, there is no better way to approach the subject than through the study of 风水/風水 *fēng•shuĭ*, often translated not quite accurately as "geomancy." *Fengshui*, at its core, is perfectly sound and is part of ecology, in the larger understanding of the term, which has become very fashionable in the West within the last thirty years or so. *Fengshui* can be said to be part of Chinese eco-philosophy, the first such in the world. Apart from *qi* (a virtually untranslatable term), the other two most important notions in such a study are water and earth, 水土 *shuĭtŭ*. If these two factors favorably obtain, then the environment would be sustainable, and hence, desirable.

In traditional European thinking, the nearest equivalent which we can find is the French notion of *le terroir*, which is invoked to justify the finer points of French wine production, such as in a recent dispute in the industry about who has the right to use the label "champagne" for their produce. The French claim that the sparkling wine from vineyards only in that part of France called Champagne is entitled to be called by that name. Sparkling wine made from grapes grown elsewhere, in California, Australia, South America, South Africa, or wherever, cannot be called "champagne." Rivals to the *Champagne* label outside France ridicule the notion of *le terroir*, holding it up as merely the expression of French protectionism. The non-cynical interpretation of it lies in saying that the combination of climatic and soil conditions which make up the micro-environment within the various regions of a very specific geographical area does play a role in determining the characteristics of the produce grown in that region. *Champagne* could only be labelled as such if the grapes from which the bubbly liquid is made actually come from vineyards in that very specific region of France called by that name. The Chinese would have no difficulty with that logic, as it is a part of its broad-based ecological approach to understanding the relationship between a living, growing thing and its environment. There is the expression 南橘北枳 *nán jú běi zhǐ* which sums up this cosmological, ecological outlook – a tangerine plant which is native to south China when transplanted to north China would no longer produce that sweet citrus fruit one calls "tangerine," but another fruit which is smaller and sourer, and, therefore, should no longer be called by that name.

Before going into further details about *fengshui*, let us take a look at the various (*jiaguwen, jinwen, xiaozhuan, lishu*) forms for *tu*, "earth":

Basically, *jiaguwen* and *jinwen* seem to show a mound of earth – the bottom horizontal line represents the ground, and the thing on top of it is the mound of earth. In *xiaozhuan*, the mound has disappeared. In its place is another horizontal line which represents the topsoil whilst the bottom horizontal line, the soil below ground; the vertical line represents a plant sticking out of the soil. Not all scholars agree with this interpretation, but it seems a plausible one. Naturally, good wholesome soil is absolutely essential for cultivation. We must, therefore, respect the soil.

Another character/word for *tu* is 地 *dì*. In modern Chinese, the two characters – 土地 *tǔdì* – are often used together to refer to not only cultivated fields but also land or territory. In *xiaozhuan*, 地 looks like this:

The character has two components: the *tu* radical is on the left and the second on the right, 也 (in Xiaozhuan). This second component renders the character *huiyi zi*, a meaning compound, not merely *xingsheng zi*, a semantic-phonetic compound as some scholars maintain. In an exploration of an earlier theme (***Nothing's more boring than personal pronouns***), it has been pointed out there that 也 refers to the female genitals and its parts. The construction of the character *di* shows, then, very clearly that the ancient Chinese considered the soil or earth as the source of all life, just as in the case of the reproduction of mammals, without females there can be no reproduction and no birth. Earth is then Mother Earth (many other cultures share this view, too, from time immemorial). So it is all very fitting that Mother Earth should be respected.

Earth, 土 *tǔ* or 地 *dì*, in the Chinese understanding of life, is basic. This is entirely in accordance with ecological reasoning which says that all life comes from, and is sustained, by the earth or soil. This is absolutely scientific, as all carnivores, to survive, must eat herbivores, all herbivores, to survive, must eat plants or grasses which grow from the soil. Without soil, there is no life or perhaps life only at the level of microbes. We, humans, are earth-rooted beings; as such, we could not, for a moment, survive without soil, whether we are carnivores, vegetarians or omnivores. Apart from food, we also make use of other resources, such as wood, fire and minerals. Where do we get them? From the ground, from the earth. Wood comes from trees, trees grow from the soil. Fire comes from burning wood, peat, coal, which ultimately all come from trees and plants which grow in the soil. We are beings beholden to the soil, to earth in all ways. Significantly, too, we cannot live without water; but the relationship between water on the one hand and vegetation (and soil) is a complex and intimate one – without water, nothing would grow, nothing would thrive, but without soil for plants to grow on, water would also diminish or even disappear altogether. In sum, to understand 水土 *shuǐtǔ*, is to understand life. It is also to understand the place of humans in that ecological web of life.

Imagine yourself leading a band or a tribe looking for a site to set up a more or less permanent settlement. First, you look at the soil – if the ground is not stony, the soil looks rich and wholesome, you would know you have found a potentially good location. Next, you must further ascertain whether there is a source of sweet and sustainable water nearby. You would then be doing nothing but practicing *fengshui*, applying the elementary principles of sustainable living. Soil without water is no use; so is water without soil. The two must be within reasonable distance of each other. Sometimes, the water could be transported to the soil over even large distances, such as the *karez* system of irrigation (traced back probably to the ancient Persians) which has been in place for centuries in places like Xinjiang, carrying the snow melt from the foothills of the Tianshan to the great oasis towns such as Turfan and Urumchi, aided by gravity through a series of wells linked together by underground channels. If there is water, one must also determine what its source is, how large is its watershed, how extensive is the system below ground, where it eventually flows out, etc. When you know all these things, you could then make an informed decision as to whether the location would make a good settlement.

There is an ode in the *Shi Jing* (*The Book of Songs*) which records precisely such an account of how a certain Duke Liu selected a site to found a new settlement in the fertile plains of Bin in 1796 BCE, when his existing territory became over-populated. He used the gnomon to measure the shadows in order to determine the compass directions as well as which side would get the sun (*yang*) and which would be in the shadows (*yin*), especially during the winter. He also ascertained the sources of water:

> *Of generous devotion to the people was duke Liu ,*
> *His territory being now broad and long ,*
> *He determined the points of the heavens by means of the shadows ; and then , ascending the ridges ,*
> *He surveyed the light and the shade ,*
> *Viewing also the course of the streams and springs .*
> *His armies were three troops ;*
> *He measured the marshes and plains ;*
> *He fixed the revenue on the system of common cultivation of the fields ;*
> *He measured also the fields west of the hills ;*
> *And the settlement of Bin became truly great .*

> 篤公劉、既溥既長、既景迺岡、相其陰陽、觀其流泉、其軍三單。
> 度其隰原、徹田為糧。
> 度其夕陽、豳居允荒。

There is a notion called 来龙/龍去脉/脈 *lái lóng qù mài* in *fengshui* or Chinese eco-philosophy which refers to water. One may distinguish water in terms of three categories: that which comes from the clouds in the sky is rain; that which runs in rivers draining ultimately into the seas and oceans is running water; that which is invisible is underground water. The *fengshui* practitioner, in determining the suitability of any site, whether the site is for a permanent settlement in the old days, for a grave for the dead, for a dwelling for the living, must look into the system or network of underground water. This is what 来龙/龍去脉/脈 *lái lóng qù mài* refers to. Sustainability depends on the availability of water, as we have seen, but it depends not simply on rain, on rivers but also on water under the ground. Chinese mythology associates water in all its forms with the dragon 龙/龍 *lóng* – hence the use of it in the expression to refer to underground water. 龙脉/龍脈 refers to the dragon's system of vital circulation which is made up entirely of water which is analogous to the major circulation system in our body, made up of blood and *qi*. This notion of "invisible" water is considered to be so important that 来龙/龍去脉/脈 *lái lóng qù mài* is derivatively used to mean "the origin and development, the whole story or the full context of something" – to understand something properly, one must understand its *lai long qu mai*.

Readers, who know Chinese, may sometimes wonder why the tap, or in America, the faucet, in Chinese is 水笼头/龍頭 *shuǐlóng·tou*, literally "the dragon's head from which water sprouts." Now you know why such a mundane object has such a colorful name.

In Chinese philosophy and cosmology, the crucial notion is 天人合一 *tiān rén hé yī*, meaning "harmony between the Heavens above and humanity on Earth below." In other words, human beings, as already mentioned earlier, live under the constraints of Nature which surrounds us. In the West, modern philosophers have on the whole thought that what we do on Earth cannot affect the heavenly bodies while what happens up there does not affect us either. While the first half is correct, the second is subject to correction. Of late, astronomers have warned that according to their calculations, a huge meteorite hitting Earth, capable of destroying us is not beyond the bounds of probability, and they have proposed various technological strategies for coping with such an eventuality. Experts in archaeo-astronomy have revealed how it was just such a meteorite hitting Earth which very probably ended the age of the dinosaurs, permitting the age of the mammals to emerge in the history of evolution. The modern scientific mind claims itself to be different from the non-scientific superstitious mind of our ancestors by distancing astronomy from astrology. While the extravagant claims of the latter would not stand up to critical scrutiny, it does not follow that the general one that what happens in the heavens above do affect terrestrial affairs is also totally unfounded.

The ancient Chinese had grasped such a link as shown in their understanding of the relationship between the sun and the moon, on the one hand, and tides, on the other. Their recognition that the times of the tide are correlated to the passage of the moon can already be found in their early literature and poetry as well as in accounts in the second century BCE about high tides at full moon. However, the most definitive material of a scientific nature about the link between the tides and the phases of the moon is found in a work called *Lun Heng* (论/論衡), translated as *Discourses Weighed in the Balance*, 82 – 83 CE) of a Han scholar Wang Chong (王充) in which he marshalled arguments and evidence for the thesis that the tides are causally dependent on the moon. The ancient Chinese knew the relation of the lunar cycle to the sun and the earth by 150 BCE as well as about the four phases of the moon – new, first quarter crescent, full and last quarter crescent – but which in Chinese astronomy were divided into eight divisions, yielding a more refined and detailed classification of the lunar phases. They also knew that the full moon comes once a month, that while the leap tide occurs at the full moon, the neap tide occurs at the new moon. Hence, the phases of the moon and certain terrestrial events are intimately linked. They had organized such data into simple forms as tables by 1056 CE.

The ancient Chinese also displayed understanding of the direct effect of such phenomena on humans such as in their grasp of menstruation, 月经/經 *yuèjīng*. It is interesting that in English the word comes from the Latin, meaning "month" – a woman's period comes once a month. In Chinese, *yue* also means "month," as we have seen. We have already discussed that *jing* (经/經) is the word for "warp" and stands derivatively for something regular and recurring. It is, therefore, equally interesting that the word for "menstruation" in French is *les règles* (literally "the rules"), which implies something going like clock-work, operating to a rule. One could even say that the English and French words combined together would give the meaning of the Chinese (two-syllable) word 月经/經 *yuèjīng*. The truly interesting thing is that such a combination would not exhaust the meaning of the Chinese word. The missing dimension comes from the fact that *yue* does not only mean "month" but also "moon." As we have already mentioned, the Chinese month is lunar, the word *yue* which stands for the moon (as in 月亮 *yuè·liang*) also then stands for month (the period of time in which the moon goes through its different phases). The onset time of the monthly period in each woman is steady and regular and the interval between periods is a lunar month. According to Chinese understanding, the full moon and the onset of menstruation are intimately linked.

Menstruation occurs because the uterus sheds its lining when conception fails to take place. The egg released by the ovaries did not manage to meet up with any sperm. The release of the egg and its entailed sequence of events are determined by the hormones in the female body; the secretion of hormones has its own cycle. According to ancient Chinese understanding and its fundamental *yinyang* principle, while the male is *yang*, the female is *yin*, the sun is *yang*, the moon is *yin*. Hence the female hormonal cycle is determined by the moon and its phases. Recent Chinese studies have shown that women whose menstruation falls squarely within the period of the full moon have a higher rate of conceiving than those whose menstruation falls somewhat outside that period.

These intimate links between the physiology of the female body and the moon is an excellent illustration of the concept 天人合一 *tiān rén héyī* , that humanity and nature are at one.

Let us end by briefly taking a look at a very curious (two-syllable) word in Chinese for "thing," 东/東西 *dōngxī*, literally meaning "east-west." It is not an ancient word, having come into existence only during the Song Dynasty (960 – 1279 CE), but since its emergence, it has taken firm root, displacing more ancient equivalent words in general. This involves a story about the distinguished philosopher Zhu Xi, 朱熹, and a good friend, equally well versed in *yinyang* philosophy but who also had a sense of humor. One day, Zhu Xi met him on the street carrying a basket. The friend said he was on his way to buy some 东/東西 *dōng·xi*. You must remember that this was the very first time that the (two-syllable) word had ever been uttered in the history of the Chinese language. This puzzled the distinguished philosopher who responded: What on earth are you talking about? If you are going to buy east-west, you might as well do one better and buy south-north too? The friend smiled and teasingly said to the great man that he should have no difficulty in understanding the allusion to "east-west" provided he recalled the philosophy of the five phases (五行 *wǔxíng*) and the five orientations (五方 *wǔfāng*)! With that remark, the friend disappeared with his basket on his arm to go and buy *dongxi*. The philosopher soon gathered his wits about him and worked out, although somewhat laboriously, what his friend was really talking about.

To understand the witty coinage, one must know a little about the philosophy mentioned. The notions of the five phases and the five orientations are a crucial part of *yinyang* philosophy which is also the basis of Chinese medicine. 五行 *wŭxíng,* in older English (and other European) translations, is referred to as “the five elements,” but that is a mistranslation. It arose because the scholars who first came into contact with Chinese philosophy were trained in Greek classical philosophy. Greek philosophy talks of four elements (earth, water, air and fire); so these Europeans, trained as Classicists, simplistically borrowed the term to translate *wuxing* as “the five elements,” observing that the sole difference between Greek and Chinese philosophy is that the latter has one more element than the former. More recently, Western scholars have realized that the term “element” makes no sense in *yinyang* philosophy and that a slightly more suitable translation is “phases” (but even that is not a perfect translation). What then are these five phases? They are wood, metal, fire, water, earth. (You see how easy it is to think that the ancient Greek and ancient Chinese philosophers all meant the same thing as they seemed to have in common earth, water, and fire.) The five orientations are: east, south, west, north, and center. The two sets are correlated as follows: east pairs with wood, west with metal, south with fire, north with water, and center with earth. On a commonsensical level, one could follow the pairings: for instance, we have already seen that the east is where the sun rises, being associated with plant growth; the south has a warmer climate than the north, hence fire or heat is associated with it; the north is cold and damp, hence water (which includes snow and ice) goes with it.

In the light of this brief account, you would realize straightaway that the witty friend, who was going to buy some *dongxi*, actually meant to say he was going to buy some things which were made of wood and metal or more generally, solid things you could put in your basket. He did not say he was going to buy some *nanbei* (south-north), as he could not put fire or water in his basket. No body in ancient China would buy (packets of) earth, so we can rule that out, although today there is no doubt a market for it, and you can most certainly put some earth in your shopping basket. So you see, this thing called 东西/東西 *dōng·xi* is no ordinary thing – the word embodies deep philosophy, although we would not like, for the briefest moment, to give you the impression that *yinyang* philosophy is no more than what a wit in the Song Dynasty had dreamed up by inventing that word to stand for things.

末

The art of war and the art of peace:
Swapping shield and spear for jade and silks

In exploring an earlier theme (***The elevated and the despised***), we have mentioned that ancient Chinese society officially recognized four classes: scholar, farmer, artisan and trader. The military class was not one of them. However, this did not mean that ancient Chinese society was so peaceful that there was no need to have soldiers or armies. On the contrary, times from the Shang Dynasty (ca. 16th – 11th century BCE), if not before, till the unification of China by Qin Shihuangdi in 221 BCE, were full of violence and bloodshed, during a long history of roughly a thousand five hundred years. In the thirteenth century BCE, the Shang king, Wu Ding (武丁), led an army of over 50,000 men. Once, he had taken some 30,000, some of whom he offered as sacrifices to gods and ancestors, others he buried alive to accompany as slaves or servants his own dead noblemen, and yet others he used in opening ceremonies of his new palaces. These figures were only about prisoners-of-war. One dreads to think of the numbers actually killed in battles and wars. Just to drive home the mind-boggling scale of the killing, here are some other figures, this time, from the Zhou Dynasty (ca. 11th century – 221 BCE): from the Spring and Autumn (770 – 476 BCE) to the Warring States (475 – 221 BCE) Periods, about five hundred years, those killed in any single big battle alone could number as many as several tens of thousands. In one, which took place in 317 BCE, the figure cited was more than 80,000. In another, occurring in 293 BCE, the number was 240,000. In yet another campaign, a general of the state of Qin (the state which finally vanquished all the other rival states in 221 BCE) killed more than 400,000 enemies. Such figures would include primarily soldiers, and occasionally male children of 15 and above, but would exclude those killed in other ways in a war such as through lack of food, illness, etc, which always ensued whenever there were disruption and destruction.

Above are two fighting scenes from engravings on bronze vessels of the Warring States Period. Conscription, on demand, was the order of the day, as there were no standing armies in the true sense of the word. (However, the king, as in the Shang Dynasty, would always keep a core of fighting men.) People had no choice but to fight for the king whenever he decided to go to war and needed to put together an army of men.

In the Shang Dynasty, a division (帅 / 帥 *shuài*) under a commander had 10,000 men. Soldiers were divided into infantry and those riding in fighting wagons or chariots. Weapons were divided into those for attack and those for defense. The bow and arrow were, of course, a part of the armory. Below are pictures of two sorts of weapons: the one on the left is an axe, the other a knife. The picture on the right shows a soldier holding an axe in his left hand and a prisoner-of-war in his right.

Let us now look at the character for "soldier," 兵 *bīng*, in its various (*jiaguwen, jinwen, xiaozhuan, lishu*) forms:

Jiaguwen shows two hands (the bottom part) holding an axe. The two hands in *jinwen* are holding the same weapon, except that the blade of the axe now faces right instead of left. *Xiaozhuan* also retains the two hands but the axe is now looking more abstract. Come *lishu*, the character has become stylised, bearing few traces of the vividness of its earlier forms – the two hands are replaced by what look like two fingers. The character/word originally meant "weapon." This meaning was extended to include military matters or war – hence, the famous classic by Sunzi (孙/孫子) is translated as *The Art of War* – 兵法 *bīngfǎ* (孙/孫

子兵法) – a sixth century BCE text which is still studied today by military academies throughout the world, such as Sandhurst, West Point, Saint Cyr, as it is regarded as a classic on military strategies and tactics. It holds that preparedness for war is the ultimate guarantee of security. It starts from the premise that the enemy would strike, but if one were prepared, having made one's own position unassailable, there would be nothing to fear. This preparedness for war, however, should not be equated with belligerence. Belligerence leads to destruction, while ignoring the possibility of war is dangerous. Preparedness for war should not be understood in a narrow, literal manner, to mean simply "amassing a lot of weapons." *The Art of War* focuses not so much on the physical aspects of fighting, as on how to outwit your enemies, to fight and win wars without even having to go into battle. This approach to warfare involves a subtle, sophisticated perspective. As a result, it is studied not merely for its relevance to military thinking, but also to business and other spheres of activity, such as sports.

Here is a rubbing of a soldier made from an engraving on a Han brick, excavated in Luoyang, Henan Province (河南洛阳/陽).

The ancient Chinese tended to use other terms, and not *bing*, to refer to soldiers, but it is easy to see how it came to stand for soldier. A soldier, after all, is someone holding a weapon in his hands, ready to kill, given the command. Indeed, what better way is there to define a soldier but as someone whose business is to kill when ordered.

The Chinese have a fondness to deconstruct their characters, as we have been emphasising. Sometimes, the deconstruction is not done for the purpose of scholarly understanding but for another, such as to create a special expression to convey, for instance, disapproval. From *lishu* onwards, when the character took on the form it has retained since, you can see that 兵 *bīng* consists of two components: the top one looking like this: 丘 *qiū*, meaning "hill" (we have come across this before as it is Confucius's name – ***What hangs upon a name? A lot***), and the bottom one, like this: 八 *bā* ("eight"). So the Chinese sometimes called soldiers *qiūbā*, to refer to the ill-disciplined, lawless variety, which plundered, raped and terrorised ordinary folks.

A whole cluster of characters concerning warfare, such as 战/戰 *zhàn* ("war") and 武 *wǔ* ("military"), has for radical the character for a particular weapon called 戈 *gē*. We have come across this when we analyzed the personal pronoun, 我 *wǒ* (***Nothing's more boring than personal pronouns***). Its various (*jiaguwen, jinwen, xiaozhuan, lishu*) forms look like:

Jiaguwen shows clearly it is *xiangxing zi*, a pictograph. This was a very basic weapon as it was adapted from an implement used in agriculture. The long vertical bit is the handle, and the horizontal bit is the sharp edge of the dagger/axe attached to the handle. The handle was as long as three meters (roughly ten feet) if used by soldiers in fighting wagons pulled by horses. When it was held by the infantry, the handle was 1.4 meter (roughly four and a half feet). During the Shang and Zhou Dynasties, soldiers used the long-handled variety of the weapon until men in fighting wagons were superseded by the cavalry, although it still remained in use beyond the Han Dynasty up to the Three Kingdoms Period (220 CE – 265 CE). By the Han Dynasty (206 BCE – 220 CE), it was, by and large, no longer a really serious part of the armory and had become, to an extent, a fashionable ceremonial ornament amongst the aristocracy.

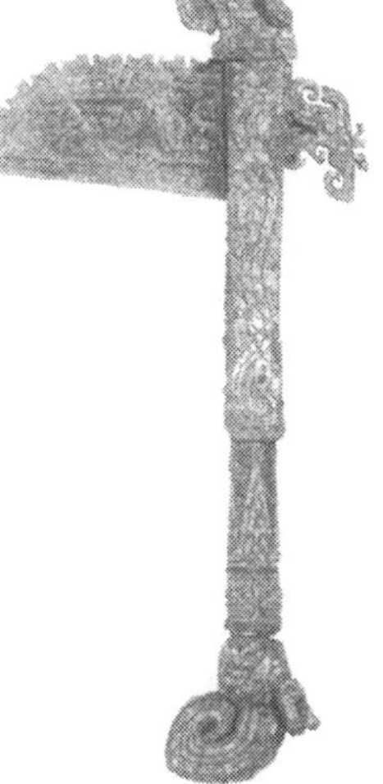

This is a picture of a Zhou Dynasty bronze *ge*, with elaborate dragon patterns. It was excavated from a site in Anyang, Henan (河南安阳/陽) province, but the object is now no longer in China but in a museum in the USA.

The *ge* illustrates well the point that China, during its long history, had no real professional soldiering class whether amongst officers or men. The former would come from the ranks of the aristocracy or the scholar class – people particularly good at martial arts or theories and strategies of warfare who would take up arms when their king issued the call to arms, or their territory had to be defended. The common soldiers were ordinary farmers. During protracted periods of warfare, when the fighting season was over, they would return to the land for the harvest and in the winter, they would hunt, and practice with their weapons, until the fighting resumed the following year. The nearest equivalent in modern terms would be the British Territorial Army, where young men join the army and are given military training for a certain part of the year, but otherwise are people with day jobs in stock-brokering, accountancy, plastering or whatever. When the UK needs additional men to send off, for example, to Afghanistan or Iraq, they are then called up. This analogy must be heavily qualified, as the ancient Chinese peasants were not volunteers like the members of the BTA but conscripts, who had no choice under the political system in which they lived but to bear arms, but who, nevertheless, felt a moral obligation to fight for the king when ordered to do so.

Wars in China's long history could simplistically be classified under two heads: inter-fighting amongst rival clans or states, on the one hand, and fighting, on the other, to protect the territory called *Zhongyuan* (中原), the heartland of the Han people, from foreign invaders and aggressors. In the latter case, the ordinary people felt a strong moral as well as an overwhelmingly emotional obligation to protect the integrity of their homeland from the invading non-Han tribes from the north, north-east and north-west. The people of *Zhongyuan* felt that they had to be on eternal vigilance against invasion by the peoples from the steppes. This threat seemed to be reflected in the various (the first is *jiaguwen*, the next two are *jinwen*, followed by *xiaozhuan, lishu*) forms of the character for "frontier guard," 戍 *shù*:

The three versions preceding the stylised and abstract form of *lishu* (which is retained in *kaishu*, up to today) basically show a person with a *ge* in hand. This person was the frontier guard, who was perhaps not meant to take part in serious prolonged fighting but primarily was posted for surveillance and watch.

We next turn our attention to a very interesting character with components which refer to two different sorts of equipment, one for attack and the other for defense. The character is 戎 *róng*; its various (*jiaguwen, jinwen, xiaozhuan, lishu*) forms can be seen below:

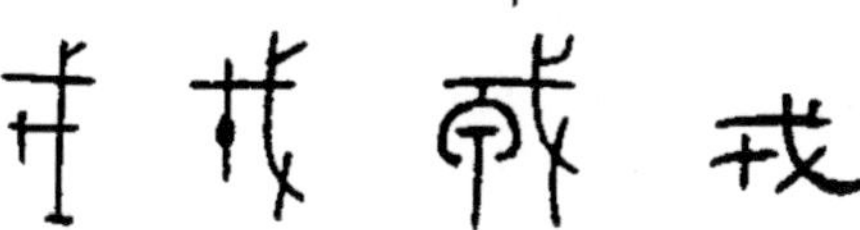

On the right, it has for radical the *ge* which, we have seen, is a weapon for charging the enemy. In *jiaguwen*, the horizontal cross attached to the middle of the *ge* looks like the side view of a shield, a device for defense. In *jinwen*, the view of the shield looks like a frontal one, but there are some scholars, of late, who think that it is not a shield but something looking like this:

It is called 毌 *guàn*, which, too, is a defensive device. But in *xiaozhuan*, this second component seems to be replaced by the character for "armor" whose modern form is like this: 甲 *jiă*. Whether the second component is a shield, a *guan*, or armor, they seem to point to defense rather than attack. The vivid juxtaposition of offensive with defensive weapons in one single character renders it singularly apt to stand for the idea of military matters; 戎 *róng* is *huiyi zi*, a meaning compound, meaning precisely that.

Here are two soldiers fighting with shield in one hand and sword in the other.

The distinction between offensive and defensive devices has given rise to a very interesting contribution to the Chinese vocabulary. We have already mentioned the shield as part of the latter group; it is 盾 *dùn*. There is an offensive weapon which we have not so far mentioned, and it is 矛 *máo*, a weapon with a very long handle (usually planted in the front of the fighting wagon) which appears to belong to the same family of weaponry as the *ge*, an offensive weapon. It is a spear. In *jinwen, xiaozhuan and lishu*, the character is written:

The character for "shield" appears (in *jiaguwen, jinwen, xiaozhuan, lishu*) as shown below:

Jiaguwen shows very clearly a man carrying something which looks like a shield. Once, a market-stall vendor tried to "flog" his shield, shouting at the top of his voice: here are the best *dun* money can buy, so good that not even the sharpest *mao* can penetrate them. Carried away by his own feverish sales-pitch, he continued in the same vein, this time, however, holding up one of the spears he also had for sale, and shouting equally loudly: here is the sharpest *mao* money can buy, so good that it can penetrate even the most perfectly made *dun*. Obviously, this fellow was long on sales-talk but short on logic. The (two-syllable) word in Chinese for "contradiction" is, therefore, 矛盾 *máodùn*, derived from the logic of the fellow's illogicality, so to speak. There is the related expression: 以子之矛，攻子之盾 *yǐ zǐ zhī máo, gōng zǐ zhī dùn*, literally meaning "to use a person's own spear against his own shield," that is, "to refute someone with his own argument."

There is another character/word 武 *wǔ* also meaning "military" which makes for some interesting observations. Its various (*jiaguwen, jinwen, xiaozhuan, lishu*) forms are presented below:

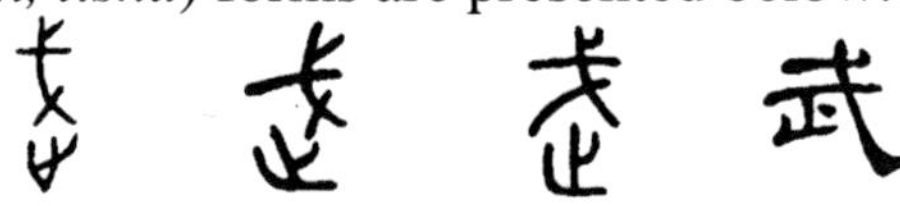

If you look at them all, it is very clear that the character has two components: the *ge* (戈) and under it something which means "foot," 止 *zhǐ*. It could mean two different things. According to the first interpretation, this amounts to talking about soldiers on the move, that is, about an army, about military affairs. The second points to something more complicated such as a war dance 武舞 *wǔwǔ,* a form of 舞蹈 *wǔdǎo*, dance movements. In the ancient Chinese context, *wuwu* would refer to the rolling of drums, the lifting and waving of flags or banners, which showed readiness to fight the brave fight as well as to challenge the foe. The aim of any war dance is to "psyche up" the soldiers for the task of killing ahead. Some scholars point out that the Chinese war dance was derived from hunting, where hunters would also be carrying weapons, surrounding the area where they thought the prey was, crying and yelling while co-ordinating one another's movements rhythmically as they advanced to drive the beast into a pit or net. The method of hunting and killing a large wild animal would basically be the same as that of organizing and leading an army to slaughter the human foe. On this interpretation, the original meaning of 武 *wǔ* would be related to "dance" and derivatively to mean "military affairs," referring to those activities involved in the planning and logistics of an army on the move to the front. Of course, today, *wu* simply means "military matters" in general.

Here is a Han Dynasty picture on stone of a soldier beating the war drum as part of 武舞 *wǔwǔ*, war dance.

There is a well-known tale which showed how one could build a whole strategy upon issuing the drum roll as a challenge to the opposing army. This happened in 684 BCE when the state of Qi (齐/齊), the stronger of two states, attacked the much weaker state of Lu (鲁). Both sides knew each other's strength. When the two armies were facing each other, ready finally for action, the chief of Lu State was eager to attack first, thinking that would be to his advantage, given his relative weakness. However, his counsellor advised against such a move. It was left to the Qi army to issue the first drum roll, rushing forward. The Lu commander, naturally, wanted to order his men to meet the enemy onslaught, but again his strategist restrained him. The Qi army issued the second drum roll, which also produced another damp squib upon the enemy. As a result, it grew more and more impatient. It then issued the third roll of the drums, to which there, too, was no response. Exhausted and frustrated, it retreated to rest. At that crucial moment, the clever Lu strategist advised his general to issue his own deafening drum roll and to attack. The Lu army, against all the odds, routed the superior enemy forces, winning a resounding victory. The strategy relied on is one of psychological warfare – the soldiers, having been psyched up but then let down each time with no action, would progressively be more and more dispirited as well as more and more exhausted. They had reached their lowest point after three such abortive attempts, and that was precisely the opportune moment for the cunning enemy to strike at them, as its own troops would be fresh, carried along by its first flow of adrenalin. This episode in history has prompted an idiomatic expression, 一鼓作气/氣 *yì gǔ zuò qì*, "to complete something at one go" ("within the breath of one drum roll").

Qu Yuan (屈原), who lived ca. 340 – 278 BCE during the Warring States Period, was the first Chinese poet to depart from anonymity and to put his name as an individual to his poetry. Below is his elegy 国/國殃, *For Those Fallen For Their Country* in which he paid tribute to his compatriots for serving so nobly their king and country with their lives. In this vivid and moving poem (translated by Yang Xianyi and Gladys Yang 阳宪/陽憲益、戴乃迭), he not only described the scene in which his side was defeated, but also mentioned the various weapons and equipment used in Zhou warfare.

We grasp huge Shields, clad in Rhinoceros Hide;
The Chariots clash; the Daggers gashing wide;
Flags shade the Sun, like lowering Clouds the Foe;
While Arrows fall the Warriors forward go.
They break our Line, our Ranks are overborne;
My left-hand Horse is slain, its Fellow torn;
My Wheels are locked and fast my Steeds become;
I raise Jade Rods and beat the sounding Drum.
The Heav'n grows wrath; the Gods our Fall ordain;
And cruelly we perish on the Plain.
Our men came forth but never shall return;
Through dreary Plain stretches the Way eterne.
We bear long Swords with curved Bows grimly set;
Though cleft the Skull the Heart knows no Regret.
Warlike indeed, so resolute and proud,

Undaunted still and by no peril cow'd;
Their Spirits deathless, though the Body's slain,
Proudly as Kings amongst the Ghosts shall reign.

操吴戈兮被犀甲，车错毂兮短兵接。 /操吴戈兮被犀甲，車錯轂兮短兵接。
旌蔽日兮敌若云，矢交坠兮士争先。 /旌蔽日兮敵若云，矢交墜兮士争先。
凌余阵兮躐余行，左骖殪兮右刃伤。 /凌余陣兮躐余行，左驂殪兮右刃伤。
霾两轮兮絷四马，援玉枹兮击鸣鼓。 /霾两輪兮縶四马，援玉枹兮擊鸣鼓。
天时坠兮威灵怒，严杀尽兮弃原野。 /天時墜兮威灵怒，嚴殺盡兮弃原野。
出不入兮往不反，平原忽兮路超远。 /出不入兮往不反，平原忽兮路超远。
带长剑兮挟秦弓，首身兮离心不惩。 /帶長劍兮挟秦弓，首身兮離心不懲。
诚既勇兮又以武，终刚强兮不可凌。 /诚既勇兮又以武，终剛强兮不可凌。
身既死兮神以灵，子魂魄兮为鬼雄。 /身既死兮神以靈，子魂魄兮為鬼雄。

Xu Shen, in his dictionary, gave a very interesting interpretation of the character/word 武 *wǔ*. He regarded it as typical *huiyi zi*, a meaning compound. He took the second component 止 *zhǐ*, not so much to mean "foot" as to mean "to stop," "to check" (制止 *zhìzhǐ*). This led him to maintain that built into the meaning of *wu*, paradoxically, is the meaning that the goal of being armed is not to have to use arms, or that the end of military might is to stop all wars and fighting (止戈为武 *zhǐ gē wéi wǔ*). In other words, be armed but using them would have to be the last resort – all other channels, such as diplomacy and cajolery, must be first explored and exhausted before sending in the military. Scholars since have pointed out that Xu Shen was wrong in deconstructing the character/word in this way, because 止 *zhǐ* meaning "to stop" is only a derivative meaning, the original being "foot." We get from one place to another by walking, using our feet and, naturally, when we reach our destination we stop. The derivative meaning is, indeed, "to stop." Xu Shen should not have relied on the derivative meaning, as that period of history during which the character *wu* was constructed, was extraordinarily busy with wars and warfare. In terms of actual deconstruction, Xu Shen was wrong, although he was right in another way. He had detected that the ancient Chinese who lived before him felt very war-weary. An anti-war sentiment, which had appeared in the face of the violence associated with the Shang Dynasty, re-emerged particularly during the second half of the Zhou Dynasty. Xu Shen had absorbed this anti-war strand of thought which was commonly expressed particularly during the Spring and Autumn Period. For instance, there are passages from the

左传/傳 *Zuo Zhuan* (*The Zuo Commentary* said to be a sixth century BCE text but more likely to be of a slightly later date) which appeared to have influenced Xu Shen on the matter of war. One such passage cites the king of Chu (楚庄/莊王) who said that to make one's state militarily strong was a necessity but its military strength should be used ultimately to further disarmament so that blood might no longer be shed in fighting wars. Such passages taken together may be said to express a philosophy and ethics of war: victory is not to be understood simply in military terms (胜/勝之不武 *shèng zhī bú wǔ*); in victory, do not oppress the weak by means of sheer strength (以强凌弱 *yǐ qiáng líng ruò*); to attack another state while taking advantage of the chaos instead of attempting to restore order through mutual alliance is not in accordance with military ethics (以乱/亂易整, 不武 *yǐ luàn yì zhěng, bú wǔ*).

There is another well-known expression: 化干戈为/為玉帛 *huà gāngē wéi yùbó*, literally meaning "to transform arms into jade and silk, to stop fighting and embrace peace." This would be analogous to the English expression "to turn swords into plowshares." We have come across 戈 *gē*, a weapon for charging; 干 *gàn*, on the other hand, is a defensive device like a shield. The two characters/words stand collectively for "arms and wars." Jade (玉 *yù*) and silks (帛 *bó*) stand collectively for peace. The ancient Chinese in their official as well as ordinary lives believed a lot in giving gifts. This tradition also governed inter-state, or diplomatic relations. We have already seen in exploring an earlier theme (***Precious as the warp***) that they held both jade and silks to be precious, but in different ways. Jade expressed rank and status, and was, therefore, given as a token of respect and honor. Silks expressed wealth and were, therefore, given as an expression of friendship. The idea, then, of jade and silks as gifts standing for respect and friendship came to embody the idea of peace.

One can say that Xu Shen's faulty deconstruction of 武 *wǔ* gives us a valuable insight into the evolution of the Chinese attitude towards war and warfare. Xu Shen himself lived in the relative calm of the Han Dynasty which succeeded the short-lived Qin Dynasty (221 – 207 BCE), and which continued the process of unifying China begun by Qin Shihuangdi. From the texts which would have influenced Xu Shen, one could also see that the anti "gung-ho" sentiment had already taken root several hundred years before him. Our very brief account of Sunzi's *The Art of War* has pointed out that it is not a crude war manual but a thoughtful treatise which recognized that like death and taxes, war would always plague human-kind, and hence the need to be always vigilant and prepared for such an eventuality. Such preparedness, according to Sunzi, should not be read as exhortation to be "trigger-happy" or to embrace "shock and awe" as the way forward. In fact, war-weariness and laments about war went back to the *Book of Songs* (诗经/詩經 *Shī Jīng*, ca. 1000 BCE). Here are two of these lamentations found in this great classical text (translated by James Legge):

擊鼓 *JI GU War Drums Rolling*

Hear the roll of our drums !
See how we leap about , using our weapons !
Those do the fieldwork in the State , or fortify Cao ,
While we alone march to the south .
We followed Sun Zizhong ,
Peace having been made with Chen and Song;
[But] he did not lead us back ,
And our sorrowful hearts are very sad .
Here we stay , here we stop ;
Here we lose our horses ;
And we seek for them,
Among the trees of the forest .
For life or for death, however separated ,
To our wives we pledged our word .
We held their hands;
We were to grow old together with them .
Alas for our separation !
We have no prospect of life.
Alas for our stipulation !
We cannot make it good .

击鼓其镗、踊跃用兵。 /擊鼓其鏜、踊躍用兵。
土国城漕、我独南行。 /土國城漕、我獨南行。
从孙子中、平陈与宋。 /從孫子仲、平陳與宋。
不我以归、忧心有忡 /不我以歸、憂心有忡。
爰居爰处、爰丧其马。 /爰居爰處、爰喪其馬。
于以求之、于林之下。 /于以求之、于林之下。

死生契阔、与子程说。　/死生契闊、與子成說。
执子之手、与子偕老。　/執子之手、與子偕老。
于嗟阔兮、不我活兮。　/于嗟闊兮、不我活兮。
于嗟洵兮、不我信兮。　/于嗟洵兮、不我信兮。

This seems to be the lament of some elite soldiers of the army, commanded by the general Sun Zizhong of the state of Wei (魏). These were no ordinary soldiers as they were cavalry. Horses were costly. Losing a horse could mean death, not only because one had lost the means of quick escape from the enemy but also because the animal carried the essentials of survival for the rider, such as his ration, not to mention weapons and armor. In such moments of dire despair and exhaustion, when they realized they probably would never return to their native land, the thoughts of the warriors naturally turned to their wives and families – war, after all, was and is one of the biggest disrupters of domestic tranquillity and destroyers of homes. Yet, the poem also conveys that wars are not of the making of those who fight. The decision lies not with them but with the powers that be.

凱風 *KAI FENG Genial Wind*

The genial wind from the south
Blows on the heart of that jujube tree ,
Till that heart looks tender and beautiful .
What toil and pain did our mother endure !
The genial wind from the south
Blows on the branches of that jujube tree ,
Our mother is wise and good ;
But among us there is none good .
There is the cool spring
Below [the city of] Jun .
We are seven sons ,
And our mother is full of pain and suffering .
The beautiful yellow birds
Give forth their pleasant notes .
We are seven sons ,
And cannot compose our mother's heart .

凯风自南、吹彼枣心。　/凱風自南、吹彼棘心。
枣心夭夭、母氏劬劳。　/棘心夭夭、母氏劬勞。
凯风自南、吹彼枣薪。　/凱風自南、吹彼棘薪。
母氏圣善、我无令人。　/母氏聖善、我無令人。
爰有寒泉、在浚之下。　/爰有寒泉、在浚之下。
有子七人、母氏劳苦。　/有子七人、母氏勞苦。
睍睆黄鸟、载好其音。　/睍睆黃鳥、載好其音。
有子其人、莫慰母心。　/有子其人、莫慰母心。

This lament is especially poignant as one of the greatest duties in traditional Chinese culture is filial piety. Alas, this poor mother would be left uncared for and unhonored by her seven sons, as war had made it impossible for each and every one of them to discharge this sacred duty. War must be a terrible thing if it could negate so elemental a value of the moral order. It is poignant for another reason. It invokes 凯风/凱風 *kăi fēng*, which Legge has translated as "genial wind" but which could also be translated as "gentle breeze." On its own, 凯/凱 *kăi* refers to the triumphant strains of battles won, to being victorious in war. Expressions such as 凯/凱歌 *kăigē* means "song of triumph (in war)" and 凯/凱旋 *kăixuán*, means "triumphant return (from war)." Yet the expression 凯风/凱風 *kăi fēng* means "gentle breeze or wind." This dramatic contrast in meaning almost seems to stress the gentleness of nature as opposed to the triumphalism of the human spirit which expresses itself so boldly and vividly in war. The anonymous composer of the lament seemed to be playing upon this striking opposition by invoking 凯风/凱風, which should be blowing not only on the heart of the jujube tree but on the hearts of all sons and all mothers. Even if there be a triumphant return, who knew who would return and who not, what anguish would consume the mother's heart while waiting. To lose one son in war is a fate difficult to bear, but to lose all seven sons, would be too unbearable even to contemplate. Furthermore, to the Chinese, for parents to mourn the death of children renders the grief even more heart-rending as it goes against the order of children mourning the death of parents, in the more natural course of events. 风/風 *fēng* on its own, in this context, may also mean "airs or songs." 凯风/凱風 *kăi fēng* means not only "gentle breeze or genial wind" but may also imply 凯/凱歌 *kăigē* , "a song of war triumph."

It seems to us that this little poem encapsulates many conflicting, complex emotions and sentiments. The anonymous author had very skillfully played upon the various different possible meanings of the key words of the poem in order to convey the complicated richness of his feelings, the state of turmoil in his soul as he confronted war and facing death in the face, while he was caught in a situation, not of his own making, which made it impossible for himself and his brothers to carry out their foremost duty to their mother.

Laozi's *Daode Jing* (ca. 500 – 250 BCE) also contributed to the condemnation of war and war-mongering, if not out-right pacifism. What he wrote has been rendered freely in the following version:

Armies are tools of violence;
They cause men to hate and fear.
The sage will not join them.
His purpose is creation;
Their purpose is destruction.

Weapons are tools of violence,
Not of the sage;
He uses them only when there is no choice,
And then calmly, and with tact,
For he finds no beauty in them.

Whoever finds beauty in weapons
Delights in the slaughter of men;
And who delights in slaughter
Cannot content himself with peace.

So slaughters must be mourned
And conquest celebrated with a funeral.

夫唯兵者，不祥之器，物或惡之，故有道者不處。
君子居則貴左，用兵則貴右。兵者不祥之器，非君子之器，
不得已而用之，恬淡為上。勝而不美，而美之者，是樂殺人。
夫樂殺人者，則不可得志于天下矣。
吉事尚左，凶事尚右。偏將軍居左，上將軍居右，言以喪禮處之。
殺人之眾，以悲哀泣之，戰勝以喪禮處之。

When Laozi said that "weapons are tools of violence," it was almost as if he had before his mind's eye something as fearsome as this ceremonial Shang bronze battle axe, although it was unlikely he would actually have seen such an object.

Such a long tradition of lamentation about war, so well-established from such early times in Chinese history, would also explain why ancient and traditional Chinese society neither recognized nor celebrated a military class. Instead, it recognized and celebrated a different social group, that of 武侠/俠 *wǔxiá*, experts in the martial arts who embodied the ideals of chivalry, who were knights-errant, roaming the land to defend the weak against the bully, the poor against the exploiting and unscrupulous rich, the oppressed against the strong and the tyrannical. These were the true warriors and heroes in the eyes of the Chinese people. Bearing arms and killing others were morally justified in the context of fighting oppression (and, of course, against invading foreigners). In China's long history, its people had three hopes: that the king/emperor be an enlightened ruler, but failing that, to have good, uncorrupt officials, but failing even that, to have *wuxia* to protect one and to enforce just order in society. *Wuxia* may no longer exist today, but the literary genre it has engendered, in the form of martial arts novels, survives and flourishes, enjoying an extremely devoted and large readership, both in China and throughout the diaspora. Films about *wuxia* are also very popular, and of late, have even won recognition in the West as art house films.

In an earlier theme (***What is to be a woman?***), we have looked briefly at the character 安 *ān*, meaning "peaceful and tranquil": it is the "roof or house" radical 宀 with the character of "woman" under or in it. This word primarily suggests peace in a domestic context. It can also mean "secure and out of danger." The expression for "safe and sound" is 平安 (a two-syllable word) or 平平安安 *píngpíngānān*. 平 *píng* also means "calm, peaceful, tranquil." So, it is very appropriate that it should also be used in the larger context of peace in the land as well as peace between countries – the word for "peace" is 和平 *hépíng* (a two-syllable word). 和 *hé* means "gentle, kind, harmonious, on friendly terms."

One tribe may beat another tribe in battle. One state may defeat another in war. To conquer on horseback is one thing; but when the conquering is done and peace takes over, one cannot rule from horseback. Peace can only be ensured by the art of ruling or governing the land and its people. The character/word "to rule or to govern" is 治 *zhì*.

It should straightaway be pointed out that its meaning is extensive, and goes beyond merely to rule or to govern. For instance 治病 *zhì bìng*, is "to treat an illness," 治疗/療 *zhìliáo*, "medical therapy." It can even be used to talk about teaching someone a lesson, 治他 *zhì tā*. Indeed, its earliest use was in the context of river engineering, to control a river to prevent flooding. This, surely, is both curious and puzzling. The character actually has the water 氵 radical. According to Xu Shen's dictionary, it originally was the name of a river, a river whose location could be traced to the North-east of China. That dictionary records the character as *xingsheng zi*, a semantic-phonetic compound, as it has two components. The first is the "water" radical, and the second on the right gives the sound. Later, the name of the river was used to mean "control of a river." This meaning of managing the flow of rivers led to talk of controlling or treating illness, social behavior, as well as ruling or governing a country and its people.

The heroic feats of the great Yu (禹) of the Xia Dynasty (ca. 21st – 16th century BCE) were to do with controlling the course of the Yellow River (黄河). That river was at once China's joy and its sorrows – joy, because without it, Chinese civilization might not have emerged or developed the characteristics it possesses, its sorrows, because the river's floods throughout China's history had wrought great destruction and brought immense grief. China's engineers had no choice but to develop techniques to control its course. These included dredging, digging channels to divert the flow both over and under ground, damming, etc. China's system of agriculture has depended on controlling water in all forms, including extensive canal irrigation. The relationship between water control and government was an intimate one. If the emperor failed to get the river under control, there would be flooding. Or if there was prolonged drought and the irrigation channels no longer brought sufficient water from another area, then there would be famine. Floods, drought, famine, disease all led to political unrest and even uprising. If the harvest was poor, the people would be unable to pay taxes to the landlords and the emperor. Faced with such precarious outcomes and dangerous threats, the emperor would feel that the Mandate of Heaven might at any time be withdrawn from him. So, it was very natural for the ancient Chinese to derive the notion of control and management, in general, as well as that of control and government, in particular, ultimately from the name of a river.

As for the relationship between controlling a river and treating illness, it is equally not so difficult to grasp its closeness once it is pointed out. As we have seen, Chinese culture was born along the banks of the Yellow River which runs like a great artery through the heartland of that civilization, in *Zhongyuan*, the Central Plains. Water is essential for life, not only in the sense that one would die very quickly for want of water to drink, but also that one would die, too, for want of food to eat. Water is required to grow food. The circulation of blood in the body would then be analogous to the great river – blood is both water and food, carried to every part of the body, just as the great river brought food and water to all parts of *Zhongyuan* along its banks. That is why in Chinese medicine, the kind of pulse felt is regarded as a key indicator of how well or badly the different organs of the body are faring, just as the political and social well-being of *Zhongyuan* would be measured by how well the river performed its task of ensuring that the essential elements for survival were made available to the people dependent on it. In Western medicine, the pulse is significant because it tells you the rate of the heartbeat. In Chinese medicine, it is much more than that, as it is a key diagnostic tool, helping the physician to determine the nature of the patient's illness as well as the treatment for the condition.

Politics is 政治 *zhèngzhì*. In English and other European languages such as French and German, the word "politics" comes from the Greek for a city, *polis*. Ancient Greek states were primarily city states, the most well-known of them was Athens. That city state was a direct democracy, where the freemen of the city gathered in the forum to discuss and vote on all matters concerning the running of the city. Politics were the affairs of the *polis*. However, ancient Greek democracy might not be all that appeared on the surface. The reference to the freemen of the city gives the game away. If only freemen could participate in the life of the *polis*, then there must be unfree people who were not entitled to do so. Indeed, there were; these were the slaves. Ancient Greek democracy was run on the back of slavery (as a full-blown institution, unlike the less extensive and less systematic efforts of the Shang state – see ***Surviving and Living***). Slaves did all the laboring, ensured that the economy produced enough to feed and clothe their masters, as well as free time for the master class to take part fully in the duties of citizenship. In today's terminology, we would say it was based on exploitation. Not only were slaves excluded from membership of the *polis*, so were women. The *polis* was, in reality, a pretty exclusive club. It was "elitist democracy" (a contradiction in terms?) at its most provocative, but is, nevertheless, often praised as the noblest expression of the human spirit.

The Age of Modernity (which began in Western Europe from the seventeenth century) had chosen to root itself politically in ancient Greek civilization. The leading modern Western states, as a matter of fact, turned out, too, to rest on slavery. Slavery was not, for instance, formally abolished in Britain till 1833 when Parliament passed the Anti-Slavery Act after about two hundred odd years of the very profitable slave trade. When such states later embraced democracy, they, too, excluded women from the franchise just as Athenian democracy had. Of course, these large nation-states differ from the *polis* in one key respect – they cannot hope to run direct but only indirect democracy. After a specified interval of time, whether four or five years, voters go to the polling booths to return rulers to run the affairs of the state, to pass new laws, etc. In certain countries which enjoy an enviable reputation for being democratic, such as Switzerland, you may be surprised to hear that women did not get the vote till 1971 (*sic*). An inverse relationship appears to hold between female suffrage and the kind of democracy involved – the more direct the democracy (such as in Switzerland), the longer it took for women to obtain the vote. The historical evidence tells a tale even more ironical than that. It appears to show that the further from the democratic ideal as advocated by Western political theory, the faster women got the vote – the Soviet Union pioneered universal female suffrage in 1917. The USA followed in 1920, and the UK in 1928. Perhaps women in the West owed their universal suffrage in part, if not wholly, to the Bolshevik Revolution, rather than merely through their own heroic efforts of chaining themselves to public railings.

While the word "politics" in the West is rooted in Athenian direct democracy, in contrast, traditional Chinese civilization did not have the notion of democracy at all. What could the word "politics" in

Chinese, then, mean? The word itself, as we have mentioned, is 政治 *zhèngzhì*. We have already taken a quick look at *zhi*; we now need to say something about 政 *zhèng*. The character has two components: on the left is 正 *zhèng* and, on the right, the radical 攵, stands for "to strike or hit." But strike what is then the crucial question. Obviously, it strikes 正 *zhèng*. In *jiaguwen, jinwen, xiaozhuan and lishu*, the charater 正 *zhèng* looks like this:

In *jiaguwen* and *jinwen* there are clearly two components: the square or circle at the top which stands for a head, hence representing a person, and the word for "foot" at the bottom which shows the person marching or walking straight up north. This combination is taken to mean being "determined to hit the target with no deviation." In *jiaguwen*, this word was normally used in the context of an army marching to war; so the original meaning was a military one. In *xiaozhuan* and *lishu*, the foot appears as 止, and the head is replaced by a horizontal line. 正 *zhèng* stands for "being upright, unbiased, balanced." It is *huiyi zi*, a meaning compound. It is a word which is rich in meanings; it has only positive meanings, such as: "straight"; "upright" (physical sense); "situated in the middle" (therefore, "balanced/unbiased)"; "precise/exact"; "honest"; "upright" (moral sense); "right"; "pure"; "just" (moral sense); "correct." Used as a verb, it means "to rectify." It implies that the ruler is expected to carry out policies which are correct, just, honest, and balanced (not favoring only one sector while ignoring the rest). These abstract desirable qualities (since Han times) were made more concrete by the Confucian ideals which we have earlier (***A virtue uniquely Chinese***) outlined. The Confucian virtues of *ren* (仁) or co-humanity, of *yi* (义/義) or doing what was morally/socially/aesthetically proper which included the Golden Rule, and of *li* (礼/禮) or acting in accordance with codes of behavior, which in turn embodied *ren* and *yi*. *The Analects* (论语/論語), one of the Confucian classics, contains a passage which can roughly be translated as: a ruler who rules in accordance with moral principles would be like the polestar around whose fixed position the other stars would move (为/為政以德, 譬若北辰, 居其所而众/衆星供之).

Confucius in *The Analects* when asked by one of his students to explain the notion 政 *zhèng*, glossed the word as follows: 政 involves 正 *zhèng*. If you, as ruler/leader were to be upright, just, and correct in your conduct, who would dare not to be similarly upright, just and correct? (政者，正也。子帅/帥以正，郭敢不正？)

The ruler's policies were expected to advance the welfare and interests of those whom he ruled, rather than his own private interests. Should he advance the latter at the expense of the former, he could be criticized. It was the task of his high officials to keep him on the straight and narrow. Of course, in reality, many rulers would simply ignore such criticisms at best, and at worst, would order the critics to be dismissed from office or even killed. Many such good officials resigned and some even committed suicide, as they were thrown into such deep despair at their own impotence in curbing and changing the corrupt ways of the ruler.

One such official was Qu Yuan (屈原) who was also a great poet, one of whose poems we have cited earlier above. When exiled from the court, he went back to his native village, and spent a good deal of his time collecting the poetry and songs in the countryside of Chu (楚) state. He grew more and more depressed when he saw the inevitable sad decline of his country and the sufferings of his countrymen owing to the ruler's determination to carry on in his corrupt ways. He had secured a near "immortal" place in the affections of the Chinese people because he committed suicide in a despairing gesture of protest. He flung himself into the river clasping a large stone. Legend has it that the people of Chu threw into the river a special wine called "yellow wine" (黄酒) which had the medicinal property of preventing decay, so eager were they to prevent Qu Yuan's body from putrefaction and attack by predators big and small in the water. Also, they made dumplings wrapped up in bamboo or reed leaves, boiled, and then thrown into the river, to feed the fish to divert them from eating him. This dumpling is called 粽子 *zòng·zi* and may be made (today) with different fillings, some savory, others sweet. You can buy them from your local Chinese supermarket, especially during the festival period. Today, after two and a half millennia, every year on the fifth day of the fifth month of the Chinese calendar, people would celebrate by racing boats on rivers, lakes, coastal waters, making leaf-wrapped dumplings to commemorate his life and his death. This festival is called *Duanwu jie* 端午节/節. (As of 2008, it has been declared a public holiday in the PRC.) Of course, it was unlikely that the dragon boat festival originated as specific commemoration of Qu Yuan. It pre-dated the event of his death, and was originally a celebration of the harvest of mid-winter wheat. Anyway, once the race had been borrowed by those who wished to perpetuate the memory of Qu Yuan, the elaborately designed dragon on the prow of the boats, the beating of drums, gongs, clappers as well as the setting off of fire crackers are said to represent the original attempts to recover his body and to scare off predators from attacking it. It is touching that he should still be remembered at such a festival after all those years, for having stood up to his principles in public life and for sacrificing himself in a fruitless attempt to promote the welfare of the people, rather than be a yes-man to a ruler intent on pursuing his own selfish good. The Chu king eventually doomed the state of Chu to extinction, as it was conquered by Qin Shihuangdi in 221 BCE.

Here is the refrain of an elegy by Qu Yuan entitled: *Thoughts Before Drowning* (*怀沙/懷沙*). The translation is by Yang Xianyi and Gladys Yang:

On and on the Rivers slow
Down their various courses flow.
Dark the Way and overgrown,
And the Future all unknown.

All my Time in Anguish spent,
No End set to my Lament
By the World misunderstood,
With no Friend or Kinsman good.

Though my Conscience is quite clear,
I can find no Witness here.
Gone the Charioteer so prized,
The swift Horses are despised.

Sad or happy, each Man's Fate
Overtakes him soon or late.
If I keep a steadfast Heart,
Fear in me can have no Part.

Death, I know, must come to All,
Nor for Mercy would I call.

Saints, I follow in your Wake!
Your Example shall I take!

浩浩远、湘，分流汩 兮。	/浩浩遠、湘，分流汩兮。
修路幽蔽，道远忽兮。	/修路幽蔽，道遠忽兮。
怀质报情，独无匹兮。	/懷質報情，獨無匹兮。
伯乐既没， 骥焉程兮。	/伯樂既沒，驥焉程兮。
民生禀命，各有所错兮。	/民生稟命，各有所錯兮。
定心广志，奈何胃惧兮！	/定心廣志，奈何畏懼兮！
曾伤爱哀，永叹喟兮。	/曾傷愛哀，永嘆喟兮。
世 浊莫吾知, 人心不可謂兮。	/世濁莫吾知，人心不可謂兮。
知死不可让，愿勿爱兮。	/知死不可讓，愿勿愛兮。
明告君子，吾将以为类兮。	/明告君子，吾將以為類兮。

Put very simplistically, the major difference between the idea of politics in modern Western and traditional Chinese political thought appears to lie in this: the West emphasizes procedural matters while the Chinese focussed on substantive ones. Democracy which defines political life in the West simply lays down certain rules of procedure for throwing up decision-makers – these involve the people casting their vote in a secret ballot every so often for candidates sponsored, preferably, by two big rival parties. Who these people are and what they stand for (always remember that Adolf Hitler was democratically elected by the German people in the 1930s), how they get the citizens to cast their vote for them (for example, through advertising campaigns run on big money as seems to be the practice in today's mature democracies), and what they do, once they win power (to lead the country, for instance, to horrific wars even) are strictly speaking not something that democracy has anything to say, provided the specified procedures are followed.

In contrast, the traditional Chinese conception of the political had little to say about the procedures by which rulers were thrown up. According to it, what was crucial was how they used that power once they became political decision-makers. Historically, rulers in China got to be political decision-makers through two routes: the first was through inheritance, and the second through revolt, dethroning the ruler already there. Sometimes the legitimate ruler was deposed because he neglected his duties and was corrupt. At other times, it was through naked ambition – a rival sibling or relative wanted the throne badly and the incumbent was weak or incompetent. Traditionally, the Chinese had put up even with brothers killing brothers, fathers killing sons (when sons were suspected of plotting against the father), and even on some rare occasions, mothers killing or imprisoning sons and other relatives. What appeared to count more was the aftermath of the fighting and the bloodshed, following the change of regime. Should the new ruler or political decision-maker act in accordance with 政 *zhèng* in governing the people (that is to say in their 治 *zhì*), the people would judge him to be a good ruler, and would be prepared to overlook the blood on his hand as he climbed the greasy pole of political power. Their judgment was influenced by the outcomes in the exercise of political power, whether it was responsibly discharged. An example of such a ruler who won approval was one of the three great emperors of the Qing Dynasty (1644 – 1911 CE), acknowledged by history and historians to have done China and its people good – he was the Yongzheng (雍正) emperor who lived between 1678 and1735 CE. He came to the Dragon Throne probably by forging his father's will, putting down his rival siblings and others who stood in his way through ruthless machinations. In turn, to ensure that his own succession would be smooth, he ordered one of his sons who had earlier allied himself with one of his uncles against himself, to commit suicide. He might have been autocratic, but he was very efficient, very severe against corrupt and wasteful practices, and reformed the financial administration. When as prince, his father, the Kangxi emperor, sent him to deal with a disastrous flood in southern China, he not only faced the extremely difficult and delicate task of extracting money from the local "moneybags" for rescue and recovery work, but he also made sure that the relief funds were properly distributed so that no one starved. His reign though short-lived – a mere thirteen years – is acknowledged to have brought prosperity and peace to the country.

This way of understanding the traditional Chinese conception of political power is often masked by saying that Chinese political philosophy is at best a form of paternalism, and at worst, no political philosophy at all but the mere acceptance of naked force. There is no point in denying it could lend itself to the charge of paternalism, as Confucian texts about ruling used paternalistic or patriarchal metaphors. For instance, the relationship between ruler and ruled was presented as that between father and son. However, we need to look beyond such metaphors to see what stood behind them. We find a body of ideas which was meant to guide the ruler in his policy-making. Central to that body of ideas is the notion of the welfare of the people. Today, many Western political theorists say that such talk is empty rhetoric and means nothing, as each individual has her own view about what counts as welfare. We have to remember that traditional Chinese thought was not based on the spirit of individualism. To it, the concept was not meaningless – the Chinese people quite understandably above all wanted (and still want today) adequate food, shelter, clothing, security etc., not to be unjustly taxed, not to be oppressed by corrupt practices and officials, to lead peaceful, tranquil and prosperous lives, with no upheaval at home, and no invasions from outside or wars. The Chinese ruler knew that was what the people wanted. Ultimately, if the ruler did not deliver on these large fronts, he knew he would be in deep trouble. Should attempts to satisfy these important goals and aspirations be simply called paternalism? We leave you to ponder the matter.

Let us say something briefly about the notion of law in the Chinese theory of ruling. Some Western scholars have been known to go so far as to say that Chinese thought had never known it. This is surprising for two reasons: first there is a whole school called The Legalist School. One of its key texts is dated to the Warring States Period. Its author is Han Fei (ca. 280 – 233 BCE). Qin Shihuangdi put the Legalist philosophy into practice in running his empire; so did the famous Cao Cao, warlord, general and poet in ruling the state of Wei during the Three Kingdoms Period (220 – 265 CE). Second, the view also ignored the actual existence of the law throughout Chinese society, whether in the area of criminal or civil law. There were clearly laws forbidding people to do certain things with specific sanctions attached should these be violated. People drew up wills, contracts in business deals and for the purchase of property. There were courts with judges to adjudicate claims when people litigated; when murders occurred, the alleged murderers were taken to court and tried to determine their guilt or innocence.

Indeed, the Chinese as early as the Warring States Period had established the office of the coroner, as shown in one of its texts, *The Spring and Autumn Annals (of the State of Lu)*. In 1975, during an excavation of a Qin tomb in Hubei Province (湖北云梦/夢), over a thousand bamboo slips comprising the book were found as well as those recording the legal system of the Qin State (897 – 221 BCE) which was carried over into the Qin Dynasty, as already mentioned. The Qin system required the coroner to conduct immediate post-mortems and to write reports about the outcome of the investigation.

There were other later texts such as one during the Three Kingdoms Period. However, the most systematic work on forensic science and the detailed investigative methods of the coroner is a Song text, written by a leading judicial officer of the Song Dynasty (960 – 1279 CE) called Song Ci (宋慈， 1186 – 1249 CE). He was viewed as a wonderfully humane person, a model of moral probity as well as possessing great intellectual, analytical rigor. His book was based on the cases with which he had been involved during his distinguished career which, not unexpectedly, ended in his resignation from office. When his investigations led him to exposure of corruption amongst the highest places, the emperor chose to ignore his findings, while showering him with honors. His book has miraculously survived, and has been translated into Japanese and several European languages. The earliest of the latter was in French in 1779, then in Dutch in 1862, in English in 1882 and 1902, and of late there is even an American translation in 1982 (*sic*). One of its titles in English is: *Collected Cases of Injustice Rectified Through Forensic Science* (洗冤集录/錄). Other books after Song Ci's followed in the succeeding centuries but his remained unsurpassed and authoritative.

The first official record of the role of the coroner in English legal history emerged in 1194 CE during the reign of Henry I. This bears such remarkable detailed similarities with the Song Dynasty system of judicial forensic procedure and investigation since 1000 CE that some scholars have argued that this might not be a mere coincidence, but that such ideas would have entered Europe from China through the trade routes. One of these ancient forensic methods was recently used (1993) in a court operating within the Common Law tradition.

Some Western scholars might have been misled by the fact that the Confucian world-view, which dominated Chinese society for nearly two thousand years, preferred moral notions rather than legal rules to govern conduct. This, however, should not be interpreted that Chinese society dispensed with the law. The Confucian philosophy should be understood as saying that morals are superior to law as law is concerned with external behavior, not so much with the character which is behind that outward conformity. A morally good person would do something because it is right and avoid doing something because it is wrong. That is why the cultivation of virtue is so important. A morally good person would not dream of harming an innocent neighbor, even if the law were to permit him to do so, and even if he were bribed handsomely to do so. A person, who obeys the law only because of the fear of being caught and punished, is a morally inferior person. Such a person would also do anything which is not explicitly forbidden but permitted by the law, even if the act is a morally ignoble one. For instance, he might walk by without bothering to stop to help an elderly person who had fallen, lying in agony on the ground, begging for his help, because he was in a hurry to get to the pub for a drink. It is true that the law does not oblige him to stop and help another in need, but morality says he should.

No society can dispense with the law as every society must ensure a minimum degree of order and harmony. Neither do we need to interpret law quite so narrowly and so negatively as no more than a disguise for the use of force. In theory, at least, if not always in practice, law is intimately associated with justice, and is intended to curb arbitrary power. So how exactly did the ancient Chinese understand the notion of law, which is 法 *fǎ*. In *jinwen, xiaozhuan, lishu*, the character looks like this:

The character first appeared in *jinwen*. Let us, however, focus on the *xiaozhuan* version to unravel a complicated and interesting analysis. It has three components: the "water" (氵) radical on the left, the top bit on the right 廌 *zhì*, the bottom bit on the right 去 *qù*. The "water" radical implies that the law is like a bowl of water: take a bowl of water and hold it steady in your hand, or if that is too difficult, rest it on a flat surface. After a while, you will find that the surface of the water is perfectly flat. The law should be like that – before it, every one, regardless of rank or status, is equal. That is the meaning of law as justice: 公平 *gōng píng*.

The second component, on the top right, actually stands for a legendary animal which is also called 獬豸 *xièzhì*. Here is a fifteenth century CE badge of the Ming Dynasty with the animal embroidered on silk, worn by the government censor, a law-enforcing agent. Should you visit the Ming

Tombs outside Beijing where thirteen emperors of the Ming Dynasty (1368 – 1644 CE) are buried, and walk along the road leading up to the mausoleums, called the Spirit Way, you would see the road lined with statues of officials, warriors and animals, some real and some mythical. The *xiezhi* is one of the latter.

We have already come across this mythical beast in an earlier theme (***Rites and rituals: how the butcher became the prime minister!***) when we looked at the character *yang* ("sheep") which is linked with the notion of justice. This animal, we said, did not have two horns but one, and so was like a unicorn (*qilin*), though not one. We have also told the story about its ability to distinguish between right and wrong, to arbitrate properly and to mete out suitable punishments to the guilty party. If this peculiar animal saw two people fight, it would butt the party in the wrong. If it found two people quarrelling, it would bite the one who had aggressively started the squabble. Its nature was said to be its love of justice. It represented fair-mindedness in administrating law and justice, that is, 公正 *gōngzhèng*. This explains why traditionally judges in China wore a hat called the 獬豸冠 *xièzhì guàn*, a cap which incorporated in its design this legendary beast, while other law-enforcing officials wore a badge, as shown above. In the West, the mythic figure for law and justice is the Greek goddess, Themis. The ancient Romans turned her into the abstract figure of Justitia, who is portrayed as impassive, blindfolded, carrying a pair of scales. The traditional Chinese equivalent of Themis or Justitia is the 獬豸 *xièzhì*.

Now, we come to the third component at the bottom right of the *xiaozhuan* version of the character for "law." It is 去 *qù*. Its various forms (*jiaguwen, jinwen, xiaozhuan, lishu*) are shown below:

Jiaguwen shows a person on the top and what looks like the opening of a cave at the bottom. It is *huiyi zi*, a meaning compound, whose original meaning is "to leave, to depart." It has numerous derivative meanings including "to get rid of (to eliminate)" as well as "to lose." As part of the character for "law," to eliminate or to get rid of a problem amounts to solving the problem before the court brought by the case in hand. This sense implies that the function of law is to settle and decide cases: 法断/斷 *fă duàn*. What could the second derivative meaning amount to in the legal context? It is equivalent to saying that the law must not lose sight of or forget its two basic functions, to regard all to be equal before the law (公平 *gōng·píng*) as well as to dispense justice in a fair-minded manner (公正 *gōngzhèng*). These two functions are captured by the notion of 法 *fǎ*, the law, which as 公义/公義 *gōngyì* could be translated as "righteousness in the public domain."

The features of 法 *fǎ* revealed through the deconstruction of the character show that the traditional Chinese conception of law approximates to certain key aspects of what in the West is called the rule of law. The Western conception, amongst other things, emphasizes the curbing of arbitrary power, equality before the law regardless of rank or class, fair-mindedness in the administration of justice, etc. In China, the beginnings of law, some scholars hold, had emerged by the Xia Dynasty in a basic form, probably merely in terms of codes of behavior and punishment. By the Zhou Dynasty, and certainly by the Warring States Period in late Zhou, the more elaborate development of law both in theory (as the containment of arbitrary power) and in institutional arrangements (such as courts, judges, appeal procedures) would have been firmly established.

In *lishu*, the more complicated strokes and content of the *xiaozhuan* version were simplified to 法 *fǎ*, a form the word has retained to this day, with only the "water" radical and the third component on the bottom right, left in place.

末

Welcome to China

Should you visit China, you may hear yourself referred to as 老外 *lǎowài*. *Wai* means in this context "someone from outside, abroad, that is, a foreigner." *Lao* literally means "old" as in 老人家 *lǎo·ren·jia* ("an elderly person"). It is also used in 老朋友 *lǎo péng·you* ("a friend of long standing"). In the first case, *lao* is a term of respect. Chinese culture cherishes longevity, and so gives special respect to the elderly. The association with respect is then transferred to other contexts, such as that of referring to foreigners as *laowai*. (The term can also be used to refer to a lay person who lacks expertise in a specified field of skill or knowledge.) It is meant to convey not only respect but also friendliness. It is so much more informal than the term 外国/國人 *wàiguórén* ("foreigners") or, even the expression 外国/國朋友 *wàiguó péng·you* ("foreign friends"). The expression *laowai* is also considered to be especially apt because of a certain implication it carries. No Chinese would be surprised or offended should foreigners do something which the Chinese themselves would consider to be impolite or inappropriate. The expression is an acknowledgement of the possibility of cross-cultural ignorance as well as incomprehension.

The attitude to foreigners conveyed by the term *laowai* is in sharp contrast to some terms used in the past, particularly during the nineteenth and the first half of the twentieth centuries, to refer to foreigners. The Europeans were 洋鬼子 *yángguǐ·zi* (literally "Western ghosts"), and the term was intended to be abusive. The non-abusive term for Europeans would have been 西方人 *Xīfāng rén* ("people from the West") or 西洋人 *Xīyáng rén* ("people from across the Western seas"). The Chinese people during that period felt the need to coin an abusive term because foreigners were imperialist invaders. Some arrived on their shores in gunboats from the west, such as those we today call "white people," while others marched from across the north-east, humiliating and exploiting them. Thankfully, times have changed and foreigners are no longer of that ilk.

In Chinese folk belief, there is a world of difference between the land of the living occupied by humans who are 人 *rén* and the shadowy beyond occupied by ghosts who are 鬼 *guǐ*. Ghosts are considered to be neither friendly nor benign to humans, but full of hatred and vengeance. It is no wonder that the living is both afraid of them as well as resentful about them. In terms of the traditional Chinese moral outlook, one should have mutual respect, care and concern for fellow humans. But ghosts are not humans, and they show no goodwill to humans. Humans and ghosts do not occupy the same moral universe. As foreigners of that unfortunate era brought no goodwill but only ill will towards them, it was not a surprise that the Chinese people should feel that such foreigners were not fellow humans but ghosts. As they were unable to drive these invaders from their shores, they could only vent their feelings by coining such an abusive term to refer to them.

Worry not. Foreigners are *laowai*, and you are very welcome.

末

Conclusion

We have used the metaphor of the warp and weft to illustrate the inextricable way in which the Chinese language in its written aspect (汉/漢字 *Hànzì*), on the one hand, and Chinese culture and history, on the other, are inter-twined. Nevertheless, we have also argued that prioritising the former over the latter may not be unjustified, as without the continuity of the written word, the course of Chinese culture might have taken a different route. It would also have meant that the Chinese people might not, to a greater or lesser degree, have direct access to their own past.

The continuity of *Hanzi*, in its most fundamental aspect, is reflected by the fact that Xu Shen's six principles of formation and use apply to the earliest forms of characters/words in *jiaguwen* as well as to the latest in *jianti*, the Simplified Standard script, an interval of at least three and a half millennia. This in turn makes it possible to deconstruct characters/words in terms of their different historical forms to make them yield interesting information and stories which lie behind them. Such linguistic excavation has told us many things about how the ancient Chinese lived daily and throughout the year as the seasons changed, how their society was organized as it changed and evolved, about their views on cosmology, philosophy, astronomy, geography, ecology, biology, physics, medicine, even neuroscience, politics and law, war and peace, and other themes.

We have seen that the Chinese use the warp (经/經) to stand for something which is foundational or regular and recurring. Certain texts are considered to be so fundamentally important to the culture that they are called *jing*, such as 易经/經 *Yi Jing* (*The Book of Changes*), 诗经/詩經 *Shi Jing* (*The Book of Songs*), or 道德经/經 *Daode Jing* (the Daoist classic attributed to Laozi). Emperors came and went, dynasties rose and fell, but for the Chinese people, what endure are these canonical works and their reception with different understanding by different generations of scholars under different sets of circumstances. The world-view of the Chinese people, in spite of changes and development as well as the continuous addition of new strands over the centuries, has basically been shaped by these canonical texts.

One can plausibly argue that Chinese writing is part of Chinese identity, whether the writing is conceived merely as a mundane tool of communication or as an expression of Chinese aesthetics via its calligraphy. These two aspects of the writing are constitutive of Chinese civilization. Although China went through anxious soul-searching during the last century and teetered on the brink of going down the road of radical language reform, Mao and his comrades, in the end, drew back from embracing such a project. They realized that one cannot detach the utilitarian role of the writing from its aesthetic expression, and that the latter would not survive should the non-alphabetic character be replaced by its approximate (Latin) alphabetic equivalent. They could not contemplate the loss of so much cultural heritage.

On this point, it is instructive to compare briefly the respective historical turns taken by China and Turkey. These two countries were faced with a similar set of problems, the challenge posed to them with the passing of the old feudal orders (the collapse of the Qing and Ottoman dynasties) and the aggressive dominance of Western powers. In the name of modernization and progress, Ataturk ordered the Arabic Ottoman script to be abandoned and the Latin alphabet installed. As a result, today, apart from some very elderly people and specialists, the ordinary Turk could only access their Ottoman past (1299 – 1922) via (Latin) alphabetic translations of some limited texts. One could argue that this is no great loss in one sense, as the Chinese people today, educated only in modern Chinese (*jianti* or *fanti*), also cannot readily read texts in classical Chinese, without additional effort and some training. However, what is important is the impact on the national psyche which is more psychological than intellectual – the Ataturk language reform of 1928 was intended to make the Turkish people conceive themselves as building afresh a "new modern nation" modelled on Western nation states. It was meant ideologically to cut the people from their old roots, so that present and future generations could no longer directly draw inspiration or pride from the past, which was considered at best an irrelevancy, at worst a pernicious impediment to progress. China, in the end, rejected this option. As a result, the Chinese people remain in touch with their rich and long past, an enduring history of cultural achievements of which they can be proud, and to which they can, to an extent, still directly access, in spite of the *jianti* in use in the Chinese mainland. This access is also helped by the fact that the Chinese language in daily use retains and employs many idiomatic expressions which are based on or derived from historical happenings and personages.

The continuity of the written tradition has made written Chinese unique in more ways than one in the history of writing in the world. It is the only living non-alphabetic language. It has probably the longest unbroken history of any written language. If the latest scholarship turns out to survive critical scrutiny, it may also be the oldest form of writing in the history of writing itself. The written language is remarkable also in the fact that it combines two techniques of character/word-creation, the principles of *xingsheng zi* (semantic-phonetic compound) and *huiyi zi* (meaning compound) – while the latter is not unique as more than one other living language uses it, the combination might well be.

In the absence of such continuity, this enterprise of linguistic excavation would, at best, only make antiquarian sense. It would not be a deconstruction of living characters/words, characters whose different historical forms could, all the same, be made to tell fascinating tales, or suggest interesting but, hopefully, plausible hypotheses in interpreting them.

This exercise would have served its purpose if it has made readers more aware of the richness of the Chinese character/word. It would most certainly have served its purpose if it succeeds in arousing curiosity and a desire to learn more about the Chinese language as well as the culture and the history which it encapsulates and in which, at the same time, it is embedded.

Chinese Historical Periods and Dynasties

Palaeolithic Period 旧/舊石器时/時代	ca. 1,700,000 – 8000 BCE
Neolithic Period 新石器时/時代 Yangshao Culture 仰韶文化 Hemudu Culture 河姆渡文化 Dawenkou Culture 大汶口文化 Majiayao Culture 马/馬家窑/窯文化 Longshan Culture 龙/龍山文化	ca. 8000 – 2000 BCE ca. 5000 – 3000 BCE ca. 5000 – 2500 BCE ca. 4300 – 2500 BCE ca. 3300 – 2050 BCE ca. 2300 – 1900 BCE
Xia Dynasty 夏代	ca. 21st – 16th century BCE
Shang Dynasty 商代	ca. 16th – 11th century BCE
Zhou Dynasty 周代 Western Zhou Eastern Zhou Spring and Autumn Period 春秋时/時代 Warring States Period 战国时/戰國時代	ca. 11th century – 221 BCE ca. 11th century – 770 BCE 770 – 221 BCE 770 – 476 BCE 475 – 221 BCE
Qin Dynasty 秦代	221 – 207 BCE
Han Dynasty 汉/漢代 Western Han Eastern Han	206 BCE – 220 CE 206 BCE – 24 CE 25 – 220 CE
Three Kingdoms Period 三国/國/时/時代	220 – 265 CE
Jin Dynasty 晋代	265 – 420 CE
Northern and Southern Dynasties 南北朝	420 – 589 CE
Sui Dynasty 隋代	581 – 618 CE
Tang Dynasty 唐代	618 – 907 CE
Five Dynasties 五代	907 – 960 CE
Song Dynasty 宋代 Northern Song Southern Song	960 – 1279 CE 960 – 1127 CE 1127 – 1279 CE
Yuan Dynasty 元代	1279 – 1368 CE
Ming Dynasty 明代	1368 – 1644 CE
Qing Dynasty 清代	1644 – 1911 CE
The Republic of China 中華共和國 The People's Republic of China 中华人民共和国	1911 – 1949 –

Map 1: *Putonghua* and other *fangyan* (regional speeches)

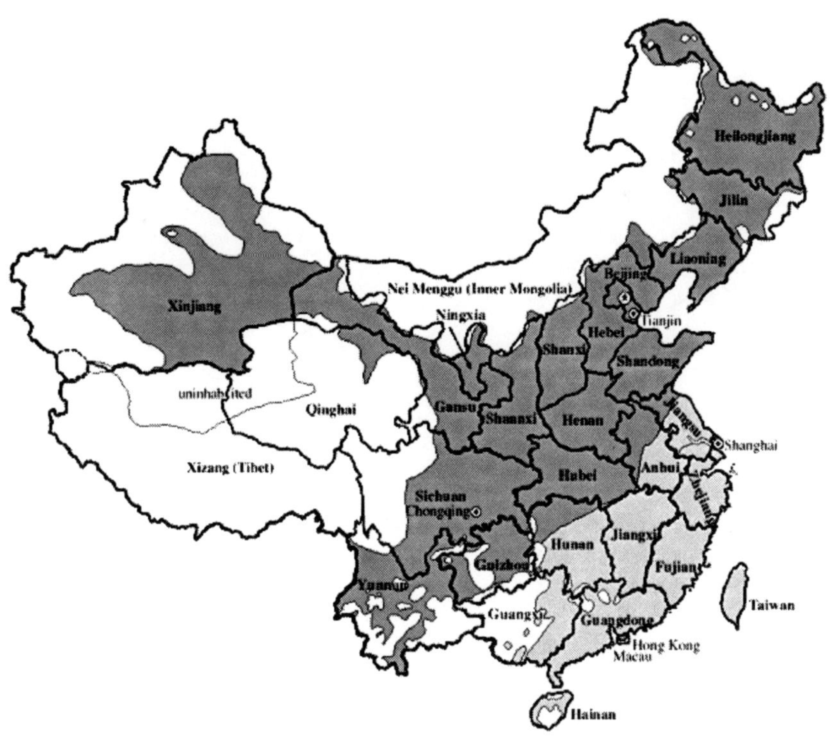

Putonghua (a northern *fangyan*) stretches in a great swathe from as far north in the east as Heilongjiang, as far west as parts of Xinjiang, as far south as Yunnan – portion covered pinkish red.
Fangyan: The major ones are: *wu* which, in the main, covers Shanghai, Jiangsu and Zhejiang; *min* covers Fujian, part of Hainan and Taiwan; *yue* (Cantonese) covers Guangdong, part of Guangxi, Hongkong and Macau – portion colored ochre.

Putonghua and the other regional speeches constitute *Hanyu*, also known as "the Chinese language" (*Zhongwen*). The languages of some minority ethnic groups, such as Uygur and Mongolian, are non-Han.

[This map is reproduced, but with editing, from the following site: http://schiller.dartmouth.edu/chinese/maps/maps.html]

Map 2: Some Neolithic Cultures and their sites

Diaotonghuan, near Poyang Lake in Jiangxi Province: excavation in the 1990s revealed rice cultivation in the area 10,000 years ago. Remains of rice, dated to 7000 years ago, were also found at **Hemudu**, Zhejiang Province during excavations which began in the 1980s.

Damaidi, Ningxia Hui Autonomous region: scholars in 2007 announced that some two thousand marks or symbols, dated between 7000 and 8000 years ago, carved on rocks could well be the precursors of *jiaguwen* (Oracle-bone Script)..

Yangshao Culture (ca. 5000 – 3000 BCE): most famous site is at **Banpo**, near today's city of *Xi'an* in Shaanxi Province.

Dawenkou Culture (ca. 4300 – 2500 BCE): Neolithic wine vessels found (in the 1980s) in some thirty tombs in Shandong Province, with inscribed symbols which have now been deciphered as similar to *jiaguwen*.

Majiayao Culture (ca. 3300 – 2050 BCE): mainly in Gansu Province as well as neighboring Qinghai Province to the east.

Map 3: Two dynastic capitals and their archaeological sites

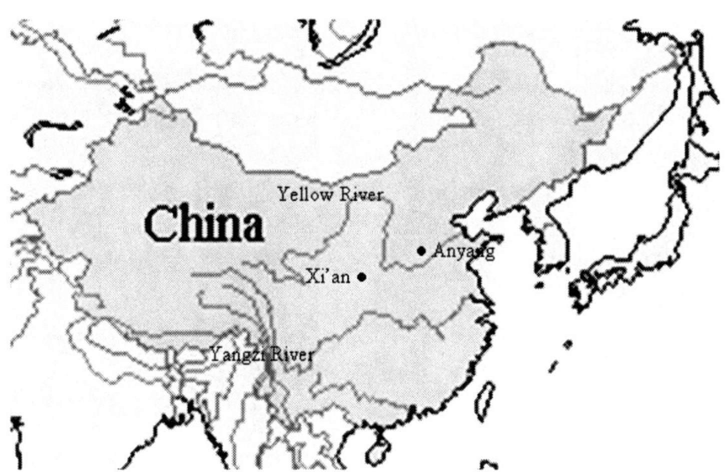

Anyang, Henan Province: capital city of the late Shang Dynasty (ca. 16th – 11th century BCE). Tortoise shells and ox shoulder blades with *jiaguwen* (Oracle-bone script) inscription on them were found near by in excavations carried out from the 1920s. These excavations also yielded magnificent Shang bronzes. In 1976, the tomb of Fu Hao, a consort of one of the late Shang kings, was excavated, yielding a sumptuous harvest of tomb goods of great historical and cultural importance as it was one of the few ancient tombs excavated in recent times, which have been left undisturbed by tomb robbers over the millenia.

Xi'an, Shaanxi Province: it and its environs had been the capital city of thirteen dynasties, including the Western Zhou (ca. 11th century – 770 BCE), the Qin (221 – 207 BCE), the Han (206 BCE – 220 CE), the Tang (618 – 907 CE). One of its ancient names was Changan. The terra-cotta army of Qin Shihuangdi, the first emperor of the Qin Dynasty was found in the area. It was also the start of the land Silk Route, begun in the Han Dynasty. The site, called Banpo (discovered in 1953), belonging to the Yangshao Neolithic Culture (ca. 5000 – 3000 BCE) is also near by.

Bibliography

Coulmas, Florian. *Writing Systems: An Introduction to their Linguistic Analysis*. Cambridge: CUP, 2003.

Curt, Richard: *Brushes with Power: Modern Politics and the Chinese Art of Calligraphy*. Berkeley/Los Angeles/Oxford: University of California Press, 1991.

De Francis, John. *Visible Speech: The Diverse Oneness of Writing Systems*. Honolulu: University of Hawaii Press, 1989.

—. *The Chinese Language: Fact and Fantasy*. Honolulu: University of Hawaii Press, 1984

Loewe, Michael and Edward L. Shaughnessy. *The Cambridge History of Ancient China: from the origins of civilization to 221 B.C.* (Alternate: *Ancient China*). Cambridge: Cambridge University Press, 1999.

Printed in the United Kingdom by
Lightning Source UK Ltd., Milton Keynes
137869UK00001B/97/P